COLORING OUTSIDE THE LINES

A Love Story in the Gray of Addiction, Recovery, and Redemption

One couple. Two voices. A raw memoir of chaos, surrender, and the radical path to healing.

KATIE AND CHRIS BOWICK

Love Through the Gray, LLC

LANDON
HAIL
PRESS

Paperback ISBN: 978-1-959955-74-0
Hardback ISBN: 978-1-959955-75-7

Cover design by Rich Johnson, Spectacle Photo
Published by Landon Hail Press

This book is dedicated to

Anyone struggling with addiction or carrying the weight of loving someone who is: *I pray you find the hope, accept the help, and experience the healing you deserve. Your only way out is through. Keep going!*

—Chris

Those who love them: *To the ones whom I call "The Anchor(s)," who lost themselves trying to save someone else, may you return to yourself with tenderness.*

You are not the wreckage. There is redemption in your rising.

—Katie

This is for those who are becoming whole, even in the messy undoing.

You are enough.

CONTENTS

Foreword

Jaime McFaden, behavior change specialist
Author, *Waves of Self-Care*

Chances are, at some point in our lives, we will love an addict, maybe even more than once. Perhaps we are the addict or in a tangled co-dependent relationship, unsure what to do.

The mass reality of those who struggle with addiction is so loud and yet often swept under a rug of concealment. It's time we open up the conversations to find healing through God: through surrender and through any means necessary to LOVE one another through life's ups and downs.

As someone who lost my favorite person to addiction, followed by many others, this book is one I highly recommend for those either "going through it" or to support those who are doing all they can to see the light and shine through darkness. To understand and acknowledge how many people are affected and devastated by this topic, and then begin to be part of the change. To break the stigmas and find solutions to this epidemic problem, we all face.

When I was introduced to Katie and Chris, I was immediately pulled into their story—the raw and real truth of what it's like to be an addict and what it's like to love someone so close to us who is struggling. Personally, I felt seen by hearing their story. Working with them as their writing coach was a joy, and it became incredibly healing for me, too.

Often with addiction, there is a stigma around one of two things: 1. There is a specific route to take and that's it; or, 2. Most people won't change. I disagree with this belief. When Katie and Chris asked me to write the foreword, I was filled with joy because I knew someone out there would read it and it would help shift their perspective, which can change someone's life.

They will learn that there is often no one-size-fits-all approach. That just like the waves in life, we can lean into the golden rules of loving each other as a whole person, without the shame of our mistakes and misfortunes.

Katie and Chris struck me as a couple who are perfectly imperfect, embracing the journey one step at a time, and cheering each other along through growth and sustainability. Learning to lean into *FAITH* and to put in the work required to make change.

This book will take you on a journey into the depths of real love and pain that can come with mental health and real-life struggles. It will also remind you that you are not alone and LOVE is really the answer. Enjoy!

Prologue

Chris

Sobriety, for me at least, wasn't achieved solely by following the Twelve-Step program. Not because I don't find value in it, I absolutely do! I have witnessed so many people turn their lives around by following that path. That just wasn't what felt natural for me.

My recovery initially began with my close friends and family surprising/saving me by hosting an actual intervention. Which was the last thing that I ever expected, and yet it was precisely what I needed. Seeing all their faces gave me the courage to lean into the truth, and the truth was I desperately needed help.

Since that day, I have focused on healing, learning, and growing. I made a simple promise to myself that I wouldn't give up once I started this process, and I have kept my word. It is worth mentioning that I never promised I wasn't going to make any mistakes… and thank God for that, because I've made damn near every single one of them! Each time I fell short or screwed up, I was forced to face myself and decide whether I wanted to keep suffering or move forward.

As you can imagine, I was terribly embarrassed when I walked into a room full of my friends and family, all sitting in a circle. I was the last person to realize that my deepest, darkest secret wasn't even a secret anymore. The guilt, shame, and pure embarrassment that accompany this moment haven't made the road easy or the journey shorter by any means. Still, I saw this exactly for what it was: a gift, a one-time chance to get my life back on track. I didn't know where I was going to be sleeping that very same night, but I already knew for sure that I wasn't going to waste this chance to change.

Until then, I always tried to live as independently as possible, rarely needing or asking for much from anyone. However, this was different; this was what I needed. And so, when help was offered, I was fortunately more than ready to accept it. What everyone didn't know is that I had already tried to quit using every way imaginable, and more than once. I'd made myself dangerously sick so many times, and all because I didn't want anyone to know my truth. I couldn't find it in me to ask for help.

So, I dove headfirst into the recovery community. It was this entirely new world, utterly foreign to me. Even so, I surrendered to the fact that I didn't have the tools to climb out of the hole I had dug for myself.

It wasn't for lack of trying or wanting to stop. The truth was, I started my journey at an in-patient facility called the Refuge, down in Ocala, Florida. That very long first day turned into seven days. A few weeks became a couple of months. All one day at a time.

Before joining this diverse community, I, like the rest of the world, had some predetermined, unfounded idea of what *that* group of people would be like. What I found was that there were plenty of people I respected, and the best resources were among them. I utilized every resource available to me back then, and the reality changed my perspective completely. I have met some of the most amazing people since pursuing my recovery.

I learned the language and the acronyms used by the recovery community and the healthcare system. For anyone like me who has literally zero experience with the addiction and recovery side of our medical system, I can assure you, what you don't know can hurt you.

To be my own best advocate, I had to become familiar with everything. I learned to navigate the ins and outs of our imperfect healthcare system. I've read the Big Book several times, with and without a sponsor. I've attended almost every "A" meeting: AA,

NA, ACA, CA, even SA. I've had a "home group," and I have attended more than 90 meetings in 90 days. I voluntarily completed roughly four months of in-patient and two years of outpatient rehabilitation programs.

During the time I spent in meetings, doctors' offices, rehabilitation facilities, etc., I listened with intention! I tried to put all that I had gathered into practice regularly. I relearned how to be completely honest with myself. I had to, but I also wanted to relearn the foundational ways that I was thinking, communicating, and behaving. I applied these newly acquired or polished principles to everything I encountered. I wanted to absorb as much as possible, then work through whether the information I'd obtained was credible, reliable, or relatable. I held onto the lessons and words that felt the most authentic, relearning to trust my gut and instinct.

More importantly, I relearned to place my sobriety and my healing in what I believe is the most genuine understanding of respect and humility. Eventually, I came to realize that, while this newfound intention was good, I was still feeling out of touch with myself. I was still feeling alone, anxious, and out of place. Fear was still the primary emotional driver in my heart, and when it weighs on you day after day, no matter how determined you are or how strong you are, eventually it will start to overwhelm your efforts.

I knew I couldn't manage this on my own. But I also felt an extreme sense of guilt that I only ever seemed to call on the Lord in my times of need. I was reminded by a friend that it doesn't matter how many steps you take away from God; it only takes one step back toward Him. And that's what I did. I took that step and began rebuilding my relationship with the Lord. I laid my fears and anxiety at His feet, and I haven't been alone since.

My sobriety came from a combination of things: therapy, functional medicine, microdosing, alternative medicine, hard conversations, spiritual surrender, and brutal honesty. It was unconventional, nonlinear, and never perfect. **But it was mine.**

There were plenty of times when I felt like I was "doing it wrong" because of the feedback I was receiving. I was made to feel like my recovery didn't "count," because it didn't look exactly like the version that society, friends, and family had laid out and believed was acceptable.

People would tell me, "If only you went to more meetings and worked the Twelve Steps, maybe then you wouldn't have struggled through this like you have!"

They may be true. The way I pursued a healthier version of myself was the longer or less traveled road. But it wasn't wholly different from the Twelve Steps. In fact, many of the "steps" I took mirrored the Twelve-step program. I tried every program, every group, anything I thought might offer me something. I took as much good from each of those and utilized the lessons as I pushed forward on my own. My journey to recovery was remarkably similar to the Twelve Steps.

I've come to believe there is no one-size-fits-all road, not in its entirety. Many programs I participated in taught me something I needed in order to grow and move forward. Some things occurred naturally, based on the circumstances. One thing I did well in the beginning was to completely surrender. I surrendered to my secret being out and to the fact that there was no going back. I surrendered to my addiction. I surrendered and accepted help.

For me, a challenging but essential part of my healing has been learning to forgive myself. That, and to speak with less shame, not just about what I've done, but also about how I have tried to frame it. The Substance Abuse and Mental Health Services Administration (SAMHSA) recommends using language that respects the person before the condition.

I started to notice that I didn't like using specific words to describe my addiction, but it turned out to be deeper than that. I didn't like being an addict, period. When I surrendered to the truth and accepted the help being offered to me, I didn't think that my life from now on had to be centered around addiction and recovery for the rest of my life. I don't think it should have to be that way. But at times, that is how you really feel while going through this experience.

Because I am not my worst decision. I am not defined by the darkest moments of my life. And neither are you.[1] If you're back in the driver's seat of your life and have accepted your past but are living for your future..., you could call me whatever you want, and I'd own it.

I've learned to be humble and grateful for this process that has let me face myself, my behaviors, my decisions, and the wreckage of my past and move toward myself again. Recovery for me has been relearning many of my best habits, which I had given a back seat to.

In my weakest and darkest moments of recovery, my faith reemerged profoundly**, and I knew God had never left me,** even when I couldn't recognize myself. Even when I was deep down the wrong path with no idea how to turn around. Ultimately, when I had given up and felt I couldn't possibly find myself forgivable, the Lord lit up the room. He began guiding me back to Him, and I started paying attention to those opportunities. I have never felt so acutely alone as I did at certain points during this process, and it was in those low moments that I reached out to the only one I truly believed could help me.

Healing isn't free. I want to set the record straight. You might go to a beautiful place and have a life-altering experience. But the most essential part of recovery is stepping back into your real life. You will not come home to a life that has been cleaned up for you. Every issue that you procrastinated or thought you had left behind will surely be there to meet you upon your return.

Hopefully, removing the toxicity and substance from your life will give you the clarity you need to realize the severity of the situation you left behind, and you will have to search within yourself for the courage to push onward, right at the point where you previously quit. It's either that or you can fall back into the fear and anxieties that drove you into the depths of your addiction.

There's a lot of negative stigma surrounding addiction. I kept mine hidden from the world for years. And that hiding? That secrecy? That's what kept me sick.

Most people don't fail at sobriety because they can't quit a substance. They fail because they've never learned how to live without it. Addiction isn't just physical. It can be a survival mechanism that helps numb physical, mental, and any pain! It enables you to cope with trauma when you don't have the tools in place. And when you take the substance away without healing the reason you needed it in the first place, you don't just get clean. You end up getting lost. And instead of trying to find your way again, you start trying to find more of whatever it was that made that pain and anxiety go away.

And I don't say any of this lightly, because it's not just about one person's story. This crisis is everywhere. In 2022 alone, more than 100,000 people in the U.S. died from drug overdoses, and three out of four of those deaths involved opioids.[2]

That number wrecks me. Because I know I could have been one of them. I came as close as you can—twice. I needed to learn to build a life that didn't rely on substances to make it tolerable, and one that wouldn't. And the foundation of that life had to be forgiveness.

I used to believe I was too far gone and too broken to forgive. And if you can't forgive yourself, you start to think you deserve to stay stuck, and the shame starts to creep in, and then you feel like there is little to no hope. That there's no reason to change. For some people, there's no rock bottom… It's bottomless. Sometimes, people need a jackhammer to keep digging because the first rock bottom wasn't deep enough.

The truth is, drugs will fundamentally *change* who you are. Every value. Every principle. Everything you thought you stood for will get stripped away, one lie at a time.

And maybe you're still functioning. Perhaps you're still showing up, going through the motions. However, the longer you use it, the greater the risk of losing it. Not just relationships or jobs or trust, but the things you value about yourself deep down. You cross one line then another and another, until one day, you look in the mirror and think, *Who the fuck even am I?* Sometimes, you do not even want to look at yourself in the mirror.

And that list of regrets? That list of things you swore you'd never do? It grows longer and longer like a never-ending grocery list. And uglier and heavier. But if there's even a sliver of you left who wants to be a good person and try to start over, I think that's enough to begin again.

Some people may not believe you can change. Hell, *you* might not think it right now. But you can, and I believe in you. I'm living proof that even if the world says you're done, even if you yourself say you're done, guess who isn't done with you? God.

This book isn't a recovery story wrapped in a bow. It's a story of survival, faith, and figuring it out amid chaos. It's what happens when you stop trying to do it for everyone else and finally decide to live for *you.*

Katie

If you're reading this, chances are you're standing in a wreckage you never asked for. Maybe you're barely hanging on. Perhaps you don't even know why you're still here in the relationship or supporting a loved one. Maybe there might be some part of you that can't let go. If these resonate with you, you are the constant anchor, keeping everything from floating away or falling apart.

I know that feeling. I lived it. In some ways, I am still living it. Our book isn't a story about how we figured it out and found a neat, clean road to recovery. Our story is unconventional. It's not a guidebook. It's not a roadmap. It's not a pretty story or happily ever after, tied up with a bow.

This is a story about what it really looks like when you love someone who is fighting addiction, and what it means to survive it yourself, whether you stay or whether you have to walk away.

It's about the ugly parts: the lies, the relapses, the heartbreak, the rage, and the nights you can't sleep because you're terrified they are not breathing next to you. It's about the moments when you feel like you're drowning and can barely get out of bed to function because your pain is holding you down.

Maybe you realize that you need to save yourself, not your loved one. Perhaps you have become so fixated on helping them that you don't even notice you are drowning, too. Maybe you have become addicted to the addiction. I sure was.

Chris and I are not experts. We are just two people who refuse to let addiction be the final word over our marriage, even when we weren't sure if marriage, friendship, or even love would survive what we were walking through.

We broke a lot of things along the way. We hurt each other. We have lost trust, hope, and our sense of safety more times than I can count. But somehow, *somehow,* we also kept fighting for something deeper, something that addiction couldn't steal.

This book is told from both of our sides. My story is for the loved one (spouse, friend, sibling, parent, etc.) who loves a person with an addiction, "the Adrift." This story is for you, "the Anchor/s." For the ones who carry the weight. It is for those who stand in the great wake of pain and keep asking, *"How much more can I take?"*

To the ones who think they're crazy or weak or too soft or too hard or too broken to fix any of it: you're not crazy. You're not weak. You're loving someone in a war they didn't even know was a war to begin with, and one they can't stop, never knowing how powerful addiction can be. You are fighting for your life, too, and trying not to lose yourself in the process. You are not broken. You are so strong. Unconditional love requires resilience.

Whichever road you are on today, you are seen. There is no magic map through this. What we found, instead, through heartbreak and relapse, rage, and repair, was that sometimes love doesn't save you by being something easy. It saves you by being real. It saves you from being messy. It saves you by giving you something to fight for.

This is our story. This is a survival story. This is a love story. This is a story about breaking chains we didn't know we were wrapped in, and then surrendering control. If you're here, you're not alone. And no matter what your journey looks like from here, you are stronger than you think.

This book is for those of you who have suffered for years, sometimes decades, inside the slow, grinding heartbreak of loving someone lost to addiction.

This book is for the past version of myself: the woman who couldn't see a silver lining, who played Detective Katie every damn day, who lived with her head on a swivel, scanning constantly for danger she couldn't quite name but could always feel.

If you know that feeling—if you're living it now or healing from it—this is for you.

You are not crazy. And no matter what the wreckage looks like, there is still life ahead of you that's worth fighting for.

Healing is an incredibly profound process, full of challenges, hard lessons, failures, and difficult storms. We can only control so much. The only thing you can ever count on staying the same is change. And change is hard.

If you're reading this and feel broken, exhausted, or unsure if you can do this again tomorrow... I see you. I've been you. And even if you don't believe it right now, you are worthy of a love that doesn't hurt—whether that love comes from someone else or, finally, from yourself.

Before we even considered co-authoring a book as a couple, we realized there was a significant gap in the literature that truly captured the intricate journey of recovery. We discovered there were no available books that explored the dual perspectives of the recovering addict, or what we like to call "the Adrift," alongside the experiences of their loved ones, "The Anchors." Our goal became clear: to shed light on the emotional toll felt, both for those battling addiction and for the loved ones, friends, siblings, parents, and spouses who walk this complicated path with them.

We wanted to share the highs, the lows, and the resilience required throughout the entire process. What tried to bury us became the soil for this story. We turned rock bottom into a rough draft, and now we are rewriting the ending.

Authors' Note

This isn't a traditional book about addiction, because our path hasn't been conventional or tidy. There's no road map you can follow, no how-to guide with specific steps, or no one-size-fits-all approach to blanket over your path to healing or recovery.

If you're reading this and find yourself in a challenging situation, whether loving someone who is actively struggling with addiction or working through your own recovery, we want you to know that *You Are Not Alone*.

We didn't sit down with a cup of coffee and make an outline filled with talking points. We brought Post-its, voice notes, half-written rants, inside jokes, personal journal entries we thought would never see the light of day, and stories we swore we'd never tell. Somehow, this is what came together.

This wasn't one journey. It was two. Katie's story of loving someone in active addiction. Chris's story of facing it head-on. There were relapses, resentments, codependency, compassion, and a lot of lessons learned the hard way. Like, *a lot*.

You'll hear both of our voices here: Katie's is more direct and raw, while Chris's is filled with humor and humility. Sometimes these voices are distinct. Sometimes, intertwined. Sometimes overlapping in the chaos that was our life together during addiction, recovery, marriage, and everything in between. Our voices may contradict, mirror, or interrupt each other—because that's how it actually felt. That's what real life and genuine relationships are like.

Our structure isn't traditional, either, and that's intentional. The format shifts. Some parts are jagged. Some are expressive. Some read like a confession. Some parts are what we call Chris's "squirrel" moments, where his ADHD takes you down a rabbit hole, but it's for a reason. Others are like a stand-up set. That's addiction. That's marriage. That's what healing looks like when you're doing it side-by-side, while still trying to find your own footing.

We wrote this because we needed to. We're sharing it because maybe you do, too.

We invite you into our story not as experts, but as two imperfect humans who kept choosing to tell the truth, even when it hurt. If you see yourself somewhere in these pages, we hope you know how strong and resilient you are. And just know you don't have to do it perfectly to survive it.

We sure didn't.

But hey, we are still standing together. Writing. Living. Loving. Healing. Creating.

Together.

The memoir you are about to read is entirely accurate, based on our best recollection of events, conversations, and memories. Many names used are real; others are pseudonyms to protect their identities and privacy. Our intention is not to vilify or cast blame; it's to show each person's place within our journey and their impact on it.

While writing this book, we had frequent conversations with close friends and family about how they remembered the events we described. We also leaned on old journals, emails, and letters to help bolster our memories. Much of the dialogue has been recreated from memory, often with support from those additional resources. Each person's recollection of this time may differ from ours—this is our memoir, and these are our memories.

Chris also obtained his treatment files from the Refuge (in-patient) and other facilities, including discharge paperwork, medical documentation, and workbooks from detox and residential care, to help inform this story.

We want to acknowledge that *language matters*. The words "addict," "addiction," "substance abuse/use," and "recovery" carry weight, and they may have different meanings for different people. We have used language that reflects our experiences, understanding that it may not resonate with everyone. Our intention is never to offend; however, we express our truth with honesty, humility, and respect.

We also want to acknowledge and show appreciation for Twelve-Step programs like AA and Al-Anon. They have saved and transformed countless lives. While those paths didn't resonate with us personally, we deeply respect the framework and community they provide. Recovery looks different for everyone. And ours is somewhat unconventional.

Trigger Warning: This book contains references to molestation, sexual abuse, suicide, mental health struggles, anxiety, addiction, relapse, drug use, opioids, hospitalization, and near-death experiences. Please take care of yourself as you read. Skip chapters if you need to. Pause if your heart asks you to. Your well-being matters more than finishing a chapter. Always.

We've chosen to speak honestly and vulnerably about the darkest parts of our story, because we know how isolating those places can feel. So, please be kind.

This is our truth. Our chaos. Our mess.

Thank you for joining us to witness it.

With gratitude,

Chris & Katie

Chapter 1

Even Superman Wore Underwear

Chris

Hey, I'm Chris Bowick—and I'm fucking awesome. I've probably always been awesome, but I didn't always know it. Writing a book, especially one about me, feels strange. Not because I'm shy about talking about myself; I've got no problem there. But the timing had to be right. And apparently, that time is now.

I'm thirty-seven years old. Recently, I had what I can only describe as an epiphany. I hate that word. It's overused, like "blessed," but nothing else quite fits. A string of traumatic events, layered with socially acceptable (and sometimes not-so-acceptable) addictions, forced me to confront something I'd been avoiding: I've been full of shit.

I've spent most of my life as a people-pleaser. That kind of behavior doesn't leave much space to figure out who you really are. You become a mirror, reflecting what other people want, what your family expects, and what your community projects. It's well-intentioned, but it's also soul-sucking.

Humor has always been my weapon of choice. It has helped me navigate life's curveballs. If you had met me five years ago, I would have introduced myself like this: "I'm Chris, I'm married to my best friend, Katie—we reconnected after our ten-year high school reunion. I once bought a house I never lived in and a lifted Toyota Tundra straight off the showroom floor because... why not? I sold my financial firm, which I had bought from my family just after college, and made six figures in a month before I could legally rent a car."

Sounds impressive, right? What a douche...

That version of me was chasing success by society's standards. I didn't know it then, but I was addicted to validation, my image, success, achievement—really anything that could drown out the truth: I was lost. I have this perfectly dysfunctional blend of ADHD and OCD. If I like something, I love it. And then, I obsess over it... until I don't.

Here's the thing: I'm not a victim. I didn't grow up in some war zone. I had plenty of opportunities. But I also wasted a lot of time on people-pleasing, doubting myself, numbing out, and, yes, getting wasted. I've often felt like I have so much to say but rarely say anything that actually matters. Until now.

This book is my shot at cutting through the bullshit. I'm going to say what I need to say, and maybe, just maybe, someone out there will see a piece of themselves in my story. You'll see my humor—dry, dark, often inappropriate. You'll also know the struggle, the failures, and the hard-earned moments of clarity.

So, here we are. I am thirty-seven years in and finally sitting still long enough to write this. I could say I've succeeded in many ways. But the truth—the uncomfortable, liberating, painful, necessary truth—is where my story really begins.

I was born and raised in Colorado. My dad is Jeff, my mom is Tracy, and I have a younger brother named Kyle, who is three years and eleven months younger than me and one of my best friends by choice. Divorce complicated my family tree, but it also doubled my grandparents on my dad's side. Some of my earliest and most cherished memories are with that chaotic extended crew.

If this were a picture I was trying to paint for you, it would become blurry whenever I try to remember anything before my brother was born. When May 14, 1992, finally arrived, Kyle came into the world, making me officially a big brother. I have a vivid memory of a brown recliner sitting right in the middle of the family room as you entered our house. It served no purpose, and it actually makes me uncomfortable to think about it now. Like, why did you guys put that there? Why wasn't there anything else near it, like a side table or a lamp? Squirrel!

Anyway, right across from the awkwardly placed hideous chair was a bay-like window with a bench seat that mirrored the front porch. That was where I was sitting when I first met my brother. My parents had me sit down, and I'm pretty sure they gave me a full tutorial, complete with their own imitations of what holding a newborn baby should look like. That was one of the best days of my life; I became an older brother, and I knew for certain I was more intelligent than both my parents. (Just kidding—maybe)

Since we are on the topic, I really should pay tribute to my parents. After all, I don't think I would be here without them… So, I just want to recognize two of the most important people to me and say, "Thank you both so much for getting married… the second time! By honoring the vows you made to each other… again… That, paired with not wearing a condom, is essentially the best thing you two have ever done! You're welcome, and thank you!"

I'm a firm believer, if you can't look back and laugh, well, you're probably really fucking boring!

My dad had this red, two-door Daytona, and that little wannabe sports car was what they pulled up to the house in, after arriving from the hospital! It was normal then, but I laugh hysterically now! Picture this…

My dad has always been a fit, athletic guy. He was/is bald…, but he refused to shave the rest of his head. The cul-de-sac look wasn't complete without his signature thick mustache. Slap on a pair of gold Ray-Ban Aviators with a frat strap (Safety first!), and paint in the most vibrant yet matching tracksuit, and you have the man, the myth, the legend! I love my dad so much, I am not going to share the music that was likely playing in that little hot rod! ;)

Obviously, I also have a mother. In 1988, there was no such thing as the Internet, so it's highly unlikely I made it here any other way. Just like it wouldn't be fair for me to give my dad's description of the times and not my mom's.

My mom, let's face it, the lady had style—swagger, if you will. Anyone my age, give or take five to seven years in either direction, likely shares one of the many things we have in common: we have seen the "glamor shots" of our moms. If you know, you know. And if you don't, well, you're probably a nineties bitch. My mom lived each scene of her *glamorous* day to the fullest! It was almost as if there was an actual wind blowing through her hair. In one shot, she wasn't even looking at the camera, and it was all so perfect, it's like she planned it that way.

I only bring this up because any time she saw an opportunity to bust out the glamor shots, the first words she spoke as she pushed that 12x12 frame in your face were, "See? I was hot!" This still makes me laugh.

The older I get, the more I grow to appreciate both my parents. They had me when they were in their early twenties. And yes, this was their second shot at marriage. But I, of all people, really can't complain. If it weren't for that second try, I wouldn't be here! Relationships are complicated, and in my experience, no two are alike. I know for sure my parents were both doing their best to learn to be parents while still trying to figure their shit out. Ya know?

When I was about six or seven years old, my parents were at their absolute worst. They fought constantly, screaming at each other and calling each other names, throwing profanity around as if there were no other words in the dictionary. There are specific memories I wish I could erase.

Our house was a split-level, and the garden level was where the TV was, so, naturally, that's where my brother and I spent a lot of our time. The level above that had only three stairs, and you could see the dining room and kitchen from the couch in the TV room.

One night, after my dad got home from work, they were having one of their fights. As the argument escalated, I looked up at them and saw my mom throw her wedding ring across the table. I don't recall what they were saying or what the fight was about. I remember feeling overwhelmed, and what's worse is that I didn't know what to call it. I wasn't old enough to understand what a *divorce* was. Still, I knew their relationship had come to an end, so whatever happened next was what I expected.

Unfortunately, not all of their fights were avoidable. My room shared a wall with my brother's room, which I always liked. At night, we both left our doors open because... well, we were children and nighttime is scary! Not as frightening as this night, though.

It was much later when my dad got home, and Kyle and I were both already in bed. I always pretended to be asleep, but really, I was awake. My parents woke me up because they were yelling at each other, so I jumped out of bed... I wanted to make sure they hadn't woken Kyle up! I shut his door, and usually, I would have left those two to duke it out. But this fight escalated. It was different.

I saw my mom grab my dad's head and literally scratch his bald head with her nails! They were doing this shuffle, trying to grab each other's arms—there was pushing, shoving, and screaming... So, naturally, I had to step in. After all, I was the only adult in the house that night, and I had a fucking three-year-old to look after! (I fucking hate thinking about this fight, so I tend to use a little humor.)

I'm not sure why I got involved, but I went and positioned myself between them, and if you can, try to imagine a seven-year-old boy in Batman underwear being bounced around with one hand on Mom and the other hand on Dad. Both of my arms were fully extended like Moses parting the Red Sea.

They both hated fighting in front of us, which is funny, because some of the best fights they had were literally about fighting in front of us! But now that I was there, they couldn't ignore the fact that I had seen them doing this. So, in what I imagine was a fairly embarrassing moment for both of them, they got desperate. They both tried to distance themselves from each other, while explicitly trying not to hurt me. But heaven forbid, they do that without simultaneously trying to land one more malicious little push, shove, slap, or pinch on the other.

The next thing I knew, my mom was in the bathtub, and the shower curtain and rod were both down. Until that moment, I swear I didn't have a worry in my adorable little head! But now, I was pissed, probably because I was wearing the wrong underwear... Superman would have been preferable. Their tone had changed, and it scared me. The entire scenario was dramatic, like a cinematic girl fight.

Neither of my parents has ever been a physically abusive person. Now, if we are talking about verbally or emotionally, that is a different story—just kidding... sorta. But that night still sticks with me. I had always been my dad's son, yet there I was, screaming at him to stop something I wasn't sure he even started! I was basically sitting or hovering over my mom in the bathtub, with one hand still up in my dad's direction.

I've never told either of them this, but the thing that stood out that night was the look of disappointment they both had on their faces—defeated, exhausted. It wasn't so much anger toward each other anymore, or worry for me; it genuinely felt like they were both upset with themselves.

They ended up separating, which was strange because, for a time, that just meant my dad moved all his belongings downstairs to the spare bedroom. I remember this specifically because he placed his big, brown dresser in the hallway near our guest bathroom. I think there might be something to this misplaced furniture *thing* I've got going on. But the separation didn't last, and they ultimately filed for divorce that same year. This is where my memory really falters, which is frustrating, because usually, it's the opposite: I simply can't forget anything!

Over the years, I have seen my fair share of therapists, counselors, psychologists, etc., and one thing they all seem to agree on is that my memory wasn't the problem, although it was subconsciously selective. We all have this innate, primal instinct, and when our brain senses pain or fear, it naturally seeks to reduce or redirect it in any way possible. Survival.

Sometimes, without really knowing it, we can bury any memories that are too painful to process or for which we don't yet have the tools. One thing I have learned the hard way is that suppressing emotions is no different than self-medicating, addiction, procrastination, and, last but not least..., masturbation! Why? Well, merely because every one of those coping strategies is ultimately just another way to fuck yourself!

I remember none of the details of my dad actually moving out of our house, but I do remember feeling his absence. Initially, several months went by before we could see him again, and in the meantime, my mom was not okay. I was only seven, but I got a front-row seat to what genuine heartbreak looks like. A relationship ending is almost like a death. You go through the stages of grief, and you aren't always in control. Therefore, everyone experiences this differently. With my mom, I saw it all: the tears, the silence, the time spent in bed, the anger, and the short bursts of confidence reemerging.

My brother and I were left living in limbo while this was going on. He wasn't old enough to fully understand what was happening, but he was much more intuitive than he let on. He knew the basics, the facts, at least the ones that mattered. Mom and Dad didn't love each other "that way" anymore, so they were going to live separately. This wasn't "your" fault. This doesn't mean we love you less, etc.

A married couple going through a divorce in the nineties wasn't at all uncommon, but there also wasn't as much precedent as there is today. Or maybe it's just that there wasn't immediate access to information like there is today. It's been said (generalizing, not citing) that more than half of marriages will ultimately end in divorce; however, over seventy-five percent of those who divorce have children. For the actual married couple, their divorce ultimately results in the change they wanted. They don't have to see each other anymore, no longer live together, and are free to live their lives on their own terms again.

Unfortunately, that isn't the case for the children of divorced parents. For me, it was overwhelmingly difficult to navigate, mainly because there was never a time when I could rely on anything. I lived with perpetual change, and there was nothing I could do about it. I was at an age where I had opinions, wants, and needs. But divorce doesn't ask the kids what they want or need. They leave that to parents to decide, which I do and don't understand. You leave the fate of the kids' happiness in the hands of the two people who couldn't manage their own?

I didn't know what to call it back when I was seven, but I was already struggling with a unique blend of ADHD and OCD. If I had to define what that feels like, I would say that whatever could grab my attention also had to be perfect… But never for long, as something else would usually distract me from whatever *that* was to begin with. Also known as *squirrel*!

I had to grow up quickly; at least that is how I felt. It started off innocently enough. I just wanted to make my mom's life easier. I wanted to help take care of her and my brother in my dad's absence.

My brother and I may be part of the last generation whose upbringing included this weird thing called "chores." I seemed to thrive in this department, and since I'd spent a lot of time helping my dad, I already knew what needed to be done around the house. It made me feel good to be busy and ultimately have something to show for my time.

I remember the first time I started the lawn mower myself, and it also took over a dozen attempts. In between, I would run inside to the beige house phone to call my dad for instructions. Everyone knows *this* phone. It was near the kitchen/living room area, mounted on the wall. The coiled cord, like a Slinky, extended and was long enough to reach pretty much every corner of the house.

The numbers were on the detachable phone itself, and they lit up a neon-greenish color when you pushed them. On the part that remained on the wall, there was an Excel-formatted printout listing all the numbers any family needed to survive: *9-1-1, Grandma, Grandpa, Pizza, Dad work, Chinese, *69, etc.*

Although my mom was navigating this difficult chapter, I was also fortunate to have a front-row seat to what resilience looks like. There is a time for everything, and eventually, her time to rise came. The three of us found solid ground again. Time has a way of healing most things. We developed a new routine for the day-to-day necessities, and I remember feeling a brief sigh of relief. We seemed to be growing into our new *roles.*

To me, this looked like our family "horse" blanket laid out on the floor in front of the TV, with Chinese food and perhaps a rented Blockbuster VHS movie. Divorce comes with plenty of noise—court decrees, custody battles, child support, etc.—but not enough relief. These are the elements that kids have no control over, yet they dictate a kid's entire existence until their eighteenth birthday.

We experienced a positive shift with my mom and dad. Kyle and I went on our family vacation with my dad and his side of the family to Destin, Florida. This was the first time we had seen him and had the chance to spend quality time since he'd initially moved out. We spent all day on the beach with some of my favorite people: my grandma and grandpa, my aunts and uncles, and my Cousin Katie, who was more like an older sister to me growing up.

After a few days of unlimited fun, coupled with the powerful sense of safety I always felt around my grandparents, my dad finally talked to Kyle and me about the divorce. He opened up to us in a way I knew was hard for him. He said he was sorry and made no excuses. He cried, which was the first time I had ever seen him do that.

I don't know if there is any one way to handle what follows for each family member after they go through traumatic changes like this; it's person-specific. After a while, I found some understanding. I knew my parents weren't happy together because I saw them learning to be happy again on their own. I saw a side of them I had never seen before. They were growing into their own and seemed noticeably better. There was a new vibe in both households, one in which Kyle and I started to regain each other's individual attention and focus. When your parents pay attention to you on purpose, it validates you and gives you a sense of calm.

The initial shock of divorce ultimately wears off, and the pain that turned to anger fades, but it never completely goes away. Even when change slows down, it never stops. So, anger shifted into resentment, and the peace I found in understanding was disrupted again. Tuesdays, Thursdays, and every other weekend were our scheduled times with our dad. Holidays were split between the two, every other year.

It's funny that, back then, no one asked me or Kyle what we might prefer, or at least I don't remember them doing that. I remember hating this new schedule, and I made that clear. I developed anxiety surrounding all the shuttling back and forth between the two houses. My brother didn't really speak… not at all, to anyone, except me. So there was a period when I did the talking for both of us. He would literally whisper in my ear, and I would relay the message.

Implementing the new schedule felt as though we would be forever on the go. Every time we had an updated routine, the schedule changed, and Kyle and I felt forced to comply. This split schedule also meant something else: both our parents could have their own individual alone time again. Like most seven-year-olds, I never liked the idea of leaving my parents to their own devices… I felt I had to keep an eye on them. It wasn't long before I noticed that my mom was dating. I would hear her talking about it on the phone. Eventually, I realized, I would probably meet some of these guys. When I did, it sparked a change in me, but I don't believe it was for the better.

I might as well have been walking around, pissing on the houseplants. I learned very quickly that I was allowed to be angry and disrespectful, even toward these douchebags my mother was dating. Otherwise, I accepted the "punishments" I received, which were usually less severe because I was, after all, going through a *tough* time.

I imagine this had a lot to do with my protective feelings toward my mom. I had just seen her at her lowest point, and it broke my little heart to see hers broken. So, I decided to hate these guys before I met them. I have always felt I possess an older soul. I wasn't a genius, but I was a smart kid. I put that all to use, first baiting these guys by initially being tolerant of their existence. When my mom looked away or stepped out of the room, I often hit them with some sort of remark that they, having just met me, had a hard time reporting back to my mom. Some did, and those fuckers didn't last long.

The longer the guy was around, the more desperate I became to get rid of him. Sleepovers were a hard no for me. "No way, Kemosabe! This is *my* house now!" I mowed the lawn, wore the Superman underwear, and therefore was king of this castle. But I knew that sleepovers were inevitable, and as I accepted this, my strategies grew a little darker. I figured, if I couldn't keep the fox out of the henhouse, then I would make that house as uncomfortable to be in as possible.

I still had a bedtime, but I was allowed to get up for a glass of milk or water or to use the restroom. If someone was staying over, I drank as many fluids as I could! Naturally, I had to use the bathroom a lot, so I peed with the door open, turned all the lights on, and maybe I flushed more than once. Sometimes, I stomped as loudly as I could back and forth, so they were forced to hear me downstairs.

My favorite technique was the never-ending "question." I never ran out of questions to ask my mom… in the middle of the night!

"Mooommmmm! Are we planning on leaving for school at the usual time tomorrow? Yeah, we are? Okay, well, you'd better get some sleep… It's probably time for the guy with the shit car to leave."

"Heyyyy, Mom, one more thing, do you think Dad could beat up the guy you're hanging out with? Should I call Dad and ask him, like right now? No, Dad couldn't beat him up? Or no, I can't call

Dad and ask him? Remember, you promised I could call Dad whenever I want…"

This wasn't as effective as I thought it would be. And now that I have much more life experience, I understand the "over/under" rule is a motivating part of the grief process. Gross. My favorite scheme came from a guy named Chris. How his parents thought he was worthy of such a name is beyond me. I could have kicked this guy's ass!

He was over at our house way too much. He sat on *my* couch, and he watched *my* TV. Then, that piece of shit would fall asleep on the remote. So, one morning when he did this, I recruited the absolute best NERF-gun sniper there ever was… Kyle never missed, and he had a fantastic arsenal! I told him to get his largest, heaviest weapon and quietly walk—no, crawl—over to the couch. And then… Well, I guess, just stand up and shoot that guy in the face!

Kyle's record is still perfect to this day. Chris woke up in complete fight-or-flight mode…. We scared the shit out of him!

In the first few seconds, he reached out to my brother and grabbed his arm. Admittedly, this was innocent. But Kyle could cry on command, and he started up a storm of tears. Knowing this, and being the mastermind that I was, I had already gotten my dad on the phone… When he asked, "Why is Kyle crying?" I simply replied, "Chris, the guy that mom lets sleep over… Well, he hurt Kyle!" *Click*!

My dad hung up, and I knew the damage was done and justice was on the way.

My mom came downstairs after hearing all the crying and yelling. Just like Chris didn't give me a chance to watch my regular shows, I didn't give him the chance to speak. Dramatically, I told my mom what had happened, but she quickly put the pieces of the puzzle together.

The first thing she asked was, "Who were you just on the phone with?"

I knew I had won this one. With a smirk, I said, "That was Dad, and he heard the whole thing, but then he hung up on me."

My mom and I were literally the only two people who realized what was going on. Somewhere out there, my dad was in his new Land Cruiser, likely speeding and running red lights on his way to the house.

Naturally, the second thing my mom said was, "Chris, you need to leave! My ex-husband is on his way here, and I am not sure what he'll do!"

I have never seen a grown man get the fuck out of a place so fast, and barely fast enough! Not a minute after Chris left, my dad's truck was in the front yard. Not the driveway, the front lawn. He jumped out in a rage that actually scared me.

I finally had precisely what I wanted: the four of us back together again, along with my TV and couch! I was so proud of myself; I felt like a director shooting a movie. I wanted to thank all the stars for their performances. Instead, this was around the time that my parents began their poor attempt at this thing called "co-parenting."

Although my parents had joint custody, we really lived with my mom. My mom didn't have to work while my parents were together. She did in-home daycare for some of our neighborhood kids for a short while. Eventually, she was offered a job by our Farmers Insurance agent. I remember this being a new challenge for our schedule, because she was no longer going to be there during the day, since she had to go to work. But it was a welcome change of pace, and it was nice to see my mom have something of her own—a sense and a source of independence for the first time in a long time.

To accommodate the new work schedule, Kyle and I would need to catch the bus to and from school. Unfortunately, the bus stop wasn't a short walk, so my mom made plans with another mom in the neighborhood who had two kids who also went to our school, and they lived right across the street from the bus stop. We would get dropped off at *her* house in the morning while we waited for the bus. Then, after school, we would stay there until our mom came to pick us up from work.

Sounds simple enough, right? A solid solution to one of the many growing pains that I assume came with reentering the workplace as a now-single mother of two! I didn't think anything of it, and why would I? There is no way that I (or anyone else, for that matter) could have known or even suspected what was in store for me. We were simply catching the bus to and from school with two other kids, and their mom watched us for a brief period while we waited for my mom to pick us up.

If you were an average and lucky eight- or nine-year-old, growing up like I did, there wasn't much to be genuinely afraid of. Of course, there was the occasional scary movie that you weren't supposed to watch at home. Naturally, you end up watching it at your best friend's house instead, and from then on, you have to sleep with a light on and would never put your feet on the ground right next to your bed! Other than that, we were taught to look both ways before crossing the street. We didn't talk to strangers, etc.

Parents are supposed to be and provide a guaranteed safe space. I assumed that *Emily*, being the mom of the two kids whom we rode the bus to school with, would be no different. But for the first time in my short life, I was about to learn that not all parents are created equal! That, and whatever innocence that remained in me up until this time, was about to be stripped away all at once.

There was no pause in life back then; it felt like we were always on the go. So, our new routine of being dropped off and picked up from Emily's house went on for a while. It was nice that our bus stop was literally visible from her front window. When it was cold out, we just waited inside and ran over when we heard or saw the bus coming. My brother and I enjoyed riding the bus together, and we also had those two kids near our age to hang out with!

This is, or was, the extent of my memory of this time in my life. I had managed to suppress what you'll soon learn about for my entire life! Age eight until age thirty.

I can't even recall the neighbor kids' names, though I know one was my age and the other was Kyle's. They weren't really friends—more like placeholders in the background—but their house was right across from the bus stop, which made it the perfect place for us to hang out before and after school.

I don't remember a husband, and I can't say how my mom even knew Emily. What I do know is that my life was spinning that year, and the pieces I do remember feel like fragments of a puzzle that never quite fit together.

In the mornings, we usually spent only five or ten minutes inside Emily's house. Once we saw the bus coming, all of us headed out to the corner, where it picked us up. In the afternoons, we stayed for two hours or more while we waited for my mom to come pick us up after work. My mom was truly coming into her own. With this new job, she had found a new purpose, and she excelled at it! It was a pleasant development in our routine, my mom regaining a sense of her independence. But we spent a little less time with her, now that she was back to work full-time for the first time in our lives.

Emily was a "grownup" to me. I never did get around to asking her how old she was, but I would guess she was in her mid-twenties. It's still strange for me to think I know next to nothing about this person—neither her age nor her last name, yet I remember everything about her physically.

Her hair was a thick, dirty blonde with highlights. In the morning, it was up in a poor attempt at a ponytail, and in the afternoon, you could tell she had spent time on it. Her eyes were blue-green-hazel, and the only reason I know that is because she told me they mirrored mine. She was tall—actually, she was the tallest of my married, adult girlfriends at the time! She had really white teeth and huge lips. She had a petite frame, so it came as a surprise to find that she was a mother of two.

In the year leading up to this, I had become the "man of the house." I had taken on adult-like responsibilities. I had always felt like an older soul: not necessarily more intelligent, but more socially evolved than other kids my age. These feelings I had about myself were just the sort of things Emily came to reinforce and validate. She talked to me like an adult, and I appreciated that. She clearly had significant issues; I think that goes without saying. But when she shared her own marital problems with me, I told her about my parents' divorce and anything else I struggled with, as if that was somehow relatable. Weird, I know!

I looked forward to going there, seeing her, and talking to her. When we were "alone"—meaning her two kids and my brother were downstairs, watching TV—I would talk with her upstairs. But I started to notice that, whenever there were other adults around, she wouldn't pay any attention to me.

She was intentional, calculated even. She used a completely different, high-pitched, fake tone, similar to how you would talk to a baby… or a dog. She avoided eye contact and spoke to everyone in the room except for me. Basically, she treated me like any other eight-year-old. Some time went by like that, where I was kind of "put back" with the rest of the kids. No more being upstairs, no more one-on-one conversation, all with no explanation. I learned later in life that this type of behavior was what my therapist described as *grooming.*

Emily had a split-level house, like my mom's house, but smaller. The kitchen was on the main floor, along with the most cramped intersection between the upstairs and downstairs. A small flight of stairs led you down to the garden level, which had just enough room for a three-person couch and a TV. This was where all the *kids* hung out after school. There were also five stairs leading right up to her bedroom door.

One day after school, we were playing a game on the TV downstairs, and I went up to the kitchen for something. Before I went back down, she called my name. So, I looked up the stairs to acknowledge her, but before I could say a word, there she was… without a shirt on!

I'm not sure how long that moment actually lasted, but I can imagine I responded like a deer in headlights. I remember turning my head and quickly going back downstairs. I was… totally cool, calm, and collected. Obviously, I had seen this countless times!

No! I was hyperventilating and feeling all *the things* for the first time. I was still at an age when I wasn't interested in girls like that. But I was curious in the most basic ways. After that, my curiosity… Well, I was going to say it *exploded,* but that would probably be inappropriate.

I thought for sure I would be in serious trouble and figured she would tell my mom. *I wasn't; she didn't!* I was waiting for her to come down (with clothes on) and yell. *She didn't.* No, instead, she never said a word to me about it.

Several days went by as if nothing had happened. I didn't know what to do with what I'd seen. I felt like I was living on an island… and that island was made of boobs! I had dreams about having a bouncy castle… also made of boobs—floor, walls, roof, and all! Lying in my bed at night, the light on my ceiling… yep, you guessed it: it became a giant boob!

If this story ended here, I would have probably been grateful for the sneak peek into the land of boobs. I imagine it would have been like that scene from *Wedding Crashers*: "What? So, some hot older lady made you feel her cans? Quit crying like a little girl!"

This wasn't where this scenario ended, though. There was a "next time" when this occurred, very similar to that initial instance. The way she got my attention was the same; only this time, rather than ignoring me, she signaled me upstairs. And I went.

This was the first time she shut and locked the door behind me before I realized where this was leading. I can't say I didn't want to, because I mostly did, out of curiosity. At least initially. This continued to happen intermittently for a short while. It wasn't every day; it wasn't even once a week.

It made me feel uneasy, because I never knew what I was walking into. Some days, most days, Emily left me completely alone. It almost felt like I was being ignored. On other days, she seemed so genuine, engaging, and nice, and she appeared to care about how I was doing. Anytime there was anything physical, that's when this cycle would reset. I found myself in a constant state of adrenaline, riding a wave of emotion with extreme highs and lows. I felt like I couldn't talk about it. After a while, I think I felt that way because I was actually worried it would stop, even though I wanted it to, sometimes.

It's difficult to revisit those feelings this much later in life. Can I know for sure that I was, in fact, feeling one way over another? Impossible. I liked the attention, no doubt. Maybe not physically, but emotionally. I enjoyed having an adult *validate* me the way she did.

But in a way, I felt trapped. If I said something, I risked everything. However, by not saying anything, I inadvertently caused more harm than good. I ultimately isolated myself with this secret.

One time, on the way home after my mom picked us up, I actually got sick in the back of the car. My brother didn't know what was going on, and I wanted to keep it that way. I felt like it was my job to protect him, and I needed to shield him from this. I did everything I could to make sure he was never alone with her at that house. In my head, if it were happening to me, it couldn't be happening to him. Another day, I was actually sick—like cold-type sick. In a way, I should have stayed home from school. Instead, though, I downplayed my symptoms and forced myself to go, so he wouldn't be alone at Emily's.

Make no mistake, both of my parents paid very close attention to my brother and me. They asked me plenty of times if I was okay during the period when this was happening. I never said anything. I learned in a not-so-obvious way that trauma's best disguise is other trauma. I was always the *talkative* one and genuinely shared anything and everything with my parents! So, when I said I was okay, I knew they believed me. If something was off, I was generally the one to tell them and wasn't shy about it.

By keeping this to myself, I didn't see it as protecting Emily. I felt like I was protecting myself. I just didn't feel like facing this, back then. Part of me knew the consequences of something like this would be severe. And, of course, it would embarrass and hurt me, but not just me—everyone who cared about me.

Around this same time, I went to talk to a counselor or a family therapist. The purpose of this, or so I was told, was for me to "work through" my parents' divorce. The therapist emphasized that everything we discussed was confidential. She really drove that home.

After my sessions, my mom always wanted to know what we talked about, what was said, and so on. In one of my sessions, the therapist asked me something along the lines of, "Has either of your parents ever physically hurt you?"

I really don't know why, but I lied and said yes.

Honestly, I can't help but laugh when I think back on this. I vaguely remember how the therapist was guiding the narrative, and I just *played* along. I was also mad at my parents for making me go there. Still, it's no excuse.

I didn't feel much like talking during this session, and instead of that being okay, she pressed on. She used hand movements and gestures, trying to piece together how I was "hurt." I was stuck, once I'd said "yes" to that initial question. There didn't seem to be a way back out of this. So, I yesed and noed my way through it. I don't even remember if I said it was my dad or my mom. I just know that this was how I found out that "client confidentiality" doesn't always apply. I learned that the therapist was basically sharing everything about our sessions with my mom.

A decent period passed without thinking again about Emily. As time went on, it felt further and further away. As I now know, that feeling never truly goes away, and it would involuntarily remind me of it periodically as I grew older.

One of the earliest times it showed up was when I was in seventh grade. I had my first girlfriend, or at least the first one I actually hung out with. Everyone should know what that means. In grades one through five, you have a girlfriend you never speak to! Those relationships were perfect… and equally a win-win! I just brought her flowers and candy on Valentine's Day, we exchanged the occasional note, and I got to call her my girlfriend.

Anyway, when I was in seventh grade. I was probably 5-foot nothing, going through that awkward stage, and experiencing all the weird changes. I had kissed a girl, but not like kissed-kissed yet. Suzie (yep, real name) was in eighth grade. (I know, a real cougar). And she had *matured* faster than most of the other girls.

Right around Christmas time, a bunch of us from school decided to go see a movie. I obviously wouldn't go on a date with my girlfriend by myself... That would be insane! We all met at the movie theater fifteen minutes ahead of time.

Please take a moment to reminisce: think back to that prehistoric world, before creature comforts like cell phones, text messaging, and even Google. These were the dark ages, when we had to look up the movie times in the TV & Entertainment section of the *Denver & The West* newspaper. Then we had to call our chain of friends, one at a time, from our landline to theirs. If someone was using dial-up Internet, the phone wouldn't ring. Yet somehow, we all managed to make a plan, stick to it, and execute it... *Squirrel*!

There were four guys and four girls. The guys got the tickets, and the girls worked out the seating arrangements, based on who they liked the most. Suzie and I sat together, obviously. (Take a minute to remember a time when you were so nervous to hold someone's hand... and you're welcome.)

So, the hand-holding began, and it was intense... We found every way to rub every side of every one of our fingers together. We did so in such a way that could be seen as trying to switch it up! Really, we all know the truth was that it was just getting kinda clammy. I must have been the most naïve guy in the world.

Eventually, the hand-holding peaked, and Suzie (bless her heart) looked over and asked me if I wanted my Christmas present. Without a second thought, I nodded my head, yes, and that's when it happened! Halfway expecting a copy of the latest Eminem CD, I went for the peck! Unfortunately, she went for nineties softcore porn! Just like that, I'd had my first *kiss-kiss*, sort of.

Sounds relatively normal, right? Everyone's first make-out sesh is a mixed bag. Well, in my case, this ignited a bunch of shit I thought was dead and buried. I should have been excited, or anything other than the way I actually felt. I started to feel weird. Was it her? Was it me? Did my tongue really just rub the exterior of someone else's braces? *Gross*!

I had to get the fuck out of there… So, what did I do? I said I had to go to the bathroom. Instead, I called home… from a payphone!

My mom answered, and I immediately blurted out, "Suzie stuck her tongue, like, all the way in my mouth…"

The line is silent, and then my mom goes, "Okay?" And I can tell she was trying not to laugh. She asked me where I was and where Suzie was.

I told her I was calling from the payphone and that Suzie was still in the movie! My mom didn't understand why I was so uncomfortable. How could she? I didn't even really understand it at the time. In retrospect, though, it's pretty straightforward: *that wasn't the first time someone had stuck their tongue in my mouth…*

I ended up doing what any gentleman would do. Rather than deal with this, I took the high road. When we got back to school on Monday, I broke up with Suzie. I know, tragic. But at least I was man enough to do so both passively and indirectly… I gave her friend a note to give to her. Listen, I don't like the sounds of it, either, but it was either that or confronting the awkward invisible elephant in the room. A combination of feeling gross, guilty, and confused.

In sixth grade, I went to Dr. Martin Luther King, Jr. Early College, a public school in northeast Denver. I was literally the only "Caucasian" in my class. Yes, I did own a pair of FUBU jeans, and no, I didn't know what that stood for when I got them. Fortunately, I was good enough at baseball, and I played on the eighth-grade team. My older teammates made my time in school more comfortable. I definitely stood out and never felt like I fit in. Funny enough, I won an award called "The Mile-High Scholar" for all sixth graders in my school district. Being that I truly was the only White kid in my class, it's almost impossible not to be skeptical about that.

Up to that point, religion for me meant we were baptized. I knew that my dad was an Episcopalian, and my mom was raised Catholic. She "converted" when she married my dad. We went to church, or so I'm told. After sixth grade, my grandparents encouraged me to go to private school. They generously paid for me to attend a Christian school for seventh and eighth grade, which was a lifesaver. It was the opposite of what I was used to. I had never even held a Bible, and now I had a class called "Bible Study." My FUBU jeans were turned in for school uniforms. And rather than attending a public school overflowing with kids, there were only twenty to thirty students per grade!

My best friend went there, too, Ryne, but I always called him *Ryno*. We grew up together, played baseball, and both our dads coached us. Ryne and I were best friends from age four through the beginning of high school, or at least until I moved to Parker. When we lived near each other, we spent almost every day together. We kept in touch and talked on the phone occasionally.

When he turned sixteen, about a year ahead of me, he came out to visit a few times. But it wasn't the same. It was noticeable how we were now walking two completely different paths. Somehow, he got involved with the wrong type of people and fell into the wrong things. I didn't recognize him anymore.

Shortly after graduating high school, I got a call from Ryne's sister. She let me know Ryne had passed away. I later learned he had taken his own life, which is never easy to process. Anger, sadness, regret… All those feelings run through your head. Could I have reached out more often? Maybe I should have. I think people come and go from our lives for many reasons, but in these circumstances, it's not always easy to understand. Gone but not forgotten.

This new school put me more at ease, and I learned so much more than I had expected. This is where I developed my relationship with the Lord. Bible Study was a great way to learn and understand the stories of the Bible, both literally and sometimes metaphorically. No amount of reading could have prepared me for the church retreat I attended with some of my friends, though.

I had never experienced anything like this before. We were up in the mountains, and the days were a mix of worship, service, and outdoor games. On our final day there, one of the younger pastors spoke about what it meant to be *saved*! That was the first time I specifically remember hearing that term: *saved*.

He described what it felt like to know that you were ultimately saved. He shared what *faith* meant to him in such a relatable way. I felt as if I was meant to be there just to hear that. Following his message, and during the final time of worship, I felt like I had found something I didn't know I was missing. Or perhaps that same something found me when I was in my greatest need.

Right when that feeling had filled me up, I quietly spoke to the Lord for the first time. I didn't know how one was supposed to pray, or if there was a "way." I simply closed my eyes, envisioned *Him* sitting just above me, and spoke to Him as if He were a friend I had always known.

From that day on, I have never gone anywhere alone, and, in the best way, I have never been the same. I have taken many steps toward the Lord, and I have also taken many steps away from Him. One thing I was reminded of recently is that no matter how many steps you take away from God, you only need to take one step back toward Him. That, to me, is the purest form of love. That is the definition of unconditional love.

If it's true that God only gives us what we can handle, I have definitely had days when I think He must believe I'm much stronger than I look. However, I have more days when I recognize patterns in His plans. The times in my life when I have placed Him at the center of everything are my happiest moments. Those are the times when my life has felt most meaningful.

I shared my newfound faith with my family. I wanted them to have an experience that I had. They have always supported me in my faith, but have been set in their own ways. And although I know they each have their own relationship with God, we have never discussed it.

My mom eventually remarried this weak imitation of a man, Clyde. He had two sons, Cody and Cory, and they were almost exactly Kyle's and my age. It hadn't even been a whole year since my parents divorced. It also hadn't been that long since Clyde divorced his previous wife. So, now we had four boys in one small house—my house—that I had to share.

And I thought I was angry… Cody was angry! Most of the time we spent together ended in some sort of fight. Cory and Kyle got along great, but Cody and I just didn't. I resented him in the same way he resented me. If we found ourselves having fun together, we almost had to check back into hating each other.

I don't make much space for these memories anymore. For me, they were simply things that happened on the way toward where we needed to be. Long story short, Clyde ended up being a bigger piece of shit than I'd initially thought…, which was impressive, because I set the bar pretty fucking low for him! Not one year into marriage with my mom, he woke up one day, went to work (in the brand-new truck my mom helped him buy), and we literally never saw him or his sons again.

I had thought my mom was devastated before, after separating from my dad. Now, we had to add the unresolved trauma of her and my dad's divorce on top of her "rebound" marriage to Clyde, and all within a very short time frame. I went back to mowing the lawn, and my mom recovered. This time, though, she went full-blown "man-hater." She wouldn't date. She wanted nothing to do with the male species.

Enter Steve. Steve was about my age when he met my mom, who had met up with a girlfriend or client after work. This was near the end of her "man-hating" stage, but she still wasn't interested in potentially more heartbreak. Steve was also a lot younger than she was; he had never been married, had no kids, and no baggage. Still, he pursued her; he wouldn't take no for an answer.

And I guess, when my mom gave him her number, she also gave several reasons why he shouldn't call. Something like. "I have two kids, and I've been married and divorced three times now. But hey, if you want that kind of baggage, give me a ring!"

He did, and ten years later, he actually did. They are happily married to this day.

Steve was different. My mom was different with Steve in the best ways. My mom had been burned and learned from it. So, she didn't let on that she had met him. They dated quietly for a while before she decided to introduce us. I was twelve, Kyle was eight, and we were both pissed off!

We had just recently retired from boyfriend-bashing. Kyle had finally gotten "out of the life" of NERF-Gun assassinations. We didn't want to deal with this shit again! Why couldn't our mom just be boring? Become a nun? Retire to the countryside?

She didn't tell us anything other than Steve was his name, and we were going to go bowling at this new bowling alley. *Bowling*? *Fuck*! *We love bowling*… So we were in.

"But we weren't going to call him Dad, ever! Not even if there was a fire!"

Much to our surprise, in walked this gigantic dude! It was no contest. I put my prison shank away and shook his gorilla-sized hand. I liked Steve right away. He wasn't too cool to be a gentleman. He was cool because he *was* a gentleman. He wasn't nice to Kyle and me to score points with my mom. He was just a nice guy. If you don't like Steve, that's because you either worked for him or you have something wrong with you.

Steve was the breath of fresh air our family needed. He moved in with us for a time, but ultimately, he and my mom decided to move us to Parker, Colorado. Douglas County and Parker, specifically, were great places to live, and the area also had one of the best school districts. I went to Ponderosa High School from ninth to twelfth grade. I couldn't be more grateful for this period of our lives. Steve saved us in more than one way. He had never been a father, yet he lived what a man looked like, setting a great example. He had never been a husband, yet he showed my mom the most unconditional devotion I have ever seen.

My mom excelled at work, and she ultimately decided to start her own insurance agency from scratch. She was great at this, and we know her success was partly due to the support she received from Steve. Kyle and I respected Steve. He didn't have to ask for that from us; the way he lived demanded it. He was the perfect blend of a role model, friend, and father figure that we desperately needed.

Our new life began in our new home and community. Even now, thinking about this time leaves me with a sense of relief. It felt like we could finally take a breath. Kyle and I felt safe enough to be kids again. I could let go of the idea that I needed to look out for my brother and my mom. I might finally be safe enough to be a *kid*—better late than never!

One thing that never really went away over time was the way my parents spoke about each other. Both my mom and dad shared their opinions and frustrations with Kyle and me. Often, we became the go-betweens. It wasn't just that we were hearing things; sometimes it felt like we were expected to carry messages back and forth. I know how that sounds, still…

My dad eventually got remarried to Diane, who was much younger and closer in age to me than to him. We were already accustomed to the pattern of perpetual change. I hadn't reacted well to my dad's earlier relationships, especially since the first woman we met was someone he had been involved with while married to my mom. I'd made my feelings known, often bluntly and rightfully so. I was angry and hurt; I was loyal to my mom.

By the time Diane entered the picture, though, Kyle and I were complicit. We couldn't control these things. We knew it, and in some ways, it was easier to adapt than to resist. Surprisingly, Diane brought out a lighter, more playful side of my dad, which was refreshing, as he had often been the stricter, more serious parent.

As both our parents settled into their new relationships, life at home became more stable—at least on the surface. But for Kyle and me, the back-and-forth between houses continued, not just physically but emotionally! We were still in the middle, still absorbing the lingering resentment and opinions. To be fair, my dad eventually pulled back from this dynamic; after an argument blew up at his house, he became more careful not to put us in the middle.

My mom, though, struggled to let things go. Talking about my dad was a regular part of our dinner conversations—sometimes it felt like it filled most of them. I've always understood and validated the pain and betrayal she felt from the marriage, and in the manner that it happened. But after a while, I wondered why her need to process it with us didn't fade.

A typical conversation might include questions about what we did at Dad's, what he said, how he looked, or what we said about her to him. When we finally had enough, she always threw one more in, like, "Well, did you remind him that he's a piece of shit?" This made us laugh sometimes. And this was how dinner ended sometimes. Too much of anything can be exhausting. Too much of this felt like I didn't know where her opinion ended and mine actually began. The lines would blur.

When I tried to set boundaries, even gently, it usually backfired. Disagreeing with her version of things or expressing a desire to change the subject sometimes resulted in friendly fire. Her frustration, once aimed at him, would turn toward me, with comments like, "You're just like your father!"

This was the constant, relentless pattern I was trying to grow up in. Eventually, without realizing it at the time, I often found it easier to go along with, laugh at, or vent about my own frustrations with Dad, which, unfortunately, kept the door open for more of these conversations.

The relationship my mom and I had and still have is complicated. We've played many roles in each other's lives, and there's a lot about her that I admire and see in myself. She can be fun, generous, and supportive; she's someone I've often turned to for advice or companionship. But she has a tendency to amplify things, making them bigger than they need to be. If you don't want to participate, she will do it without you, for you. There seems to be a level of calculation, as if considering how a conversation today might serve her in the future. Her insecurity in relationships has often meant she needs a lot of reassurance, and she gravitates toward gossip and drama, which sometimes leads to conflicts and fallings-out. Her words can cut deeply, and she rarely apologizes.

Anyway... My high school class had a good group of people. Like anywhere else, there were many close groups, but mostly everyone got along. I had a few groups of friends, including a guys' group that got together on Tuesday nights at our pastor's house. I played baseball and hung out with that group, too. I bounced around a lot; I became sort of a social butterfly.

By the end of my sophomore year, I think I'd grown out of my "awkward" stage; that year alone, I grew almost a foot. I was always the youngest in my grade, the last to grow, and the last to get my license. Having a summer birthday, so you could technically start school a year sooner or a year later, was a double-edged sword. Being able to drive gave me a sense of independence that I'm sure everyone can relate to.

In my junior year, I met *Ashley*. I liked her right away, and in a way that I had never experienced before. She was almost as funny as I was, very smart, and she quickly became my best friend. We ended up dating throughout the rest of high school. She was my first love and my first heartbreak. She was all those *first* things.

Before I met Ashley, I had a well-practiced boundary around any intimate encounter I found myself in. I only took things as far as I felt comfortable, which is crazy, because I'm a guy... and we are typically such selfless partners! I had been slowly, infrequently, and awkwardly evolving over time. I mastered hand-holding, kiss-kissing, and yes... I touched several boobs. Three to be exact, although technically two of them belonged to the same person. However, anytime things drifted past a certain point or "base" that triggered my suppressed sexual trauma, I bailed! I changed my name, my number, moved countries… you get it.

Because I had never told anyone, I was able to go for long periods of time without remembering that it had even happened. Whenever it came to mind, it was usually a fleeting image or feeling that I could beat right back down quickly. I buried those memories so deep that when I felt uncomfortable doing something that was supposed to feel good, I just assumed that was how everyone must feel.

However, at a certain point, I just accepted that abstinence was highly unlikely. And for the first time, I wanted those things to happen. Each step just took a little longer for me. Ashley obviously had no idea about my hidden struggle, and I went out of my way to maintain the façade that I was more seasoned and more comfortable than I really was. She was always patient, kind, and understanding. I think it was those things that helped me normalize, while at some point, I had gone from an asexual behavior to a more hypersexual one.

When the time finally came to sleep with Ashley, I was terrified—and not for the usual reasons. I wasn't afraid she'd laugh or judge me; I was worried I'd vanish. That something in me would snap back to that night I'd spent years pretending hadn't happened.

Ashley thought I had experience. I let her believe that. I had the swagger, the jokes, the fake confidence. But inside, I was shaking. Not from excitement, though there was that, too, but from this low hum of panic I didn't know how to name.

It's strange how trauma hides in the body. I'd spent years compartmentalizing the molestation, burying it under humor, ego, and distraction. I'd convinced myself it was just something that happened, not something that happened to me.

But with her, something shifted. She didn't rush me. She didn't make me feel broken. Her patience and kindness disarmed me. For the first time, sex didn't feel like a reenactment of pain; it felt like a reclaiming of something I'd been robbed of.

She helped me break free from the minimization I'd built around that event, the walls I didn't even realize were still standing. With Ashley, I learned how to stay, how to be present in my own body again.

That was the first time I started to believe that maybe I wasn't ruined. That maybe what had happened to me didn't have to define what intimacy meant anymore.

Just when I started to believe in safety again, life reminded me it could vanish in an instant.

Todd was a friend of mine from school. We were acquaintances more than friends, really. That is, until one of my best girlfriends started dating him. Todd and I had the same birthday, but I had to wait about a week longer to get my driver's license.

One night, while I was at my dad's house, I got a call from my friend, Anthony. It was early in the morning, around 4:00 a.m. When I answered, he calmly told me that our mutual friend and teammate, Tony, had been in a car with Todd and two other friends, when an accident occurred. He spoke as if this conversation wasn't his first call and wouldn't be his last.

He said that Todd and Sean were in bad shape, but they were at the hospital. He didn't really have to say much more than that. That night, four of my friends were driving down a poorly lit, one-lane back road in the rain. They ended up in a head-on collision with another vehicle. The driver of the other car, along with all three passengers in Todd's car, had passed away.

For a little while, it felt like all of Parker stood still. It's hard to know how to act or what to say when something that serious happens at such a young age. Tony's funeral was the moment when I just couldn't hold it in anymore.

Carlo was closer to Tony than anyone. Carlo played on our baseball team and became one of the better friends I have to this day. When he spoke at Tony's service, it was the purest silence you can imagine. He made it just long enough to get through what he had to say, and I won't ever forget those final words as he came down from the stage.

He pointed at the sky and said to Tony, "You're the man."

Our baseball team walked his coffin to the car, all of us wearing our jerseys. Everyone handles loss in their own way. For most of us, we were learning just that for the first time. Parker was already a small town, but it felt even smaller after that. The bond you make with people through something like that lasts a lifetime.

Would you believe me if I told you I didn't really know I was supposed to apply for college? I'm not kidding. I thought that was something that... someone did for you. You know, like your parents just handle that for you, while you're busy living your life.

I came to school at the beginning of senior year and found out that people were already getting their acceptance letters. WTF, Mom?

I went home that day, made my mom sit down with me at the computer, printed out all the forms, and filled them out to send in. I applied to all the universities in Colorado; I was basic that way. I also strongly considered Doane College in Lincoln, Nebraska. But after a quick weekend visit with a buddy of mine, I decided raccoon hunting wasn't for me.

I didn't even have my own email at this point; I was using my parents'. Colby, a buddy of mine from high school, can vouch that I literally got my first email during the second week at CU-Boulder. I think he said something like, "How have you managed to live this long?"

I should have set up my @colorado.edu email during orientation. Unfortunately, due to extenuating circumstances all beyond my control, I was too hungover to attend the week-long orientation. I heard it was good, though.

I drank my first full beer in high school. I also drank often during that time, which carried over into my freshman year at Boulder. I was taking twelve credit hours per semester, the exact minimum credits to be considered a full-time student. That year turned out to be fairly average, meaning I got straight Cs, which I thought was a miracle, but my grandparents didn't see it that way.

I was living the dream and even signed a lease for my second year in Boulder. Then, I got a call from my Grandma Susan. It was high time we had a chat, she said.

"Cs might get degrees, but not at $50,000 per year!"

Not even I could argue with that! This was a great change of pace. I was able to work *and* go to school full-time, which was a good fit for me. Initially, I was an accounting major, but when I transferred from CU Boulder to the Denver Campus, I found out I would have to take calculus for a second time. Rather than go through that again, I changed my major to business. In my final year, the business school changed its requirements, and I ended up having to take calculus after all.

During college, I got the four main insurance licenses I needed to sell insurance. I worked with my mom in her agency, and by the time I graduated, I had gotten pretty good at that job. I was living with a girlfriend, and our relationship ended dramatically. But it turns out that was just what I needed. That and a couple of months bouncing around in Europe with some buddies from school after I graduated.

I thought seriously about not coming home. I also considered being able to afford food. So, I came home and moved into a shit-hole, mother-in-law apartment on South Pearl Street in Denver, next door to a friend from high school. It should have been condemned, but I had never lived completely alone before. At the time, there were lots of bars and restaurants in this up-and-coming neighborhood.

Everyone should have the chance to live completely alone at least once in their life. For that little while, I was a ghost. I was everywhere and nowhere, whenever I wanted to be. I made no plans, but I was always busy. I got close to seventy ski days in one season, hiked a half dozen 14ers (peaks over 14,000 feet), and went on my first solo road trip. I liked that version of me, and I was motivated to seek out a little more for myself.

I moved in with a good buddy of mine, and if it's true that you become who you surround yourself with, I was in good company.

While I lived there, I secured a business loan and purchased my family's insurance agency in the Denver Tech Center. The company had sophisticated software that could analyze my business in every which way, all in hopes of revealing some profit at the end of the tunnel.

Instead, it ultimately showed that the business as it was would not earn enough to cover its ridiculously high amount of overhead! Not to mention paying myself or my bills. In buying the business, I had to factor in that I would also lose clients; it was just a fact of the transition. So, to offset the shortage, I would need to consistently bring in twice as much new business… No pressure.

I had a window of time when I was prequalified for a large business loan, and I also had to get my securities licenses, the Series 6 and 63, to be qualified to purchase the business. I always did well enough in school, and I'd passed the insurance exams simply enough without studying, but this was different.

The licensing test consisted of 150 general questions and forty-five state-specific questions for each. I needed a passing score of just 70%. I took it seriously, studied, felt confident about it…, and ultimately ended up with a 68%. I wish they hadn't told me I came within one question; it just made it feel worse. I was able to get an extension from the bank, though, and ultimately pulled this together.

The next nine to ten years of my life seemed to pass by at an accelerated pace. I became obsessed with *winning*. In every way imaginable, I wanted to win. And in every category, I didn't want to simply place well. I wanted to be the best at it. In the insurance and financial services industries, our production numbers were trackable daily, so we always knew where we stood. These trackers became the ways I determined my success, and at some point, I simply got used to seeing my name in one of the top slots on the board at all times.

In the first couple of years, I grew substantially and organically. I found a way to hold on in business through that tight financial transition period when I was going to be short. I measured every

KPI and pulled every report the system could give me. I learned that my business's greatest strengths and weaknesses were just opportunities waiting to happen.

If I knew we couldn't write one product, but we were competitive in another, that is where my focus would be. I viewed quality and quantity as one and the same. My response to a question about focusing on one over the other was usually just "Yes." *Yes,* I want the best clients, *and* I like enough of them to keep me busy. Still, I made just as much, if not more, time for existing clients as I did for new clients. I felt it was easier to keep a client than to replace one.

My first goal at the start of all this was to make enough money to pay my bills. At some point, it felt like I was playing games within the game, and my goals became doubling my earnings year over year. So, I tried to be smart. I bought a new truck, sure. But then, I bought a house. I dated plenty during this time in my life, but I always felt it held me back in some ways. As though the people I was dating didn't quite get what I was trying to do.

My network became more like family. I associated with people like me, who put their souls into their businesses and weren't ashamed to admit that. Like many, I started feeling like a bigger fish in a smaller pond. Restricted. Mostly in ways that didn't matter, but I didn't know that then.

I felt like, if I wasn't growing, I wasn't moving forward. I started being consistently awarded my company's top accolades, which was validating. Success had a way of making me feel invincible. Like I could outwork, outthink, and outrun anything—even myself. I kept chasing the next win, the next title, the next version of "enough." But the thing about constantly climbing is that you forget to notice when the ground beneath you starts to crack. I didn't know it then, but all that drive was just a distraction from the one thing I couldn't outwork: my own pain.

Chapter 2

Little ol' Complicated Me

Katie

Why is it always so intimidating to tell someone who you are? You must dig deep in your curated collection of "yous" for specific occasions.

I can pull out "professional" Katie, who covers up her tattoos with makeup and Band-Aids, takes out her nose ring, and wears appropriate yet stylish clothes, while sharing only tiny pieces of her life.

I can pull out "vulnerable" Katie, who is profoundly layered and multifaceted, and you are a lucky individual who gets welcomed into my rich soul, which only a few have seen.

I can pull out "vivacious" Katie, who is tenacious about life, music, books, snowboarding, golf, food, travel, friends, God, and family. Who knows how to be positive and everyone's biggest cheerleader, while keeping my bright smile as I welcome new experiences and faces.

I can pull out "argumentative and mean" Katie, whose tongue is sharp and cruel, knowing how to pierce through the thickest of hearts.

I think you understand the idea. We become educated shape-shifters, crafting an ever-evolving collection of what influences us and how we wish it to be "presented." God forbid someone notices a flaw or two.

As I began writing this book, I found the process of confronting the traumas I had successfully compartmentalized and neatly tucked away to be incredibly triggering. Unpacking this without slipping into a dissociated state has been both challenging and rewarding, and I hope you can hold space for my vulnerability. Unfortunately, there are some empty pages that no amount of therapy or EMDR can fill, due to my brain's protecting my little ol' complicated self, plus a brain injury I sustained in a car accident that affects my memory. But I am ready to share the parts of myself that need to be released. So, here goes.

Hi! My full name is Katherine Elizabeth Farland, but I now go by Bowick (married woman). I was born and raised in Colorado, which I still proudly call home. I grew up in a house where we blasted the Beach Boys, Bananarama, Kenny G, and Tears for Fears on Sunday mornings during breakfast, before heading to church. During my adolescence, I was surrounded by Disney movies, Polly Pockets, Power Rangers, American Girl dolls (Molly, of course), Legos, and an imagination I exercised daily. I still sound out Wednesday as Wed-*nes*-day when I spell it, and if it weren't for spell check, I would always spell *definitely* incorrectly. I love reading; I love getting lost in stories and the power of words they carry.

On a snow day, there is nowhere I would rather be than on the mountain, snowboarding in between trees or bombing down a well-groomed black or blue run. The sound of waves crashing on the shore, with my feet dug deep into the sand, soothes and recharges my soul, and the warmth of sunlight on my skin awakens every cell in my body.

I adore the somber feeling a full moon gives me when I stand outside in the cold grass, staring up at the night sky in awe, basking in God's heavenly creation. I love the smell of freshly pressed coffee in the morning, and I enjoy lying on my warm laundry atop my bed, the second it's out of the dryer. I hear past the surface level of conversations to the root a person is speaking about. I give people the benefit of the doubt and see them for their good qualities, rather than their darker sides—considering we all have them, and I think we all wish not to be defined by the perfectly imperfect messes at our core. I am incredibly trusting and can be very naïve. I will accommodate others to a fault and will sacrifice myself by people-pleasing to the point of personal destruction.

I am constantly torn between my two loves: music and movies. Occasionally, to recharge, I require hot tea or a glass of red wine, coupled with plush blankets, Harry Potter, and no conversation. Other times, I crave the energy of people, parties, midnight walks, and deep, frenzied discussions. I blossom in the joyful. My mind works deeply, and I feel like a walking paradox when it comes to how I see the world and its hypocrisies. I see magic where others do not, and I fiercely need to believe in magic. Being a Libra, I struggle with the delicate balance—a perpetual tug-of-war—between feeling fierce and taking up space versus feeling soft in the solace.

I adore calm people, because they bring peace to the busyness of my life. I speak to Jesus quietly in my head throughout the day, having full-blown conversations with Him about the complexities of our world, even down to insignificant things like why I keep stubbing my toe in the same spot. I cry *a lot*. And sometimes, I simply need to feel sadness. I need to experience the struggle of being alive.

My mom, Kay, was incredibly active in the church while I was growing up; her faith is one of the strongest pillars on which I'm grateful to lean. She is the salt of the earth and my refuge, providing a space where I always feel understood and offering me a life worth living. Her light and kindness shine upon our family daily, and her voice is the most comforting sound when I call, and she says, "Hi, sweetheart!"

I inherited her freckles and infectious smile, and she has taught me to love, forgive, and pray for those who hurt me, allowing forgiveness to release and wash away their pain from my heart. She is uncommonly selfless and provides a quiet strength that we all take for granted.

My father, Dan, worked incredibly hard to build the beautiful house they built over forty years ago on a few acres with horses. He provided for our family in every way. He is the strong, silent pillar who absorbed and protected us from harm. Because of him, I learned to value myself as a complete person rather than half of a whole. He is intelligent, witty, and a force to be reckoned with. He always provided for our family, even if it meant sacrificing his happiness and time. He gains respect and deserves it. And now that I am older, Dad, I am ready to hold the flashlight for you and keep it still. Maybe…

I am smashed in the middle between two sisters, and I feel more at home here than anywhere else on the planet. The older I get, the more grateful I am to be the middle Farland girl, buffered from the world by one big-sister (Ashley) and one little sister (Jessica).

Ashley and I are eighteen months apart. She lives a beautiful life with her husband, Cole, and their two children, McKinleigh (nine) and Teryn (six), who mean everything to me. Since Chris and I have chosen not to have children, these two bring us so much joy and laughter, we would do anything for them. I love seeing the world through their eyes, and my inner child smiles every time we get to play. Ashley is full of tenacity and kindness; we often find ourselves unintentionally matching outfits, and she is my steadfast source of validation while lovingly challenging me. She drops everything and hops on a plane for every surgery and heartbreak, providing a support system I rely on immensely.

Jessie and I are four years apart, and she towers over us in height. She's sarcastic, incredibly generous, and full of sass. She and her husband, Brad, live an adventurous life with their handsome dog, Atlas. She is extremely loyal and always quick to smile and offer encouraging words. I also don't have to worry, since she worries enough for both of us.

All three of us are incredibly close, and a day doesn't go by that we don't talk or text; there is very little we don't know about one another, and we love one another through our imperfections and know precisely what buttons to push. Sisters are a rare combination who see you at your best and love you through your worst. Talking to them daily isn't just a habit; it's a welcome reminder that, no matter how dark it gets, I have someone who truly understands me, flaws and all, and will still love me just the same.

We bear each other's burdens and have healed together, even though scars remain. The hidden scars from mental illnesses, suicide attempts, too many hospitals, sexual assault, eating disorders, car accidents, babies, natural disasters, and surgeries (just to name a few), into shared tattoos—etched not only in ink but in resilience and shared understanding.

I grew up believing that arguments should be handled privately, behind closed doors. We rarely heard yelling; instead, we learned the art of the silent treatment, which I have carried over and perfected in my relationships (something I'm not proud of). I am a master of stonewalling and compartmentalization. Occasionally, we acted as messengers between my parents. And in any marriage, the D-word arises from time to time. However, our parents consistently work through their problems, just as any couple does. They have taught me that vows are taken seriously and values and morals are among the highest treasures, which one should wear proudly, along with the power of forgiveness.

Interestingly, my parents met at a Mormon church. My dad was raised Catholic and even served as an altar boy, lighting candles and performing the usual duties. My mom grew up in the Methodist faith and has wholeheartedly embraced her beliefs. They found the teachings of Mormonism quite intriguing, first appreciating their emphasis on family and community.

My dad noticed my mom's regular attendance at the church and immediately recognized her beauty. One day, he mustered the courage to sit beside her in the pew and intentionally shared a hymnal with her. Years later, they married in the Mormon church in Utah, and the stories my mom told about that day and their ceremony felt both intense and peculiar.

Since their families weren't Mormon, they couldn't enter the church, but a few weeks later, they hosted a backyard gathering to celebrate their big day with close friends and family. My mom worked as a nurse and was helping my dad through school at BYU. She felt pressure from the church, which constantly asked, "So, Kay, when do you and Dan plan to start a family?"

This remark irritated my mom immensely. Here were my parents, working tirelessly to finish school while juggling multiple jobs and living in a small basement, where my dad's head nearly brushed the ceiling, yet they were being asked about having kids. Eventually, they moved back to Colorado and left the Mormon church when my mom became pregnant with Ashley, choosing to raise us girls in the Methodist church.

Growing up, attending church gave me the space to discover my faith on my own terms. As a child, my relationship with God was innocent and surface-level, and I took the Bible very seriously. I was a sensitive, quiet kid, full of curiosity and just enough perceptiveness to make things interesting. If my sisters ever misused the Lord's name, I tattled immediately—which McKinleigh now does to me occasionally. Karma is a bitch, am I right?

One time, during a fight with Jessie, I looked her dead in the eyes and said, "You are not welcome at God's table!" I have no idea where I picked up that holier-than-thou attitude, but thankfully, I grew out of it.

By middle school, I became deeply involved in our church's youth group at PEPC—Parker Evangelical Presbyterian Church. One of the most life-changing experiences I had was during a Young Life camp in Frasier, Colorado. It was a three-day retreat, but the last night is still etched in my memory. The preacher invited us to accept Jesus Christ as our personal Savior and to welcome Him into our hearts, if we felt led. As we worshipped, I remember listening, truly listening, for His Spirit.

And then it happened. I fell to my knees, overcome with emotion, tears streaming down my face. I cried out to God with everything in me, surrendering and committing myself to be rooted and established in His love and glory. I felt an overwhelming warmth rush through my body, accompanied by full-body goosebumps, a sense of fullness I couldn't quite explain, and the most profound peace I had ever known. At that moment, I knew His work had begun in me. And I knew my life would never be the same.

Growing up, my parents did everything they could to provide for us girls. My dad started an insurance agency from scratch, while my mom worked as a nurse intermittently, to help supplement our household. I will never forget the day when, to afford my tuition, they sold one of my dad's favorite cars.

While I bounced around three different colleges each year (Hawaii, CU Denver, Boulder), they never complained and were fully engaged in the experience, supporting me through graduation. My gratitude toward them is something I'll never fully grasp, but *Thank You* for letting me figure out life and for welcoming me back home after college and during Covid.

I'm sorry, Dad, for not majoring in business management, but hey, at least I graduated! Throughout college, I always felt guilty, knowing they were doing so much for me financially. At one point, I worked three jobs to help ease some of the financial burden.

One of the jobs I enjoyed most was working for Kroenke Sports Enterprises on the Game Entertainment team. I love hockey, so I was fortunate to be part of the team that assisted with the Avalanche and Mammoth games. Unfortunately, during my junior year, just twenty-four days after my twenty-first birthday, I was involved in a traumatic car accident on Highway U.S. 36, heading east to Denver.

When traffic stopped near the Broomfield exit, I was driving to work for an Avalanche game in my black Jeep Cherokee Sport. Suddenly, a girl struck me at 65 mph, causing me to crash into not just one but four cars in front of me. Remember, I had a full car's length of space in front of me; that's how hard she hit my completely stopped vehicle. It felt like I was in a slow-motion movie.

Stopped in traffic, I had just turned down the radio when I glanced in my rearview mirror and saw a white, lifted Jeep Cherokee barreling toward me. A girl with brown hair was texting on her phone, completely unaware of the chaos she was about to cause.

My airbag failed to deploy, so I immediately slammed my forehead into the steering wheel—*BAM*! My head then rolled to the left, striking the side against the window—*POP*! It rolled back to my headrest and forward again, crashing into the steering wheel—*BAM*!

I don't know how long I was out cold, but when I regained consciousness, I saw the contents of my trunk sprawled out in front of me. My seat had buckled, pushing me forward and crushing my chest against the steering wheel. In front of me lay shattered glass and the completely wrecked engine, steam billowing from my car.

I have no memory of physically exiting the vehicle, but my head was ringing, my vision was blurry, and I could taste the metallic bitterness of blood. I apparently walked to the car in front of me, where I saw a newborn baby being pulled from the back seat, and I immediately lost it and broke down, feeling sick with worry for the child. Fortunately, no one was hurt by the cars I was propelled into. I believe the main reason for that was the space I'd kept between myself and the red car I was forced to hit.

This moment drastically changed my life in every way. As I was taken to the hospital and fitted with a neck brace, not in a million years could I have known this car accident would still affect me to this very day. I couldn't get behind the wheel for months because of PTSD. My 3.8 GPA dropped to 2.5 in a matter of months. I couldn't stand for over thirty minutes at a time, and the number of doctors I had to see was overwhelming. I also had to see a range of therapists: speech, cognitive, behavioral, physical, massage, chiropractic, psychotherapy, neurological, and occupational. Recently, I went in for another MRI, and as I lay there, listening to the clicks, vibrations, and alien-like noises, I couldn't help but reflect on the past sixteen years and all I have experienced since that horrific car accident.

- I've undergone numerous MRIs and X-rays
- Caudal epidural injections
- C4 through C7 disc bulging
- L4 through S1 disc bulging
- Hip injections
- Radiofrequency nerve ablations in my neck, back, and shoulders
- Medial branch blocks
- Facet injections
- Regennex: stem cell procedure
- Glute med/min/piriformis/hamstring injections
- Platelet-rich plasma injections in my hip and the L4/L5 and L5/S1 regions aimed at enhancing blood flow to the degenerative disc and annular tears in my spine
- Bilateral injections at C2-C5
- Discogram with an injection of my own bone marrow
- Trigger point injections
- Injections in the IT band and pubic symphysis
- Bilateral iliac crest injections
- Consultations with TMJ specialists
- Physical therapy
- TENS system
- Chiropractor
- Essential oils

- ⌘ Acupuncture
- ⌘ Massage therapy, two to three times a month
- ⌘ Therapist for food sensitivities and intolerances to address food inflammation
- ⌘ Pain management specialists
- ⌘ Functional wellness providers
- ⌘ Herbal supplements
- ⌘ Cognitive specialists for my traumatic brain injury
- ⌘ Spinal stenosis
- ⌘ Coccygectomy (yes, I had my tailbone removed)

When I discovered I had a brain injury and needed to relearn basic skills while working on my memory, which remains a daily struggle for me, I felt as though I had to find myself all over again. Now, with complex PTSD, anxiety attacks, migraines, and a constant pain level of six to seven every day, I try to put on a happy face because I have come so far and endured true, gut-wrenching pain. At the end of the day, this accident does not define me. It took many tears, anxious moments, and a lot of suffering to reach where I am today.

I will never forget the day I cried out to the Lord in tears in Gatlang, Nepal, during a mission trip. We had a free day, and we trekked on a beautiful hike into the Himalayas. I fell to my knees while hiking in this small town, in front of magnificent snow-capped mountains, and cried out to Jesus, asking Him to take control of my pain, stating it was now in His hands, not mine. I asked Him to look after me, and I have never looked back.

Coincidentally, someone in our group took a picture of me on this hike after I had a prayerful, heavy meltdown. A bright ray of sunlight shines through the clouds, cascading down my neck and back, while my side profile reflects a look of rest, contentment, and pure surrender. The photo reminds me of what I told myself then: "You are strong, you are enough, and you are not broken, Katie."

To heal, I had to lose the identity I'd built around my pain. When we experience trauma or prolonged stress, we develop coping mechanisms to survive, and these mechanisms become our identity. This behavior isn't a flaw. It is a survival strategy. But as we grow, they limit us, keeping us trapped in patterns that no longer serve us, even though they once helped us feel safe. Healing is not about erasing these parts of ourselves. It's about understanding them, letting go of patterns that no longer serve us, and creating a new way of being that is not defined by our pain.

When it comes to trauma, and especially trauma involving car accidents, there's one story that has stayed with me ever since I was sixteen. It was a rainy Colorado evening, June 18, 2004, and it changed my life forever.

Fun fact: my teenage weekends didn't involve Keystone Light or sneaking vodka from my parents' liquor cabinet (later refilling with water), like most high schoolers. Instead, our house was a haven. Friends came over to play pool or air hockey, gamble on an old-school slot machine, or race each other for hours on a sit-down arcade car racing game. We had a cozy movie room, too, with an oversized, overstuffed couch and a DVD collection that made it feel like our own mini-Blockbuster.

For any of you young ones who don't know Blockbuster, it was a store filled with movies you could rent or "check out" like a library book for a few days. And before there were DVDs, you actually had to rewind the bulky VHS tapes yourself before returning them. If you didn't, you would be hit with a fee!

That evening, my then-boyfriend, Kellen, and I were in my red-painted basement room. I was sitting at my repurposed vanity, putting on makeup and chatting with him as we got ready for a group of friends to come over. What I didn't know was that four boys had already arrived a little early, after grabbing dinner at Chili's: Michael Budge and Sean Student, both seventeen; Tony

Majestic, sixteen; and Todd Stansfield, who had just turned sixteen a couple of days earlier.

Our neighborhood was built on a long, winding road called Inspiration Drive, ironically named, given the pain that would soon be attached to it. There were no stoplights, just a stretch of rolling hills that invited any driver to speed.

Todd pulled up in his dad's Lexus, parking beside Michael's and Sean's newly purchased trucks. Then, for reasons we'll never fully understand, the four boys piled into Todd's car, likely to test out his dad's car by taking it for a spin.

Todd was speeding when he crossed over the center line. The Lexus collided head-on with a Chrysler driven by a man named Mike Gilchrist, who had alcohol in his system. Mike was killed on impact, along with Todd's passengers, Michael and Tony. Sean was rushed to the hospital and placed on life support, but he passed away ten hours later.

Todd survived.

Todd woke up to the unimaginable weight of knowing that three of his friends were gone, and he'd been the one driving. I can't begin to imagine the depth of pain, confusion, and guilt he must have felt or what it was like to open his eyes and realize he was the only one out of the group still alive.

While the rest of us grieved from a distance, I think Todd was suffering from within. He unfortunately became the face of the accident. Some people projected their pain onto him, with rage, questions, and a need to blame someone. He was just a kid, only sixteen, who made a mistake with tragic consequences. But it was a mistake that any of us could have made at that age, caught up in the thrill of freedom of turning sixteen and the illusion of invincibility of our youth. I will never forget watching Todd carry this unbearable burden.

Grief doesn't have rules, and Todd had every right to mourn, to fall apart, to rebuild, and to try to make sense of what happened. There were court proceedings, whispers in the school hallways, empty seats in classrooms, and attempts at group therapy, as we all sought to make sense of it all. He lived with the burden of survival. I don't know what healing has looked like for Todd over the years, but I know that bearing such a loss requires a kind of strength most people will never understand.

What still takes my breath away, even after all these years, is how truly amazing those boys were. Michael Budge had a magnetic personality. He was funny, sharp, and deeply kind. He was the kind of guy who could light up a room without even trying. People were drawn to him, and he vocally expressed his love for Jesus. He had a quiet leadership quality that made others feel included and seen.

Tony Majestic was full of energy and heart. He was funny and spirited, with a spark in his eyes that suggested he was always on the verge of saying something hilarious or insightful. Sean Student possessed a gentle strength. He was grounded, thoughtful, and kind. There was a steadiness to him that provided comfort, and he was a confident friend who didn't need to speak loudly to be heard. He had big dreams and a quiet fire inside him that you couldn't put out. I am convinced he would have been a professional hockey player if he'd had the chance to grow up.

They were all so young, yet they had already impacted many lives in such a short time. Their deaths didn't just shake our community; they left an irreplaceable void. It made us hold our friends tighter, prompting us to say, "I love you" a little more often. To this day, their names still come up in conversations. Stories are told, and laughter echoes in remembrance. They are not forgotten, and they never will be. I still have the rubber bracelet we had made with their initials etched on it: *TMS*. Their lives, though so brief, truly mattered. While I may never understand why they were taken so soon, I do know this… They left behind a bright, shining light.

I could go into how we discovered they'd been in that crash, how we followed the sirens, stood at the crash site with its scattered belongings, saw pools of blood, the overturned car, the scorched metal, and the smell of ash still in the air. I could tell you about walking into the hospital waiting room, where grief poured out of the eyes of families and friends, filling every corner with unbearable pain. I could describe the funerals…, three of them. And how I carried a casket across the cold floor of an ice rink, feeling its weight in both my hands and my heart. But nothing I could put down on paper can fully capture all that I had experienced.

What I can't fully explain is the guilt and the shame. The unbearable heaviness I carried for years afterward. Some people blamed me, too. Said it was my fault. That if they hadn't come to my house or if I had known they'd arrived, this never would've happened. Teenagers can be cruel, but when you add trauma, grief, and death to the mix, the cruelty takes on a whole new shape. This was one of the first times in my life when I became the unjustified scapegoat. And I carried that quietly for a long time.

The trauma resulting from the aftermath of this accident took years to heal. And as scapegoats, we are conditioned to believe it is our fault. I truly convinced myself it was my fault that they had died, and it was my responsibility to fix it. The burden I secretly carried wasn't just grief; it was the blame that others, overwhelmed by their own confusion and heartache, projected on me. Todd and I weren't especially close before the accident, but after that day, we found ourselves linked in a way that no one else could truly understand, because we both became scapegoats.

For a long time, I let that blame shape how I viewed myself. I held onto it like it was only for me to bear. However, people don't always think clearly when they are hurting. They try to make sense of the senseless, and if they can't find peace, they grasp for control. After years of therapy, I can rewrite my narrative around shame, and I no longer carry the weight of blame.

Thanks to finding a proper trauma therapist for complex post-traumatic stress disorder (C-PTSD), I no longer internalize what I had experienced. I've learned that, with a traumatizing event, PTSD can trigger a negative loop in our brains when the experience had such a significant impact on and meaning in our lives, and sometimes we don't process the event fully.

I also found eye movement desensitization and reprocessing (EMDR) therapy to be beneficial; it treats trauma and reduces anxiety. During this process, you bring up emotionally uncomfortable situations or memories (often related to trauma) that are causing you distress. While doing so, you focus on bilateral stimulations, like the light bar, pulsators, or tapping. This method helps the brain process the stored trauma and memories, so they don't continue to trigger you. You integrate it and dissipate it, so the past doesn't have to haunt the present. When you revisit these traumatic memories and work through them with this technique, you will remember them differently and become less likely to feel triggered by similar events and emotions.

What I love about it is that your brain naturally makes the connection, and your memory loses the emotional charge. Over time, EMDR enables you to be more present and helps you to acknowledge and process emotions, ultimately fostering a deeper connection with others. Most importantly, it stops you from living in survival mode. Talk therapy helps me to an extent, but I am too self-aware and intelligent for my own good. So, if you feel you are stuck in the past with trauma or have present anxiety from work, relationships, school, etc., maybe try it!

EMDR therapy helped me process specific traumas and challenge the beliefs I held to be true. It allowed me to realize I was not the problem, nor was it my responsibility to fix things. I needed to understand that the issue lay with them, and I was the only person I could control; I was only responsible for myself.

Oddly enough, getting a tattoo in memory of the boys helped me process this situation, especially considering my age. Since I was sixteen years old, my dad wouldn't allow me to get anything larger than a half-dollar, so I chose a side profile of a butterfly shaded in the colors I associated with the boys: red for Michael, orange for Tony, and blue for Sean. To me, butterflies symbolize transformation and resilience, growing into something entirely new and beautiful while overcoming hardship. The tattoo also matched my vibrant personality during this dark and painful time.

After carefully considering the best spot for my tattoo, I chose my left hip, but I wondered how bad the pain could possibly be there, right? Wrong. It's apparently rated as moderate to high on the pain scale, typically between six and eight. *OUCH*. I also didn't want too many people to know I had a tattoo, so I figured this would be an easy place to hide it. Years later, I expanded the butterfly to make it more visible, since it had seemed to shrink a bit, and I added three crosses below it with sparkling dust.

A fun fact about me is that on my birthday, October 15, I experienced a Category 5 hurricane named Wilma in Mexico, as well as a 5.0 earthquake, a tsunami warning in Hawaii, and one of the most significant recorded freak snowstorms in Colorado, all within three consecutive years after I turned eighteen.

Growing up, I felt lucky that my birthday fell during fall break. When I turned eighteen, my parents organized a trip to Cancún, Mexico. My dad loves the beach, so he always made sure our vacations included all five of us gathered under an umbrella, enjoying the sea breeze in our sandy swimsuits. With my invisible halo, I was excited to celebrate my birthday at the beach, where I could legally drink.

After checking in, my sisters and I settled into our own suite, a room near my parents'. After settling into our routine of food, beach, nap, food, beach, shower, food, and beach for a few days, the morning of my birthday finally arrived. Instead of a mariachi band singing "Cumpleaños Feliz" when we opened the hotel door, we found a vital bulletin letter that had been quietly slipped under our door, waiting for us to read.

In large, bold letters, it read something like:

> **We regret to inform you that, due to the imminent arrival of a Category 5 hurricane heading directly toward Cancún, all guests must evacuate the hotel immediately for their safety. Please prepare to leave today, as authorities have ordered a complete evacuation of the area. Each guest may bring only one personal item and essential documents. Our staff is here to assist you in making the necessary arrangements. We understand this is an unexpected and stressful situation, but your safety is our top priority. Please follow all instructions from hotel staff and local authorities. The front desk will offer additional information about evacuation transportation and shelter locations. If you need assistance, please contact hotel management. We appreciate your cooperation and urge you to respond promptly. Stay safe, and thank you for your understanding.**

My perfectly planned beach birthday slowly began to unravel. We all rushed to pack our backpacks with personal items we couldn't live without, thinking it would only be a few days. I packed my brand-new purple iPod Shuffle, headphones, a book, my pink Razr flip phone, my pink childhood blanket, a change of clothes, and makeup—because what eighteen-year-old doesn't think makeup is a priority during an evacuation?

As we approached the front of the hotel, lines of buses were loading with vacationers, while multiple staff members held clipboards and recorded relevant information. While we were standing to board the buses, filled with anxiety, my mom pointed out a row of insects skittering away from the storm in a long line, trying to escape, and marching like the rest of us in an organized fashion. As we boarded the overcrowded, poorly conditioned bus, my dad secured us a few seats together. Our group was the last to evacuate from the hotel, all of us soaked after standing in the torrential downpour of wind and rain.

As we left the hotel, the road began to look like a white-capped river, steadily rising above the bus's wheels as palm trees slowly toppled. After what felt like hours, we finally stepped off the bus and found ourselves at what seemed to be a college. The volunteers greeted us, asking for our names and the hotel from which we had arrived, before escorting us to the last five available chairs in the entire building, where we would wait out a Category 5 hurricane. The eye of the storm was barreling toward us, seemingly indifferent to our vacation plans. We were all packed in tight as sardines, though some were fortunate enough to find space to spread out.

Once we settled on the plastic chairs lined up against a busy stairwell, they began to close the heavy, gray doors behind us, trapping us with hundreds of strangers for the next five days. We would face hunger, angry outbursts, and lack of sleep, with our survival instincts starting to kick in.

Luckily, a fair number of the hotel employees came to the evacuation center with everyone else, so at least we could see a few familiar, if frantic, faces. One in particular took a liking to my oldest sister, Ashley. He was named Santiago and would sneak us extra fruit and even bring us a liter of pop (which we needed to hide, but was such a treat after drinking questionable water for a few days straight). He even helped our family find a new spot to camp together, up on the top floor, behind a long table that served water. This was a godsend. You can only sit down for so long. The supplied food consisted only of hot dogs with no buns, some fruit, and water, and even that became scarce the longer we were there. When people are hungry and scared, the energy in a room feels constricted and suffocating.

It would be fascinating for a psychologist to study hundreds of survivors sheltering in the same environment, especially as doom looms and food runs low. What we observed was both reassuring, showing humanity's capacity to remain civil, and frightening, due to the uncertainty. Specifically, a group of British women tackled the overcrowded and now filthy bathrooms. They guided us to the toilets that could accommodate either #1 or #2. They helped us with buckets of water to ensure the toilets flushed properly, and they even supplied hand sanitizer! All hail these queens of the disorganized bathroom!

In my free time, I walked around the college, observing how many people were packed into each classroom while searching for extra food. Surprisingly, I managed to make a few friends. Each classroom full of evacuees formed its own tribe with its own rules. In one room, you had to take off your shoes at the door before entering. Another had gathered all the food and medicine on a community table in the corner. While yet another was filled with people shaking from a lack of cigarettes, their patience wearing thin by the second. On top of all this, an angry bee colony attacked the college, deciding we would be their primary target. Did I mention I am deathly afraid of bees?

One night, my mom heard that a family needed help. With her nurse's degree in play, she headed down a flight of stairs to them. Just then, a two-story window completely shattered, showering her and several families with shards of glass. The eye of the storm was officially over us and showing no signs of letting up.

We compacted our space along with blankets and towels to help a family of five who had been bunking under the glass window before it shattered. As I replay this traumatic experience in my head, I can only remember small chunks of time. I think a lot of that is because my mom gave us girls some anxiety medication while we were there, for which I am incredibly thankful. I hope I never feel this dark, surreal survival mode again; it's such an ugly, unrelenting, powerless feeling.

Once Wilma dissipated, we were all frantic to get outside and feel the sun and air on our skin. Then, madness ensued:

"Who wants to go back to the hotel to grab any belongings?"

"Cancún's airport cannot fly out planes because of the damage from the storm. How will we get out?"

"Be careful. There are looters and individuals released from the prison, if you leave this area to look for food!"

A small group of men volunteered to go back to the hotel to see if there was anything to salvage, but my mom felt uneasy and didn't want my dad to join them. She had heard that a bus was coming from the airport to take us in groups to the Mérida International Airport.

My dad's phone had excellent service, and word quickly spread, leading people to line up to call their loved ones. When we got back home to the States and he saw his monthly bill, he quickly realized that international calling isn't cheap.

One of the fathers who had chosen to go to the hotel kindly stopped by our room. He retrieved Ashley's laptop, but he told us our balcony had been torn away entirely and fallen into the water. In the end, we finally got the oceanfront room we had paid for.

After watching everyone else evacuate to the airport, we finally boarded the last bus to Mérida International Airport. After four long, grueling hours through the jungle, navigating trees and debris while rocking back and forth over rocks and potholes, we finally arrived. Unfortunately, our driver provided little direction. He just turned off the engine, and we sat in dark silence and slept the night on the bus, unsure when we would get a flight out.

As sunlight peered through the muddy window, I awoke to the sound of people yelling at the front of the bus. It was between my dad and the bus driver, who were having a heated argument. The driver wanted us to exit the bus, and my dad overheard someone say that, once we were off, they would leave us stranded with no directions on where to go.

The situation escalated. My dad snagged the keys to the bus and turned it back on, holding his ground that we weren't going anywhere. Tensions rose as other evacuees on the bus chimed in with their opinions as to whether to keep the bus running or listen to the men laughing and mocking my dad.

My mom ran to the front and begged him to back down, to think about our family and how we needed him to come home–whenever that would be—not spend the night in jail. My dad's face seemed exhausted. He had been trying to keep his calm since being evacuated, and his survival instincts had been put into high gear, with no downshift of relief in sight. My mom quickly turned the engine off and handed the keys to the angry driver. Then, everyone on the bus had to exit.

As we walked into the small, overcrowded airport, a news crew member was speaking on camera with someone I assumed was a local mayor. They welcomed us, stating they were happy to help look after tourists and get them home safely. As the camera rolled, showcasing our sweat-soaked clothes and six-day-old hair, we grabbed a few blankets and a couple of water bottles. We walked around briefly, settling down by an inoperable suitcase carousel, and pow-wowed as a family. Because we had booked our trip privately, not through a travel agency, we quickly learned it would be a while before we'd be offered peanuts on a flight home.

Unfortunately, we had to stay at that airport for two more days. We slept outside under the stars near the entrance, on rough, hard grass, and we ran to the toilet every chance we got. Tensions brewed among all the stranded travelers, and the airport workers kept parading us around the airport to different gates and sections, giving us no new information but attempting to keep us confused with little glimmers of false hope. Our ticketed airline, Frontier, didn't have privileges at this airport. Any flights departing from Mérida were full.

I don't remember which airline flew us home, but I do recall there were about five other families on the Boeing 747, and we all stretched out in our own rows. The flight attendant was unhappy that we weren't respecting the "keep buckled and stay seated" sign, but our stomachs were in knots, and we kept rushing to the bathroom, both during the flight and during our descent.

When I looked out the window and saw our blue Rocky Mountains, I cried, finally letting out all the built-up anxiety and uncertainty. I've never been happier to be home. After departing the plane and not needing to stop at baggage claim, we finally made our way back to the house.

Once we got home, everyone rushed for a shower, and we quickly ran out of hot water. However, I didn't mind; I was just so happy to shave and didn't care about the clumps of hair falling out due to stress and lack of brushing. It took us a few weeks to get back into our routine.

I remember going back to school around Halloween. My girlfriends all matched in their cute costumes, and I was so disappointed and felt left out that I couldn't take part. A part of me was also incredibly bitter, because no one understood what we had just gone through, and it was hard to find the right words to describe it. I also had a big cheerleading competition a week after returning home; I had a panic attack from the loud noise in the arena. I remember crying on the ground in the hallway with my mom, overwhelmed by my anxiety and desperately searching for my headphones to listen to music.

My parents arranged for us to talk to a therapist, which helped us unpack our experiences as a family. I found having a safe space to discuss how this situation affected us incredibly helpful. My dad took this experience the hardest; I imagine, when we got home, he went upstairs, finally let his guard down, and cried behind closed doors.

As a family, we have faced other highly traumatic issues that I won't address specifically in this book, to protect them from further harm or judgment. We do occasionally brush things under the rug, because it is so much easier to pretend something didn't happen than to address it. But what we went through was another traumatic experience that ultimately strengthened our bond as the Farland family.

Did I mention we are incredibly supportive of one another and always focus on the bigger picture of forgiveness and love? This mindset has especially influenced me. I have carried these values into my future relationships, and as a result, I am quick to forgive. My biggest flaw, however, is that I can be incredibly naïve, allowing someone to hurt me repeatedly until it eventually goes too far. In the past, I have also stayed in toxic relationships, but I still stayed.

When I was thirteen years old, I made a promise to God and myself that I would be abstinent until marriage. I bought a purity candle to light on my wedding night, and I wrote letters to my soon-to-be husband, telling him how excited I was to meet him. I also told him about my faults, wants, and desires around sex and pressure.

My parents also showed their support for this decision. They bought me the most beautiful opal ring (for my October birthday) with a gold band, which I wore proudly all the way through college. The ring also put a big, red target on my back for boys, as well, that read: "Do not go out with her, because she won't put out," "Her staying a virgin won't last long," "What a goodie-goodie," "Maybe I should see how far I can push her and give her a note in English asking for a blow job."

After high school, another kid at a school I hadn't even attended said to me, "Oh, *you're* Katie Farland. You were what we called an 'untouchable'."

As you can imagine, my relationships in high school didn't last more than a year. Often, once we broke up, my exes quickly moved on to someone new, finding what they didn't get from me. I also didn't go to the big parties in high school, and there are days when I feel like I missed out on being young and carefree. However, during that time, I became deeply immersed in the church, the youth group, and my faith, which mattered more to me. Still, that didn't lessen the sting of those experiences.

There were moments when I felt pushed too far. In my senior year of high school, with prom just around the corner, I decided to attend a house party with familiar faces, thinking it would be a safe environment. I was wrong. Everyone there seemed excited to see me drinking, and within an hour, I was throwing up. I ended up lying down in an extra room while the room spun around me.

I don't remember a lot of what happened, but the gist is that multiple boys I had a lot of respect for came in, one at a time, to try to hook up with me, while I was passed out. One of my friends noticed what was happening and came into the room, choosing to sleep on the floor in front of the door to keep anyone else out. The following day at school, rumors spread that my friend had locked the door and that things had happened. It was awful. I never received an acknowledgment or apology from the boys who entered that room, and to this day, I don't think they even cared. This event was the beginning of my trust issues with men.

In my early twenties, when I was entering my junior year of college, I met a boy who was seven years older than me. We had both recently come out of serious relationships, and we really enjoyed each other's company. We had a great time together. I had been waiting until marriage to have sex, and he was aware of this. However, over time, my morals were pushed aside, and I felt pressured into intimacy.

I convinced myself I had to stay in the relationship no matter what, with the hope of eventually getting married, since we had already become intimate. The amount of guilt I felt during this time was overwhelming. Throughout the relationship, I had major blinders on; I ignored any red flags that came up and convinced myself that everything was fine.

Our relationship was messy. I moved in with Chad after graduating from college, but he was in a dark place, something I did not know about. I knew he struggled with drugs and alcohol, and I caught him in many entangled lies, but I stayed. I stayed because I thought things would eventually change, and I didn't rock the boat or challenge him, either. I thought I could "fix" him.

I realize this was the first time in my life I had fully embraced ignorance. I ignored the signs when I heard he had cheated on me and didn't ask him about it. I allowed his family to make me feel like I wasn't good enough for their son, and I believed it. I disregarded the fact that I was moving in with someone who frequently lied to me. I was so naïve; I didn't question why he kept the basement in his house locked.

One day, when I was home alone, I noticed the basement door was ajar. As I cautiously made my way down the stairs, I heard the loud whir of fans and the sound of plastic shifting. When I peeked around the corner, I found over twenty marijuana plants being grown in our basement. He had never mentioned this to me. I know you are asking yourself, how on earth did I not smell it? I always just looked the other way and kept telling myself things would get better and that he would eventually change.

Ultimately, we grew apart. One day, while he was out of town, I called my mom and said, "I need a U-Haul and some help to move out of Chad's house. I can't do this anymore." That same day, I moved into my sister Ashley's spare bedroom, just a neighborhood away. I began the emotional process of moving on, but I was left with confusion, guilt, and a lot of shame.

A month later, at my new corporate job, I received a call from my dad. He said, "Chad just came over here in a black tuxedo. He has a ring, and he just asked for your hand in marriage. He's headed your way at your work. I didn't give him our blessing, but he would still like to try."

I was stunned. As I gathered my belongings and ran to my boss to ask to leave early, I saw Chad outside, blocking my car, red roses in hand. I went outside in disarray. He got down on one knee and proposed, apologizing for not treating me well and begging me to give him another chance. He expressed that he would like to make it up to me for the rest of our lives.

As the snow fell around us, I asked if we could talk in his car. I don't remember exactly what I said, but I thanked him for our time together and told him the ring was stunning and that I would always love him. Ultimately, I said no. It broke me, knowing I had hurt him even more, but I didn't trust him with my heart.

To this day, I remain grateful for our time together, and I have learned a great deal about myself. He is a great man, incredibly generous and funny, and he deserves a wonderful life. Deep down, I also knew I wouldn't be able to give him the children I believed he wanted. And today, he has exactly that. I couldn't be happier for him.

Relationships are a challenging journey that everyone eventually embarks on wholeheartedly. We all yearn for some form of partnership. However, to find authentic, gut-wrenching love, we must be ready to love another person completely. But we also must be prepared to love through suffering, disappointment, and sometimes hatefulness. These circumstances are constantly changing and often conflicting, and each person will continually discover new aspects of their true selves.

When you first say, "I do" to the promises you intend to make, one aspect that I think deserves more thought is "through sickness and health." I encourage you to reflect on this carefully. Can you genuinely love your partner during their struggles with addiction? Maybe it's pornography, drugs, alcohol, gambling, sugar, or even excessive workouts. What if they face serious health issues, like cancer, losing a limb, or becoming unable to walk? If you have any doubts about your ability to support them through such challenges, I advise you to reconsider your commitment to them forever and always.

There is a quote I love that reads, "When one falls in love with someone's flowers and not their roots, they don't know what to do when autumn comes." Make sure you can love a person even when things get ugly, even though rebirth and new growth can happen.

We need to ask ourselves: do we know how to love the person we want to spend our lives with? To love is to celebrate, and we must celebrate their life in all its facets, the amazing and the ordinary, everything and anything.

To truly love involves some self-sacrifice, even when it feels destructive. We must endure hardship to find our place in this harsh world. And showing kindness matters most. When I was in my twenties, my heart grew increasingly uneasy and neglected, and I sensed that the small openings I had for a love partner were slowly closing, making it harder for anyone to find their way back in. Occasionally, after a few heartbreaks, I called my mom late at night from the bath, sobbing. I told her my loneliness was palpable, and I wondered if I would ever find someone who knew how to love the real me.

One of the best gifts I could have given myself in my twenties was the experience of living alone. There is something so beautiful about making your condo or apartment reflect your own personality and about learning to truly be silent with just you and your thoughts, embracing the loneliness. I realized I may have been lonely, but I was never alone. I learned how to lean on myself, and this is where I really grew into my whole being and found out who Katie is and why.

You have your whole life to live with your significant other, if you are lucky enough to find one. But how many chances do you get to live alone and become confident about living with just you? This is the reality of loving oneself, which then allows space for others to love you, as well.

And to open your heart to the prospect of finding love, you must also prepare to open yourself up to hurt. It is our perceived hurt of a future loss that has us put up our walls and not even let love in. At what cost? So, trust yourself, and unguard your heart.

Chapter 3

The Ten-Year Detour

Chris

I wasn't intimidated by Katie. That would imply I thought I would ever be anywhere on her radar. I knew her, and she knew me. Surface level, she wore a halo, and I swear she even had two tiny moles on her back, perfectly separated…, as if her little angel wings had been clipped at some point. Me? I had horns and a tail, and I wasn't sorry about that.

I'm not really the type of guy who says things like, "I love the story about how we met." But in this case, I've become that guy. The story of how Katie and I met isn't close to the story of how we ended up together. In fact, exactly one decade separates those two moments. When I think about it, ten years might not have been enough time for her to venture a little my way and for me to make my life-changing journey in her direction.

I can't say I ever "met" Katie. At some point, I learned her name, and I assume the same is true for her, as well. In high school, she seemed to have life wrapped around her perfectly polished, adorable little finger. She has always had this infectious smile… (I literally just smiled.) Back then, we had several classes together every year, yet we never really spoke to each other. She seemed to be in her own world, happy and content. Everything I knew about her had been told to me by other people.

I'm sorry, that's a lie. I never failed to notice her in her short shorts, and I came to that conclusion on my own. Though I wasn't the only one. She always seemed to have a boyfriend. We had many friends in common, but I guess we just ran in different circles. My circle was fun, beer-pong and house parties. McCormick's green apple vodka and… throwing up…

After high school, she took off to Hawaii, and I went to Boulder. I didn't know it, but in our sophomore year of college, we both transferred down to Denver. Even then, our paths never crossed. Then she transferred up to Boulder, where I had started. I know, it's like the universe was teasing us. We were living parallel lives, like two sitcom characters who don't share a scene until season three or ten.

The first time I really hung out with the adult version of Katie was in Boulder. She was living with some mutual friends of mine, and I went up to visit with my girlfriend at the time. As stated in the Geneva Convention, you always pre-game before going out on Pearl Street in Boulder. For the first time, Katie and I had some drinks together. I felt like I was partying with a saint! Then we went out, and I forgot I had a girlfriend. *Whoops*?

There was this weird gravitational pull between Katie and me. Everyone seemed to notice, including my then-girlfriend, who didn't understand she was killing our vibe! But it was the first time I considered Katie to be more than just a familiar face.

Over the next few years, our lives kept brushing up against each other. She'd show up as the fourth in our golf foursome, or she would sub for my softball team. We ended up carpooling together on a few ski days. I started seeing her more at backyard BBQs, birthday parties, Broncos games, and tailgates. Meanwhile, I was hopelessly dating around, wondering why I couldn't meet someone I had more in common with. Still, nothing really happened, and I admit, Katie started to make me nervous.

By nervous, I meant she made me… not me? I was annoyed with myself when she was around, because I couldn't keep my shit together! I always had the gift of gab, but around Katie, I was a toddler who stuttered. So, I stayed as far away from her beautiful face as possible, limiting my exposure to my inner teenager.

But then there was *the* Broncos game.

I showed up at a friend's house for the perfect Sunday Funday. There she was! I'll never forget it: she walked right up to me and asked if I could make her a Moscow Mule. I froze and just looked at her. You see, my "gab-gifter" had officially stopped working. So, I sort of nodded a yes-type response, and then I physically ran away. Yes, ran… like a jog, but quicker.

And let me be clear: confidence has never been my issue. If anything, my problems stemmed from having too much confidence. But there was something about her that unnerved me. It wasn't just that she was beautiful; I've always known she was. She was disarmingly confident and electric! It felt like I had just met her, like the real her. We didn't fall in love that day. But that was the day the spark was set… Call it what you want.

I saw her. Who she was right then, paired with who she was trying to be and everything in between. I had spent most of the time I'd known Katie thinking we were these two polar-opposite people. And we were/are? But at the core of what makes us *us*, we had more in common than not.

While Katie built a life, I built a life. When Katie bought a condo, I purchased a house. She sold art at a gallery to support herself and to live the life she wanted, which was/is attractive. I always saw that as her silent way of saying, "I don't need you, I want you." Ya know? *Squirrel*!

I was doing the same, except my version was a little more conventional. I was working my ass off…, but it wasn't for "me" anymore. It was, at first. I bought all the shit I wanted… Then I realized I didn't really want much. The house I'd purchased, I didn't live there… It felt like I was missing something. The way I'd pictured success was just different, if that makes sense. I wanted someone to do (verb) life with. Yeah, I said *verb*.

I don't know why it bothered me so much, but this was pretty much the last straw. Katie came by for a get-together we were having. I didn't know if she was seeing anyone. For a while, it had seemed like she was single, so that night, I innocently asked her if she still was.

She told me about this older guy from her old job, how they had been on and off for years. I thought, maybe… he had developed dementia! Ya know, since he was so old?

She politely explained how, during the *years* they were together, she had never met his family. It sounded like there were plenty of opportunities and the same number of excuses. I told her the truth about what that means. I didn't sugarcoat it.

Shortly after that, our ten-year high school reunion was our next meetup. Gross! I had no intention of doing that. Not a chance. So, naturally, when Katie asked if I would go with her, I told her I would pick her up! She could have asked me to do just about anything, and I would have agreed just as fast.

We'd hung out plenty before this, but this time felt different. I was nervous! Like, change my shirt twenty-five times nervous… Which is like… my highest level.

It might have been different if she hadn't asked me or if we'd just been meeting there. I still wonder how much different it would have been, if we hadn't started with margaritas at the Rio.

We had planned to meet some mutual friends for dinner first. You know, to ease into the night with a group buffer. But they got stuck in traffic. So, it was just the two of us. A dinner that was supposed to be pre-game and food ended up feeling a lot like… a date!

We talked. A lot. It was easy and light, but there was this energy I couldn't place. We already knew each other, but we hadn't talked to each other about the things we did that night. No awkward silences, thanks to me. Some awkward tension, thanks to Katie. She can't help it; her face is so readable.

The reunion itself was… fine. Do you recall why you sometimes forget certain people? It was sort of terrible. None of the people I associated with during high school were there. Katie and I smiled, we mingled, but neither of us was really feeling it. So, we bailed. Just a few of us headed downtown into the chaos of Oktoberfest.

Somehow, Katie and I got separated from the group. We were waiting for a friend outside this bar, and it was late. There was a dull-yellow light overhead, and we were leaning on a brick wall behind me. We were perfectly tipsy. We were standing around. We were talked out, but we kept making eye contact. A few grins were thrown back and forth.

I was literally thinking to myself, *I am definitely gonna have a make-out sesh tonight!* But, of course, true to how I had become around her, Katie beat me to it.

Out of nowhere, she looked at me in this way I've come to know. She was smiling, but it was a different smile, mischievous. She said, "How have we never kissed before?"

Fuck, this girl has stolen my game and is using it as a weapon to seduce me! I laughed awkwardly and mumbled something like, "I do not know… We should try that."

And we did. Once, twice, a third time, just to make sure it was good. Katie is never who you think she is, and when you think you know, she surprises you. This version of Katie was bold—something that was usually my job! She was also, historically, kind of a prude (she'll admit this!). She didn't make the first move, flirt, or chase, but here I was.

We called an Uber to head home, and I figured we'd had a moment. Maybe we'd hang out again some other time. I'd take her home, say goodbye, and be left to my conflicting thoughts.

But no.

As we're heading to her place, Katie leans forward, cool as can be, and says to the driver, "One stop, please."

I had seen movies start this way. I also would have bet every dollar I had against this exact thing happening. I also felt like, "Holy shit, I am going home with Katie *Farland*!"

And that night… is none of your business! Just kidding, I'll tell you all about it, but you have to pay me $100 per word.

We both had plans the following day, but I wanted to see her again. I also had this gut feeling: if I went back the next day, I wouldn't ever leave. Was I ready for that? Did I want to second-guess what I already knew I wanted, for the chance to screw it all up? I remember being vague with her, saying I might stop by, but I wasn't sure when. Truth is, I already had a bag packed in my car.

I was right, though. After that first night, Katie and I never spent a night away from each other for almost three years. It escalated quickly! That same first week, I mentioned to her that I was planning to take a day trip to the Maroon Bells, but honestly, in the back of my mind, I figured I would find a hike near Evergreen, instead.

She immediately sent a text back: "I'd love to go. Pick me up tomorrow?" *Ummm*, what?

What better than five long hours in the car to get to know each other more? There wasn't a second of awkward silence.

We started to talk. Like, really talk. The kind of conversation that feels like you've known someone your whole life but are somehow meeting them for the first time. We'd both lived enough life to appreciate what the other person had gone through. We were no longer those high school kids… thank God! We were more complicated. More layered. A little banged up, sure, but better for it.

Something real started to build. We found each other during a time when we weren't looking to date or settle down. It just happened. Turns out, we'd needed half our lifetime for it to come together.

I suggested buying a house together. She was excited and entirely on board. I got the ball rolling, and then I found myself at this standstill. I realized we weren't married, but if I was buying a house with her, that's essentially what I was saying I wanted, right? I knew that's what she wanted! *Shit*!

Then, I began to spiral. She's going to want a really expensive house! She's going to want an even more expensive ring. She said she wanted a Frenchie, and I hate those dogs! Perhaps this wasn't the right time. Maybe I wanted to sell all my belongings and move to Thailand. I didn't want that right now, but I *might* want it, someday… I won't be able to go, if I get married.

She knew I was scared, too. I was excited, don't get me wrong; I was fully invested. But man, reality was setting in: grown-up decisions. Shared mortgages. Tying our lives together. It was happening. It was real. And real really comes with a weight to it, even when it's the thing you want most in the world!

The truth is, I wasn't scared of the house or the expense of it all. And I knew I wanted to marry Katie. I just needed a minute. I needed all of that to settle in.

We bought a house and moved in! All of a sudden, we were seemingly a power couple with three houses. I liked it. So, I wanted to put a ring on it. Ashley, Katie's older sister, helped me pick out the perfect engagement ring and custom setting. It wasn't just any ring, either; I used a diamond that had belonged to my grandma, one my grandpa had given to her. It meant everything to me. It felt like it carried a story with it, and now it was about to carry ours, too!

I remember picking out our Christmas tree the day before I planned to propose. Just me, the future tree of our first engaged Christmas, and about 500 internal monologues about whether she'd cry (she did) or laugh (also did), or whether I'd completely black out and forget my entire speech (almost did).

But before I could ask her, I had to ask them.

When I talked to her parents, I thought I would be more nervous. We had developed such a great relationship that I was excited to share the news with them. Her parents are incredible people. They gave me their blessing with warmth and support.

The next day… was going to be "the day." We played hooky from work and were on our way up to Winter Park. Now, for this part, I was so nervous, and I think she could tell. I was definitely annoying her on the drive up there. I couldn't stop talking! But I felt like I had a live grenade in my pocket. I kept reaching for it in my coat, then putting it back. I knew I couldn't wait any longer, so I proposed on our first run on the top of Mary Jane Mountain on 12-12 at 12,000 feet, doing something we both love. (And yes, I got down on one knee in ski boots.) I'm amazing, I know.

At that exact same time, I was in the middle of selling my business. It was scheduled to close just three to four months later, on Feb. 1, 2019. I had the new agent coming into my office to shadow me for the six months leading up to the closing. I also had to hire and fire several people to remain/regain "compliance."

During the happiest time of my personal life, I felt like I was getting the cold shoulder from the people I'd worked with for the last fifteen years. I tried not to take it personally; I was leaving, and that was business, I guess. There is so much that goes into selling anything worth having, and selling a business is no exception. After I closed on the sale, I agreed to stay to help with the remaining tasks.

At the same time, I started a new role with a new company. I was having a hard time separating myself from the issues at the agency that, in part, were some of the reasons I'd wanted to move on. That made the transition into my new role somewhat more challenging. I was the only person in the Denver office at my new company who focused on insurance. The company was based in Chicago, where the rest of my department was also located.

After selling the agency, I made a decent amount of money. I had planned to make less in my new position, but after about a year, I started to get uncomfortable. I worried I was going to burn through too much of what I had made. We had the wedding to pay for, and honestly, I wanted to handle all that. We also got undisciplined financially. The money I had saved, plus the proceeds from the acquisition, provided a nice buffer on top of what I was making in my new role. I was grateful and confident for our financial cushion. I also had moments when I'd wake up in the middle of the night in a panic, thinking we were going to run out, and Lexi (our fur-child) was going to have to return to the streets, turning tricks for money!

Getting vulnerable enough to talk to Katie about this was hard for me. I always "had us," and I took care of everything because I wanted to. I made enough to cover our bills, and she made our house a home. If I could go back and change anything, I would have just fully included her in everything. Back then, I thought I was doing her a favor, keeping her from the stresses of bills and all that. But ultimately, it was a disservice. If she can't see it, how can she be expected to adapt or change when we need to?

She was surprisingly understanding about it. Not happy, but understanding. Which is more than I could ask for. We agreed to sell our house, and ultimately, we were so glad we did. It wasn't really where we wanted to live, and the truth was, we had two other places. Why not consolidate and get one we wanted?

The market had cooled down completely, and it took almost eight months to find the right buyer. During that time, Katie unfortunately lost her job, which was just a blow we didn't see coming. We closed on the house at the end of February and planned to move into the mother-in-law apartment at her parents' house. We didn't know exactly how long we would be there. We even considered renting a place until we figured out what we wanted to do with my other house and her condo.

Yep. This is precisely how I'd imagined it! Thirty-something years old, engaged, and living with the in-laws! It was humbling at first. But hey, at least the world wasn't ending. Wrong! Fucking Covid! Literally not two weeks into being at her parents' house. So, we were officially going into hibernation, a.k.a. quarantining. We got to focus on some real First-World troubles, like whether we were ever going to find toilet paper again.

It might not have felt this way all the time, but looking back, all of this brought us closer together. Here we were, living with her parents. She'd lost her job, we'd just sold our house, and we were planning a wedding during a pandemic! We had to get creative, be patient, and try to find humor in the stress.

Between Zoom calls, rescheduled plans, and navigating tight quarters with her parents as our stuff began to pile up and fill all their extra space (bless them), I had to stay focused on moving forward and building our life together. I tried. There's nothing like planning a wedding while living in your future in-laws' apartment during a global pandemic to really test a relationship. Katie and I were suddenly spending all our time together. No more healthy space, like the time you get when you go to work. It was just us. All day. Every day. Plus, her parents, the dogs, and a partridge in a pear tree.

Going to the grocery store became an event! Not just an ordinary errand anymore. Katie put on real pants, like jeans—with a button! Shopping felt more like we were in some apocalypse-type movie, with everyone in masks, trying to avoid eye contact, but really, we were all blatantly staring at each other, as if the masks were tinted windows. No basic pleasantries like "hello" or "goodbye." In fact, everyone developed this anxiety bubble that popped and spread anytime you got within six feet.

Katie is amazing. Katie's mom is originally from "Amazing," which is a suburb in Heaven. Katie took on the added stress of finding a job, unaware that during the first six to twelve months of Covid, the world would stay on pause. She wasn't used to this lack of routine, order, or social gathering. She didn't try to get used to it; she fought against it.

She continued to pursue opportunities and continued to plan our wedding. She learned to fill her time with home workouts to keep herself sane and fit for the wedding. When she had a moment of overwhelm, I'd find her downstairs with her mom. We all experienced what felt like daily moments of overwhelm, and we could often be found downstairs with Kay.

What about me? I was fine! No, I wasn't. I was far from fine. But that didn't stop me from putting in more and more effort to appear fine. Every day, I woke up with this sense of desperation. *How can I fix this? How can I make Katie's day? What can I do that might make a bigger difference in her happiness?*

I spent so much time and energy on thoughts like that, and at some point, I stopped asking myself those same questions. It's crazy what you're willing to give to that "one" person. I've had relationships end because I wouldn't give more time, energy, thought, etc. But Katie, I would give anything and everything for. And in a lot of ways, I did precisely that.

Pay attention, this is important! When you're not good for yourself, you can't be good for anyone else. Easy, right? Heard that before on a Snapple cap or in a fortune cookie? For me, it wasn't easy. I felt responsible for taking care of Katie, and rightfully so. But when we got engaged, I felt like I needed to take on that responsibility.

At first, I paid for it. Literally. I know money can't buy happiness! But it buys gifts: Louis Vuitton, first-class, and plenty of other creature comforts. When that ran its course—and it always does—I tried "acts of service," such as cooking and cleaning. I was doing that for me, for Katie.

Katie's sister, Ashley, and I had a conversation about this. I was venting to her, upset, because all I was doing didn't seem to make a difference. I told her I felt like I needed to wear a cape and be a super-husband!

She laid some Yoda-like wisdom on me. She said, "Katie doesn't need you to wear a cape. She doesn't need you to change because you're getting married. You don't have to walk in front of her, but don't walk behind her. Just walk beside her and hold her hand!"

I know… she's like a teeny, tiny Yoda!

Weddings! It's absurd how much money, time, effort, and energy all go into *one* day! We made spreadsheets, then abandoned them. We fought over fonts. I didn't know there were so many shades of cream. (Ivory? Eggshell? What even is cool-tone?) I also didn't know it was part of my job to care about whether we used tiny forks or toothpicks, or what to do with a 34-minute time lapse between happy hour and dinner? I wanted to make Katie happy. Period.

I knew the budget I had set for us would be doubled by the time this was done. (Thanks, Cole.) I just wanted Katie to be happy in this stressful time. I really tried to lean into my not-so-new job, and I ended up having a phenomenal start to that year. I had already made one of their achievement clubs based on production, and I still had about half the year left.

I proactively checked things off as we approached the wedding. But during this time, there was hardly any way for us to be sure of anything. Change was no longer within the realm of control. We couldn't "plan" or anything with any level of confidence. Katie, being the planning type, and I, being the Katie type, made it all the more stressful. It was also magical.

We didn't voluntarily learn to embrace this volatility. We were force-fed it. We had to accept where we were at or postpone. We agreed, no matter what, we would get married! I told her that, if it were just the two of us and God, we would not delay it. Takeaways from this time included everything from fighting fairly (most of the time) to communicating (without sarcasm... mostly), to sitting in the mess and still choosing each other, over and over.

I'd be lying if I said that reminiscing back on these times wasn't bittersweet for me. I see these challenges and chapters of our lives with the clarity and confidence I was missing in real time. While life on the surface seemed chaotic enough, underneath all the noise, I was slowly drifting.

There really was no bachelor party. No wild Vegas weekend, no single moms to support us, or vague stories I'd later refuse to explain. I told people it was because of Covid, which was fundamentally true. I also made excuses, such as it having something to do with the budget or logistics, and the constant changes.

My hidden truth was that I didn't feel like I deserved one. That's hard for me to admit even now.

I was giving everything—my everything—and I was constantly distracted. The devil must love addiction. The two have so much in common. Both prey on our weaknesses when we are most vulnerable.

I had a hairline fracture in my foot, and I was prescribed Vicodin by my primary doctor. I didn't truly need it, but I thought it might be nice to have a few around. The following month, it was refilled. Surely a mistake, but I took it as a sweet surprise. The month after that, the same thing, and it continued that way. Those of you who can't relate to the lies we tell ourselves to justify our bad decisions, I challenge you to look inward and encourage you to be honest with yourself. We all have... something. Call it what you will, a coping mechanism, self-medicating; we all have an addiction, even if it's unique only to us.

I'd had no issues with this specifically since I was sixteen years old, almost fifteen years prior. But I still knew almost immediately that the first time I picked up that prescription, I was playing with fire. Unfortunately, in my moments of vulnerability, any clarity was overrun by noise, justifications, and excuses. I'd tell myself I wasn't a kid anymore. I could handle this. I wouldn't let this affect me.

My moments of doubt quickly succumbed to proactive thoughts of entitlement. "I hardly drink anymore. I deserve to have something to take the edge off." My least favorite internal monologue is this vivid, raw, and genuine emotion that sounded more like this: "This part of life is hard right now. I just need to get over this part and back on solid ground. And these will actually help me ride out those inevitable difficulties."

Which is pretty fucking spot-on, but it's also delusional. I might as well have been accepting defeat in the long run to cope with failure in the short run.

What I had going for me was *camouflage*! I was going through a lot, and at this point, it wasn't a pity party. It was just a fact. Having a lot going on meant I could hide in plain sight. Keep in mind, at the time, I wasn't really aware that I was doing this. Katie was in full wedding-planning mode, with vendor calls, floral mockups, and dress fittings. Yes, *plural*. Meaning multiple dresses... (I know!) I became a showman, outwardly present, inwardly vacant!

Addiction is an "ick" word. For those of you who don't know what "ick" is (God bless you!), you should watch more TV with your wife! The slang term, "Ick," was first "discovered by the Germans in 1904; they named it 'icky,' which, of course, in German means a whale's vagina!" *(Squirrel).*

No, really, though, addiction has become a taboo word. This is something I hope to see changed in my lifetime. Addiction covers such a vast range of issues and behaviors, not all of which are tied to substances. Yet when we hear the word, the first two terms that instantly come to mind are *alcohol* and *heroin*. Am I right? If you disagree, approach your spouse and tell them you want them to say the first two words that come to mind when you say the word, "Addiction." If one of those words isn't "alcohol" or "heroin," I will give you five words describing Katie's and my first night together, at no extra cost to you! That's a $500 value, yours absolutely free!

I eventually told Katie about the prescription. She wasn't thrilled. She wasn't mad. She just asked why. I told her the truth: I was getting these by mistake. She asked to see it, and I gave it to her.

Then she asked, "Why do you only have X amount left when you just filled this last week?"

This was my first lie. "I left some of the pills at work." And just like that, I told the first of countless lies.

I didn't tell her how bad it felt. I couldn't. I thought, if I admitted the shame, the failure, and the cracks in my armor, she'd see me differently. I was supposed to be her protector, her provider, her soon-to-be husband. Instead, I was unraveling by the day, battling addiction in the shadows, all while picking out table linens and worrying if our guests would like the entrée choices. I was terrified. Of getting caught. Of losing control. Of being fully seen. Somehow, I thought it would make sense for me to give Katie half of the prescription I was getting, to hold on to. She was constantly having lower-back follow-up procedures from her car accident. She was periodically given pain medication. She managed it, though, and she didn't abuse it.

It's funny how life can look so shiny on the outside, with registry gifts stacking up, tuxes being fitted, the countdown to "I do," and yet inside, you're barely treading water. After a month or so of the new arrangement, which was initially my idea, I came up short. Meaning I wasn't honest with myself about how many pills

I was taking, and I had run out before my non-guaranteed refill. Do you see where I am going with this? Addiction doesn't happen overnight. It's sneaky.

Then boom! It was mid-October, within two months of our wedding. My boss scheduled a Zoom with me, which I thought was to talk about a larger account I'd recently placed.

No. I was being let go. No warning. No write-ups. Not a lack in production. I didn't think I had done anything wrong, which somehow made it worse. It knocked the wind out of me; I had never been fired before. I took it a lot harder than I thought I would.

When Katie had been let go earlier that year, she'd handled it like a badass, honestly. But me? I spiraled. My shame showed up dressed as sarcasm, a short temper, or silence. I started pulling away.

I felt like I had to rebuild my self-worth from the ground up, secretly. I didn't tell Katie how scared I was. I didn't admit how much of my identity was wrapped up in my job, my paycheck, and my ability to provide for others. I just told her everything was fine. That word again… ***fine.***

The morning of our wedding, I felt like I was on cloud nine, with a mix of excitement and anxiety. But when I saw Katie for our first look, everything around us just... paused. There she was, standing in the snow like she'd stepped out of a magazine. Her cheeks were pink from the cold, and her white smile matched her wedding gown that was blowing in the wind. I had thought it before and knew then for sure: I was the luckiest man alive. Still am!

I thought our ceremony was like a fairytale. Fireworks burst behind us in the cold mountain air after we said our vows, surrounded by the people we loved dearly. We danced all night long. We had all been so cooped up due to Covid, so it was fun to see everyone dance, laugh, and be around other people, not staying five feet apart and wearing masks. That day, we didn't have a pandemic or job-related issues. We had no problems. It was a perfect day.

There were moments that night when I forgot the weight I was carrying. When I looked at Katie in her dress, smiling, dancing with her whole heart. When I saw our parents tear up during the speeches. When my buddies pulled me onto the dance floor, but even in those fleeting moments of joy, this secret was still there. I had just promised forever to the woman I loved, but I wondered, was I already breaking that promise? In the quiet of my mind, it felt like it.

That night was magic. In the photos, we looked like a couple starting a brand-new chapter. And we were! But for me, it was also the beginning of the slow, painful realization that something had to change… or everything would fall apart.

Chapter 4

Three Margaritas Later...

Katie

Interestingly, Chris and I met in high school, although I knew him more than we actually interacted. He was part of the "popular crowd," while I floated between different friend groups. During high school, we were both in relationships and spent little time being single.

Once in college, Chris attended the University of Colorado in Boulder, while I traveled across the Pacific to Hawaii to study at the University of Hilo on the Big Island. I left Hawaii after my freshman year and transferred to CU Denver, while Chris later transferred to Metro State University. Eventually, I transferred again and completed my junior and senior years at the University of Colorado Boulder.

Throughout our many transfers, we crossed paths a handful of times because of a mutual friend group. However, we started seeing each other more consistently after college, when we were in our twenties. Since I didn't have any girlfriends who enjoyed skiing or golfing, I would reach out to my male friends to join their golf foursomes and go snowboarding with them. Chris was part of those groups on multiple occasions. It wouldn't be until our ten-year high school reunion, though, that I looked at Chris differently.

A few days before our reunion, I reached out to a few girlfriends to see if they would attend. One was planning to go with her husband. Being desperately single as I was, I thought about who else I could call to come with me, as a friend. I had recently seen Chris over the previous few weeks and thought to myself, "Well, that could be fun." So, I shot him a text asking if he wanted to go as friends.

He initially said, "*Ummm*, no way. That's lame." Then, after some convincing, he agreed.

Chris decided to pick me up in an Uber to head to the Rio Downtown and meet mutual friends, Katie and Ryan Pelton. But, in classic "universe laughing in the background" fashion, they were stuck in traffic, so Chris and I were able to have some one-on-one time together. Most of our previous interactions had been in group settings.

I remember texting Katie P. under the table, saying, "This feels like we are on a date. When will you be here?"

Once dinner was over, we walked to a bar downtown called Jackson's, where the reunion was being held. From there, a bigger group left the reunion to go to another bar down the street.

Because we embraced the three-margarita max at dinner, this part of the night was a bit hazy, but I remember stopping at a brick wall, looking at Chris, and asking, "How have we never kissed before?" (Believe it or not, I made the first move!)

Immediately, Chris's face turned bright red, and he bashfully laughed before leaning in to change that. This moment felt like we were in our own rom-com movie. Suddenly, the loud noises of Oktoberfest and music blaring from a band playing on Larimer Street went quiet. As the background noise faded, time seemed to slow.

I looked at Chris's freckles littered across his nose. I noticed a scar on his lower chin (and wondered how he had gotten it), and then I met his bright hazel eyes looking back at me, smiling. I was trying to capture his subtle features, which I had overlooked for over sixteen years, all the while wanting him to kiss me.

From there, we skipped around a few more bars while trying to maintain our composure around our friends, hiding our hands under tables. Ultimately, we headed home to share an Uber, and I made a very loud request, something I had never said before.

Once we slid into our seats, I told the driver, "Just one stop, please!" I proudly leaned back into my seat and felt my cheeks flush red, as I smiled with a mischievous smirk. Who is this girl?

I had never been so forward in my life when it came to dating, but for once, I felt empowered by my sensuality. Ultimately, we spent every waking moment we could together after that night. I remember thinking, "If this plays out like I think it will, I think this could be it."

And it was. He made me feel safe and cared for, and I will forever be grateful for that. My forwardness continued when he mentioned he was heading up to Aspen that following Thursday to hike the Maroon Bells. I didn't even ask if I could go, I just said, "Oh, how fun! I've never been. I'll take PTO that day, and you can pick me up early to head up, yeah?"

This quick day trip turned out to be one of my top-five favorite dates with Chris. The night before, I stayed up late, putting together the perfect playlist for our long road trip. Since we were in the final weeks of September, when fall makes its beautiful debut with vibrant green, yellow, and burnt-orange leaves, we couldn't have asked for a clearer, crisper day.

Once we had all our gear, we headed up the trail. We asked each other a million and one questions about recent relationships, family dynamics, life endeavors, travel experiences, music, movies, skiing—you name it, we discussed it. After a few hours, we finally arrived at the Maroon Bells and took some pictures together, but we also shyly asked if we could take individual pictures, too. We weren't ready to soft-launch the relationship yet, but wanted to document the spontaneous venture.

We found a patch of soft grass, unpacked our little picnic, and lay back on the blanket to relax. Soon, we were trying to pick out clouds and see what shapes they made. We tied blades of grass in knots out of nervousness and burst out in deep belly laughs, reminiscing about high school and replaying all the times we'd run into each other. It had been so long since I was actually nervous on a date, yet I was my 100% authentic self: no mask, no bullshit. My feelings were raw and genuine, and I embraced them fully.

The relationship progressed quickly, and everything moved quickly. Two months into dating, I was invited to be my little sister's plus-one for a wedding in Mexico. Being a "yes" person, she knew she could count on me to attend and have a great time.

To my surprise, when Chris picked me up from the airport, there was a medium-sized pit bull mix—white, tan, and orange—in the backseat of his truck. I said, "Oh, well, hello! What's your name, and where did you come from?"

Chris quickly reassured me, saying not to worry, because Lexi wouldn't be around for long. He was helping a friend in the military for a little while. At first, I didn't think much of it, but I had been saving up for a brindle French bulldog that I intended to name Moose. I explained to Chris I hadn't gone through with it yet, because I would be an absolute emotional wreck when it came time for them to be put down.

As weeks turned into months, I tried hard not to get too attached to Lexi. At one point, Chris sincerely asked me if I even liked dogs, because he could tell I was giving her the cold shoulder. I felt awful and admitted I would be sad when she left, so I was trying very hard not to get too attached.

He quickly revealed, "Well, actually, she is ours. She's always been ours. I'm sorry for not telling you sooner. I didn't know how you would react."

Immediately, I got in the car, went to Petco, and bought the fanciest dog bed, five toys, lots of treats, and a new collar with both our contact information on it. Lexi became our first child and built-in best friend.

After a year of Chris packing a bag every night and shuttling Lexi back and forth from my place in Cherry Creek North to his house, where he was renting a room with a few of his best friends as roommates, we noticed that the drawer I gave him was overflowing with clothes. We sat down and had a serious conversation about buying a house and moving in together. My condo was only 701 square feet (that's right, don't forget that additional 1), so I wanted to find something we both owned, while I could rent out my condo and he could rent out his as his first home purchase.

From the beginning of our house search, I got the impression that Chris was dragging out the process. I later found out it was because he was terrified of combining finances and revealing the "dirty secrets" in our bank accounts. My secret was being an impulsive shopper, coupled with high medical bills from sustaining my injuries from the car accident. Chris's secret was an obsession with shoes, hats, sweatshirts, and anything related to golf and skiing.

We quickly contacted our mutual friend and talented real estate agent, Michele Ciardullo, to find our first home. Shortly after, we arrived at the first house on our list to begin our tour. The ranch-style home was located in the heart of Sunnyside, near LoHi, and Chris recognized the seller's name on the sign; it was a significant commercial client he had worked with. I secretly thought this was a positive sign.

We both fell in love with the house, and Chris even allowed me to convert one of the four bedrooms into a walk-in closet—*Ummm*, yes, please! What I loved about this decision was that we both came to the table with equal money, so the house was equally ours. I refinanced my condo to afford this big venture, and the remaining funds were to decorate the house and make it a home. A fun fact about me: I *love* furniture. I enjoy the quirkiness it can bring to a space and love picking colors to match our taste and style. I thoroughly enjoy the decorating process.

After settling into our new home, it felt as though we were racing through life. Both of us were working full-time, and Chris was managing most of our household bills, including the mortgage. He was excelling at work and surpassing his quotas, which allowed us to go on trips and let him treat me to beautiful gifts I had never received in any previous relationship. We were riding this incredible wave, feeling as though we would maintain consistent, steady momentum with no setbacks.

A favorite memory of mine is waking up on a random Saturday and turning over to tell him I had an itch to get matching tattoos. He smirked and said, "Let's do it." I showed him my private Pinterest tattoo board, which I had been secretly adding to for the last few months, and it was full of ideas.

We settled on two triangles. They are my favorite shape, and we loved the meaning of each balanced pointed side representing Chris, me, and God. Chris got his tattoo on his inner right bicep, with the triangle filled in and the point at the top. We read somewhere that an upward-pointing triangle can symbolize stability, strength, and masculinity. It can also represent the fiery journey toward spiritual awakening and enlightenment. I had my triangle inverted, with a thicker outline, leaving an open space on the inside with its peak pointing downward on my inner left bicep. This symbolizes feminine energy and grounding. It can also represent the flow of a river and its transformative change over time. Tattoos don't always have to have meaning, but they can be a fun and creative outlet when they do.

Two years into dating, Chris and I decided to play hooky and go skiing at the Mary Jane Ski Resort on a random Wednesday. During the car ride up, Chris seemed nervous. He kept changing the radio station and was jittery.

Jokingly, I asked, "Did you take your ADHD meds today? You seem fidgety." Little did I know that I would soon discover why he was acting strangely.

When we arrived at the base of the mountain and put on our gear, Chris mentioned that his boot was "fitting funny." Once we got on the first chairlift, he surprised me by asking if we could take a picture. While it's not unusual for me to ask for photos—as I'm the one who loves documenting memories—Chris's request felt a bit suspicious. Usually, I would be the one begging him to take pictures and encouraging him to smile. It was odd for him to ask as soon as we sat down on the ski lift.

As I strapped into my snowboard and turned up the music in my helmet's built-in headphones, Chris mentioned again that his boot was bothering him and he was going to go around the corner on our first run to fix it. As I pushed off and picked up speed down the run called High Lonesome Trail, I noticed Chris still up high on the mountain. He began yelling down to me about needing help with his ski boot, which I thought was odd, since I didn't know the first thing about skiing, especially not how the boots worked.

Strapped to my board, I attempted some bunny hops up the run to reach him, but after a few hops and out of breath, I annoyingly yelled back that he would have to meet me halfway.

Chris, in his bulky ski boots, wobbled down to me and shakily dropped to one knee while opening a brown lacquered ring box. He smiled up at me. I was speechless. The moment happened so quickly, I didn't have the nerve to stop his well-rehearsed speech, but my music was also blaring in my ears during this unexpected moment.

I instantly said, "Yes! Yes, of course I will marry you!" After lifting my goggles, I wiped away my happy tears.

Chris stepped back into his skis, looked at me, and said, "Ready for our first run as an engaged couple?"

I responded, "Lead the way!"

This moment felt incredibly intimate. There were hardly any other people on the mountain that day, just a few skiers overlooking from above, clapping from the chair lifts. I will never forget that first run of the day, where we both screamed down the slopes, "*WE JUST GOT ENGAGED*!" with our hearts beating rapidly and smiling ear to ear. The customized ring was set relatively high, so I couldn't even fit my glove over it, but I didn't care when my hands went numb. This ring was never coming off my finger!

We spent the rest of our powder day at the lodge at the top of the ski resort, FaceTiming our closest friends and family to share the exciting news that we'd gotten engaged on December 12, 2018, at 12,000 feet. Once we arrived home, we opened a vintage bottle of

Châteauneuf-du-Pape. We sat on the floor in front of our newly decorated Christmas tree, smelling of fresh pine and reminiscing as we added the new ornament that we'd bought earlier at the resort to remind us of this special day. Then, we began brainstorming ideas for our engagement party and wedding, envisioning our solidified future together.

Before long, we were deep into wedding planning and discovered a fantastic wedding planner in Vail, Jennifer Pletcher of Gemini Event Planning. She became our saving grace in the months that followed. As I got caught up in selecting color schemes, décor, and flowers, and planning our engagement party and photos, I said yes not only to one, but to two wedding dresses. We also discovered the wedding venue for our 2020 celebration on New Year's Eve in Vail. Everything was falling into place, and we couldn't have been more excited.

Up to this point, Chris had been involved in a handful of wedding decisions, but I noticed he was under a lot of pressure and stress due to selling his insurance agency and starting a new job. One morning, as we were being lazy in bed, Chris turned to me with a concerned expression and asked if he could vent about something that had been bothering him. Unsure of how to bring it up, he hesitated for a moment.

I encouraged him, saying, "Of course. What's on your mind?"

Eventually, he opened up and explained that this new job wasn't providing the same financial stability he'd had before, and he couldn't afford the mortgage, the HELOC, and home expenses by himself much longer.

I responded with something like, "All right, so let's sell it! We can move in with my parents to avoid feeling rushed into finding a new home, and we can save some money while we plan for the wedding."

It took us over eight months to sell our home, with more than sixty showings—it was insane! We finally sold it in late February 2020. Just weeks before the sale, I was the sickest I had ever been, suffering from Influenza A and bronchitis, which kept me out of commission for almost two weeks.

Before I got sick, I successfully organized two holiday parties for the fifteen corporate locations I managed. One event was a casino night at the aquarium in Denver, and the other was a yacht party in California with a DJ. However, on my first day back to work after being incredibly ill, I was fired without any explanation.

I was shocked. I had dedicated myself entirely to this job, and it often felt like nothing I did was ever good enough. I had never been fired before. I felt distraught, confused, sad, embarrassed, angry, and bitter.

After packing up my office with tears streaming down my cheeks, I got in my car and drove home in icy conditions. Just five minutes away from my house, I slid into another car. I completely lost it and began to cry uncontrollably. Luckily, my car was the only one that sustained damage, so after exchanging insurance information, I parked it in the garage.

Once inside the house, I began drafting an email to the C-suite, requesting an explanation regarding my termination. I also inquired why no one followed up with me after I'd reported my boss's passive-aggressive and bullying behavior to upper management a few weeks earlier, especially since there was no HR team in place.

After hitting "send" on my unemployment application, I shed a few more tears, but then I realized it was time to move on. The pity party was over. I began the exhausting process of packing up our home, organizing which boxes would go to my parents' house and which would be stored in our unit. And I had no idea the huge news that would be announced in two weeks, and how that would change the trajectory of all our lives forever.

I will never forget where I was and what I was doing when 9/11 was announced on the news. The same goes for when Covid-19 was declared, and we needed to shelter in place for the foreseeable future.

Since I was having a hard time finding a job, I tried my best to stay positive by focusing on wedding planning, exercising, and studying for my insurance licenses, so that I could start an independent insurance agency with Chris. Throughout 2020, Chris and I had some really tough conversations regarding the wedding. We considered eloping, having a micro-wedding, and even thought about postponing. My heart carried such a heavy weight of emotional and financial loss for any bride who had to make the difficult decision to delay or sacrifice their wedding day. Along with the vendor teams who worked their butts off for their clients and reinvented business offerings just so they could pay their own bills right now and make (what is supposed to be) wonderful, exciting days feel still just as special.

Covid was not going away anytime soon, so we decided, no matter what happened, we would get married on December 31, 2020. Planning a wedding during Covid presented so many hurdles, and we tried very hard to maintain a positive outlook in our "make it work moment," but it felt really stop-and-go. Chris and I had a unique opportunity to dig deeper and strip the celebration and "expectations" around weddings back down to the core of their purpose.

Three months before our wedding, we received a call from Jeni, our event planner, informing us that Vail Resorts had gone "red" and would shut down, including our wedding venue. Cue the anxiety and all the panic. Luckily, Jeni had already put our names down at another location without telling us—a backup spot called The Larkspur. This was a saving grace. Around this time, it felt like it was getting harder to get excited about anything, though, because everything that could go wrong went wrong.

Over the course of the year, Vail's status fluctuated from red to orange to yellow and then back down to orange levels. During this time, we had to restructure our guest list, initially aiming for 175 attendees but then cutting it down to twenty-five. We were later able to increase it to fifty, then seventy-five, before finally settling on a headcount of fifty-five guests. As you can imagine, it was exhausting and confusing to contact people and encourage them to book rooms, especially since New Year's Eve is incredibly busy for Vail. I had to go from telling some guests they could come to later informing them they could not, and then, after further updates, calling again to see if they could come after all.

On top of that, we faced numerous restrictions on what we could and couldn't do. For instance, we were not allowed to have a designated dance floor, which would put a specific square footage, affecting the maximum number of people who could dance. Two of my bridesmaids could not attend—one had her baby's due date close to the event, and the other felt uncomfortable, so, unfortunately, she backed out just two weeks before.

We initially wanted a live band, but that would have increased our guest list, so we decided to go with a DJ instead. We also planned to have beautiful draping to conceal certain aspects of the venue, but the vendor couldn't risk their business. Additionally, the custom tuxedos we selected for the groomsmen would not arrive in time due to the factory closing because of Covid. The fireworks schedule changed on the day of the wedding, so we had to work around a different schedule, and my poor nephew, who was our ring bearer, spent over a week and a half in the hospital before our wedding. Thankfully, after his surgery, he made a dramatic improvement, and he was discharged on the day of our rehearsal dinner.

Uncertainty about my nephew's release meant my brother-in-law, who was set to play guitar during our ceremony, might not attend, either. As a result, we had to find a backup guitarist, which we thankfully didn't need. To add to the challenges, our pastor forgot the marriage certificate, but luckily, a friend grabbed it on their way up. We also learned that alcohol service was limited until 10:00 p.m. Fortunately, we found a loophole around that restriction. On top of all that, the constant negativity and fear-mongering in the news led many people to drop out at the last minute.

I believe that a failed or faltered dream can be the fuel that ignites the bigger dream you were meant for, and Chris and I were destined to get married during those crazy times. I am so glad we persevered. The following year brought just as much chaos and uncertainty, and by the time people began planning their weddings in 2022, everything was booked up and prices were significantly higher. It's hard to believe, especially since the wedding industry is already a considerable investment. No bride or groom should have to go through what we did, but despite all the anxiety and negativity, it was worth it, because we got married before God and our closest friends and family on New Year's Eve!

We did our first look with my first wedding gown by Miss Hayley Paige (a girl you might know, as she has since reclaimed her brand and name!) on top of Vail Mountain. I felt so special, walking around Vail village and up to the gondola to see Chris for the first time before committing our lives together.

People sped past on their skis, yelling, "*CONGRATS!*" "Good for you guys!" "You look beautiful!" while they slapped their ski poles together. It was a rush of excitement and emotion, mixed with the odd feeling of not being fully equipped in ski gear as I rode up to the top. I will never forget the rush of emotion, with Chris in his tuxedo, facing toward the mountains and his back to me, then the moment he turned around after I placed my hand on his back. And it was the perfect bluebird day, so it wasn't too chilly.

After taking numerous intimate photos of just the two of us, it was time for me to change and head over to the venue. With our guests sipping on champagne, it was finally time to walk down the aisle. As my father walked his last little girl down the aisle, my brother-in-law, Cole, played "Say You Won't Let Go" by James Arthur. This song held a special place in our hearts as a couple. The first time I heard it was four weeks into dating Chris. He hijacked my Bluetooth to play a song for me, telling me it made him think of me. Safe to say I was crying in bed when it played.

Our ceremony was intimate and felt very us. My old pastor, Gary McCusker, fortunately agreed to marry us. He'd played a huge part in both our lives—our relationships with Jesus and the community—and he really made the ceremony feel incredibly personal and special. Each year, we watch the ceremony on our anniversary and are reminded of five important rules every couple should follow in their marriage every day, according to Gary:

1. Put God first.
2. Forgive often and quickly.
3. Serve each other.
4. Pursue each other.
5. Have fun!

My favorite part of the ceremony was when Gary asked our family to come up and join us in a circle, and everyone went around, giving advice, reading poems, and saying how they would support us through our marriage. We ended with an emotional prayer. I don't think there was a dry eye there. It was truly beautiful and encouraging to know that we had this amazing support system through both good times and bad.

I often reflect on the bittersweet moments of our celebration, but one in particular really tugs at my heart. Many cherished family members couldn't join us. Yet for those who could attend, we took every precaution to ensure the gathering was safe and comfortable for everyone. Together, we welcomed the New Year with open arms at midnight, indulging in delicious food, vibrant fireworks, and champagne flowing. Tears were shed, and laughter filled the room with the warmth of great company and music.

We worked diligently to create pockets of pure love and joy, and I was so appreciative of everyone's resilience in choosing joy over fear. It truly was a night to remember, and no one got Covid!

Unfortunately, we weren't able to have the honeymoon we'd initially planned in Europe due to travel restrictions, so my two sisters and their husbands joined us in Mexico. We had the best week together, hanging out on the beach and enjoying one another's company.

Covid created numerous pivot moments for us, but we tried our best to remain resilient and keep the positive energy flowing during what felt like a heavy, confusing, and dark time. But also, during this stretch of time, I didn't notice the Devil was seeping into the corners of Chris's life until it was too late.

Chapter 5

Slipping Away

Chris

I didn't wake up one day and decide to be an addict. No one does. No matter the person, no matter what their journey is or was. For me, it was a slow drift, unperceivable at first. A series of moments, decisions, and circumstances that silently compounded within me until I found myself drowning. Initially, addiction was self-medicating my suffering, and ultimately, it became the center of my suffering.

When I think back on my experiences with substances, it's easy to remember the first time I encountered opiates. I was fifteen years old and a sophomore in high school. I think I was approximately 5′2," but by my junior year, I was closer to six feet. So, I grew almost a whole foot in a year, and I wasn't exactly graceful during that growth spurt. It felt like I had been transferred into my own avatar.

I was playing on a fall baseball team when I was fifteen. I was always one to two years younger than the rest of my teammates, but this season, I also hadn't grown into my body. I felt awkward and clumsy, as if I had lost my center of gravity. A friend of mine used to joke that my legs flailed sideways just about as far as they moved forward.

Now that I have explained and made some reasonable excuses for myself, I'll tell you my glory-horror story! We had an elimination-style tournament scheduled for one weekend, with the overall winner of twelve teams advancing to a tournament in Las

Vegas. Heading into this, I hadn't had a hit in two games, which was an embarrassing slump.

In this specific game, the overall score was low, and we were down by one, heading into our last inning. I was 0-for-3 that day, but I managed to get a hit and was now the potential tying run on base. I had made my way to third base and was therefore in position, but we also had two outs. If I didn't score, we would lose the chance to go into extra innings, let alone win. I have never been very fast. I knew this. Everyone knew this. But in this scenario, if there was a wild pitch or that ball made it past the catcher, I had to go, had to try to score. Otherwise, we were done, and we'd lose.

Sure enough, that's precisely what happened. A pitch was thrown, hit the dirt, and got past the catcher. My coach yelled, "*GO!*" and I took off toward home.

Just my luck, the ball had a good bounce off the backstop and came back toward home plate in the catcher's favor.

I was barely halfway down the ninety-foot stretch toward home when I saw this, but I was already committed. As the catcher and I both sprinted toward home, I knew either he was going to beat me there or we'd arrive at the same time.

We met at the plate at full speed. I leaned my head down, ready for us to collide and selfishly hoping I'd be able to knock the ball out of his hands.

I felt my right arm pinned between us as we collided. My elbow was at the center of my chest with the full force of my body behind it, and my hand, raised up and open, met his ribcage. That's when I heard it—this pronounced *POP* sound inside my body. It felt like lightning and thunder striking simultaneously! Anyone who's broken a bone knows this sound. I'd never felt adrenaline like this before, and I didn't even know what had happened to me yet.

I remember hearing the umpire say I was safe, and all of a sudden, my team was surrounding me in celebration! *That's* when I felt it: as my teammates were trying to high-five me, the most excruciating pain I had ever experienced.

When I made it to the dugout, the adrenaline wore off, and I knew something was seriously wrong. My arm looked bent. One play after I scored, that last inning ended, and we were going into extra innings.

I showed my coach my arm, and he looked disgusted. He told me to get to the ER right then and there. Fortunately, my friend Tony was there and could sub for me. I didn't want to admit I was in as much pain as I was, but there was no more hiding it. What's worse, we were in the middle of nowhere in Colorado for this tournament, over an hour away from the nearest hospital.

The more the adrenaline wore off, the worse the pain became. I started to feel every bump and turn in the car ride. When we got to the hospital and they saw the bend in my arm, they rushed me back and gave me an IV right away. I hated that, because I was recently terrified of *needles.*

Only a few weeks before my broken arm, I went to the nurse's office at school to donate blood for the first time. They said I had to get out of class and could even leave for the rest of the day, so, naturally, I told them to take their fill. What I didn't know is that they typically send only nurses-in-training to cover blood drives. So, my nurse missed not once, but several times. On her final attempt, she didn't think she'd *stuck it,* and when she withdrew the needle, a long, thick, dark-red stream of blood shot out of my arm and several feet past her! I passed out... and have hated needles ever since.

I didn't know IVs were how they gave you medicine. In an instant, I went from the most unbearable pain to this tranquil, euphoric, pain-free state, one I never knew existed. With the medication on board, I was told this ordeal was far from over. The doctors reviewed the X-rays with us, and we could clearly see that both bones in my arm were broken almost perfectly in half, and then, they had doubled over on top of each other. I needed a manual procedure that involved pulling on my wrist to stretch the bones back out, then readjusting them at the break lines!

The doctor said they were going to give me the maximum amount of pain medication allowed, hoping I would pass out. I did for about thirty seconds, but then I woke up just in time to see and feel the procedure entirely. Then, I passed out for good.

If I'd had any experience with opiates before this injury, I don't remember it. I believe this was my first serious-enough injury to require it. This was also the first time I learned these things even existed. They put me in a cast and sent me home with a large bottle of Percocet, which I took exactly as prescribed: two pills every four hours or as needed for pain. As I spent the next five days in bed, I began to appreciate how the drugs alleviated my physical pain, but even more than that, I liked how I felt on them.

That was my first encounter with opiates. I felt like a hero, having scored the tying run, and I'd broken my arm while doing it. I thought learning to wipe my ass left-handed was the worst thing to come of all of this. However, only five days later, I had my second encounter with opiates.

I stayed at my dad's house for the week while my arm healed. I didn't have the energy to go back and forth between my parents' homes. Whenever I was injured, I tended to gravitate toward my dad for help. However, after five days of missing school, my dad encouraged me to return on a Friday to try to catch up on the work I had missed that week.

That morning was exceptionally cold, and it was the first time I left the house with my arm in a cast and sling. It felt good to be showered, dressed, and ready for the day. However, I remember feeling this fog over me, like a hangover without a headache. It was my first day off from pain medication in about a week, but fortunately, I attributed the way I felt to my injury. Knowing what I do now, that fog was my brain begging for more dopamine and serotonin.

If you went to high school in the early 2000s, you know how we carried everything in our backpacks and that our lockers were always empty. Because it was so cold, my dad went out to start the truck. I came out shortly after. He warned me more than once that there was black ice everywhere and to be careful, but my bad mood drowned out his warning. Being in the daze I was, while carrying my heavy backpack and trying to get my casted arm situated in the sling, I stepped out onto the driveway pavement.

It happened so fast. But this time, I knew exactly what had happened. I somehow slipped on the black ice, instinctively trying to protect my newly broken right arm. Somehow, my left leg was the only leg to slip, while my right leg remained perfectly grounded. This caused the full weight of my body and backpack all to come down on my right leg, and that's when I heard and felt the loud *POP* sounds again: three cracks that sounded like one!

I let out a blood-curdling scream, surprising myself that such a loud noise had come out of my mouth. The adrenaline felt all too familiar, and I was literally shocked that this had just happened.

My dad rushed over, thinking I had hurt my arm. When I told him it was my leg that was broken, he tried to correct me, saying, "No, Chris. Let me see your arm!"

I was in and out of consciousness. The immense physical pain of this has no equal. My usual reserve of adrenaline was depleted, since I had used it up just five days earlier. So, as that dissipated, my dad rolled up my jeans and was looking at my leg. He didn't have to say anything: the look on his face confirmed what I already knew. I doubt any parent likes to see their kids in pain, but I could tell my dad felt so bad for me. His military mind kicked in, and he immediately went into instruction, delegation, and action mode.

I couldn't move, I had no adrenaline left at all, and the cold had settled into my toes. My brother came out with pillows and blankets to make me more comfortable in my hobbled state. I felt relieved when I heard the ambulance coming down the street, but that relief was short-lived. As they tried to stop, their tires locked, and they began to slide down the hilly street, showing no sign of stopping! They plowed right into my neighbor's black truck, which was parked on the side of the street.

One of the paramedics tried to get up to me, but he also fell and hurt himself so badly that he had to join me in the ambulance ride to the hospital. The remaining EMTs got the gurney out and slid it along the icy ground, crawling on all fours to reach me. My dad assisted me to get on top of the gurney, and once I was lifted and placed on the mat, I blacked out from the pain. When I woke up in the ambulance, they had already given me an IV, which was great, because, like I said, I hate needles.

"Hydromorphone," I heard one of the EMTs say. "We just gave you some to start getting your pain under control."

And almost instantly, with a moment of clarity, the medicine entered my bloodstream. Warmth spread throughout my body, and I felt like stretching out to capture each tingle. My pain improved, but so did my mood. I can't explain it to those who have never had it, but this drug does so much more than control your pain. "Hello, darkness, my old friend."

The hospital's entire emergency room was packed; I wasn't the only one who had fallen on the ice, and the waiting room was overflowing with patients. After a long wait, they prepared me for X-rays, which meant removing my shoe.

Any reasonably intelligent person might suggest untying the laces or, shit, cut the shoe off, for all I cared. But no, my nurse began tugging on my shoe, flexing my foot front to back and side to side. We'd later learn why that was so painful: the X-rays showed my leg was in four pieces, with three whole breaks. So, each time they tried to take my shoe off, the break points in my leg were forced to rub together, nerve on nerve. This all made sense, since my leg was visibly curved and misshapen!

For me to heal, they needed to insert two twenty-inch titanium rods through the broken bones to hold them together, which meant I had to undergo surgery that night. It also meant that, once I healed in four to six months, I would have to come back for another surgery to have them removed.

My nurse quickly became my favorite person. She brought me ice chips and even delivered my pain medication early. After spending all day in the hospital under her attentive care, I had consumed way too many bags of fluid and really needed to pee. I told her about it and assumed she would bring me a portable urine container or instruct me where the bathroom was.

Instead, a doctor came back and started explaining to me what a *catheter* was. *I would like to go on record and state that catheters are also a type of suffering.* The doc explained what the procedure entailed, including the best part: where a large tube was supposedly going to be shoved into my… *what*? While explaining all this, he was literally playing with the exact tube, waving it around like I was suddenly going to get comfortable with it.

What's worse, they had planned to wait until my surgery, when I was under anesthesia, to insert the catheter. But now that I needed to pee so badly, they had to do it right away, because I wasn't going to be able to wait that long.

I'm not going to lie… I threw a childlike tantrum! I yelled, I pouted, and yes, I cried. The doctor explained that it just had to be done, and I would feel much better afterward. He then left, assuring me the nurse would be in shortly to assist.

Last time I'd checked, my nurse was a nurturing, attentive, and attractive lady. But, as my luck lately would have it, she was replaced by this body-builder version of a male nurse who didn't strike me as the *delicate* type. I resorted to begging…

I eventually summoned up enough courage to let them grab hold of… *me*. But when that tube got within inches of… *me*, I panicked, tossed and turned. Keep in mind, I was now basically paralyzed on the right side, since both my right arm and leg were broken and bound. I basically put myself through more pain than the catheter would have been.

They gave me some medication to help me sleep, but I resisted the urge to doze off, because I knew what was about to happen. Eventually, they reached the point where they couldn't administer any more medication and agreed that, if I could stand up to use the restroom, they would allow it. So, with my broken arm, broken leg, and multiple IVs in place, my dad somehow helped me to stand. I felt like I had just won a gold medal! I was relieved that I was going to be able to pee without a catheter. The only problem was, once I stood up, I couldn't go... I had put myself through hell to get to this point, and then I froze!

I wasn't sure what hurt more, my arm, my leg, or my bladder full of fluids. I had to resort to using the catheter, and the best way to describe that is traumatic. I firmly believe that anytime something must enter your urethra, you should not be conscious! During the initial attempt, my nurse reached for a large catheter but then had to stop and ask for a smaller-sized tube... adding insult to injury.

I spent a few nights in the hospital and was utterly miserable, aside from the luxury of a morphine drip and a button I could push every fifteen minutes. I suspected that misery would last the next four to six months. I had to undergo surgery to insert the rods, then return to have them removed.

I knew there was no way I would be able to return to school, so I would be bedridden for the next four months or so. I hated the idea of being cooped up that long, but I didn't imagine I would be in such outrageous pain that entire time. When I felt better, what was I going to do with all that time?

While checking out of the hospital to go home, part of that process was for me to evaluate my pain. On a scale from 0 to 10, with zero representing no pain and ten representing the worst pain possible. I remember the doctors giving my parents a bag full of medication with these instructions, almost verbatim: "Give him as many as he needs. He is in a lot of pain. When you run out, we will get him more."

Growing up, medicine was never the first option in my family. If I had a headache, my parents would tell me to drink more water. Depending on the time of day, they might tell me to eat some fruit. My dad's mother, my Grandma Barb, had a significant influence on the nursing school at CSU, and she owned several medical clinics. Despite spending much of her life tied to medicine, I can still hear her say, "Put some Bacitracin on it," as this was her signature and universal treatment. Headaches to broken bones... Bacitracin oughta do it!

I had never had any experience with these types of injuries, never anything this unusual or severe. This will sound naïve and sheltered, which I was, but I didn't even realize that Percocet was a sought-after drug. To be honest, in my family, we never needed to have a sit-down conversation about this shit, because we were never exposed to it, and it wasn't necessarily identified as an epidemic-sized problem back then.

I found myself lying in bed with around a hundred and eighty 10 mg Percocet pills on my nightstand. That first week, I needed them. That first month, I needed them. I would wake up in the middle of the night in excruciating pain and had to take a couple of pills just to get comfortable enough to lie back down. Then, in the morning, I would have to eat something, so I didn't take the pills on an empty stomach.

During the first couple of weeks, I didn't feel "high." I just used the pills to manage my physical pain, precisely as I was told to. As time passed, I had no choice but to settle into this mundane daily routine that never included me leaving my bedroom.

My mom was the only one managing my medication, and she had no reason to question my intentions. I was a good kid; I didn't drink or smoke pot. Though after a few months and several refills later, she started to notice I was going through them fast and asking for more pills than I had in the beginning. She began to feel uneasy.

During her final conversation with my doctor about a refill, she expressed her concerns about how much medication I was taking and for how long. Instead of responding with concern, the doctor said, "Give him what he needs. He is in pain!" Which, at this point, didn't matter. No one, including me, could have foreseen what this experience would unlock within me.

My mom didn't listen to the doctor's suggestion and decided to take this into her own hands. She looked at this simply as it should be: if I need *more* now than I did before, but I'm healing more each day, then the result should be that I need *less* medicine as time goes on.

For those of you who don't relate to addiction, specifically with prescribed opiate medication, there are two sides to it. One's physical and one's mental. Both are equally difficult to overcome.

First, my mom took the bottle and kept it in her room, because she was tracking what I had, and I was taking more than I should. This was the first time I experienced a mental withdrawal. I know this now, because I experienced it the same way, later in life. When I lost immediate access to what my body was craving, that changed my entire demeanor. I became desperate and would go from intentionally acting like I didn't care about them to yelling and screaming that I should have access to the meds.

Then, she started giving me only half of the prescribed dosage. This was the first time I experienced a physical withdrawal. I realized I had built a tolerance, and I wasn't happy about it. I was partially in pain, practically paralyzed, and now experiencing mild withdrawal... Needless to say, my mom was a saint, and I was not pleasant to be around.

She then found a Tylenol that looked like Percocet. So, if I wanted two every four hours, she would give me two Tylenols instead. This is ultimately the "placebo" effect, which was genius on her part. I would take those two Tylenol, thinking they were my medicine, and would sigh in relief. She'd ask me an hour later how I was doing, and I would tell her I was feeling so much better. What I didn't realize was that I was getting two Tylenols instead of two Percocets.

The crazy thing was that I had no idea. This went on for weeks, but eventually, I began to question what she was giving me.

One day, after she left for work, my curiosity got the better of me, and I decided to make the long journey to her bathroom. I slowly crawled across the carpet, using my only functional arm and leg. I was sweating profusely, partly because I had been immobile for too long, and partly out of withdrawal. Finally, I reached the bathroom door. I could see the pills on the counter, but with less than ten feet to go, I heard the garage door open!

My rule-abiding inner child was freaked out. It had taken me so long to get to this point. I couldn't go forward or backward in time so that she wouldn't see me.

She walked partway up the stairs and asked, "What are you doing?"

I did my best to make her feel guilty. I found every excuse to explain the pain I was in, crying out in desperation, "I *need these*! I am in pain!"

In the past, my mom would have yelled back, matching my energy. Instead, I was met with an uncharacteristic silence. She calmly said, "You must not be in that much pain. Look how far you crawled."

I backed down, unable to believe that these little pills had so much power over me. Here I was, desperately dragging myself across the floor, trying to get to them, when just before, I couldn't even go to the bathroom without help.

That was the last time I took a pain pill for this injury. I let my mom continue the process of weaning me off, even after I had that additional surgery to remove the rods from my leg. I never sought out any sort of drug after that and didn't take anything for years.

However, I wasn't naïve or sheltered anymore. I knew these things existed, I'd learned what they were for, and I knew what they could do. I knew they could give me a feeling I couldn't find anywhere else. So, in a way, by having this experience with opiates, I wasn't shielded by ignorance anymore. Whether I knew it then or not, I was permanently changed.

The sound of car keys jingling, the change in my pocket, or the sound of pills rattling around in a bottle seemed to catch my attention more. Fortunately, for my sake, I was able to make a clean break from that initial exposure to opiates.

It's never one thing that saves you; it's a combination of things. My mom questioned the doctors and surgeons and then applied her intuition in deciding to wean me off the way she did. I was also at the end of my age of "innocence," I guess, and still listened to my parents. I healed from all this by the time I turned sixteen, just in time for me to begin a new chapter in my life. And although it didn't include painkillers, every chapter seemed to have something.

In high school, I partied like everyone else. Booze was just part of the culture. I was always up to grab a thirty-rack and a bottle every weekend. I was never the mildest person at a party, but I wasn't consistently the most out of control. I had tried weed but preferred alcohol. But then, I went to college and turned the volume up a notch.

Drinking was fun, and it was nice to let loose. I occasionally skipped some of my 8:00 a.m. classes because I was hungover, but who didn't? Justifications and excuses were my favorite ways of lying to myself back then. I started drinking way too much and much too often. For whatever reason, I have always felt the need to touch the fire and make sure it's hot.

This one particular night… the fire was extra hot, and I got burned. By *burned,* I mean I woke up zip-tied to a hospital bed! Groggy, confused, and with no memory of how I got there.

All I was told was that someone found me at a bus stop. I was lying on the bench, and they called for help. The day before had been the infamous annual CU - CSU football game. I went down to Mile High Stadium to tailgate and party with some friends.

Apparently, at some point during that little fourteen-hour drinking binge, I'd been roofied. I had to ask the doctor to repeat that to me once more. Yep, roofied. No wallet. No keys. No phone. No dignity. I just panicked, and technically, I did have one of the two shoes I'd been wearing.

Everyone who drinks is likely to have that "one time" with alcohol that just goes so much further than you ever could have imagined… I'd had those plenty of times. This wasn't that. Or it was like that, just amplified by roofies, apparently. It was the kind of wake-up call that punches you in the dick and sprinkles anxiety all over you.

After that personal low, I didn't look at alcohol the same way anymore. I felt embarrassed, but deeper than that, I was ashamed.

I felt like alcohol had become this pastime I had gotten all too comfortable with. I didn't feel like myself anymore, and I didn't like the version of me who was emerging when I drank.

So, I stopped drinking for about a year. I still was social; I still went to parties, birthdays, and games. And I realized that I liked myself better when I didn't drink. I also realized I could successfully change when I needed to. I redefined my relationship with alcohol and set boundaries for myself. Ultimately, I became what people now call *sober curious*.

I was fortunate to have two sets of grandparents on my dad's side. His mom, Barb, and my Grandpa Dave. And my dad's dad, Earl, and my Grandma Susan. Growing up around all of them and taking those relationships with me into adulthood became an anchor in my life. One I was extremely grateful for. In their own ways, they were the matriarchs of our family.

My Grandpa Earl and Grandma Barb passed away within a few years of each other. I expected to miss them; I expected grief. I didn't expect the rest of the fallout. They were the glue that had held our chaotic, complicated crew together, and they carried the traditions I had grown so fond of. They gave me a sense of being *home*. But change is just as inevitable as death, and it can't be avoided forever.

I know that everyone grieves differently, and I expected loss to complicate my already divided and dysfunctional family, but I didn't think it would happen to the extent it did. Everyone had an opinion, a claim, and a version of the truth. I was seeing sides of people I wished I hadn't. Conversations got sharp. Loyalty got weird. And I felt slowly weeded out of the place I'd thought I had within the chaos. Ultimately, it was like grieving for them twice: once for who they were, and again for the family they'd held together.

By the time Katie and I were dating, I was pouring everything I had into building my career and business. The hustle felt good. It gave me purpose, direction, momentum, and validation. Katie and I were slowly but surely tying our lives together. First, the house.

Then, we were engaged. In between our getting engaged and our wedding, life knocked the wind out of me! I had too much on my plate, and it felt like I was being picked apart.

I was selling my insurance agency, which wasn't easy, and I knew I'd be stepping out of my comfort zone. I didn't even want to do it, initially. It was so stupid. It all came about because the company had previously given pre-approval, but years later, they wanted to rescind it. It would have six-digit ramifications for me in bonuses. I looked at it like I'd tripled my business's revenue during my time with them. I had followed their direction to the letter. I was this consistent "rising star," leading by example. If something this minuscule couldn't be fixed now, what larger issue was I going to face later?

I was also interested in the independent side of what I did. It would be a good time to switch it up. I had no idea how much of my self-worth was tied to work. But it made sense. I found validation around every corner: awards and bonuses! No one tells you, when you're climbing the ladder, sometimes it's leaning against the wrong wall.

I was fried, slowly burning the candle at both ends. I asked myself whether work/life balance was a real thing or just a bunch of buzzwords companies used to keep you from quitting. I kept chasing this illusion of freedom, believing if I just worked harder, got bigger, and made more, then I'd finally have time to breathe. That's not how life works.

I had a specific dynamic with my mom. We had worked together, and she took up a *lot* of my time. Our relationship got blurry. She was my mom, then she was working with me, and sometimes we were each other's unpaid therapists. Sometimes, all of the above in the same phone call.

She was tired of her job at the district office. She hated driving all over Colorado from office to office and following up on life insurance leads for other people. I figured she could work from home with me while I finished selling the agency. That wasn't the healthiest move.

My CPA was one of the main individuals who helped me start my business. She provided direction on everything from business entity options to itemized deductions. I found out, much too late, that my taxes weren't being updated as quickly as they should have been and weren't keeping pace with my income. Not for one year, but for several. I had gone from paying her once per year for tax preparation to monthly payroll/bookkeeping, plus quarterly taxes and annual tax preparations. As that relationship ended—coincidentally around the time my sale went through—I had a basically standing appointment with the IRS, and it felt like another full-time job.

In the last two months of my acquisition process, I was audited four times! Once by the Department of Labor for a more accurate unemployment rating factor (which, if you don't know, determines the amount or multiplier your business needs to pay toward unemployment). Once was by the IRS because my bookkeeper had prepared my taxes incorrectly. Once by our Broker-Dealer, which was normal—just more of a time suck required for me to exit the business. And one more time, following my very first complaint, which a former client sent in. When it rains, it pours. I was exhausted, and I realized that the only person I could rely on to see this all through was myself.

Work was just one thing. It was admittedly a big thing I was dealing with. But my personal life? It didn't feel like I had enough time to even have a personal life. My life became so busy that there were no boundaries, no compartmentalizing. I didn't have a work/life balance because establishing healthy boundaries takes time, and it was easier to be "on" all the time, rather than to turn it off and on again.

A good example of this came about when I wanted to buy a house. I told my uncle I was looking, and soon after, he called to let me know he had seen tenants moving out of his neighbor's house. I was excited; I got the owner's contact information and followed up. Ultimately, the owner and I made a handshake deal. I would pay for an appraisal, then pay the appraised price.

I told my uncle about this and also said to him that, at the time, I was naïvely nervous about whether I would qualify for a home loan. I asked him if he would co-sign with me, if I couldn't purchase it on my own. He agreed. I went through the forty-five-day process, qualified for a great interest rate, and even put more money down.

Simultaneously, I introduced my uncle to my mortgage broker (she's fantastic), as he wanted to do a cash-out refinance on his own house. Long story short, I found out my uncle had lost his job at the time, but he didn't tell me. So, technically, if I had needed a co-signer, he wouldn't have qualified. So, I closed on the house on my own. Inspections, earnest money, down payment, title, water, trash—everything.

Shortly after closing, I was over at the house, cleaning it up. My uncle asked me how much he owed me.

"For what?" I asked.

The down payment... He still wanted to split it with me. To be fair, I hadn't told him that I knew he had lost his job. But to be fairer, he still hadn't told me, either. I should have just quashed this right then and there.

But he was the uncle I had idolized growing up, and I simply didn't want to let him down, even though I secretly knew he was already a bit down. Does that make sense? This scenario could be categorized as my life's "theme," where I avoid my own discomfort while trying to accommodate someone else's.

This quickly became a double-edged sword. I was getting busier with work, and he lived right next door to what would become this project, treating it like a job with a salary.

The house absolutely needed updates, repairs, and improvements before it could be rented. But the way those came about was the problem. He would take on the odd jobs he could do himself and hire out anything major. On one side of the sword, I had help moving these things along, and on the other side were the details...

I started getting messages letting me know how much I owed him for the work he was doing. $1,000 here, $5,000 there, week after week. It didn't take long before I was feeling uncomfortable. Not only did I not realize what I was paying for, but I didn't realize what he himself was charging me for his help. As it turns out, help came with a significant hourly rate. But he explained that, to account for his part as an owner, he was only charging me 50% of that said rate.

I don't know how many uncomfortable sit-down conversations we had about the difference between owning and having equity in something versus being compensated for services rendered. This all started to take up so much time, and it dimmed whatever excitement there was in the beginning.

It became a lose-lose situation. I know this sounds ridiculous, but without a better conflict-resolution method—one I felt had some upside—it was easier for me to just ignore this problem.

During the final year that I owned that house, I was referred to a potential tenant. I met her, and she had good references. She seemed shy and odd, but I felt that was almost the perfect type of person to rent part of what was an unusual, dual-living situation. The basement had been turned into a makeshift apartment with its own bed, bath, and kitchenette.

I was so distracted, I should have vetted her better. And I admit, she sold me, because I wanted to be sold. I wanted it to be easy to keep my place rented out. When you get as busy as I felt, you become unorganized and start taking shortcuts. Innocently, at first, but then the shortcuts start to feel like your main highway through life.

I accepted her deposit, which later bounced. Rather than running a full background check, I allowed her to move in early, after she told me her heartfelt story of domestic abuse, which she was escaping. And just like that, I ended up on the most fucked-up rollercoaster with what I was learned was a "professional squatter."

This was another level of education I learned the hard way, including the ins and outs of how ridiculous it is to legally evict a tenant. If you try to navigate it yourself, you will fill out one wrong form and end up back at the start. If you hire an attorney, there goes

$40,000 and twelve to eighteen months of your life..., which is ultimately what I had to do.

This was not the only legal proceeding I had. I sold my agency at a reduced valuation due to forecasted commission reductions and a compliance-related issue with my office lease, which was previously agreed upon in writing—some of the variables that led me to want to sell to begin with. I reached out for advice. I was told by specific union representatives as well as several reputable attorneys, to investigate a breach of contract. I didn't want to do that, though. I just wanted to be done. But I explored it. I figured there was no harm in running it by professionals when I had already gone this far.

I was told I had a "smoking gun" type of case. I paid a sizeable retainer for them to review all my contracts. Ultimately, it turned out to be a waste of time.

When something unfortunate happens, it's not unlikely that more misfortune will follow. I had to get corporate approval to share an office with another agent, which we did to afford a larger/nicer space. It had become a compliance thing: the company wanted the big agents to have big offices, and lots of them. We were in different districts, both top performers, and the company put it in writing that it agreed to our proposed new five-year lease.

With two years remaining on that lease, they came to us both and said we wouldn't qualify for bonuses for the next two years, because we'd officed together and were no longer "compliant." (In that year alone, my bonus totals were a third of my income.) We were compliant when we entered the lease, and we'd gone one step further to get corporate approval. So, when I sold my business, the buyer had to factor in that my office was now not compliant. I was then personally liable for the remainder of that lease, which I was no longer in because I'd sold the business. My portion for two years' rent was about $73,000. And that wasn't the end of that, either.

Everything, and I mean everything, felt like it was falling apart. I had worked so hard to put myself in this exact position, and when

I got there, it was much harder to "shut off" than it was to start. I started weighing things in simple dollars and cents, and nothing much made any sense. One common denominator was me. I was feeling like such a pushover. In the long run, I can tell you, I learned some lessons, but the primary thing I figured out is you can't really trust anyone to do right by you. Which contradicted the mentality I needed to build myself up at the start, when I believed I couldn't do this alone.

Burnout doesn't really have any symptoms. Not when you're going as fast as you can. You don't necessarily make time to notice, and it doesn't always look like exhaustion. Sometimes, it seems like success. On paper, I was crushing it—thank God, because it costs money to make money, and it costs even more money to actually liquify that money.

I know this wasn't exactly true, but during this period when all this was going on, it felt like everyone I talked to either wanted or needed something from me. It felt draining! My family, clients, employees, and even Katie. I say that, but that pressure period had more to do with me than any of them. I put a lot of pressure on myself, and when I don't measure up or make good, I take it just as hard, if not harder than anything else.

I had this idea of the man I was and the man I wanted to be. Successful, stable, and sharp. A provider. A leader. And I proudly wore that "cape". I kept pushing past warning signs and ignoring the anxiety, the lack of sleep, and the constant feeling that I was behind, even when I was ahead. My self-worth got tangled up in output, and I just didn't know who the fuck I was anymore.

I had money coming in, but it went out just as quickly. It felt like it went faster than usual, and I felt like that was my fault for not being more on top of it. The reality was I just had new types of expenses that weren't ordinary. Every time I turned around, I was writing another check or putting out another fire. Everything felt equally important, and it was all on the same emergency timeline. I found myself going to bed at midnight and waking up at 5:00 a.m., and even that sleep window grew shorter and shorter.

I had gone a long time without needing anything from anyone, and that was important to me. When you are self-sufficient, you're naturally going to have fewer people checking in on you. Maybe most people assumed I was perfectly fine or that I'd figure it out. I always had, so far. Except I wasn't okay, and I didn't know how to ask for help.

To this day, I still don't know exactly how I would have asked for help back then. When I was in the thick of all this, who out there could have helped me with all that I had going on? I was at the center of all these things that, ultimately, were my responsibility. But I was tired. Resentful. Feeling pulled in a million directions, yet somehow, I was falling short in every one of them.

After what had been a rigorous and lonely acquisition process, I closed on the sale of my business. I started a new job, one where, for the first time in years, *I wasn't the boss.* I didn't own my calendar anymore. I didn't control the budget. I couldn't even schedule a dentist appointment without checking someone else's schedule first. It was exciting, which sounds backward. But I'd never had to do that shit before… Or maybe I was supposed to, but I hadn't. All I knew was that I was really used to being my own boss, but I was excited for someone else to be in charge now.

After the excitement subsided of having a big company match my 401(k), I'm not going to lie, I started having some "seller's remorse." I was still able to influence my own success, but it wasn't mine to define anymore. It was based on someone else's numbers and someone else's goals. I went from being the guy who was at the top of every leaderboard, attending every achievement club, and earning every bonus, to virtually starting over. I think I mentioned before how I had felt like a big fish in a little pond. The company I moved to made me feel like I wasn't even a fish… I was more like a fruit fly, buzzing around a puddle in the backyard of their seasonal home. *Humility*

Covid was announced locally in the first days of March 2020, which just so happened to be the first days after Katie and I had moved in with her parents for what we thought would be just a short time, while we figured out where we wanted to move. We finally sold and closed on our house after it had been listed for over eight months. Five days before the home closing, Katie was let go from her job! On her way home, she got in a car accident. You can't make this shit up!

She was so incredibly strong. She lost her job, moved in with her parents, and a global unprecedented pandemic started, all while she just wanted to finish planning our wedding. I had closed on the sale of the agency just six months before this and had hardly gotten away from it. I was still dealing with the aftermath in more ways than one.

Our wedding day was on New Year's Eve, 2020, and it was so much fun. Such a perfect day. It was hard to want to go back to our day-to-day life after that, though. What had consumed so much of our time, energy, and money had finally come and gone.

So, as we returned to the everyday world, with all that I was dealing with, I knew I had to do something. And I knew Katie would need to do something. I didn't want her to just take a job to kill time until things got back to some version of "normal."

As for me, at this point, I was thirty-two years old. I had really only ever had two other jobs and worked for a total of three organizations, so I didn't think it likely that I would find a position within any company worth my time in the short run or their time, in the long run. I had suggested to Katie a few times the idea of starting an independent agency. Her dad and both sisters worked in the industry, so she usually shot down the concept of us working together. But I brought it up again because I really thought it would be a good opportunity for us to build work into the lifestyle we wanted. I had experience as a captive agent and an independent commercial agent—why not merge the two worlds?

I told Katie the steps we needed to take right away to get this moving. She got her license within sixty days, plus she had a corporate tax ID number for us even sooner. I looked at this as an opportunity for her to learn how these things were done and why. I had already gone through the steps needed to set up a small business. This is how I pathologically rationalized her taking the lead.

While Katie was busy following my crash course, *Insurance Agency Set-Up for Dummies.* I was busy trying to manage the battle of good versus evil going on inside me. There is really no other way for me to relay this story to you without first explaining some facts.

In my experience with addiction, there were two versions of myself lying under the surface. There was me. Like *me*-me, the person I have become on purpose, over my lifetime. We like this *me.* This is the version of *me* you want to take home to Mom and Dad. He'll make you laugh, open your door, help you move...

There is also a version that, right now, this very second, is still hard to admit can exist. When I'm under the influence, there is a familiar but unpredictable and actually *more* charming than normal me. The word *cunning* comes to mind. Not smart or creative, but *cunning...*

This version of me is someone you meet at a bar or have a one-time thing with, where he gets off, but you didn't, and he's totally fine with that, because *HE* is all that matters! He has also learned to lie and can do so pathologically, if it means avoiding an uncomfortable situation. Everything necessary to me-me is not at all necessary to this version of me. Honesty, integrity, respect... those become mere interchangeable tools he uses to get what he needs. They can be opportunistic ways for him to hide in plain sight, as well. Everything that I am and everything I have are at the disposal of this implicitly evil version, and it has access to all the tools and feels free to use and abuse them.

When I try to understand this myself or explain it to those I care about, it's next to impossible for me to give you an educated response as to *why* I would risk falling into the cyclical dysfunction that is addiction. Why? Why would I fill that prescription, and why would I not stop it? Especially knowing I had developed a bad relationship with opiates when I was a teenager and knew what that could look like? Desperation.

Even though I had experience with this drug before, I returned to addiction out of desperation. I had become desperate for relief, from the anxieties that surrounded almost every aspect of my life. I used the drug I had on hand because that's what I had. I don't live in a state of regret anymore, but for argument's sake, if I could go back, I would have sought help for my anxiety. I would have started going to therapy to talk through the mess that was my life.

So, for six months or so, I kept refilling the prescription for Vicodin that was first prescribed for my fractured foot. Like the first time, it just kept getting refilled by mistake. For the first few months, there really wasn't anything to report, though. I didn't take these every day, but they were exactly what I hoped they'd be: an escape. Not total oblivion; that's hard to control, like with alcohol or gummies. These were dependable little breaks that I started to give myself. I totally convinced myself that my life was tough. Even though, ten years before, I would have begged to have the problems I was currently facing.

At first, I split my monthly pills with Katie, giving her fifteen and keeping fifteen for me. But by the second or third month, I began to feel resentful, though, because I knew I was going to run out by the time I got my next refill… *IF* I got my next refill, that is.

What if I don't get a refill next month? I really should be saving these for when this eventually stops! Maybe I should say I'm not getting them anymore and just hold on to them for a rainy day. This was approximately half a second of internal debate battling back and forth within me nonstop. Again, this didn't happen overnight, but there are always signs that you're slipping.

I had never lied to Katie up to then about anything. That's true about anything until the first time you cross the line. One month finally came when I officially ran out of Vicodin. I had run out of my fifteen pills in fourteen days… I know…! That escalated quickly. But I told you, if I like something, I *love* it!

I was still in the denial/delusion state. I think I genuinely believed there was nothing wrong with what I was doing. I genuinely felt like my life had become overly stressful (and it was), and what I was doing with pills was no different than if I came home from work every day and had a beer. Or a Scotch or a glass of wine. I didn't drink, so, at the time, this was the way I was mitigating my stress.

I wasn't looking for a "high." My addiction began in the same way it does for so many innocents. A prescription. A reason. There was pain that needed managing. I just wanted relief. And that is precisely what I got. They worked!

I was able to quiet the anxieties and my restless irritation. The pills gave me moments of pause, when I didn't know how to proceed with everything that was chaotically going on in my life. The weight I was carrying on my shoulders melted down into a warm haze, where nothing really mattered. This was my attempt at control. Everything I had going on felt so out of control, and no matter what I did, how hard I tried to push through like I had done countless times, it wasn't working like it used to. I didn't have things under control like I was accustomed to. So, I attempted to control one thing: turning the volume button down on my life.

I was irritable. Restless. I had cold sweats, and I wasn't sleeping. My daily schedule had been hijacked and held hostage: all my thoughts drifted toward these pills, and when I thought I could take the next one. Was it too early? Should I wait an hour? *Fuck it.* Slowly, slowly drifting...

I figured out you could fill a prescription five days early if you told them that you were going on vacation... I went on vacation every single month for a while.

At home, I was still trying to pretend nothing had changed. But it had. I know *I* had. I was more distant. Mainly, I stopped talking to Katie about what was going on with me because I genuinely felt we had just gone through a period when everything was negative. I wasn't a negative person, and I felt so guilty that I had nothing positive to say sometimes, when she asked me about my day. And that's just the truth. I convinced myself I was basically doing her a favor by not constantly talking about things. But that didn't help, either. My life problems just festered, and the distance made it worse.

Katie approached me. She said she should still have forty-five Vicodin, which I had given her over the last three months, and she had not taken. *Well, how many* do *you have?*

She eventually grew to hate me for asking these types of questions. She would just look at me with this "you tell me" look. She was right. I had resorted to going into her things, to the spots I knew she kept her medicine, and I'd taken back the same meds I had given her. Which meant a couple of things, none of them good.

If she should have had forty-five left, that meant she hadn't taken any, but, during that same time, that meant I had taken all the pills I'd been holding onto, plus hers. This also meant I had stooped to the low of lying and stealing. I, of course, justified that in my mind: *Well, these were mine before I gave them to her…* So, I guess it's either stealing… or I'm taking my gift back?

I'm not exaggerating when I say I was so embarrassed. I crossed a line with her.

That pretty picture of her I painted in previous chapters: yes, she's all those things. She's sweet, kind, and gorgeous. But she is also terrifying.

Katie and I have had plenty of fights about plenty of things. Sometimes, she's a little brutal with her words, and sometimes, I'm an asshole. But *this* fight. This fight we would, unfortunately, continue to have wasn't like any of the others. Because in all the others, I actively participated in the fight. I pushed back and argued my points.

But this wasn't like that. I fucked up. I used so many other words when I could have just used three: "I need Help." Or "I am Sorry"

"What do you mean you went through all yours?"

"You have none left? Are you taking these during the day?"

"How many per night?"

"Chris, I think that's a problem!"

That's the watered-down version of how it went. She was furious, and rightfully so. It's hard to be completely honest when I think back to those moments. But I know that, initially, I went mute. I didn't say anything. What could I do? She couldn't have the math wrong: it was just fifteen times three. That plus whatever date was printed on the bottle.

I was almost in disbelief myself. When she used the word *problem,* though... There it was. I could get a little worked up over that. Well... I could try...

"What? It's my prescription..."

"I'm also like twice your size!"

"Well, technically, I get the next one five days early, because I found out, if you lie about having to go on vacation, they will do it for you... Shit."

I calmed the situation down. I apologized, and I meant that shit. I told her the truth... that or I told her what I also believed to be the truth at that point. I was past the point of being burned out. I was exhausted. The stresses I was carrying had reached my limit.

She asked me what I was going to do about it. I told her I would essentially get my shit together. Neither one of us had any reason to doubt that: I had fallen behind and come back from it before.

Then, I returned everything to her. Even so, Katie ended up locking her things up from that point on. And I had strained our fragile boundary.

As if that wasn't bad enough, I started to experience some significant physical discomfort, on top of some heightened levels of emotional distress. Now what was I going to do? I had to give all those pills back, and they'd been locked away. I'd have to wait two weeks until the next refill.

The internal monologue for this type of battle is endless! Back and forth like a pinball machine. On one side, you have good; on the other, you have bad. If I had been honest with someone—anyone, I was still at the point where I could have turned around.

Unfortunately, the addiction started to emerge as the victor more often. I still fought myself the entire way, because, on the surface, I ultimately knew what I was doing was wrong. Just below the surface, it was entirely out of hand and beyond my control. But, with addiction, you're fighting something that doesn't fight fair. The scales start to balance, fifty-fifty, and then it starts to go in the direction of addiction.

When I was in active addiction, everything felt extremely distorted. (No shit, really?) My sense of time, my sense of urgency, my priorities… It would be easier to say, I might as well have tipped everything upside down, then shaken it all up, and maybe spun it around a hundred times.

My physical symptoms started to dictate where my mind went, and it was always on this tiny pill. It had taken me over, and I started having desperate thoughts. Thoughts like, I *don't ever want to run out of this…* Thoughts like, *What might I have to do? Where can I look to find some more?* The thoughts were always impulsive and hard to control.

Once my mind went down that path, it was next to impossible to change course. It was so impulsive that my brain started to send me through the grieving process in advance. I literally would have an intrusive, impulsive thought about me potentially doing something that would be upsetting not only to me but to Katie… and I would begin to go through the grief process before any thought was ever put into action.

How fucking efficient is addiction, am I right? *Oh, you're* eventually going to feel bad for doing this thing that you know is wrong, so let's speed that process up for you and do it *now*!

I started going through my mental Rolodex: Who do I know who might sell the most degenerative type of drug known to mankind? Ah, of course! I knew someone from college, which, ironically, wasn't how I knew him back then. I just happened to know he had access to these things.

In my delusional state (as if no time had passed; meanwhile, it'd been ten-plus years…), he could be a celibate monk for all I knew. He could be Dad of the Year and married to the woman of his dreams. Nope. He lived between Denver and Kansas, and yes, he still sold drugs. *I know... shocking!* But great news for me, right?

I kid you not, I didn't know this person very well back then. But after all this time, I just sent him a text, asking if he sold a particular type of drug. He answered right away and happened to have exactly what I asked for. It was like he was frozen in time!

This brings me to my next "pay attention" moment. In my experience, this particular type of drug doesn't numb anything. It *delays* everything, like pressing pause. You can *pause, procrastinate, and avoid* everything you want, for as long as you want. It will still be there for you to deal with whenever you're done, though. If you have the chance to come back to it, that is. I started taking these as a way to escape life's stresses. It didn't take very long for that *escape* to become the primary cause of my suffering.

The first time I met that old college acquaintance, I was so excited. Why did I feel excited? Well, I'd found a way to avoid what I'd initially avoided. Basically, I was excited because I had begun living day to day in like two-hour time blocks. When I found that I could just pay to have my creature comforts in bulk, well, I was excited. I felt like I was going to have to stress about it less. After all, the original idea was to worry less.

The writing on the wall was all over the place, but I just didn't see it. In my mind, my deluded, dysfunctional little brain, I swear to you I told myself things like, "This is going to solve my problem. I'll never fall short again, and Katie won't have to worry..., because she'll never know!"

I don't know how many times I have met up with college dealers. There are too many times to count.

I started to stash drugs away. Literally, if I had a hundred, I would put ten in a bag and hide that bag in a coat pocket I never used. My thought behind that was, I had some tucked aside, if I needed it... And maybe, one day, I'd wear that coat, and it would be like finding money in the dryer.

I don't entirely understand this part. I did get a little dramatic with the hide-and-seek game. I started buying Velcro and attaching pill containers to the inside of my closet ceiling. Then, Katie found those…

I used to put Baggies full of pills into a wound-up pair of socks, and then I moved the socks to the middle of my drawer. Then, Katie found those…

I bought travel-size Tylenol containers, put drugs in there, and just carried them around with me…. Shockingly enough, Katie found those, too.

The ratio of times I successfully hid any of these things to how often she and I had to confront them was maybe one in twenty. One out of every twenty times, she came across something I'd promised not to have or something she hadn't seen and wondered how I'd gotten it.

In real time, it is disgusting how many lies I told. I used every logical excuse, and I treated each argument like I was on trial for murder… *"You can't prove any of that!"* It was awful.

Katie's light is and always has been so bright. After enough of this shit, paired with the country's looming anxious state during Covid and the added stress of starting the agency… even I began to see her light dim. That's how I measure this era. It broke my heart. She still did her hair, put on her hoodie, made coffee, and pushed through, but the spark didn't jump like it used to.

I can say this to you now, because I was fortunate enough to have been given a chance(s)—plural—to see for myself what this was.

It was never my intention to hurt Katie. It was never my intention to hurt myself! My intention initially was to remedy my pain, and I got lost in that. The "highs" do not stay that way. The tolerance you develop guarantees this. But that doesn't matter. For me, I wasn't taking these anymore to "feel" anything. I was taking them so I could feel normal. I was taking them to avoid feeling like needles were coming out of my legs. Like my spine was going to shoot through my skin. I was taking them to wake up. I was taking them to sleep.

It wasn't long before I came to this natural moment. I wasn't experiencing the same euphoric effects anymore, and I had plenty of times when I was going to quit. I've done it all, cold turkey... I don't recommend it. Weaning yourself off? Yeah..., because you were so responsible while you were "weaning on?" But I tried that, too.

Somehow, my life and everything in it became unmanageable. Now, the medicine I'd used to manage the unmanageable was even more so. I knew I was powerless to fight it. But I couldn't or wouldn't admit it. For a time, I strove only to get through to the next day. I developed this victim mentality, toxic, and lazy. I was in the most primal, disgusting, and reduced level of basic survival I had ever been in.

I wasn't this person. I don't know how I wound up taking so many steps backward. The truth was, I had taken them one undisciplined decision at a time. I spent so much time being the victim in my own life, but I lacked the will to do anything about it.

I had effectively unlearned so many good habits I had picked up over the course of my life. Basic habits... like eating right, drinking plenty of water, and getting outdoors as often as possible. Doing things that made me happy started to feel like a chore. Covid didn't help this at all. Between having to quarantine, working from home, and spending less time with the people I enjoyed. I wasn't only in active addiction, I was depressed.

Depression is a term thrown around too lightly. There is a significant difference between being anxious and being depressed. You can always do something about anxiety: drink more water, exercise, go for a walk, do breath work, etc. Anxiety is temporary. This was the first time I could say I was authentically depressed, and it was a dark place.

I was constantly tired. Physically and mentally exhausted without exerting myself, and I was sleeping eight to ten hours a night. I started to feel like I was living in a fog. Everything was hazy, and I didn't feel that normal sharpness, alertness. All jokes aside, I imagine this experience—from start to finish—felt a lot like a slow death.

I took care of Katie when she didn't need me. But during the time when she did, I wasn't able to rise to the occasion. I still wrestle with the guilt and shame of this. I believe the Lord gives us a handful of chances in life. These chances don't always appear the same way, but they all have one thing in common: they are an opportunity to rise. To lead by example. To be dealt a hand of cards and to play that hand as best you can. I know I have been given this opportunity in the past, and I felt I'd met the challenge and was better for it.

I didn't know my path would lead me here. I do know (now) that I stopped being prepared. I stopped caring and quit fighting to greet the day. The fact is, we don't all know where our paths are leading us every day; that's not new or new news. If you take one thing away from this, let it be this: wake up each day, and, at the very least, be willing and ready for the day to take you where you're meant to go. If you're not ready, you won't go anywhere.

In my "efforts" to simply survive each day, Katie and I were reduced to unrecognizable. Katie, my best friend, my girlfriend, my fiancé, my wife. I felt solely responsible for her unhappiness, and I have only ever wanted her happiness.

I would look around at some point each day, and when I saw her, I almost had to distract myself to avoid this feeling in the pit of my stomach. I fought to overcome this, and I had fleeting moments of clarity and energy when I would try to do something, anything, that might make a difference in her day and make her happy.

We drifted apart. She could only do so much, only ask me how I was doing so many times. She was dealing with life as we knew it then as best she could, too. At some point, as a way to self-preserve, she put up a wall. I don't blame her.

It was like one long repeat of *Groundhog Day*. You don't wake up and decide, Today's the day I blow it up. You make a hundred small, stupid choices and then suddenly, the blast radius is bigger than your life. Things were about as bad as they could be, don't you think? By that point, I had only ever taken or purchased prescription pain medication. I didn't chop it up and snort it. I didn't boil it and shoot it, and I didn't smoke it (not sure that's possible?). I just took it "normally."

One time, I went to meet that guy to re-up my supply. He didn't have the prescription he normally did—usually, every month, he got an actual prescription from a pharmacy, and I always saw the bottle. This time, he didn't. He said he didn't have the bottle with the label, because they weren't his, but he swore they were the same legitimate, prescribed medication.

They looked exactly like the ones I had gotten before. They were actually even more "clean" looking. He told me he could get these for less than the ones I usually buy from him, but they were actually stronger! I believed him because… that's just how my brain was operating. Under sober circumstances, I would have been so much more suspicious, knowing full well that if it sounds too good to be true, it usually is. And nothing in this world worth having comes for free.

Unfortunately, I bought them and brought them home. They were outrageously strong, which meant I could take less of them! And they were less expensive, which meant I could get more of them. There is a difference between ignorant and negligent, and then there was me during this time… I didn't ask too many questions. I didn't know what to ask? I paid the man and probably said, "Thank you."

Not long after this, I started to hear about the new, emerging fentanyl epidemic, which had become very pronounced in Colorado specifically. One day, while watching the news, a story came up about eight kids in Aurora who had all died instantly after coming in contact with this new (to me) substance. The story went on to talk about how fentanyl was showing up in everything… including those small, blue pills marked exactly the same as prescribed opiate medications.

Not only was I bringing this deadly drug into our home, but I was also essentially on the wrong side of the "front lines" of this deadly trend, soon to be known as an epidemic. And there was really no going back after taking those. They were so strong, anything else by comparison might as well contain nothing at all.

With one of these tiny blue pills—you could fit about two and a half of them on your pinky fingernail—just a quarter of it was equivalent to about fifteen to twenty 10 mg Percocets, maybe more. So, each whole pill was the equivalent of approximately seventy-five to one hundred 10 mg Percocets.

Oh, and there's more! Because these pills weren't carefully made in a laboratory, and they happened to use the most potent synthetic opioid agonist known to mankind, the chances of you getting a "wet pill" or a "loaded pill" were about one in ten. Similar to the way that THC shows up in edibles, where one might have 2 mg and another from that same batch has 15 mg, these pills also varied in strength.

That's what slipping away looked like: not a dramatic fall, but a hundred quiet surrenders that weren't stronger than the pills that numbed my pain. Fortunately, these pills were only part of the picture for a short while. I obviously didn't know it, but there was a day of reckoning coming right around the corner. Just in time to save my life.

Chapter 6

Curiosity as a Privilege

Katie

I grew up in a family where, if you had a headache, you were given medicine paired with a glass of water. Especially since my mom was a nurse. It was simple: medicine helped. I was also taught to be respectful and aware of the power they can have over someone, beyond just healing, and how, occasionally, medicine can become a crutch.

Because I wasn't overly curious about drugs during my younger teen years, I think I entered my twenties with a healthy sense of respect and curiosity, approaching new experiences with the mentality, "Sure, I'll try it," as long as I felt safe and surrounded by people I trusted. I won't name the specific drugs I tried, but I can say this: they expanded my awareness. They made music feel deeper, colors more vivid, laughter more alive. They shifted how I interacted with the world and encouraged me to be present in ways I hadn't felt before. They never became part of my lifestyle, but they were part of a season of exploration.

At some point, most people experiment with drugs or alcohol. Whether it's dancing at Red Rocks under a sky full of stars, passing something around at a house party, or unwinding with a glass of wine after a soul-sucking week at a job that drains your light. We are all searching for something. A spark. A sigh of relief. A glimpse beyond the gray. The settings might change, but the yearning is the same: release, connection, a moment of freedom that reminds us we're more than what we've been told we have to be.

I've always loved that about us humans: our curiosity. Our desire to reach for something more. And for a long time, I thought that kind of curiosity was universal. That we could all experiment with altered states in an exploratory, even innocent, way. I thought substances could be part of the story without rewriting the whole damn plot. At some point in everyone's life, we have looked for something to help escape our feelings or numb the emotional pain.

But as I got older, I realized something I hadn't seen clearly before: curiosity, at least my kind of curiosity, is a privilege. I could try something once and walk away. I could flirt with the edge without ever falling off the cliff. I never had to dig myself out of a hole or question whether I could function without something in my system. My relationship with substances was casual, like a guest that came and left without leaving a mess.

That's *not* the case for everyone. And before I noticed this wasn't how it was for Chris, it was too late.

Curiosity is only safe when you can walk away. The moment it starts to feel like you need it, the game changes. It can also feel like a trap when the lines between reality and fiction begin to blur. And the thing is, you don't always see it right away.

For Chris, the substances started just about pain management, but later became a refuge he couldn't escape, and it turned into a crutch to survive. He never intended the substances to change his intentions around helping physical pain, but later, down the road, they were used to help him numb and escape his reality.

There were seasons when, in our effort to unwind or manage pain, Chris and I shared what we had access to. For me, that meant taking a prescribed pill here and there after a procedure or on days when my physical pain was over a pain score of seven. For him, it was often prescribed. And on some of those long, heavy Sunday evenings, we'd let ourselves settle into comfort together… splitting a small dose, like someone might split a bottle of wine. It felt like a moment of relief in a life that was becoming increasingly difficult to bear.

I didn't understand how my "harmless" use could be so different from Chris's. It didn't feel like it was taking anything from me. It was something we did together, a temporary break from the pressures of life. I thought, "This is normal. This is what people do." I thought, at first, when we were sharing specific substances, we were on the same page, but I would soon find out we were not. Eventually, I was in the shallow end with my floaty, enjoying the sun, and he was drowning in the deep end, gasping for air.

I had access to Vicodin here and there over the years, after surgeries, injuries, or if the pain in my body from the car accident refused to quiet down. And I was grateful for it. Living with chronic pain teaches you to listen to your body, to honor the signal it sends. But it also teaches you discipline. Because, though painkillers can offer relief, they can also quietly build dependence if you're not careful. That's the tightrope of pain management: it asks you to use just enough to function, but not so much that you forget how to feel.

I never felt the need to take it daily. For me, the majority of the time, it was about pain management, not escape. But even with good intentions, I can see how easily that slope could've become slippery.

There have been times when I have turned to a glass of wine or a pill to numb the day and better manage the uncomfortable. However, as long as you acknowledge it and understand that this can be a tight line to balance on, it comes down to being mindful of your intentions. Because when you're in pain, especially the kind that lingers and wears you down, anything that softens the edge starts to look like a lifeline. That's where I was lucky. I had a healthy fear of that line. I could do what I needed when I needed it and walk away when I didn't. But at any point, the Devil can creep in and blur the lines.

But what felt helpful to me became foundational for him. And by the time I noticed that the habit had taken root in him, it was too late. I thought we had a shared understanding of these drugs. We didn't.

I had a boundary I didn't even know I was holding. Chris started with one, but it eventually became distorted. He was trying to numb the bad emotions he felt, but unfortunately, that meant he was also numbing the good ones. It was his attempt to deal with years of unresolved trauma, plus his current stress levels, by dulling his emotions. And slowly, quietly, he began taking them every day, multiple times a day.

Not in a million years did I think that our sharing a pill here and there would lead him down a darker road, making it harder to find his path. But my naïveté got the best of me.

I didn't know about his history with addictive tendencies or how his relationship with substances had been shaped long before I entered the picture. But what was manageable for me became unmanageable for him. And I didn't see the shift right away. Because dependency doesn't announce itself. It disguises itself as bonding, as shared pain, as love.

At first, I brushed away any alarms that went off in my head. An extra pill here or there found on the floor, pills I found in odd places that weren't his prescription, and him sleeping more than usual. The vague explanations for why his prescription seemed to run out faster than expected. I still wanted to believe we were on the same page. That we were managing our pain, our stress, our lives… together.

But something in me started to feel unsettled. His use didn't look like mine. It wasn't occasional anymore. It was quiet, daily, and increasing. I wanted to believe him, that it was under control. I mean, I *did* believe him, mostly because I needed to. It was easier to trust his words than to confront the quiet feeling in my gut that something was off.

It was like watching a shadow slowly form over him. I didn't want to be suspicious. I didn't want to be the nag, the worrier, or the one who couldn't just relax. But, deep down, I knew we weren't just managing pain anymore. He was feeding something I didn't understand.

Things slowly began to cross the unspoken lines I had drawn between myself and him. Our Sundays bled into weekdays. The pill we used to share became something he reached for without me and, eventually, without saying anything at all. There was a shift in his energy I couldn't explain. He'd wake up groggy. Fall asleep mid-sentence. Pull away from conversations or would disappear for hours. He became super-irritable.

Soon, I asked if I could split his prescription in half, in hopes that he wasn't dependent on taking thirty pills in a month, then I would keep the other half in my safe, collecting pills over time. But then they started going missing, leading me to question my counting or to wonder how he was getting into a locked safe.

But the clues started to stack up. I noticed bottles refilled sooner than they should've been. I became hypervigilant, scanning for any shift in tone or change in body language. I didn't realize it then, but I was already slipping into survival mode. There would be nights when I would lie awake next to him and wonder, "Is this how it starts?" Other nights, I would pray it was just a phase. That he would eventually snap out of it. That it wasn't as bad as it seemed.

But addiction doesn't come crashing in… It creeps in slowly. And denial becomes its closest ally.

Soon, my new reality became a constant series of confrontations. I even found myself rehearsing how I was going to frame the sentences in my head before even daring to say them out loud, plus finding the right tone that wouldn't set him off.

"Have you taken something today?"

"How many are left?"

"You promised this was the last refill."

I asked the questions to see whether the answers, as I knew them, were spoken honestly. But no. Those never came. What I once thought were innocent Sundays turned into tense arguments and lies. I felt like I had a second job as a detective in my own home, scanning for clues, chasing for truth, and finding the culprit.

There was no big explosion at first. It was just a slow, steady flow of lava, eroding all trust, safety, and affection. Love was obviously still there, but it was now tangled in constant fear, laced with skepticism, lies, and doubt. I wasn't trying to control him. I was trying to reach him and understand. But every time I tried, I felt like I was losing a little more of myself.

Somewhere in the chaos, I stopped trusting my gut instincts and myself. Any time I gathered the energy and courage to confront him, I questioned whether I was overreacting. He was so good at deflecting and turning the situation back around, with all fingers pointing at me. He told me I was dramatic and overreacting and that everything was under control. I wanted to believe him so badly, I started to think I was the problem, that it was my fault where we were.

Soon, I was second-guessing my instincts, walking on eggshells, and watching my confidence drain away piece by piece. I'd whisper excuses to myself, *He's just tired.* Or, *It's the stress of selling his agency. This is just a rough patch.* I carried the weight of it all like a dirty secret, ashamed to share it with anyone. When the excuses ran dry, I eventually stopped interrogating him, but then, I switched to action.

I became a detective, tearing through his pockets, his closet, his shoes, his office. Always searching, always hoping to find proof I could destroy. Instead of welcoming him home with a hug, my hands went straight to his backpack, rifling for anything that might betray our trust. Instead of trusting his words, I stalked his movements.

Every trip to the store, every detour on the way home became suspicious. You stopped at the gas station? Prove it. If I spotted him near an unfamiliar corner, I'd jump in my car and tail him, heart racing, sure I'd catch him in the act. Tracking him like prey.

Little by little, I lost sight of myself. I was unraveling. The woman who once trusted her instincts and knew her worth twisted into someone unrecognizable, coiled tight like a snake. Guilt slithered through me. Exhaustion wrapped itself around me. I didn't realize it then, but I wasn't just trying to save him; I was drowning with him, gasping, clawing for air that never seemed to come.

I thought to myself, *How did I get here?*

I was so incredibly patient when I was dating and deciding who to let into my heart. I thought I had found someone who would protect my heart at all costs. I knew when people said, "Marriage is hard," but I figured that meant a few arguments over which side the toilet paper sat on the holder or choosing where or what we should eat for dinner. But never in a million years did I think I would face what I had to deal with over those critical years.

Addiction, lies, dishonesty, yelling, deceit, jail, drugs, manipulation, hospitals, rehab, losing family, and friends. Standing in the kitchen, shaking, because I'd found pills again. Sitting in the ER at 2:00 a.m. Crying in the car before walking into work, pretending I was fine. Staying up late to monitor his breathing, unsure of what he'd ingested. I was so tired of playing referee, therapist, detective, lawyer, and hostage negotiator all at once.

Over the last few years, I had doubted my already horrible memory due to my traumatic brain injury and my personal Katie instincts, so I was constantly asking myself, "Okay, am I just overreacting? And maybe this is my fault?"

I was exhausted from constantly having to manage Chris's emotional state, while walking on eggshells and trying to avoid any explosions or fights, which left me mentally, emotionally, and even physically drained. I became lonely, even in our marriage and our relationship. I felt utterly alone. I felt unseen and unsupported. I was just stuck and felt helpless. I was in a constant state of hypervigilance and a wound-up ball of anxiety. I was always bracing for the next outburst or finding more pills or a shift in mood, afraid to speak up or be available for any concerns. Over time, this led me to become incredibly insecure, and my confidence took a significant hit.

I began to believe I wasn't enough, that I was somehow broken, too, and that what we were living through couldn't be fixed. I slowly detached from my own needs and started internalizing

Chris's addiction as my own responsibility to manage. I thought, if I just loved him better, supported him more, stayed calm, stayed present, and stayed strong, maybe it would change. But the weight of that responsibility crushed me. I stopped sleeping. I had constant headaches, knots in my stomach, and a kind of exhaustion that sleep couldn't touch. My body was screaming what my heart wasn't ready to say: *This isn't sustainable.*

Without realizing it, I developed codependent tendencies as a way to survive. I became the caretaker, the fixer, and the one who held it all together. And then, I started to break. Resentment crept in like a slow leak. I stopped crying. I stopped yelling. I just… shut down. I emotionally detached from our marriage, not because I didn't care, but because it was the only way I knew how to protect myself from further harm.

People love to say, "God gives the hardest battles to His strongest soldiers." But that saying just made me want to scream, "When did I sign up for the war? *Who enlisted me?* Because I don't remember choosing this battlefield!" And yet, there I was, armored in silence, bleeding from wounds no one could see, fighting a battle I'd never asked to join.

I have desperately prayed, whispered into the darkness, "God, do you see me? Why are you not intervening? Can You not see how much pain I am in?"

I begged for signs, for mercy, for anything that would show me I wasn't alone. But sometimes, the silence felt louder than the chaos. And when the life you imagined (the marriage, the love, the hope) doesn't match the life you're living, it's more than disappointing. It's devastating. The gap between expectation and reality became a kind of grief I didn't know how to name. A slow, aching loss that didn't come from death, but from watching something you love die in front of you.

In the middle of that heartbreak, everything felt so heavy. The weight of loving someone who couldn't always love themselves. The pressure of trying to hold up a life that kept crumbling beneath me. And sometimes, I couldn't find God's hand in it at all. I wanted to believe He was there, behind the scenes, working things for good, but some nights, all I could feel was absence. Faith was supposed to be my comfort, but sometimes, it just made me feel more alone. And it was quiet, because I'd stopped listening. I thought maybe I was being tested. Or worse… forgotten.

At some point, the truth stopped knocking quietly and barged through the door. I found pills in pockets, tucked into jacket linings, and hidden in drawers I hadn't opened in months. There were texts from numbers I didn't recognize with code words, meetups, and drop-offs. The money disappeared with no explanation. He'd leave the house for long stretches and come back dazed, with stories that didn't line up with the location I had been tracking. I once found hundreds of pills stashed away, and when I confronted him, he told me it was just cheaper to buy in bulk. Like he was Costco shopping, not spiraling out of control.

I started second-guessing everything. His tone of voice, the way he moved, and how dilated his pupils were. I even bought a drug-test kit (and those aren't cheap!), grasping for truth in the constant deception. He acted nonchalant, like he had nothing to hide. The test showed negative, but I could feel it wasn't warm. So, I went into the bathroom and started to investigate. And then I found it… a yellow Gatorade bottle, tucked under the bathroom counter, already filled and lukewarm. He'd planned to fake the test ahead of time. I wondered how long that had been there, waiting for its mighty moment to shine.

I stood there, holding it, stunned, as the weight of manipulation settled in my chest like a stone. This wasn't just secrecy. This was a strategy. A performance. A lie rehearsed down to the last detail.

I'd come home to find him passed out on the couch in the middle of the day, mid-conversation, mid-sentence. There was no hiding it anymore. It wasn't for physical pain. It wasn't controlled. It was an addiction, in its complete and terrifying form. And no matter how many prayers I whispered, no matter how many times I tried to love him into healing, I couldn't unsee what was now all around me. And the lies and manipulation were heartbreaking.

The breaks in trust weren't isolated. They become constant. Small cracks soon became huge gaping holes. I'd ask the simple question, "Did you take anything today?" And he would lie to my face with ease. He'd say what he thought I wanted to hear. He'd promise to stop, to taper, to flush the pills. But I'd find more. In coat pockets, Velcroed under cabinets, behind books, in socks. Every time I confronted him, he'd come up with a story, a half-truth, a justification, or just complete and utter denial.

And I started to break, right along with the trust.

It's not just the lying that wounds you. It's what the lies do to you over time. They make you question your memory, your instincts, your worth. They make you feel crazy for noticing what's right in front of you. And with every broken promise, something in me hardened.

Living with someone in active addiction isn't just heartbreaking. It's all-consuming. Every day felt like I was holding my breath, waiting to see which version of him I'd get. I stopped making plans, because I never knew if I'd need to drop everything to clean up a mess, cover for a lie, or keep him from falling apart. Enabling was in full effect. I was constantly scanning his eyes, his energy, and his tone of voice, looking for clues. Detective Katie had a full-time job. Hypervigilant. Exhausted. I couldn't focus. I forgot things. I stopped laughing. The joy that had once lived inside me turned into survival instincts.

I felt like I was living two lives, one where I tried my best to cover my pain with a smile, and one that I carried alone, rotting away in silence. And here's the thing, people like me don't usually get help. Not because we don't need it, but because we are too busy trying to hide the mess. Too ashamed to admit how bad it is. Too afraid people will judge us or, worse, judge the person we love. We become the keepers of secrets, the managers of chaos. We wear our exhaustion like armor, telling ourselves we can handle it. But the truth is that we are crumbling quietly in the dark.

I didn't know how to ask for help. Did no one else see that we were both drowning? I felt invisible, unraveling thread by thread, building walls I didn't even know I was putting up. Emotional detachment became my survival strategy. I loved him. God, I loved him. But I couldn't trust him. And when love and trust no longer live in the same house, you start to lose your home.

What I didn't realize then was that I was sick, too, not with drugs, but with control, obsession, and the illusion that I could save him. His addiction consumed him, but mine was just as powerful: I was addicted to fixing, addicted to rescuing, addicted to the belief that, if I just tried harder, I could keep us both afloat.

And then, one rainy February day, my phone buzzed. I didn't know everything was about to change. A gentle act of concern ignited a series of events that would save Chris's life and, though I didn't realize it then, save mine, as well.

Chapter 7

Crisis Management

Chris

Here is a part of my story that I journaled about in February 2022, leading to a remarkable event in my addiction journey. I hope you learn more about me and who I truly am as I describe this experience. There's a reason I included the times in my life that were not so gray, too. Before I turned thirty, I'd accomplished so much and had absolutely everything to lose…

Wednesday, February 16, 2022

My name is Chris, and I'm an addict. My routine has drastically changed. Instead of waking up at 5:00 a.m., taking care of the dog, cleaning up around the house, and showering to leave for a full day of work, I wake up just in time, ready to complete the bare minimum, enough to look alive, not enough to actually live.

What I didn't realize then was that my morning shower wasn't about hygiene anymore. It was about pain management. The hot water was my warm-up before I gave my body what it really wanted—opioids. Eight hours of sleep meant eight hours without a fix. Every nerve in my body hummed for it.

Like most weekdays in the early post-Covid timeframe, I could work in or out of the office. Covid messed things up—not just for me, but for everyone. I thrive off a sense of community, specifically interpersonal connection and interaction. Faced with mandated confinement and isolation, I suffered. Isolation is like gasoline for the fire inside an addict.

Before I allowed drugs and compounding traumas to take control of my life, I was an enthusiastic entrepreneur who was proactive in every way. Afterward, simple tasks became a chore, instead. The fact that I was showered and dressed by 9:00 in the morning was a small win.

And how do you celebrate small wins when you are broken and the world is in shambles? You reward yourself! My treat came in the form of two or three small pills, though I can't tell you exactly what they were at that time, as the lines blurred between "prescribed" and "purchased." My appetite and tolerance, paired with my complete lack of regard, left me vulnerable to the most intoxicating high levels of euphoria, followed by the most lethal withdrawal. That came from fentanyl.

Near the end, I could get 1,000 fentanyl pills for the same price as my monthly prescription of 7.5 mg Vicodins, and it was cheaper to buy significant amounts of fentanyl than to purchase additional Vicodin. *Fentanyl*: it is a word I had never heard before. I had ingested fentanyl on multiple occasions before I even knew what it was, or without knowing that what I'd bought through "a friend of a friend" was laced.

I put on a show just for some background noise, since I just needed to wait about fifteen to twenty minutes for the pills to kick in, and then feel at least the version of myself that I had become. I knew I was addicted. I knew exactly what to do about it. What I *should* do, anyway. And every day, I lied to myself; I convinced myself that everyone has a vice, something they don't share with the world or even keep from those closest to them.

As if lying to yourself isn't bad enough, I almost had to convince myself I deserved it. In some fucked up way, I worked as many hours as I had, made as much money as I did, and suffered in the ways I had. This was mine, my treat. In my eyes, then, it wasn't hurting anybody. It made me feel calmer, and it was a perfect pairing with my daily struggle with ADHD and anxiety.

I never mentioned my experiences with ADHD to anyone, because, when they heard that, they knew I must have Adderall. If most anyone else took Adderall, it would be a high for them. But for me, it was an attempt at normalcy, a way to achieve the quiet most people take for granted. However, on this day, as I fell back asleep, nodding off, I woke up on the couch to see my two best friends hovering over me. It's crazy, but I knew exactly why they were there, and I was relieved as well as scared shitless.

They said little, mainly, "Good morning. Get yourself together, and join us downstairs when you're ready. Many of us want to talk to you." My inner child was panicked!

As soon as they walked out of the room, I took another pain pill, because I knew there was only one possible thing I was about to walk into: an intervention. And I was right.

As I walked downstairs alone, I realized Katie, my wife, wasn't with me. My mind was racing. As I tried to put the puzzle pieces together, I thought for sure she'd organized this intervention. And it made sense. She'd been watching me disappear in slow motion. Before I opened the door to what would surely be my most humiliating, humbling, and life-changing experience, I decided, if help was offered, I would take it.

I was surprised, grateful, and confused when I opened the door to a large open room filled with a dozen chairs in a circle. It was like a preview of everyone who would attend my funeral. There were people from my immediate family, my chosen family, some of my best friends, and one or two who caught me off guard, and I wondered why they were there.

This was not the group of people whom I wanted to see me at my weakest moment, and I was not just the self-medicating addict version of myself. I was the broken, helpless man I felt I'd become. Before the intervention, I had acknowledged my addiction and how it was taking everything from me instead of healing what I thought was hurting. I'd tried at least a dozen times to stop. I became an expert at avoiding the truth; I refrained from using terms such as *addict*, because I could not accept my reality.

I looked around the room a few times and didn't want to make eye contact with anyone. I focused on where I would be sitting. My eyes landed on my Grandma Susan. I have always admired and respected her. She's brilliant and multifaceted, the definition of grace under fire. Even though I was humiliated that she was there, which meant she *knew*, I immediately went to sit with her. Neither of us needed to say anything, not aloud anyway. We communicated through eye contact, small facial gestures, and energy.

Fortunately, I did not have time to get emotional, as I was immediately introduced to Bobby. I will get this out of the way right now: Bobby is one of my least favorite people. He's an interventionist, and on this day, I learned that some interventionists are really just opportunists. And what better opportunity than a key family member falling down the wrong path, especially if they can pay cash?

Bobby did a great job. He didn't let too much dust settle. He just jumped right in, and I think the only reason I remember his words is that I could've written them myself in a how-to guide on being an interventionist.

"Well, Chris, I think you know why we're all here. And it's because everyone in this room loves and cares about you, and they're worried about you."

At this point, only one person other than my wife had asked the tricky question, "Are you okay?" I understand how uncomfortable it must be to ask somebody who is usually okay. My opinion of myself may be different now than it was then, but I know one thing that always brought me the most joy was helping other people. So, I don't hold in the animosity, and I don't wonder whether things would've gone differently if someone had just asked. In this book, you will learn a lot about what my wife Katie and I went through, and dammit, I wish it had been done differently.

After the introductions, I was told that some of my closest friends had letters they wanted to read to me. Up to this point, I hadn't said a word. I don't remember the order; honestly, I don't remember every word they read. I do remember the genuine ones.

And I am eternally grateful to have a best friend and older-brother figure who wasn't afraid to ask me if I was okay. He wasn't even upset when he found out I had lied. His letter was short, because it could be.

Also, throughout this experience, I learned that boundaries are valuable and necessary to live a healthy and happy life. Because there were people in that room who I believe had good intentions in their attempt to "help me," I pray they've learned some things about themselves.

Sitting in that room in that circle was the most uncomfortable emotional experience I've ever had. I couldn't even look at Katie above the neck. I couldn't face her, knowing the pain and trauma I'd caused and the good time I had defrauded her of. The most painful thing for me has always been to see her crying. She doesn't cry normal tears. They are more significant, and each of them has meaning.

I had seen plenty of her tears in the years leading up to this—tears of physical, emotional, and psychological circumstances. I'd also seen her cry plenty of happy tears. But on this day, I knew that all those tears were also mine. There was nothing she needed to tell me, and my feeling ashamed and emasculated was the least of my worries. While each person read their letter, I wasn't always keen on paying attention; I just wanted to stand up and hug her. I was already so sorry. And she had been carrying so much of my weight. But in this circumstance, with what was before us, that became my most common words: "I am sorry."

After my last friend finished his letter, the interventionist Bobby stepped in and tried to make a joke. He was a redneck, and I guess, in that way, he was funny. He could quote every line from every dumb fucking movie you've ever heard of. I'm sure that's useful in his line of work. I didn't know what to say, even though I knew the floor was mine, so, somewhat cowardly, I said as little as I could.

I said I was sorry, and that couldn't be more true. I mentioned my embarrassment, and everyone told me I shouldn't be. I hugged everyone in the room and thanked them for being there, and they assured me I'd be okay.

Then, somebody told me the high-level details of what was in store. In a nutshell, "Your plane leaves in two and a half hours, and you need to pack a bag."

But I wasn't given details about what to bring or for how long. I found myself in our upstairs mother-in-law's apartment with my mom, just the two of us. I remember she was talking. She's always talking, but I don't remember a damn thing she said. At some point, I just asked if Katie could come up and be with me for a while.

Depending on what I did or said, there were instructions and more codes of conduct for how everybody should act and react. One instruction was that Katie wasn't supposed to be alone with me. I had fought nothing so far, so asking for a few minutes with my wife didn't seem much to ask for.

She popped through the door, and we hugged each other in a way that I don't think we've ever hugged before. It wasn't romantic or cinematic. It was survival. It was desperate. It was a shock. It was a sincere lack of knowing what to say and knowing that whatever I said wasn't about to change what was coming. In that moment, it occurred to me that I didn't know how to exist without her anymore.

This wasn't by design, and it was not in our nature, but since the day we'd started dating, we'd never spent more than a few hours apart, just when we'd had to go to work every day. I'd miss her.

People like to put words in others' mouths, and I heard the phrase *codependent* so many times over the next sixty days. Each time made me laugh a little harder than the last. I had dated relentlessly, hoping to find someone who could sincerely check at least most of my boxes. I'd dated some great women, and some even checked a box or two.

When Katie and I started dating, I knew she checked *all* the boxes and added a few more I didn't think I needed. She is my whole heart and the best part of my soul, and we share a friendship like I have never had. I choose her every day, and I love her more fiercely with every moment. So, if that makes me codependent, fuck off. I'm happy to be.

Unfortunately, our request for space was not really granted. The large group continued to occupy our tiny apartment. You must understand, I still believed at this point that Katie had orchestrated all of this, so I found it almost frustrating that she couldn't tell me what to pack! Jeans or shorts? Cold or hot? Is there anything specific I need? How far am I going? For how long?

That was the first time I'd thought about it, and I realized this was all carefully orchestrated because she shunned me and didn't give me an answer other than, "For right now, we don't know."

I've always been the type to struggle when I don't know what's in store, and control has always been a defense mechanism. In my heart, I had already surrendered without a fight and no negotiation. I remember thinking, *Am I not showing the characteristics of someone humbled and ready for change?* So... why won't anyone tell me anything about what I was blindly signing up for? And because I wouldn't let it go, I was finally told I would be going to a fantastic place in Florida for at least thirty days.

You can imagine how I felt about that! Was that necessary? And how could I be away from Katie for that long? The questions were endless, and the so-called answers I was given were scripted and rehearsed. Later, I'd find out why.

Katie and I ran around the apartment, grabbing miscellaneous things we thought I might need. Then, in walked my mom with a bag fully packed with everything she'd described as what I needed. Believe it or not, it still didn't dawn on me that this was not Katie's plan. Katie is my person—my wife, my best friend, and so much more. I couldn't imagine in any fucked-up world how my mom would've solely facilitated, orchestrated, and implemented this entire thing...

I remember feeling it was time to go. So many people in such a small space had just endured an emotionally charged experience. We were living in my in-laws' house, in an apartment they had above the garage, and I am so happy they occupied two seats in that circle. If this had been executed anywhere else, those two would still have been the first people I wanted there. I've never met a family so sincere, genuine, and kind-hearted as Dan and Kay.

Saying goodbye to them was my first feeling of being a true and utter failure. I had come to their house after work only a few years earlier to ask for their daughter's hand in marriage. I'd promised to care for her like they had and protect her like Dan did.

Yet here I was, leaving on a selfish, self-inflicted, and utterly contradictory journey. There's no way of sugarcoating it: that was the first time in my life when I hated myself! Unfortunately, these random emotions I was having were just the beginning.

Before leaving, I made my rounds of hugs and saying thank you, and when my mom was next, she whispered to me, "Just don't be surprised if Katie might not want to be in the marriage when you get home. I'll always be here for you."

My best friend from high school, Cam, offered to drive me to the airport. Then I was told I would travel with an escort. Bobby, the interventionist, was the last person I wanted to be around, but he was, unfortunately, the company I kept for the next eight to twelve hours, driving to the middle of nowhere in Florida—a place called the Refuge.

That was my sendoff: one part mercy, one part manipulation, and one giant leap into the unknown. I didn't know it yet, but that day, in that upstairs apartment, with those goodbyes and that whispered warning, it was the end of my old life. The man I'd been didn't get on that plane. He stayed behind, somewhere between guilt and surrender, watching me go.

Chapter 8

We Now Interrupt This Marriage...

Katie

Wednesday, February 16, 2022

I feel depleted. I have been surviving, not living, for the past few years, and it all comes to a head today. My eyes are heavy from the lack of sleep and swollen from crying quietly next to Chris, last night. The buildup of anxiety is palpable as I wait for this bomb to drop on him in a few hours, one that will change our lives forever.

Strangely, it feels like I have helped plan a surprise birthday party for him: inviting close loved ones to witness this event, and instead of gifts, they bring a letter they wrote to Chris about how they hope he will accept help for his addiction, and if Chris doesn't, they list their bottom line, instead of well wishes.

I hate that the intervention must be held at my parents' house; it feels like an invasion of privacy. But I just went along with the plan as it was presented to me at my mother-in-law's house a few days ago. I had no say in the team hired for the intervention. I had no say as to where Chris would go for rehabilitation.

And I had no say in the treatment plan, which was already in place for after he leaves the Refuge in Florida. It entails him living in a halfway house for men in Tennessee for upwards of six months. Everyone was more worried that I would blab to Chris before their plan went into action than they were about checking in on the one person who would be left behind, once he left on one-way Flight 2984 to Florida later this afternoon.

Two weeks before the intervention, I received a call from a mutual friend named Chris, but we call him by his last name, Strubel. I picked up, excited to see his name on my phone, as we hadn't caught up in quite some time.

He immediately asked me, "How are you?"

I responded with a high-pitched, "I'm fine."

"Katie, come on, how are you?"

My throat began to constrict, and my nose started to tingle as if I had just taken my first small sip of ginger ale. My eyes slowly filled with tears, and I said, "I've been better."

He sighed, then replied in a monotone, "I know."

But how on earth does he know? I've kept this secret so close to my heart that I hid it under years of bitterness and resentment that had taken up residence in my mind. I'd worried myself to the point where I was physically sick. I lived in a constant state of worry, and it had caused a frenzy on my mental health. I suffered and was mentally ill with worry, anxiety, fear, and frustration. Physically sick with IBS, panic attacks, loss of hair, and weight gain because of my high cortisol and inflammation. I'd lost sleep because I would stare at the wall at night, fearful of this disease that was slowly taking over both of our lives.

And I was always on high alert. I screamed at Chris constantly, I threatened him, cried, and confronted him. I tried to hold my tongue, but I felt like I was barely hanging on by a thread.

As these thoughts raced through my head, Strubel explained that Chris's mom had formed an intervention team and wanted me to come to her house to hear their game plan. I couldn't comprehend why I was receiving this news from a friend instead of my mother-in-law just calling me and, God forbid, asking me how I was doing. My only guess was that people had to tread lightly around me, as the wife, and they didn't want me telling Chris and ruining their systematic plan, which didn't involve me.

And, mind you, this was all based on speculation. The only hint I'd seen that his family might have had a clue Chris was losing his sparkle was on the previous Christmas, when he nodded off at the dinner table on Christmas Eve. That's it.

As I got off the phone, I had a glimmer of hope. The idea of intervention had come up in past conversations, but it was for Chris to go to rehab to help him quit tobacco. However, when we'd talked about rehab briefly, I didn't know Chris had secretly hoped he would go in with the intention of stopping his chewing, but hidden deep in his heart, with his genuine desire to stop his addiction to drugs.

Ultimately, I didn't know how bad it was and how much he was hurting. When you are knee-deep in your own shit, all you can think to do is keep trudging along, pretending things aren't that bad, and you can fix it yourself. Instead, you find yourself in quicksand, sinking lower and lower slowly, while being held down by the Devil and his lies.

A week before the intervention, I lied to Chris about where I was going, and I went over to his mom's house. As the sun set, I found the intervention team and his grandma on a Zoom call set up in their kitchen.

They asked me questions: "When did the addiction start?"

"How long has he been using?"

"What has he been taking?"

"We thought these specific family members and friends should come to the intervention. Do you agree?"

I wondered why on earth they wanted to do an intervention when they didn't even know the answers to these questions! How did they decide to go down this road without calling me to ask how things had been and whether I even thought we should do an intervention?

Don't get me wrong; I was incredibly thankful that, finally, someone could help me in this dark space where I'd been living in for a couple of years all alone, a space filled with lies, fighting, deceit, broken promises, pills in pockets, pills hidden in secret compartments, pills hidden in socks, pills hidden in so many places I lost track, money slowly leaving the bank account, and arguments filled with anger and resentment and concern.

And the fact that his treatment would be paid for was an immense relief off my shoulders. There was no way I could have afforded this on my own, and I have trouble asking for help, especially financial aid. I am incredibly thankful for his family. *Thank you, thank you, THANK YOU!*

As we sat down to discuss the details of the intervention, I disagreed with the people his mom planned to invite, and I asked them to be removed. The intervention team said the only people who should be there were the people whose lives Chris's addiction had directly impacted and who knew about his addiction.

Honestly, the only people who should have been at the intervention were my mom, my dad, and me. We had been living together since we sold our house in February 2020 (before Covid hit), and they'd seen everything firsthand, whether they knew it or not. They had seen Chris and me struggling in our relationship but couldn't have known what was truly happening behind our closed doors. They'd always supported us as a couple and given us advice and a safe space to vent.

Everyone else who thought they should attend should have just written their letters, and we would have read them aloud. But in hindsight, I feel like Chris would have gone if I had gone upstairs after that phone call with Strubel and said, "I think you should go to rehab." It seems like such a simple thought.

Katie, if it was indeed that bad and traumatic, why didn't you ask for help sooner? Or why didn't you get Chris the help he needed? Up to this point, I'd thought I was helping, but I still don't know how to answer this for myself. And this is the deepest regret of my life.

This journey is not for the faint of heart, and I'd tried to fix it all alone because I thought our dirty laundry should be cleaned behind closed doors, not aired for everyone to see. I thought, if I played my "Detective Katie" role well enough, I could find all his hiding spots and throw away unwarranted pills. I could trace where he went and who he met for drugs. If I held onto his prescription, he wouldn't take as much. If I bought a safe with pill bottles that had time stamps once locked, I could catch him if he tried to break in or take my medicine. I'd tried to control every aspect of his active addiction, and I'd lost sight of why I was trying to control the situation. I became *addicted to his addiction*.

When you are constantly surrounded by someone toxic, you become part of the sickness. I lost parts of myself I could never get back. These stolen, isolating moments made me forget my passions, my favorite color, and who I was. It slowly became a part of my personality, consuming my thoughts, plans, actions, and life.

I stopped focusing on myself and became an uncontrollable psycho, focused on catching him in the act, so I could stop him from taking pills. I was in such a place of distrust, and the disease of being in a constant state of survival manipulated me. I did not know what the cure was. I feared judgment, gossip, and the profound, hard truths I didn't dare ask Chris, because that would make it real.

During this time, the addiction didn't feel like an addiction, because what I thought was terrible wasn't even scratching the surface. I wanted the sober man I had fallen so madly in love with to come back whenever I saw a tiny glimmer peeking through the darkness; it gave me small bits of hope and reasons to stay. I kept holding on to hope that, one day, he would wake up from this nightmare, and I would get the old Chris back. In all honesty, I could have lived with him being addicted for the rest of our lives, but I would have been the one to slowly die of a broken heart and the sickness that took over.

Addiction is chronic and progressive, and it is fatal if the correct support systems aren't in place or if it is untreated. Chris's disease always required feeding. Not to starve, he found different manipulation tactics to keep me in his life and continue eating this bottomless buffet of drugs.

After listening to the intervention team discuss their plan for Chris over the coming week and the following six to eight months,

I stayed behind for a bit. It felt like his mom and stepfather were interrogating me. I am a sincere and open person if you ask me a direct question. I'd thought they had my best interests in mind, so I opened my heart, thinking I was in a safe space. But I divulged too much. I got deeply personal with some of my traumas, which later turned into gossip and ammunition against me and my family.

This is another one of my regrets. Chris's mom later used her sharp tongue to share things I'd told her in confidence, turning my private stories into "fun facts about Katie and her family." She pulled out the ugliest fragments of my childhood and built a narrative that painted a big, red target on my back for her vengeance. It was damning. I understand she is Chris's mom, and I can only imagine the love she has for her firstborn son. But actions like this made it hard to understand why the focus couldn't stay on Chris's health instead of on me.

A few days after the initial Zoom call, I had to lie to Chris yet again, so my mom and I could sneak over to Chris's mom, Tracy's, house to meet the intervention team. Everyone who was set to attend the in-person intervention on February 16 sat around a long, square table in the formal dining room. Everyone was handed a laminated binder titled, *Family Playbook*. I couldn't help but joke to myself that this process is so complex that we needed a *playbook*? I pictured all of us on the sidelines, getting ready to storm a football field, with our head coach (intervention team) yelling plays from the sidelines. We'd rush the field into our designated starting positions. I wish I could say I was the quarterback making the calls, but I felt like I was the kicker coming in at the last minute to drive the big goal home for the win, a.k.a. getting Chris to agree to rehab.

First on the agenda, the interventionist provided a brief background and outlined their goals, followed by a quick recap of the expectations for the intervention. Then came the bombardment of questions that only I could answer.

"When did the use begin for Chris?"

"Is it alcohol, is it just drugs, or does he use nicotine?"

"What is the progression of his use?"

Then, they discussed a family/loved one's treatment plan, mentioning Al-Anon and how we could get involved. We then dove into the packet. Page one was called "An Agreement to Change," where it emphasized that addiction is often seen as the central issue in a struggling family system. Still, it's only one part of a broader, unhealthy dynamic. The intervention team helps the family/loved one recognize and address these deeper issues themselves. To support Chris's long-term recovery, everyone involved (not just the addict/the Adrift) needs to commit to change.

They discussed how we can all become more aware of enabling behaviors and then take steps toward healthier patterns. Some key points were that addiction is not the only issue, and the family system may also contribute to ongoing problems. They outlined how they would assist us with education and awareness around understanding both the addict's struggles and our own roles in Chris's life.

Additionally, each group member was required to make a one-year commitment to actively change their own behaviors, allow for personal growth, and acknowledge areas where we could all improve. We also needed to attend our own support groups. They warned us to expect emotional difficulty and that, as a group, we should hold ourselves accountable and consult the intervention team before making any decisions related to Chris. The ultimate goal was to support Chris's journey toward healthier choices.

The ten of us each signed the dotted line.

In the next section, we covered information on substance use disorder (SUD). It spelled out different criteria to evaluate how severe the substance use is, depending on how many symptoms are identified.

> *Two or three symptoms indicate a mild substance use disorder; four or five symptoms indicate a moderate substance use disorder, and six or more symptoms indicate a severe substance use disorder.*

Unfortunately, I wouldn't find out how terrible Chris's substance use was until he was enrolled in his rehabilitation facility, or even after he left. Still, ultimately, based on what I could guess, Chris had over six of the listed symptoms, showing a severe substance use disorder.

Next, we had a summary explaining the effects that various drugs have on the body and mind over time. This led to ways we can reframe how we understand addiction—not that the Adrift has a problem with drinking or using drugs; the issues are their not knowing how to live a sober life, especially when they need to deal with life's inevitable discomfort.

Basically, addiction is a coping mechanism, and using substances isn't the core issue. It is often seen as the solution to avoid pain; at their core, the Adrift are wired to seek pleasure and avoid discomfort as a survival strategy they have developed over time.

The materials then explained how addiction often forms early in life and is usually the result of a slow, steady buildup of uncomfortable experiences from trauma. Substance abuse is a way to numb. True recovery helps focus on the underlying emotional and psychological issues, not just maintaining sobriety.

The next page explained that addiction is not about the environment, meaning you can change the external circumstances for thirty, sixty, or ninety days in a rehabilitation facility and do all the right things. Still, until the internal issue is addressed for the Adrift with long-term recovery work, professional help, structure, and accountability, then nothing truly changes. They will not be cured when they get home. Proper recovery demands more than just detox or a lifestyle change. It requires a new way of thinking, reacting, and living.

This was followed by a diagram illustrating the ever-evolving changes required on the road to recovery, along with a reminder that relapse is a normal part of recovery. The Adrift will have shortcomings and fall back into old patterns/actions/behaviors. Each relapse brings new insight and knowledge, leading to fewer setbacks and less frequent relapses. Additionally, it outlined how true recovery requires a system-wide change, not just sobriety, from the Adrift. When the family takes responsibility for their own healing and stops supporting the status quo, the foundation that addiction rests on crumbles.

I think the most challenging section for me was reviewing the twenty-seven different forms of an addict's manipulation. I checked off twenty-three. Addiction truly trains a person to survive through manipulation. While it's important to recognize these tactics, it's equally important to remember they often stem from deep pain, fear, and an inability to cope with life while sober or an attempt to stay in their addictive tendencies. Awareness is the key for both the Adrift and the family/loved ones (the Anchors), to interrupt these patterns.

Being on the receiving end of all these tactics had, over time, led to a layered emotional impact on me and had eroded my trust in Chris. I could feel my cheeks turn red as I read this part, and my body felt zapped with anxiety as I tried to hold in my emotions around everyone at the meeting.

I had just spent a significant amount of time trying to hold it all together and keep the peace in our relationship while trying to remain strong. But I hadn't even noticed the emotional toll of it, how it had slowly chipped away at my soul, to the point where I barely recognized myself. I felt so small, sitting at that large table, and incredibly misunderstood, as well.

As we turned the page, we then discussed what PAWS (post-acute withdrawal syndrome) was. Essentially, it is a set of long-lasting symptoms that develop after the initial withdrawal period. Where withdrawal focuses on physical symptoms, PAWS involves the psychological and emotional recovery, which can last for months or years after a person stops using substances.

If someone has a history of prolonged substance use, this eventually disrupts the ability of their brain to produce its natural "feel-good" chemicals, such as dopamine, serotonin, and oxytocin. Once the Adrift stops using the substance, the brain struggles to recalibrate, leaving the person feeling numb, depressed, and sometimes overwhelmed. It is also important to avoid emotionally demanding conversations. Understanding PAWS is crucial for anchors to provide support and patience during the recovery process, which can last from six to twenty-four months. And with substances like opiates, symptoms can last for up to eighteen months!

Next came an outline and suggested structure for writing an "Emotional Appeal Letter." Each of us had to write a letter to Chris that would be read at the intervention or sent to him while he was getting help at rehab (if he accepted the help).

Basically, it should begin with a brief introduction about our relationship, listing specific reasons why we love and care about Chris, and it should share fun memories that remind us of Chris's best traits. Then, we needed to apologize for anything we felt responsible for or any behavior that required forgiveness. Next, we would shift to discussing Chris's problem. We would acknowledge the need for Chris to seek professional treatment and, if relevant, mention any family history of addiction.

We also needed to mention that we understand he is hurting and how his actions reflect this, and express our commitment to supporting him through recovery, as it will require all anchors' involvement. Finally, we needed to paint a hopeful picture of life after recovery, sharing how his sobriety will positively impact our lives. Then, ask if he will accept the help being offered.

Easy, right? Not so much.

We briefly touched on examples of what our bottom lines could be or what we would no longer tolerate, moving forward, if Chris refused help after our intervention. The last page was the "Accountability Letter." It was to express love for the person's decision to seek help and to acknowledge the difficulty of making that choice. It then addressed the painful reality that, if Chris left the treatment program, the Anchors had to set clear boundaries, since continuing to live in fear and enabling their behavior was no longer sustainable.

The letter emphasized that, while the decision was ultimately theirs, the Anchors could no longer prioritize their loved one's well-being over their own or take responsibility for their actions. Finally, it outlined specific consequences for leaving the intervention program, reinforcing the importance of completing the treatment for both their well-being and the Anchors' peace of mind. We all signed on the dotted line.

I left the meeting feeling emotionally taxed and exhausted. When I returned home, I had to start on my letter to Chris. I had no clue where he was (later, I would find out he was out getting drugs), so I had ample time to write.

This was one of the hardest letters I'd ever written, and I didn't know what to say as my ultimatum or boundary. But Bobby, who was the head of the intervention team, said he couldn't imagine how difficult it must have been for me to write this letter. He said it was one of the most well-constructed letters he had ever seen from a wife. My humility overwhelmed him, and I should not change a single word.

This is incredibly personal, so please try to be kind.

Letter from Katie:

Christopher, I am lucky to have married my best friend and started a marriage with you. I want to tell you that since that fantastic day, every single day, I am overwhelmed with how much I know deep in my heart that we are truly lucky to have found one another.

Chris, I will always look back on the night of the reunion and that first kiss. I have never had a moment surrounded by so much noise and people where it all faded away, and it was just you and me. I love that I made you blush. I love that I was so forward with a man for the first time in my life and knew that I just wanted you. Only you. Every time I play a record, I always think of our time in my little apartment, dancing, laughing, making dinners, lying in bed next to each other, and just talking about our most intimate fears and *our dreams and getting down to who we are when everything is stripped away.*

I loved building a life and a home with you. You are such a proud man who *wanted to take care of me and give me literally the world. You built an empire and to me, you were one of the most talented and successful men that I ever let into my guarded world. You put everyone first, all the time. You always speak so highly of me, and you SEE me.*

When you sold your agency, I was so proud of you for knowing when to let go. You worked your ass off to get to that point, and not many people would have been able to build that book and business into what you accomplished. You are a force to be reckoned with, and you gain people's respect. I thank the Lord above for bringing you into my life every day.

There was always a strong force that wanted me to be near you and your delicious Moscow Mules… even though, throughout the years, you would physically run away from me most of the time I tried to come and talk to you. I have known you for over 18 years, which is crazy to me. But the qualities that make you, Chris, the man I have been waiting 33 years for, come as small, everyday moments.

It's seeing you sing on the right side of your mouth when your favorite Chris Stapleton song comes on in the car. It's your return from the store with an orchid or a candle (even though let's be honest, the candle is for you) to brighten my day. It's every encounter with somebody to help them with their problems, even when you're struggling on the inside with your own. It's the notes you leave me telling me how much you love me and admire me, making me feel less alone in this loud world. You are one of the most remarkable, intelligent, cunning, driven spirits I've ever met, and I love you.

The day you tried your best to bend down on one knee in ski boots was the best day of my life. You know me so well that you did it without many people around and that it was doing what I love to do most—spending time with you outside and snowboarding. I will never forget that run we took and just screaming down the mountain WE ARE ENGAGED! *I felt so free and comforted knowing I met the man I want to run through life screaming from the mountaintops. I found my person.*

Chris, I am so sorry for picking fights with you. I am so sorry for going to bed angry and not saying I am sorry, or I love you, or even not trying to talk it out. I am so sorry for physically running away, for slamming doors, and for emotionally abusing you. I am sorry for taking out my anger, insecurities, and lack of trust with men on you. I am sorry for asking what you have taken almost every day and when. I am sorry that it may have felt like I'm smothering you and don't give you space to breathe. I am sorry for causing you any sort of pain because of my actions.

I am sorry to take control out of the conversation, control over our relationship, and control over what I think is more important. I am sorry that I have gone through your belongings. I am sorry that I have not been the easiest person to be around sometimes. I am sorry that I have set extremely high expectations for you, and the pressure I have placed on you has made you feel that you will never measure up, because you do.

You know how much it bothers me, not knowing what you have taken. Remember that night when I almost called the cops because of your weird breathing, and I did not know what you had taken? I feel like that every day, scared if you are going to wake up or not. I sneak over to you when you sleep sometimes to see if you have a breath coming out. I worry how fast your heart beats; I worry if your heart will stop.

Chris, you are hurting. And I don't know how to help you any longer. I am sick of fighting over finding pills littered across our floors. I am sick of finding them in random containers. I am tired of finding hiding places for my PERSONAL prescribed medicine. I am tired of writing what I have and knowing when things go missing that, you are stealing from me. Then lying about it.

I have tried monitoring how many were in the safe, and how many were left. I have tried convincing myself that this kid from Kansas, who you are getting these drugs from, is safe to take. But in the last year and a half specifically, I am so frustrated to see you pass out in your work chair, on the ground, mid-speech talking to me, seeing you spill Gatorade, water, ice cream, tobacco, on our pillows, beds, floors, couch, because you passed the fuck out.

Remember when I surprised you on our anniversary with the picnic up on our patio? I spent weeks putting that all together, getting food, setting it up, and hanging up lights, and you were late. You fell asleep before we even had dinner. It was our anniversary, and I wanted to show you how much I value our relationship. Instead, I was worried about your safety, and I was angry that my plans weren't valued.

Do you remember falling asleep at Christmas dinner at your mom and Steve's two years ago at the table? Your eyes rolled back behind your head. I lied to them, saying you were under a lot of stress, and you were just tired. You know I HATE lying!!! Do you know how many pills I have flushed down the toilet? Not knowing where and who you got them from, and at what cost?

What about our promise of going out like The Notebook*? You are my person, but I have lost my best friend in so many ways over the last few years because of these tiny, easily to hide pills that have taken over your life and now our marriage.*

Chris, I will be here every step of the way, holding your hand. No matter what, I will never give up on you. And you know what, I forgive you. I have tried everything that I know how to do, but unfortunately, I no longer have the tools to monitor what you take, when you take it, and how it affects your mood and your day. I trust you love me, and I trust our love.

The journey we need to take right now is to help you be the best man that I know you can be. That man hasn't been here for quite some time, but I know he is in there. That happiness and joy will be found again. I promise. And I am not going anywhere. I also commit to getting better for you and for us. Because you deserve that.

And I do, too. I also need to recover. We are trying to start a business and a life that I know is going to be GREAT, but I need you to be healthy for us to do this with the right mindset. It has been FUCKING rough. I know. Let's get our life back, Chris, together. You are exhausted, and so am I. This is our cure, babe. This is our millionth life chance for change, grace, and trust to come back into this committed marriage. I promised to be here for you in sickness and in health, and this is sickness right now.

And I am holding your hand so tight. I want the man who changed his shirt fifteen times before picking me up; I want the man who would not fall asleep at dinner mid-conversation; I want to feel beautiful again because you made me feel like I was the only girl in the room. I have desperately been looking at you, and you aren't seeing the pain that I am living in every day.

I have lost myself. And I miss having the confident, witty, supportive man that I made blush standing against the wall that night. He's not here anymore. I miss the man I married, and I hope you'll say yes to getting help. I will handle all the affairs at home until you come back. I can take care of all this, knowing you are taking care of yourself to be the man I know you are.

You must be EXHAUSTED. Because I am. Physically, I am losing sleep; I have more anxiety than I know what to do with it. I need you to say yes to getting help because I can't lie for you anymore. We need to get better for us and for our marriage. I am here because I love you and because I care for you.

Please accept the help and this amazing opportunity we are offering you today.

I love you,

Katie

After I was done writing the letter, I sat back in my chair and bawled my eyes out—like deep, wailing noises I hadn't made since the boys died. I cannot even explain how nervous I was for the intervention the following day and for the unknown to reveal its deepest, darkest secrets. But I mustered up the energy, pulled myself up to get some sleep, and headed up to the apartment.

I barely slept. I remember texting someone on the intervention team that night, telling them how scared I was. He said, "I know it is scary. I'm going to ask you to close your eyes and put your faith into this process. Trust the process! It is the only way that will work. And you are the Keystone Katie. You got this! Together, we can get through this process. Everything will be okay."

As I counted my thousandth sheep, I got four hours of restless sleep. Finally, it was morning. I raced to the window to see if cars had been filling the driveway. People were trickling in.

Chris was sound asleep when I quietly shut the door behind me and made my way down the creaky wooden steps. I headed through the garage to the hidden side door that led to the game room. There, a circle of chairs had been arranged for the gathering. My heart raced as I stepped inside.

As I greeted and hugged the family and friends who had arrived, I struggled to hold back my tears. I quickly found my seat, sat down, and stared at the carpeted floor in a daze while two of Chris's friends headed upstairs to wake him up and ask him to come downstairs when he was ready.

As Chris came into the room, he looked surprised, confused, and a little out of sorts. When he sat on the chair next to his grandma, Bobby began his speech to Chris. If I am being honest, I don't remember any of the letters that were read or what Bobby said. I just stared at my outgrown nails, pretended to pick at my cuticles, and cried. I was numb. I could barely muster the strength to even look up at Chris. I felt like I'd betrayed him in some messed-up way.

After a handful of people read their letters, Chris agreed to get help and go to rehab immediately. The pushback we had prepared for was not necessary. He wanted the help and didn't know how to ask. He headed upstairs to pack for the unknown.

I was incredibly proud of him because it takes immense courage to enter treatment and get the help he needed. I could not have been prouder.

One weird rule the intervention team made for him and me was to not be in the same room alone while he packed, so I stayed downstairs, still in disbelief that this was really happening. After Chris was told to pack a bag, without directions on where he was going or for how long, it didn't take long for him to ask if I could come upstairs and help. His mom and I had been texting earlier in the week, trying our best to organize items he might need and could easily pack, so that had helped a bit.

During this time, it was really tough not to let him know what was in store for him in the upcoming six months. And I wasn't sure what he needed to pack, either! One thing I did pack for him at the last minute was a book he was currently reading. Also, I quickly removed his Valentine's gift from its glass frame, which I had given him a few days prior. It was a poem I'd had professionally written for him by Beau Taplin. It read:

May this simple verse
ever serve as a gentle celebration
of the light that you are;
how you carry within you
the splendour of stars,
and all of the shining joy
of the dawn. You have held
from the moment of our meeting
this burning place
in my heart; for the way I feel always safe and protected
with you here at my side;
for the way I feel completely seen;
and understood for the first time in my life.
You face each coming day
with such strength and such courage, and give with kindness
always without concern for yourself; your simple presence aside me
is a treasure more precious than all the rare gifts of this Earth.
I didn't choose you because I
believed this would
always be easy. I chose you because loving you was never a choice.
These years with you have been quite simply every dream I ever dreamt:
you are the love, you are the heart, of my life.

Just moments before he was about to head downstairs to get in the car with Bobby for their trip to the airport, we held each other in a deep embrace that lasted what felt like minutes. We shed uncontrollable tears and took gasping breaths. Those long, necessary minutes were filled with a mix of uncertainty, fear, and heartbreak, as we surrendered to a plan that wasn't our own.

Finally, we released our hold on each other, knowing this would be the longest time we had ever spent apart.

After watching the car drive down our winding driveway, I turned around and went inside, where I broke down, falling to my knees on the carpeted floor, and I prayed. I felt incomplete; I was missing my puzzle piece.

We texted every second until he landed in Florida. Then, he stopped responding, and his phone was turned off. Unrelenting, cruel silence.

Chapter 9

Silverback Gorilla

Chris

If *Slipping Away* was the slow slide, this was the snap. The kind where everything you have been barely holding together drops at once.

The intervention had happened earlier that day—the letters, boundaries, the whole performance my family had rehearsed for a fight I did not put up. Five minutes in, I said I would go. I meant it. I was exhausted with being the director, the actor, and the cleanup crew for my own disaster movie.

I didn't think my first time going to rehab would mean going to Florida on a one-way ticket to the middle of absolutely nowhere. That's probably because rehab wasn't really high on my bucket list. No beaches. No theme parks. No spring break. Just me, a duffel bag, a lot of emotional baggage, and a stranger I'd just met earlier that day. Bobby…

How do I paint this canvas to accurately capture the mystery that was Bobby? Used car salesman energy, hillbilly charm, and volume set to permanent eleven. If Ricky Bobby from *Talladega Nights* put on a recovery Polo, you have the silhouette. He was the interventionist and had flown into Colorado the day before my intervention. He then flew with me to Florida as my sober escort. I never knew this role existed, and "his expertise" was far from necessary.

The entire day with him felt like a bad dream. Bobby didn't understand how to be comfortable in silence or read a room, but he certainly knew how to overshare. Sitting next to me in the exit row, he watched me like I was a kid on a leash at Disney World. Except, instead of a leash, it was shame, withdrawal, and a duffel full of regret. He was calm. I was spiraling internally but tried to look composed, which mostly just made me sweat profusely. I couldn't tell if I was detoxing, panicking, or just deeply regretting getting in a car with an absolute stranger.

And then, somewhere over Georgia, he leaned in with his coffee breath and said something I wasn't expecting. "If you brought anything with you, take it now. All of it. However much it is."

I blinked.

"You want me to... take it?"

"Yup," he said calmly, like he was suggesting I try the in-flight snack.

This was apparently my "last hoorah." A final escape hatch before rehab locked the doors. But what he didn't know, and, honestly, what I didn't know, was whether or not what I had on me was even clean. Because, at that point, the risk of fentanyl showing up in your stash was about as certain as TSA taking your full-size shampoo. So, there I was, staring down the barrel of one last pill that might be laced with poison. Not exactly the kind of roulette you want to play at 30,000 feet in the air.

Part of me wanted to say no. Another part of me, a much louder, more desperate part, told me I needed it. Not wanted. *Needed.* Because I didn't know who I was without it anymore. And going into that *unknown,* as sober, raw, and terrified… felt worse than the risk.

There is a saying you hear in these places: "You need to get well before you get sick." And essentially, that is what Mr. Intervention was telling me. I wonder how that liability lawsuit would work? He had just accepted responsibility for me and was encouraging me to take drugs en route to rehab?

So, I did it. I took a few stashed pills and braced myself for either relief or disaster.

I survived the flight. Barely. Mostly because my overpaid and underqualified escort had a story for every one of his stories. I am not trying to bash this guy, at least not without good reason. In his effort to become my best friend, he told me his life story, which wasn't pretty. He was in his mid-forties, and he told me he was addicted to everything from crack to booze, and he had even gone through several years in his life where all he knew was huffing paint. And I believed it. He had relapsed a total of eighteen times, and he repeatedly added, "But that breaks down to only one or two relapses per drug that I was doing at the time."

None of this bothered me; I didn't care and didn't judge. Why or how would I?

My friends and family swore Bobby and I would get along great, said we had so much in common. Somewhere between story number 3,982 and the plane starting its descent, I tuned him out long enough to wonder what that meant. What did it say about me that the people who have known me my entire life thought that this obnoxious, self-proclaimed recovery guru and I were cut from the same cloth? That pissed me off a little bit.

What was appalling was that my family had clearly placed their faith and trust in him and his team. He was a showman, and he was good at it. He was excellent! When it was just the two of us, however, he dropped the act. He made comment after comment about my family's financial position. The houses we had, the cars my circle of people drove.

I am not sure how many times he said this, but once was enough: "Recovery is a cash business. All I have to do is park outside a rehab center or get the phone number of the parents for a few trust fund kids, and it is guaranteed income."

Bobby, obviously, didn't know me. He just thought he did. So, he was clueless that not five minutes into our travels, I had already figured out that he was full of shit. My engaging him in these conversations was purely out of curiosity. I wanted to see just how much he would share with me, while thinking we were "buds."

He told me way too much about how this system works and how people like him capitalize on it. Periodically, he would ask me for my friends' or family members' phone numbers, like a referral! Ha-ha, the guy truly had zero shame!

The final straw was when he asked me for my pastor's phone number and email. He said something along the lines of, "That guy seems like he has a flock of the one-percenters, and I would love to tap into that network."

I was furious but nodded my head in agreement. I pulled out my phone, scrolled around for a little while, and ultimately gave him the phone number of this random person I had sold a car to on Craigslist a few years earlier.

We landed around midnight and drove deep into Florida for over three hours, to a town that sounded like a cough, Ocklawaha. Finally, we approached a black-iron gate waiting to open and greet me. I had arrived at the Refuge, and it was like walking into a different universe. Bobby took a selfie with me on the curb, flash on: proof of delivery for my family. After taking the picture and seeing it, his grin fell flat, and he asked me to take another, "But this time, smile, please!" This was the first time I realized recovery could be staged like a pageant, with the gate buzzing and my face used as a receipt.

I was greeted by a nice older woman who instructed me to use the outdoor facilities to complete a urinary analysis. I was terrified, and right then and there, I almost "outed" Bobby for telling me to take drugs on the plane. But Bobby beat me to it.

He spoke for me, saying, "I'm fairly confident that Chris's UA is not going to be clean."

She ignored him, looked at me, and smiled. "We just need to know what you have in your system before you are admitted. Everything is okay, sweetie, and this is normal protocol."

She instructed Bobby to leave, as I was now in the Refuge's care. I heard from the bathroom stall that he insisted on waiting to say goodbye.

After peeing in my cup, I left the bathroom and followed the nurse. Bobby, believe it or not, was asking me to smile in an attempt to take a final picture of me walking my cup of piss into the medical building. I hope he took the photo, because if he did, it would be me waiving him the finger as my fond farewell.

Inside, they took my phone, my belt, and the illusion that I was still in charge. They asked me a hundred intake questions that I mostly mumbled through, still in denial, still convinced this whole thing was temporary.

I had brought my stash with me to rehab. Not like a comforting duffel of essentials. No, I mean a literal stash of pills, in my very hidden pocket in my jeans. Look, it wasn't part of my master plan. It was panic. A backup parachute. A "just in case" scenario. I was terrified of what was coming, and something in me needed to know I had a little control left…, even if it was delusional. Yes, I brought drugs to rehab. They didn't have to strip search me, as I politely said, "I'm so sorry, but I have brought substances with me. Will you please throw them away? I don't have the heart to." Handing those over… ouch!

The Refuge had doctors and protocols. They screened my blood, urine, and eyes. The toxicology report would become a horror show in black and white: opiates, fentanyl, benzos, and something called K2/Spice that sounded like a gas station candle. I did not know what half of it was. I knew all of it was inside me. Their assessment was clear. I would need medication-assisted treatment, MAT. If you have never been here, those letters look like a shortcut. If you have, they look like a chance.

Here is where the elegant family plan started to fray. A whole year had been mapped without anyone asking me, before I was enrolled in rehab, what I was taking, how much, or whether MAT would be necessary. Florida now. Afterward, a men's program in Tennessee for up to six months.

Tennessee did not offer MAT. The thing that might keep me alive was not available at the finish line. It was the first time I understood that this was not only about survival, but it was also about what made my family comfortable. But comfort and survival don't speak the same language.

But the real detox was coming. And there would be no more exits after this.

I thought the plane ride would be the hard part.

Turns out, I was wrong.

The detox was supposed to last maybe three or four days. But my body didn't follow the script. Every morning, the doctors checked in and tilted their heads as if I were a new species. I wasn't sweating or convulsing the way they'd expected. I was deteriorating slowly and quietly, which seemed to freak them out more.

I arrived with one active prescription and the extra pills I had been purchasing to turn down the noise of my day. Within that first week in the medical unit, the prescription list ballooned to fifteen new medications! My system was saturated, then kindly topped off on the plane by the man paid to escort me to safety.

So, whatever was in my system then mixed with a ton of other drugs the facility began feeding me, and it caused me to have an extremely delayed-detox response. Withdrawal did not arrive like a storm; it circled like a shark. I could not eat for eight days. Hands shaking against a Styrofoam cup, my body felt borrowed.

I remember how, at one point, security came into my room and took a knife to the inside of my suitcase, to see if they had missed confiscating pills from me. I felt like I was a character in the world's worst episode of *Border Security: Florida Edition.* They thought I had been actively taking drugs. They gave me the MOCA (Montreal Cognitive Assessment), a tool that assesses cognitive function, with a score out of thirty points. I scored a six. Ambulance to a hospital, CT, panels, the works. Everything came back unremarkable, which is medical for your brain is not broken the way you fear, it is just on fire. The problem was that my brain wasn't ready for that level of stress.

Once the staff realized what was happening, everything changed. The director met with me, and said, "We're going to need to change course. What we're doing isn't working, and it's getting dangerous."

That's when they introduced buprenorphine, Suboxone, to force the detox to begin more aggressively. Timing matters. My receptors had been marinating for months, then I had my airborne last hoorah. The first dose lit the fuse. Acute withdrawal came fast and mean, like someone yanked an emergency brake inside my spine. Then, my doctor went home for the weekend.

This is how people die at home. A little knowledge, a lot of desperation, and bad timing. Once you start Suboxone, you need enough to keep the seesaw from tipping you over. Within twenty-four hours, I was gone. Like... *gone*. Delirium. Psychosis. The lights were on, but the house was on fire. I did not get Suboxone for two, almost three days. Reasons, charts, shifts—none of that matters at 3 a.m., when your bones try to crawl out through your skin.

The room is too white. The fluorescent hum lives inside my teeth. I lie down, sit up, forget I lie down. The sheet is sandpaper. The floor is water. There is a gorilla in the corner, massive and quiet and impossibly patient. He is not on the med list. I name him Silverback, because naming makes bargaining feel possible.

My legs are full of bees. My back is a radiator. My head is filled with helium. I sweat and shake and hear coins falling from a pocket that is not mine. I talk to people who are not in the room. Night terrors. Paranoia. Hallucinations. Ants that turn into sentences. A song from childhood hides in the air conditioner. I ask for ice and believe there is a message in the cubes. I am thirty-two, I am twelve, I am eighty. None of those ages knows how to ask for what they need. Silverback waits. He thumps his chest sometimes. Mostly, he reminds me that I am small and that powerless is no longer a metaphor.

I thought people were watching me. Following me. I was paranoid, talking in circles, convinced I had somehow ended up in a CIA holding facility instead of a rehab center. Especially since I kept looking up at the many cameras facing my bed.

I tried to explain this to a nurse named Tara, who patted my arm and said gently, "Okay, sweetheart, let's just breathe together."

I don't remember breathing.

They gave me medication to help with the withdrawals. I don't know what it was, but I started to feel... strange. Not good-strange, not coming-back-to-life strange. More like, "Oh great, I'm losing my mind," strange. At first, I was shaky. Then sweaty. Then confused. This is the only time in my life when my reality, my dreams, and everything in between had no bounds. I had no bearing on what was real or not.

At one point, I was absolutely convinced that I saw my friend, Cam, standing in the hallway, just chilling like it was totally normal for him to be in rural Florida, watching me twitch from a safe distance. He put his hand to his mouth as if he was trying to whisper, and said something like, "Hey, buddy, we came to take you home!"

This was so real to me then that I began telling all of the rotating staff members I was going home. For almost two days, I created a narrative that genuinely convinced the staff that I had a visitor who was going to take me home!

Eventually, the detox team had to monitor me 24/7. They were this close to sending me to the hospital for IV fluids and stabilization. My brain was shutting down. I couldn't remember my own name, let alone what day it was. I went from being the guy who could quote movies line for line to someone who couldn't hold a sentence.

I knew Katie was watching all of this from afar, calling the staff, asking questions, and feeling terrified. I had never felt so far away from her or from myself. At this point, I had no idea of the difficulties Katie was facing due to the backlash from my own family.

Detox hit me like a freight train. Not all at once, but slowly, like my body and brain were staging a revolution. The nurses (God bless them) had seen it all before. They spoke in soothing tones, gave me water, and helped me into a room that smelled like antiseptic and shame. I had a hospital twin-size bed, a cold floor, and one of those plastic mattresses that crinkle when you move—more like a quarter-inch-thick pad. Being six feet tall, it's safe to say my feet got cold, hanging off the edge of the bed with a blanket that only covered up to my chest. They didn't want you to get too comfortable, since this process is anything but.

But honestly, the worst part wasn't the room. It was what was happening in my head.

Then, someone turned the knob in the right direction, and the fog started to lift. The medicine arrived on schedule. The hallucinations eased. The psychosis backed off. I slept for a few hours. The hum became just a light. I recognized my hands. I could tell the difference between a thought and a story.

Day seven. My head broke the surface. I woke up sober and clear in a way I had not been for years, and I tried not to cry from the relief of simply being back inside myself.

The staff was patient. And the moment I realized I had made it through? I didn't feel like a warrior. I felt like Bambi, legs shaking, unsure how to walk. It was humbling. My therapist, Billie, called it, "the moment my head popped out of my ass."

Cam was no longer in the hallway. And I realized this was it. Day One. No more shortcuts. No more exits. This was the first time my blood and urine toxicology report read, "N/A" in a long time.

Detox had dragged on for over a week, and it almost broke me.

But it didn't.

The first call I make is to Katie. There are two rotary phones for the whole center, five minutes at a time, no callbacks. If no one picks up, you lose your turn and sprint to breathwork class, which you do not believe in yet. I was scared out of my mind to call her.

Not because she'd be angry. But because I thought I had finally crossed the line, the one you don't come back from. I thought the last call we had would be just that: the last. When I dialed her number, I was ready for the worst. I had rehearsed it:

"Katie, I understand. You don't owe me anything. I messed up. I get it if you're done..."

But when she answered, she didn't sound angry. She sounded steady. Sad, but steady. Her words were given to me before I could even ask for them!

"I forgive you," she said. "I love you."

I broke, frozen in this long-lasting moment of pure gratitude. I'm in awe of her!

This woman, who had already endured so much of my chaos, who had every reason to hang up, held space for me. Not just as my wife, but as my person. My anchor. She had every reason to be cold or cruel, and instead, she chose compassion. Again.

But while Katie was keeping the door open, my family… wasn't exactly rolling out the welcome mat for her.

From what I pieced together through fragmented updates and whispered phone calls, she was doing damage control on my behalf. She was navigating group texts and side chats and "concerned" relatives trying to paint their own version of the truth and place blame on her, while all of this had to do with me and *my* decisions. And while I was out in Florida, trying not to hallucinate the ceiling turning into water, she was fielding cold shoulders and passive-aggressive commentary from people who should've had her back.

People asked her, "How could you not know or get help sooner?"

They asked her, "Are you sure he will want to be married to you, once he comes home?"

They whispered, "She's enabling him, and she is just as sick," while she was taking care of our life back home.

She wasn't just holding *me* up; she was trying to hold *herself* up while people quietly tugged at her foundation.

That's the thing about addiction: it's not just your crisis. It becomes a storm system that hits everyone in your orbit. But what people don't understand, what they still don't understand, is that the person going through it doesn't need a lecture. We don't need judgment, accusations, or shaming of someone who's already been stripped down to nothing.

If you're walking through hell with someone—family/friends/loved ones—don't make the fire hotter. Why not try to help put the fire out or lower it to a simmer, by asking how you can help?

Don't give ultimatums when we're barely clinging to hope. Don't act like we planned this. Don't treat the person we love like collateral damage.

The irony? I wasn't even well enough to defend her. I couldn't be her protector from the whispers and tension and backhanded sympathy. I was in a plastic chair in the middle of an oak-moss-treed facility built to treat all walks of life through their addictions and struggles.

That guilt of knowing she was out there, fighting for me, while also being punished for loving me, was more complicated than detox.

But that call with her reminded me of what I had waiting for me when I got out. Not a perfect life, not a magic reset… but love. Loyalty. A partner who still believed I could get better, even when I didn't believe it yet.

I decided right then and there that I was going to give this my best go. But also, I was going to fight like hell for her. Because she never stopped fighting for me.

I cleared medical and joined the outside program. Groups stacked from 7:30 a.m. to 7:30 p.m.: trauma, process, EMDR, yoga, breathwork, education. Syllables that sound soft until they make you cry in a room of strangers. I scheduled grief in five-minute blocks. I scheduled guilt. I scheduled my marriage between the jam-packed agenda.

So... what *is* rehab?

Before I got to the Refuge, I pictured rehab like a sterile hallway lined with people in matching robes, sipping lukewarm tea and speaking in hushed tones about "letting go." Like a cross between a hospital and a meditation retreat led by someone named Harmony with a face tattoo of a lotus flower.

Instead, what I walked into was a human fucking petting zoo. They had it all here. I met a woman who carried her inner child around with her, and the doll was customized to look just like her! I met a woman who was there for, in her words, "slutty-social," where she was provocative on social media specifically. Lots of he/she/they/them and everything in between. I met a person who, when I asked what had brought them there, simply said, "I'm lonely."

But that's not all. Almost everyone there was genuinely pursuing their own happiness and doing their best to figure it out. I was no different.

The place was beautiful, to be fair. Lush, large mossy trees, a river that surrounded the property, and buildings that looked like log cabins, as if you were at summer camp, ignoring the fact that no one had shoelaces.

But the people? The people were *wild.*

You had every flavor of broken:

- ⌘ Guys who looked like they should be in a *Sons of Anarchy* reboot, but were in rehab because they were obsessed with CrossFit.
- ⌘ Finance bros detoxing from their phone addictions while still somehow wearing Patagonia vests in 85-degree humidity.
- ⌘ And one girl who was much older than she looked, carried a baby doll with her everywhere because she'd been molested by her dad, and was gripping onto her inner child and never wanted to let go.

I met a younger woman, maybe eighteen or nineteen years old, who was missing an arm and had significant burn scars covering her body. She was an artist, constantly drawing with her non-dominant hand. She was amazing. I'd run into her several times in passing, in groups, etc., but finally, she mustered the courage to speak in one of our closed group sessions.

When she was about nine years old, she lived in a town in rural Sierra Leone, West Africa. During a time of civil war, a terrorist or militant organization entered her village and her home. Her grandmother was executed right in front of her. Her mother was raped repeatedly, also in front of her. When the group was done, they removed her mother's breasts and clitoris.

When they shot her grandmother, a bullet hit this young girl's arm, and it took so long for her to get adequate medical attention that they had to amputate it. Both she and her mother managed to survive, and both were there, at the Refuge, bravely telling their stories of actual survival and actual suffering.

And then there was me: the guy who'd brought his stash of pills to rehab and wondered why his detox took longer than expected.

I swear, at one point, I looked around and thought, "This is like a playground for silverback gorillas who partied too hard in Vegas."

My weeklong detox was rough, but the food, though? Shockingly decent. Like, "Why am I eating grilled salmon with mango chutney on a plastic tray in rehab?" decent. I still don't know how they swung that chef. Someone said he'd worked for John Travolta, and I believed it, because the tilapia had a wine reduction sauce, and someone once got crème brûlée for their birthday. Meanwhile, I couldn't remember my middle name.

The atmosphere was bizarre. Picture a place where you cry in group therapy at 10:00 a.m., do art therapy with popsicle sticks at noon, and play competitive sand volleyball at 4:00 p.m. with a guy named Goose, who has a Bitcoin tattoo and unresolved mother issues.

The campus is Jurassic Park without dinosaurs. Staff in golf carts, clients on charity bikes. If you are lucky, your tire holds air. If you are unlucky, your seat spins like a weather vane, which becomes a spiritual practice if you let it. I learn fast to shut up and listen.

Now, part of the charm and challenge of this rehab experience was the cultural education I received. I was relatively open-minded, chill, and aware. Turns out, I was a walking HR violation with a "what's up, dude" attitude.

There were many transgender individuals there, and the staff made it very clear that this was a *respectful*, inclusive, and affirming environment. Which I was totally on board with! In theory.

But then there I was, just trying to survive detox, wandering into the cafeteria like a confused squirrel on mushrooms, and I'd casually say, "Hey, dude" to someone I thought was Frank from my art therapy group. Next thing I know, there's an all-campus announcement about how "*Fran* now uses she/they pronouns and would like to remind clients that misgendering is harmful and will not be tolerated."

I swear it was targeted. They might as well have added, "Chris. Chris B. from Colorado. Stop screwing this up."

I spent the rest of the day mentally rehearsing everyone's names and pronouns like I was prepping for a spelling bee. "Okay, James uses they/them, Fran is she/they, Goose is just Goose… like Prince or Madonna. Got it."

At one point, I found myself in a gender-identity processing group by mistake, because I misunderstood what "Exploring Transitions" meant on the weekly schedule. I sat through the whole thing because it felt too awkward to leave once it had started. Honestly? Learned a lot. Still very confused… but humbled. Will be back.

All of it, the wild transportation, the pronoun slip-ups, the mix of broken brilliance around me, was a crash course in getting over myself. I shut up, listened, and realized that while I was busy freaking out about my own disaster, everyone else was navigating their own storm, too.

And that, my friends, is how I got a spiritual awakening and a lesson in gender inclusivity... all before lunch.

It was funny, tragic, and surreal. Like summer camp, if everyone was court-ordered there and trying to unpack their trauma before karaoke night.

And yet... somehow, in that madness, it worked.

Because, in between the psychosis, the IV fluids, and somewhere in the noise, I started to feel again. The fog lifted. I began to see myself, the real me, under all the junk I'd buried him in.

Rehab wasn't what I'd expected. But it was precisely what I needed.

And then… I met Billie.

I had barely survived the bike situation, the detox rollercoaster, and the gender etiquette crash course, and was thinking I had a handle on this place—*BAM!* Enter Billie, stage left.

Picture this: a leathery tan that said, "I've been smoking Cowboy Killers since the Nixon administration." He had slicked-back, thinning silver hair pulled into what I think was a man bun, though it could've also been a rogue paintbrush. White pants. A bright-pink Polo. Purple shoes. A cigarette was glued to the corner of his mouth like a nicotine sidekick. And his face that, no joke, was printed on his own T-shirt and sold in the rehab's gift shop for a cool $12.99 before tax.

He put one hand on his hip, squinted at me through mirrored aviators, stuck out his other hand, and went, "You, Chris?" in a thick New York accent.

I nodded.

"I'm Billie. I'm your therapist."

I couldn't tell if I was hallucinating again or if this was just Florida rehab energy in human form.

Turned out, Billie was seventy-five years old and a walking contradiction. Recovering junkie in every derogatory sense of the word—you name it; he did it. Heroin. Meth. Crack. Pills. Booze. Women. Men. Gambling. Maybe even pyramid schemes. I wouldn't be surprised if he'd once robbed a KFC using a kazoo and a headlamp. Let's put it this way: he was an addict before they sent him to Nam.

But here's the thing: Billie was sharp. Like, really sharp. He was raw, no-bullshit, unfiltered, and yet he had this way of cutting straight to your soul without even trying. He'd ask one question, and your inner child would immediately try to hide under a coffee table.

Our first session was about thirty seconds long, because I almost shit my pants… literally. The unspoken Refuge slogan came into play: "If you don't shit your pants, you're doing it wrong." The detox meds, the nerves, the cafeteria food—it was like a gastrointestinal rebellion timed perfectly with my first emotional breakthrough.

Billie just pointed toward the door like, "My personal bathroom is around the corner, bud."

But session after session, Billie started cracking me open. He didn't care about what I thought sounded good. He didn't want polished, shiny, "let me impress you" Chris. He wanted the wreckage. The ugly. The scared kid. The shame. The lies. The pills. He dug until it hurt and then kept digging.

And this is where the Refuge started to make sense, why it was so expensive. Why was it so respected? Because while the golf cart mafia ran the grounds, the staff? They were next-level. Wounded healers. Professionals who had been where we were and weren't afraid of our worst. They met you in the muck.

Billie didn't try to fix me. He sat in my swamp of shit (not literally) with me. Smoked through it. Cursed through it. And for the first time in a long time, I didn't feel judged; I felt seen. For once in my life, I gave someone my unfiltered truth and trauma, and I didn't hold back. And for the first time in my life, it felt good.

Another favorite memory, one I still think about when I'm feeling jaded about the world, was from one of my twice-a-week group workshops: Sound Therapy for Healing. This was three hours of sweaty, soul-expelling drum work, with a professional drummer who basically moonlighted as a spiritual drill sergeant.

We would vocalize our affirmations to the rhythm. You'd start small, "I am strong," or "I am enough," and eventually build up to your own personal power mantra. Mine?

"I AM FUCKING AWESOME!"

(With *oomph,* obviously. You don't whisper that shit.)

Then, we'd move to a narrow drum, and everyone in the group would join in, mirroring the way you hit the drum. Soft, loud, chaotic, controlled—whatever you wanted to do.

But here's where things got dicey.

The instructor pulled me aside before class and kindly asked me to remove my wedding ring, so it wouldn't damage the drum. Fair, no big deal. I slipped it into my pocket.

Reminder: this was the first time I had ever taken off my wedding ring.

Three hours later, after hiking half the damn property during our breaks, we finished the session, and I reached for my pocket and felt nothing.

No. Ring. I felt like Gollum in *The Hobbit,* crying out, *"Lost it is, my precious. Lost. Lost! Curse us and crush us, my precious is lost!"*

My stomach dropped like I'd just watched my life flash before my eyes on a Spirit Airlines flight. Total panic. But I didn't want to make a scene, so I told just one person: my roommate, Carlos. He was Native American, wise as hell, and always calm, like the human version of incense.

We were chatting quietly when the drum instructor overheard us, and she immediately yelled out, "Chris lost his wedding ring!"

And just like that, the entire group, like thirty people, stopped walking to their next class and started looking. It was surreal. Within minutes, it felt like everyone at the Refuge knew Chris Bowick's new wedding ring had vanished and was part of the search and rescue team.

And while looking for it, people were whispering, "Katie can't find out about this. He is already on thin ice as it is."

And what happened next was… human.

In a world where people are terrified of getting involved, where everyone's waiting to sue or snap back or ghost you completely, I was witnessing thirty strangers stop what they were doing, miss their own support groups and classes, bend down, and look, with kindness, with effort, with no judgment.

Even Fran/Frank/They, who had corrected me like three times that week for misgendering them (fair), was crawling on hands and knees in the dirt with a smile, searching. It was community. Pure, honest, messy, beautiful community.

They even rolled out a giant magnetic wheel, like it was a missing-person case. I, naturally, was the only one who didn't believe we'd find it. Everyone else had faith.

After nearly an hour of searching through Spanish moss and God knows what else, I turned to Carlos to tell him I felt bad people were missing their groups. And as we walked toward each other, ready to give up, he just lifted his hand...

He'd found it.

Just like that. No big speech. Just a nod. A knowing smile. Carlos's magic.

And I swear, I've never put something back on my finger faster in my life.

Back in the phone line, I kept trying to protect Katie with my five minutes of rationed words. I jogged between buildings to hit the phones at the top of the hour. I learned the names of nurses who could find me, if a call came through. I wrote notes for five-minute windows: ask about sleep, ask about work, say you love her first, in case the line drops. Absurd and holy, and it was all I had.

Physically, the hardest days were those three without steady Suboxone, when the gorilla moved into my lungs and bones and made everything hurt the same amount. Emotionally, the hardest was knowing that people who loved me were rerouting their pain toward Katie, because she was visible and I was not. Mentally, the hardest was the loop at night, when grace finally ran out, and the mistakes outweighed the man she married.

Slowly, the groups stopped feeling like punishment and started feeling like practice. I learned to breathe like I meant it. I knew that surrender was not a sentence; it was a tool. Powerless is not helpless; it is humility that lets others hold you up while you relearn how to stand.

Somewhere in those weeks, the nickname made sense. Silverback is not the drug and not the withdrawal. He is the part of me who believed I could dominate every problem by outworking it, outtalking it, out planning it. That chest thump had built businesses and a prison. He is not my enemy; he is my teacher, patient and immovable, waiting for me to understand that force will not save me. Surrender will.

Day by day, the fog thinned. I added Katie to my release of information. The calls home felt less like triage and more like stitching. The story of who'd sent me and why stopped feeling like betrayal and started to feel like human beings flailing in a storm, grabbing whatever floats. I was still angry. Anger is allowed. I am less interested in being right than in being here.

By the time the calendar clicked toward Family Week, it had been forty-five days. My mom and Katie were coming on different flights, renting different cars, and driving the same Florida roads to the same place, to sit across from a man who was finally starting to look like himself again.

I was terrified. Family Week felt like opening night for a play I'd rehearsed in fragments—apologies, boundaries, and the quiet, new truth that I did not get to control how anyone heals. The sun went orange over Ocklawaha. The campus settled. In the corner, Silverback stopped thumping his chest. He just watched. I could breathe. I could wait.

The next part is what happens when the people you love take a seat across from you and tell you the truth you could not hear when you were slipping away. Power looks like listening. Surrender becomes a choice you make with your eyes open.

Chapter 10

Rehab for Him, Hell for Me

Katie

There are days when I wake up from crying myself to sleep. With salty, crusted-over eyes, I roll over, ready to greet Chris, "Good morning!" Then, when I roll on my back and look up at the ceiling, a tear builds in the right outer corner of my eye and begins to fall down my cheek.

The silence is deafening, and it's like my mind doesn't allow me to actually remember he is away at rehab continuously 24/7, because it is too much for my heart to handle. I have to go through the pain all over again each day he is away. *Oh, yeah, he is in Florida.* Did that intervention really happen?

Sometimes, before that thirty seconds of reality hits me, it feels nice to remember our morning cuddle sessions with our pit bull mix, Lexi, before I open my eyes. We would laugh together, going through our reels of chopped-up dreams, trying to piece them together and figure out what they meant.

Today, I woke up to a continuous nightmare of my teeth cracking and falling out. I immediately typed into Google, "What does it mean when I dream my teeth are falling out?"

The search comes up with a quick answer: "*It is often interpreted as a symbol of feelings of insecurity, lack of control, anxiety, or fear of significant life changes; essentially, it could represent a sense of losing power or confidence in your life, as teeth are associated with appearance and ability to bite down (assertiveness) in waking life.*"

"Well, duh. Of course, that's what it means, Katie," I said sarcastically to myself, as I set down my phone.

As I rolled out of bed and sat on the edge of the mattress, I quickly placed my feet on the carpeted floor. Our king-sized mattress sat directly on the flat floor of the apartment above my parents' garage, as there wasn't enough space to fit a bed frame. I grabbed my phone from our makeshift side table and unlocked it to find fifteen unread text messages in the group chat created by the intervention team.

This chat was set up exclusively for updates about Chris while he was away at the Refuge and included a select group of friends and family, ensuring we presented a united front. Some texts sent over the past few weeks were inappropriate and ultimately dissolved the group texting, such as sending baby pictures of Chris, people expressing how they are feeling, and people going down memory lane, acting as if they were grieving a sudden loss of him, like he had died.

As I stretched my arms up to the ceiling and twisted my body from side to side, I reached for his favorite blue sweatshirt, which still carried his scent, resting on his pillow. I pulled it over my messy hair. Once it was draped across my body, I scrunched the front of the material and brought it up to my nose, inhaling deeply. I did this every morning, and every day, Chris was gone.

I quickly checked to make sure my phone's sound was on, so I don't miss his calls, wondering how many times and at what times he would ring to give me his daily updates. Every day, I found myself wondering if he'd slept well, had breakfast yet, and was making new friends.

I couldn't imagine how scared Chris must have felt as he arrived at the rehab center in the middle of nowhere in Florida, contemplating how long he would need to stay and what kind of life awaited him when he was discharged. I still couldn't grasp the uncertainty he must have experienced. Little did he know, I was just as much in the dark as he was, entering a plan that had been crafted without us knowing any details.

Our new adventure of starting an independent insurance business also had to be put on hold during this time. We were incredibly grateful for the pause from our Master Alliance Group. They were so supportive, even though they did not know the full details of why Chris needed a leave of absence.

He was the show pony and the expert at work, so there was only so much I could do for us, and unfortunately, I wasn't able to bring in stable income or new clients during this time. It was also terrifying, not knowing if Chris even wanted to do this line of work still when he came home. Especially since Chris was damn good at insurance, specifically the complicated layered policies for commercial clients. He has a way of identifying gaps in policies and knows where to add value without sounding salesy, because he is that amazing at it. And he loves helping people!

Let's face it, insurance isn't sexy, and my eyes will glaze over when I have to read through policies occasionally, but his eyes light up. He is so brilliant and savvy, and people would be lucky to work with him and have his attention.

The first few weeks after he left were the toughest, as there was no rulebook on handling this massive change. The day after he left was tough. That was when I learned, whenever I called the Refuge and asked for any updates, they had to say the stupidest line: "I will give the message to this individual if they are here, as we can't confirm or deny they are here. Thanks." *CLICK.*

The first time they said this, I wanted to throw my phone and yell, "*Of course he is there!* I just want to talk to my husband!"

It was challenging to determine what level of communication was acceptable once he entered the facility that first night, and it was somewhat awkward for me, as this was my first interaction with the facility. Before this conversation, I was unaware of their protocol; I hadn't called to inquire about the cost, the food, whether both men and women would be present, where he slept, or what they did all day. Does he get a therapist? Are there any forms or documentation I must also sign or be aware of?

I'd blindly gone in with faith that things would work themselves out. And why should I second-guess his family, whom I'd just married into, and who I thought had both of our interests in mind? I thought they wouldn't admit him into a facility that they didn't think was acceptable. And never in a million years would I have guessed the treatment I was going to receive from his family in the following weeks.

When someone we love struggles with addiction, the focus shifts entirely to the person in recovery. Their needs and treatment will be the primary concern. And yes, that makes sense, but it also means the person who stays behind—loving, supporting, and occasionally carrying the weight of the chaos—will feel left behind, overlooked, and exhausted.

I've come to understand that this role has a name; we like to call it *the Anchor.* The Anchor is the person who stays grounded, holding space for the one who is addicted, or what we name as *the Adrift.* We provide the stability, support, and love often at the expense of our own comfort. Being the Anchor doesn't mean you've done everything perfectly or correctly. It doesn't mean having all the answers. It means the person is doing their best to show up consistently, set boundaries, and take care of themselves while holding space for the Adrift.

For those of you facing the situation of watching a loved one enroll in a rehab center, I want you to know that what you are about to experience may be incredibly challenging, especially if you are the significant other left behind. The primary focus will be on the person who needs medical help, but it is also crucial for you to seek help for yourself. You've probably heard the phrase during a plane emergency: "Always put on your oxygen mask first before assisting others," because if you pass out, you won't be able to help anyone. This principle applies here, too. You need to take care of yourself first, to effectively support others.

However, I understand you may have neglected your own needs for a long time, and it's likely you've forgotten how to care for yourself. I can relate. During my experience with Chris's substance use, there were moments when I had to stop and think about what my favorite movie was anymore; I'd lost sight of who "Katie" was, apart from his addiction.

So, go get a massage, treat yourself to a movie, get yourself in therapy immediately if you aren't already, build a support system (you can't do this alone; you've already done so much by yourself), meditate, sleep, journal, sleep some more, and pray. The side of addiction that doesn't get talked about is when the addict finally gets treatment, you get the trauma. They receive a bed, a therapist, cooked meals, and all responsibilities are removed, along with a dedicated team of support who guides them through rebuilding their lives. Meanwhile, we get sleepless nights, panic attacks, and flashbacks of the lies and manipulation, plus we have to clean up the mess they leave behind, while wondering if we will ever be whole again.

While your significant other gets the help they need, I think it's essential for you to seek help for yourself, as well. You are never taught how to live life without someone you love, and when they are gone, this time might feel incredibly isolating. I should have spoken up and asked for help, as well. Especially because I did not feel taken care of by Chris's family during this time.

One of the most challenging aspects of this journey—and something I never anticipated—was the impact of family dynamics. Addiction doesn't just shake the person struggling; it shakes the whole system. And in our case, it exposed every crack in our foundation.

There's this unspoken trust that, when a man struggles, his mother often steps in with a kind of primal urgency. I get it now; in a way, I didn't then. He's her baby and her son. And watching him in a rehab center, broken and unreachable, must've felt like her whole world was slipping through her fingers.

However, that maternal urgency, if left unchecked, can become something entirely different. It can become possessive and territorial. And suddenly, the wife... *me*... becomes a threat.

That's what happened.

Instead of collaborating, I was shut out. Not explicitly, but subtly. My instincts were questioned. My love was scrutinized. I wasn't seen as a partner trying to help. I was cast as the villain who didn't do enough, did too much, or didn't do it their way.

His family didn't have to hold all the roles I did as wife, caregiver, detective, advocate, boundary-setter, lover, and sometimes, reluctant enabler. They didn't have to wake up every morning, wondering if today would be the day everything unravels again. They didn't carry the emotional weight of watching him nod off, lie, hide things, and promise to change. That was mine to carry, and mine alone.

To them, their world felt more black-and-white. Love him. Support him. Believe him. Forgive him. No questions asked. But addiction lives in the gray. And in the gray, I was alone.

I felt there was little understanding or empathy from most of his family toward me. I never asked to be put in this situation. I didn't even know how bad it was until he was admitted into a treatment center. There is no preparation for what to do when your loved one becomes an addict. That doesn't even happen until *AFTER* the problem.

I was desperately trying to keep my head above water, and I had tried so incredibly hard to keep everything from falling apart around Chris and me. I had the best of intentions for us, and I was honestly trying to help. I was being told by everyone how "sick" I was from what I'd had to endure from his addiction, and they were telling me to stop enabling.

No one was there to explain to me what decisions were unhealthy. No one lovingly walked me through the step-by-step actions I was taking that weren't working. Or saying empathetically, "Okay, I see why you were trying to handle this all alone, but I wonder, could we try it this way instead…?" And, "Katie, by doing X, Y, Z, you have been supporting Chris in his addiction and attaching him to his delusion." I am lucky I searched for this help on my own.

But where is the support for the Anchors (the loved ones) who have been directly affected? Why can't they be included in the rehabilitation programs and have their own coaching? Coaching to unpack what you just experienced, coaching for what to do, and how to prepare when their loved one is discharged and coming home.

We who are left behind *also* need the education around addiction and coping mechanisms; we need to understand the what-ifs that could come down the pipeline, once rehab is complete and the person in recovery comes home. When there is no education around the Adrift's problems and what they are facing, fear has no bounds.

Why not have direct question-and-answer support groups with licensed professionals who have practical solutions? Coaching on how to avoid enabling, creating healthy boundaries, navigating mental or physical relapses, and learning how to detach with love, among other topics. In one location for the recovering addict, and another location for the people left behind, who are traumatized, codependent, angry, resentful, anxiety-ridden, etc.?

I did the best I could in the moments I had when Chris was in active addiction, because I was motivated by fear, and I did enough with what tools were available in my box. So, loved ones, please don't point your damn finger at the one person who stood by your loved one through the pits of hell, trying their best to save them, while they lost themselves. Show them love and unwavering support.

What I wanted, what I *hoped* for, was harmony. I wanted an open dialogue. I wanted to collaborate as a team, to unite around Chris's healing, and not to compete for ownership of his pain. But the path they took felt predetermined. They all followed his mom's lead, often without question, and the opportunity for true partnership between all of us slipped through the cracks.

I still try to hold compassion for where they were coming from. Everyone responds to trauma differently. Everyone tries to make sense of the chaos in their own way. That was their way. To follow and not ask questions or get information elsewhere. But it came at a cost. And the price was our connection.

One of the best resources I received from the intervention team was Experience Onsite. While it is expensive, I believe it was essential for anyone's personal growth during this traumatic time. Another regret was not attending this program. I had signed up and even put a deposit down to participate in the location in California, while Chris was away in Florida, but I backed out at the last minute due to the steep cost. I couldn't afford it.

Deep down, I know this opportunity could have led to a life-changing journey toward rediscovering "me" more quickly. I believe going to Experience Onsite would have immersed me in a profound transformation and brought me more awareness of the challenges I'd developed because of Chris's struggle with addiction (isolation, codependency, trust issues, resentment and anger, emotional neglect, and hypervigilance, to name a few). I hope to be able to afford to go there myself one day, possibly even as a couple, with Chris. However, I encourage you to check it out either way.

Fortunately, I am a curious and self-aware individual, and I have made some crucial discoveries. I will continue to recover through various unconventional holistic medicines and therapies (stay tuned) that have transformed me into a healed woman. Although I carry insurmountable unseen scars, they are no longer open wounds.

While your loved one is at the rehab center, the restriction of communication is going to be rough waters, especially since they will most likely be undergoing detoxification from the substance(s) they've been dependent on. You will be in the dark for a while, which is terrifying.

This period will be just as crucial for you as it is for them in terms of healing. Take all the time in the world for whatever you need, and do your best to communicate that, so you aren't feeling alienated and lonely. Luckily, I am fortunate to have an extraordinary support system. I had spent years building a foundation of open and honest communication with my family and friends, and they are the only reason I survived this uncharted time.

I am incredibly grateful to all of you who were there for me during my most challenging moments, while Chris was away. You responded to my calls and texts at odd hours, allowing me to vent and cry when I was spiraling. Some of you flew thousands of miles just to sit with me on the couch, watching *Harry Potter,* and holding me as I cried. Others brought me cookies, flowers, and soup. You offered silent companionship, listening, and holding my hand through it all. Thank you to everyone who supported me during this dark, confusing, and earth-shattering time. Words like "thank you" will never fully express how you helped heal the broken parts of my life.

I am especially grateful for your commitment at our wedding to honor the promises Chris and I made to each other at the altar: to support us in being who we are, to believe in us, and to love us through every challenge we face together. Thank you for encouraging, supporting, and praying for us throughout this covenant commitment we made to each other, in both good times and bad, in sickness and in health.

To everyone reading this, I urge you to be there for those who are "left behind." They need your support now more than ever, even if they may not have the courage to ask for help or just need someone to keep them company. When they say, "I don't need anything" or "no thank you," show up with food, or a hug. Don't let them be alone. Get them outside of the house and go on a walk!

Ideally, when you decide it is time for outside help, I hope you can make that decision as a couple, so neither of you goes in blind. I know when you are deep in the trenches for someone else's addiction, you are in pure survival mode, and your brain is just attempting to get through one day at a time. And none of this is your fault. I repeat, *this is not your fault.* Louder for those in the back, *IT IS NOT YOUR FAULT.*

Your loved one's addiction is the product of years of untreated trauma or possibly a rough patch. They don't have the tools to properly cope, or they simply enjoy the feeling of being numb, or maybe they just like substances! This has nothing to do with you, though; it has everything to do with them, and they are not your responsibility to cure.

You are not in control. God is. Loosen your grip and let go. I am sorry you are in the line of fire, and I know you are tired. I know you haven't been able to unpack the manipulative tactics that have been constantly thrown your way, and I know you are deeply hurt. It's going to be okay, I promise. I understand.

However, I hope you never have to go through what I did. There is an important form called an ROI (release of information), an unbreakable document allowing the patient to share their protected health information with a point of contact. And drug rehabs are medical facilities that must follow HIPAA policies regarding privacy. If you aren't listed on their ROI form before your significant other goes under the detoxification process, you are shit out of luck.

Additionally, there is an accompanying document that lists the primary contact for medical updates. Make sure your name is on there. Because I didn't pay for or sign up my husband to this facility, his family did a *huge* disservice to me and "forgot" or didn't care to or even think to add me as a contact, to get real-time health updates and information on *my husband*. I had to depend on information from Chris's mom, Tracy, as she was the self-assigned contact on the ROI.

His family lacked any understanding of the complexities and depth of Chris's situation, as I did, so I was deeply concerned and confused when I found out I wasn't listed on this form as well. Unfortunately, I'd seen how Tracy likes to indulge in gossip, treating it like a sweet treat to enjoy and share, regardless of its accuracy. I may never know her true intentions, but I am aware of the damage that resulted, and I can never trust her again. But I do forgive her.

My only saving grace from this attempt at keeping me on the sidelines was Chris contacting me before, during, and after the detox process and giving me honest, firsthand information from his experience. Ultimately, the differing stories led to conflicting information between Tracy, Chris, and his doctors. But the timeline was not my own, and before I mentioned this bullshit piece of paper to him and asked him to give me access, he was admitted to their medical clinic to begin detox. I thought it would be only for a few days, but it ended up being over a week.

When Chris arrived at the Refuge late at night on a Wednesday, he was admitted to the medical building, and for over two days, he showed no sign of withdrawal symptoms. The medical team strip-searched Chris because they thought he was taking the drugs he had brought. They even tore out the liner in his suitcase! But what actually happened was a significant error on the part of the Refuge, our intervention team, *and* Chris.

While Chris and Bobby were traveling to Florida, Bobby told Chris this was his opportunity to take whatever he wanted before being admitted, to "feel comfortable." So, what addict wouldn't think to themselves, "This is my last hooray before getting sober. Let's party!"

Because Chris had flooded his system with his drugs, and because the medical team gave him dozens of antipsychotics, antidepressants, and muscle relaxers upon his arrival, his body couldn't keep up with the accumulation of drugs. His body was not able to break down what was supposed to help versus what substances could potentially kill.

That following Monday, Chris was given an additional medicine that, as we learned much later, was the magic charm to this puzzle of initiating his real withdrawal: Suboxone. Five days after being admitted, Chris spiraled into acute withdrawal syndrome.

His doctor later admitted an error on their part, that they had tried too many drugs at once. Then, their team had taken away all medicines when Chris fell into a state of psychosis and showed signs of cognitive impairment. Things escalated so quickly that their new plan was to get Chris admitted to a hospital for an MRI and a CT scan. Then, he could be monitored there.

Waiting on an update on how Chris's detox was progressing was debilitating to me, but we all finally heard word from Tracy after she spoke to the Director of Medical. She said it wasn't good news.

At admission, they had found a lot of drugs on Chris, which I couldn't help but laugh at, since in what world does someone who is on their way to rehab think to themselves, "Well, I'd better bring my stash with me!"

Obviously, they confiscated them. His admission drug test had come back, and it was like a punch to the gut: Percocet, hydrocodone, oxycodone, fentanyl, and K2/Spice. *Excuse me, WHAT*?

Regarding this concerning update, the doctors were puzzled as to why Chris was showing very few symptoms of withdrawal. They asked Tracy to disclose any relevant information about his involvement with other substances. It was hilarious when I heard this, because they are asking the *wrong* person for this kind of update. But because my dumb, naïve ass had opened up a few weeks before to his family about our recent experience with ketamine, when I thought it was a safe space, they'd taken everything I said out of context and tried to fill in the gaps they couldn't.

The night I went over to Chris's mom's house to find out about the details of the intervention and what was to follow, I'd informed them that both Chris and I underwent an intramuscular ketamine treatment, coupled with integrative therapy, on February 8. Before we started the ketamine therapy, we'd had an in-person consultation. We'd met the clinic's team, and we'd individually discussed our previous health history and our goals with ketamine therapy. They had reviewed the integrated treatments with us, including what to expect from them and us. We then agreed to their presented personalized treatment plan, which entailed our going two times a week for a month, coupled with integrated therapy the following day after each session.

One big reason we had looked into this treatment for Chris was that the therapy is used to treat the root causes of addictions (traumas, unresolved wounds, narratives, etc.). They are cautious not to introduce ketamine too early into recovery, as there needs to be time between substance use.

After our first ketamine sessions, the clinic director came into my room and inquired if Chris had taken anything or was on any medications, because he had exhibited an unusual reaction to the ketamine. They could sense something was off.

Feeling frustrated and defeated, I'd felt tears welling up and sighed. "No, I hope not," I replied, reminding them that Chris had struggled with opioids in the past, but to my knowledge, he hadn't been using them for a while.

I thought he had been honest, so this discovery was both shocking and disappointing. I had just undergone a life-changing guided journey, with the intention of working through my anger and resentment toward Chris. Instead of leaving my session feeling proud of my newfound insights, I left wondering how we had reverted to his hiding and lying about his drug use once again.

My excitement toward my own healing was immediately quashed, and I had to redirect my attention back to Chris. On top of all of this, the clinic and I needed to establish a plan for the next ketamine session to ensure Chris wasn't using opioids. We ultimately decided on a mandatory drug test before each session. Big surprise—Chris did not like this, so he said he wouldn't continue with his treatment. I digress.

When his family found out he had K2/Spice, a form of synthetic marijuana, in his system and heard about our recent ketamine therapy, the story twisted in a game of telephone. Somewhere along the way, K2/Spice was mistaken for ketamine, and people started throwing around street names like "Special K." Before long, a false narrative took shape, and the blame landed on me. The truth was, I didn't even know what K2/Spice was.

I remember being on a Zoom call with everyone when his toxicity report was shared from the Refuge. They all wondered why I was so concerned, and I yelled out, "I'm scared because I might have taken this stuff, too!" They did not know I was referring to Chris's prescriptions.

I started to wonder whether what Chris gave me was indeed from a doctor or some pills that Chris got from his other sources.

The fact is, intramuscular ketamine metabolites are out of our systems ten to twelve-and-a-half hours after injection, so this still doesn't explain why Chris wasn't experiencing withdrawal symptoms. As the ROI contact, Tracy distorted her conversation with the Medical Director and then assumed ketamine was the reason for his delayed detoxification.

They asked me how I could have been so foolish as to introduce more drugs to Chris, implying this was all my fault. (Cue eye roll.) This was the first time I got this conflicting perspective from Tracy, who shared updates via Zoom or the message chain, compared to what I heard from the Medical Director and Chris weeks later.

The Director then said they might need to change their plan and alter his medicines to trigger his detox better, since his condition was deteriorating daily. They also ordered a MOCA test (Montreal Cognitive Assessment). On it, a strong high score is 30; a normal score is between 26 and 30, and anything below 26 indicates cognitive impairment. She said dementia and Alzheimer's patients score around 16. Chris was at a 6.

Six.

I remember thinking, "Wait. Out of ten?" No, Katie. Out of *thirty.*

After they'd given him different medicines, my brilliant, funny husband was now struggling with psychosis and delirium, coupled with intense hallucinations. I found out later that this happens when you have to induce withdrawal using buprenorphine (Suboxone) medically. Psychosis can sometimes occur as a complication, contributing to hallucinations and severe confusion. Luckily, when the acute psychosis resolves, the detox can proceed gradually, reducing stress on the brain. And since Chris had not been honest about his intake, this impacted their strategy for getting him back on track.

The Director said they would need to keep him through at least Monday, and if he continued to decline, they would need to take him to the hospital for IV hydration and further medical help. The only thing they could get him to eat was applesauce and bananas, and he didn't know what to do when they put his tray in front of him. She said he was confused, did not know how to eat, was experiencing profound hallucinations, and was paranoid. She said he did not want to go home and was now speaking only in short words, not sentences, but that he was very cooperative, not aggressive, and pleasant.

On our weekly Zoom during this stressful week, Tracy gave us a grim update. Deep down, I knew it was exaggerated, but still, it sounded terrifying.

She said the doctor at The Refuge thought Chris may have had a stroke. We were awaiting the results from the MRI, but he had apparent neurological and psychiatric abnormalities. It was possible that the drugs—Chris's *and* the Refuge's—may have done irreversible damage to his brain.

When this was casually reported on the Zoom call, I called out to everyone that it was bullshit. Not for one second did I believe this to be true. Tracy then added more of her delusional salt to the unaddressed wound, saying Chris might not come back as the same person, and there was a chance he might not want to be married to me.

As all the blood rushed to my face and a knot in my throat grew bigger, I yelled out of anger, *"Well, maybe I won't want to be married after all of this, either!"*

I stormed out of the room, leaving my poor parents in front of the camera. Then, I dropped to my knees in another room and started crying uncontrollably, which led to a panic attack.

Unfortunately, I didn't learn the truth from Chris's doctor until after he was in a good mental state, and just days after he signed the HIPAA form. At no point did the doctor mention any concerns about the possibility of irreversible brain damage, a potential stroke, or neurological and psychiatric abnormalities. Chris's hospital discharge papers support these facts, as well.

The night Chris was at the hospital, I got a call from a random phone number. It was Chris! Calling from his doctor's cell phone. He sounded sleepy but was calm and alert.

He began to give me a full update on the past week and what had been happening. I updated him about my not being on the specific HIPAA form, and he was pissed.

I also told him about the "concerns" around brain damage and a stroke, and he broke out in laughter, saying, "Katie, I've been better, but I am fine. We are trying to figure out why I am not experiencing withdrawal. Now, I am at the hospital to do some tests for them, to make sure everything has been properly assessed. Don't worry, I am fine!"

Apparently, the fire department was called to the Refuge to take Chris to the hospital; they were mad about being used as a "shuttle service." But once Chris arrived, they performed two tests and couldn't discharge him, because his blood pressure had skyrocketed. We would find out later that this was because of his first dose of the Suboxone being administered, plus the Refuge not continuing the medicine appropriately.

As you can imagine, this week was incredibly confusing. I was receiving calls from Chris, and he was telling me the opposite of what his mom had reported to me and the group. I was also still in this manipulative limbo with Chris, so a part of me was unsure what to believe. Then, at any given moment, the intervention team and Chris's supporters saw me being argumentative and confrontational and upset because I wasn't on the HIPAA form, and they didn't know why I didn't trust Tracy and her intentions.

However, I appreciated James on the intervention team keeping me level. He kept saying, "Katie, don't worry about the form. Chris is fine, and that is all that matters. You are not alone. You have many people who love you and will be with you through this. Help has already begun, and unfortunately, we have to go through pain to get through it. It's the only way to get through pain. We and God are here to support you and hold your hand.

"Addiction is a deadly disease, and we are trying to save Chris's life. Just focus on that for now, take a deep breath, and know you've done all you can do. Pull in your oars and stop trying to steal your boat right now. Just take a deep breath."

Little did he know, Chris's family was making me feel alone and judged, pigeonholing me into a narrative I disagreed with. A big regret is being honest with them about my personal relationship with drugs, my family's mental health history, caring about their one-sided narrative about Chris and me, getting involved with their drama, and ultimately becoming their scapegoat. And I also never entirely pulled in my oars to allow God to take control until it was almost too late.

So, during this time, I encourage you to pull in the oars sooner and really press hard against the Lord or any pillar in your life who will be able to withstand all the pressure being flooded your way. Because this is too heavy for you to carry alone. You deserve a break from the burden of your significant other's addiction to take care of yourself for once.

After being released from the hospital, Chris was back at the Refuge's medical center, finally detoxing with all the "fun" symptoms of withdrawal: muscle aches, trembling, sweating, fatigue, excessive sweating, confusion, nausea, diarrhea, frequent yawning, anxiety, etc. The following Monday, Chris's medical team finally saw the comatose veil lift from Chris. His therapist, Billie, said it was like "his head popped out of his ass." Over the next few days, the medical team saw Chris's inherent self shine through as the intelligent, witty, smart-ass, caring human that he is. So much for being "brain dead!"

Once Chris came down from the intense withdrawal and detox, he could finally call me coherently and give updates on his day. Let me tell you, it was *so* comforting to know he was going to be okay and that the narrative being spun behind his back was not accurate.

One of the first things I immediately told him was, "I forgive you, I love you, and I am here for you."

Since packing meant throwing a bunch of clothes together for us, he called and asked for a couple more items, so I sent him a few more gym shorts, sweats, a couple of white T-shirts, and my letter. (*GULP.*) He physically felt able to attend the community group that morning, where they read stories and passages from books, and he spoke about how friendly and welcoming everyone was toward him.

The topics discussed were self-awareness and music appreciation. Each person picked one song they'd like to share with the group that expressed what they were feeling, and Chris chose, "Trying to Find Balance" by the band, Atmospheres. And let me tell you... When he told me this, I was shocked. During the time we dated and shared our music tastes, this band had never come up. So, the Devil crept in for a moment, leading me to think maybe he wouldn't be the same man I'd fallen in love with after he was discharged.

Music is a massive part of my life. It is always playing when I work, during my workouts, when I am getting ready in front of my vanity and putting on my makeup, when I am in the shower or in the car, and my favorite is when I put on one of my vinyl records while I cook dinner. I also enjoy creating playlists for others and have even put one together for when I pass away, to be played at my memorial. (I know, I am weird!) Music is this unspoken love language that can be interpreted in so many ways. It just hits you at your core, revealing the darkest corners of your soul.

During Chris's absence, music was my saving grace. It also doesn't help that I lean on sad songs on a daily basis, because I thoroughly enjoy tapping into my emotions, especially ones that make you just want to sit on your bathroom floor after taking the best, most relaxing bath. At the same time, your hair is still drenched, and you curl up your knees, press your weight against the side of the tub, and surrender. I surrendered all control during this time. I surrendered to the people in my life who were going to think what they wanted of me, and if they didn't take the time to get to know the real, deep, true *me*, that is their loss. I surrendered to the cold isolation I had been surviving in for too long; I hadn't been living.

Since Chris wasn't allowed to use his phone, I devised a thoughtful way to send him a customized playlist that took him through our relationship, using songs that had recently tugged at my soul. It's hard to believe, but I still use my purple iPod Shuffle when I go snowboarding. So, I did the unthinkable… I deleted my curated playlist on my Shuffle to create a new one just for Chris. What I like to call, "Addicted to Us."

I was so giddy when I sent it off to him, I felt like a kid back in high school, spending hours downloading music from LimeWire (Sorry, Mom and Dad, I most likely put a lot of viruses on your computer), to give to my crush—don't worry, I purchased all the music legally this time. Back in high school, I would even go above and beyond, writing a letter to my crush and sing the actual title of the songs to be witty. Okay, I think you get the gist. I am obsessed with music and sharing it with those closest to me.

Some of the songs that got me through this dark time and that I put on the playlist (which I will share with you at some point) were:

- ⌘ "Back on the road" – Billy Stonecipiher
- ⌘ "Shelter" – Joy Oladokun
- ⌘ "Storms" – Mr. Carter Davis
- ⌘ "Flickers" – Wrabel
- ⌘ "Carried Away" – Lauren Preuss
- ⌘ "Playing with Fire" – The Careful Ones
- ⌘ "Sweet Disposition" – The Temper Trap
- ⌘ "Gratitude" – Brandon Lake
- ⌘ "Almond Eyes" – Brandon Lake
- ⌘ "Lord it's a Feeling" – London Grammar
- ⌘ "Say You Won't Let Go" – James Arthur
- ⌘ "Chasing after You" – Ryan Hurd, Maren Morris
- ⌘ "First Try" – Johnnyswim

⌘ "Wildfire" – Cautious Clay

Each day in the medical unit, Chris was progressing, and his doctors couldn't have been more elated. He went to another group, and the topics discussed were recovery and relapse. They each talked about how difficult addiction is and then reviewed a few coping skills and ways to get out of that mental trap.

Chris was now waking up on his own internal clock around 6:00 a.m. every day and eating independently. I remember him telling me he had developed a weird tick: his arm, leg, or shoulder would suddenly move and jump really quickly. He said the doctors told him this was a normal occurrence.

Then, I received news that he was finally being moved to one of their cabins. That was where he would stay for the rest of his time. There are up to five people per cabin with two bathrooms. He made a comment that made me laugh. He wasn't looking forward to having a roommate, preferring to stay in the medical unit with his own bed and room, but he said he wouldn't mind having a door again.

I said, "Well, this isn't the Hilton, and knowing you, you will probably get your own room, anyway."

Chris also started receiving some of the letters his loved ones had written but could not read during the intervention. One was from my older sister, Ashley, her husband, Cole, and their two amazing kids. They wrote about how proud they were of him for getting the help he needed, expressing their worry about him, and stating that they would be there for him no matter what. (And they have kept that promise.)

He called me after reading that one, crying, saying, "Geez, I feel like I have cried more in here than I ever have. Are they wanting me to break down even more in here?"

Mind you, these two kids *adore* their Uncle Chris, as they should. He is always down to play hide-and-seek with them, he always makes them laugh, and he will take any opportunity to throw them up in the air, trusting that he will always catch them.

They knew Uncle Chris was sick but were not sure to what extent, so they used every crayon and marker they could to draw him colorful pictures. I knew those brightened his day.

While Chris was at the Refuge, I kept a daily recap in my notes app. On February 26, I wrote, "Chris signed HIPAA form!! Thank you, Jesus! I can finally breathe and hope the drama will subside. The truth will come out!"

Unfortunately, the weeks that followed were marked by even more drama and deception. To preface, we were given a rough outline in the intervention team's playbook—what to say, what not to say, and not to bombard or actively call Chris while he was there, as well as how we should react and/or act when he called any of us. Just to give you an example, here are a few prompts they provided us for when Chris would call:

"I love you so much, but I will not engage in this argument. I suggest you find a counselor and tell them how you feel."

"I understand right now you don't feel you fit in, but you have just gotten there. Why don't you talk to someone who has been there longer about their experience?"

"I am so glad you are feeling better, and I love you very much. I'm not a professional, and I'm not equipped to help you right now. You are in the right place with people who can help you here. I can't."

"I understand you feel you are ready to leave. Let's have a conference call with your therapist tomorrow to discuss."

But nothing prepared me, or the intervention team for that matter, for what would unfold over the next few weeks. During one of our weekly Zoom check-ins with the family/friends and the intervention team, his mom decided it would be a good idea to answer a phone call from the Refuge. She placed the call with Chris on speakerphone, so that everyone else on the Zoom call could listen intently.

At no point did she announce to Chris, "Hey, I am on a Zoom call with such-and-such people, and you are on speakerphone." She just immediately put him on speaker.

All you could hear was Chris in distress on the other end of the phone, looking to talk with them about a rumor he had heard from a Refuge employee about his possibly being sent to another facility after the Refuge.

Tracy immediately responded to the numerous prompts provided by the intervention team, while barely listening to Chris, who just needed to be comforted and heard. She ignored his concerns.

Chris abruptly got off the phone, sensing that something was off, and I immediately saw his name appear on my cell. I quickly stood up, saying I needed a second, and walked out of the Zoom call. I answered his call.

He said in a shocked voice, "Katie, what is going on? I just had the weirdest call with my mom, and I am feeling really isolated. Can you tell me if something is up? Or am I just overanalyzing this?"

Now, I read the playbook front to back and had some reservations about some items, but my radar was extremely high, homing in on the many steps of manipulation. I knew in my heart this was *not* one of those moments.

I immediately calmed Chris down and said, "Yes, I am sorry to be the one to confirm this, but your family has set up a men's program in Tennessee for the next six months, after you are discharged from the Refuge. I have not been involved with any of this personally from the start, as this was all set up when I went over to your mom's a few days before the intervention."

Silence. Then, I heard him take deep breaths of anxiety coupled with tears and confusion. He asked, "Are you on board with this?"

I paused, feeling a little guilty, then I said, "Yes, you need to do everything in your power to get better. Face your demons and come back to the best version of yourself. Sobriety can be your biggest weapon. You just don't see it yet! I love you." I told him I was sorry, but I had to leave, because my parents were still waiting for me to return to the group, visible on the Zoom screen. The rest of them did not know where I'd gone. I also told him his mom had just blasted their conversation on the Zoom call for everyone to hear without his consent, and that I was so sorry for this invasion of his privacy. He was pissed to say the least.

A few days later, I got a call from James. He asked me simply, "Is everything okay between you and Tracy?"

I immediately responded, "Well, yeah, everything is fine. The past few weeks have been quite heated, but I think we're all good now… Are we not?"

Silence. "Well, I think, for now, you two should look into stopping any communication with each other and take some time apart.

"*Umm, what*? We literally were just planning flights, hotels, and rental cars for the coming week to go out during Family Week at the Refuge."

James replied, "Yeah, I think some healthy space between you two would be advised. Some mean things are being said on her end, directed at you."

Noted. You know the moment in movies where everything builds to one dramatic *thing*? This was the first of many. I texted her, saying we should take some separate time, and that distance would be suitable for now. And true to her form, it turned into more drama. Regardless, we ended up with two separate plane rides, separate rental cars, and separate hotel reservations for the upcoming Family Week.

I found out later from the intervention team that she was mad that Chris and I were "in cahoots." She was angry that, after everything, we were still putting on a strong front. She thought Chris was manipulating his therapist, Billie, who had developed the impression that she had always wanted control over Chris and his life.

He noticed she was creating her own "team" to be anti-Katie, using her crafted narrative, while the rest of the family drank the Kool-Aid. To this day, I have received no apology from any of them, nor an admission that they put blinders on during this time and didn't get both sides of the story. It's wild how fast people turn on you when you stop playing the role they assigned you.

Navigating the challenges of a loved one's addiction is undoubtedly difficult, and facing those challenges alone can be even more daunting. Deciding when and how to seek help is one thing. Actually asking for that help is another. I urge you not to make the same mistake I did by trying to take on Chris's addiction as if it were my responsibility to fix it. Ultimately, it is the addict's responsibility to address their issues, not yours.

Seek outside help and opinions! If you believe an intervention is necessary, proceed with it. However, once they agree to enroll in a rehab facility, be sure to collaborate as a couple on a rough timeline. Loved ones, please try to avoid planning an entire intervention and rehabilitation program without involving the partner of the addict first. Although the goal is to get the addict the help they need (whether or not they want it), it is crucial to include the significant other as much as possible, since they are likely the one the recovering addict leaves behind during rehab and the person they will come home to. Neglecting to involve them is a disservice and fails to consider their feelings during this challenging time. Open communication and staying aligned throughout this process are vital. Remember, don't be afraid to stand up for your truth. Please do it for me, because I wasn't able to in time.

Back to our regularly scheduled programming of Chris getting better… I will recap a few updates that made me giggle during his calls to me:

- ♥ "Today was specifically around relationships and dealing with validation and repression." Chris said that, in his life, he had needed validation, and if he didn't get that, he would suppress others. It never went away. It just would switch "characters," and now he knows to take that suppression to his higher power.

- A Raccoon tried to climb into Chris's backpack and steal his chips. He left and yelled, "You little bandit, you little fucker! You know what? I'm just gonna give him what he wants." Chris gave him some popcorn, adding, "Well, now he just needs a movie!"
- "Meditation drumming is so amazing, with this dense canopy of oak-moss trees above us, and it is beautiful. I loved that we drummed along with our affirmations. Mine was, 'I am the man. I am powerful.'" *Aannd,* side note, he lost his brand-new wedding band! I will let Chris tell you more about this :)
- "I had to say bye to a few friends and am feeling low." Chris compared himself to being a gorilla, constantly under surveillance. His self-selected name is 'Niko,' since he feels like he is a silverback gorilla at a broken-down zoo.
- "Katie, I need to tell you something that happened when I was younger. It was incredibly traumatic. I suppressed it for the majority of my life, but I need to be honest with you and myself."

While Chris was busy with a strict schedule at the Refuge, I made an effort to spend time with friends and family, instead of waiting by the phone, which was easier said than done. One weekend in March, during Presidents' Day, my family and I went to our cabin in Granby, Colorado, to spend a ski weekend with my sister, her husband, and my niece and nephew. However, when we returned home, we noticed that something was off.

A large rock had been thrown through my parents' glass back door, completely shattering it, and we'd been robbed.

The people who broke in rummaged through the house and left with significant valuables. Since we were still living at my parents' house right after getting married, all of our bridal and wedding gifts were still in unwrapped boxes, neatly stacked in the basement, ready for them to take. They also stole all of my Tiffany jewelry, diamonds, rings, designer purses, gold bars, coins, and my safe, which contained my passport, social security card, and all of my medications (the list keeps going).

I have never felt more violated, angry, and fearful, constantly worrying about our safety and wondering if each noise I heard at night could mean it was happening again. Your home is supposed to be your haven, and this experience caused significant anxiety over the loss of sentimental items.

In the months that followed, my sleep deteriorated (even more, which I didn't think was possible), and my parents and I were on edge. Sleeping became even more difficult without Chris by my side.

However, after forty-five long days, I could hardly believe it. I was finally packing my bags to visit Chris for Family Week at the Refuge.

Chapter 11

Giving that Ass Away

Chris

As Family Week crept closer, my nerves were shot. I wasn't sleeping. I was fidgety. At one point, I think I stress-cleaned my room in rehab, which is hilarious because… it was a temporary room. There wasn't anything to clean except a twin bed, a Bible someone left behind, and a desk with a plastic chair that had bite marks on it… Don't ask.

Both Katie and my mom were flying in. Katie, I could handle. I needed her. My mom? That was like lighting a cigarette in a fireworks factory — something was bound to explode, and I wasn't sure if it'd be her emotions, my guilt, or the unspoken family dysfunction we'd all learned to dance around for years. Probably all three. Still, I was weirdly excited to hug her.

The Refuge didn't just throw families into a therapy Thunderdome without warning, though. We had prep sessions. Lectures. Workbooks. Role-playing exercises. We practiced "grounding techniques" and "boundary tools," all phrases that sounded great until you tried them on the people who activated half your triggers.

The team there kept saying things like "this is going to be healing" and "opportunities for deeper connection." Still, I was over here, wondering if they had a Plan B for when my mom tried to gaslight the entire room or if Katie politely throat-punched her with an innocent look.

Because here's the thing, I had done a lot of damage, yes. But my family? They weren't just innocent bystanders in this mess. They came with their own baggage, projections, and what I now know were some extremely unhealthy coping mechanisms disguised as "concern."

Heading into Family Week, I was torn in two. I wanted Katie to understand everything. But I also tried to shield her from it. I wanted my family to support me. But I also didn't want them anywhere near her if they were going to treat her like she was the problem.

I was the human equivalent of a tug-of-war rope, guilt pulling from one side, fear from the other. And yet, there was this tiny flicker of hope that maybe some of this pain would be worth it. That things could finally be said out loud. That Katie and I could walk out of this stronger.

I can remember the day Katie arrived at the Refuge for Family Week like it was yesterday.

You'd think I'd be excited. I mean, this was the woman I loved, my wife, my best friend, my partner in all things messy and beautiful. But in that moment? I was sweating bullets. My stomach was flipping. I was nervous as hell. And not the "first date" kind of nervous. This was, "I've got a full folder of red flags, and she's about to read them all," kind of nervous.

Because here's the thing: when you're in rehab, you have time to reflect (a lot of time). You start to realize just how much your actions hurt people, especially the ones who loved you the most. I had already come to terms with some of the damage I'd done, but having Katie show up meant I was going to have to *say it out loud...* to *her face.*

I was scared she'd look at me differently. That the weight of everything I'd hidden, everything I'd lied about, would finally crush us.

Instead, she showed up like she always does, strong and calm in the chaos. Her eyes met mine across the parking lot, and I braced myself for judgment, disappointment, and maybe an "I can't do this anymore." But nope.

She hugged me.

Tight. Like she meant it. Jumping up into my arms. I know I lacked strength in some avenues of our life, but holding her in my arms? No problem.

And in that second, I could breathe again. I smelled her Chanel perfume against her neck, and I was home again.

Of course, once we got into the first group session, all that warm and fuzzy stuff went flying out the window, and we were tossed into the deep end of some very real shit. But even in the challenging moments, she showed up with love. She asked hard questions. She didn't sugarcoat anything—she never does—but she never made me feel like I was beyond redemption.

That week, Katie didn't just support me; she showed me what grace looks like in motion.

You could feel it in the air, though; Family Week was a big deal at the Refuge. The staff was buzzing with nerves, pacing around as if the president were coming. I found out they hadn't hosted one in a long time because of Covid, and this was the first whole group back. Everyone wanted it to go smoothly. Everyone wanted it to be transformative and powerful.

No pressure...

Billie, my walking contradiction of a therapist, with purple shoes, leathery skin, and a cackle that could cut glass, pulled me aside a few days before and said, "Chris, I want you to represent me."

Apparently, every therapist picks a client to showcase during Family Week. I didn't realize this was some Hunger Games of Healing, but okay. I nodded, trying to act honored. Meanwhile, my insides were screaming.

He said he chose me because I showed promise, because I was doing the work, and I could hold space and speak my truth. And I wanted to believe that. But what I didn't say out loud was that my truth felt impossible to tell. Not with my mom flying in with her martyr complex and Katie, my wife, my person, still wounded from my lies and addiction.

I had written a letter. Actually, two letters. One to Katie. One to my mom. I thought maybe, if I read them out loud, something would click. Perhaps I could finally make everyone understand, and we could walk out of that room lighter, freer.

But every time I tried to practice reading them, my voice cracked. Because the truth was, I wasn't focused on *my* healing. I was trying to mediate a war I didn't start, one that had been festering in whispers and fake smiles for years. I was still being the peacekeeper, the fixer, the buffer—just wearing designer boxers (I had to retire my Superman pair)—putting out fires instead of standing in my own truth.

Billie sat me down after one of our prep sessions and just looked at me, that cigarette dangling from his lip. "This is crazy, Chris," he said. "You shouldn't have to carry this. You're here to get well. Not to be the damn referee for your family."

And in that moment, I felt seen.

Because he was right. I was still choosing everyone else's comfort over my own recovery. I was still trying to control how they experienced me, rather than just being honest about who I was, what I'd done, and where I hoped to go.

They put us all in a mixed circle of clients, therapists, and family members. The room was warm, and I could feel the sweat pooling behind my knees. Chairs were in a distinct circle, with boxes of tissues in every corner, and everyone breathing heavily through their masks.

Katie was already sitting next to me as we waited for my mom to walk through the heavy doors. She smiled that tight, polite smile she uses when she's unsure if she's the victim or the hero. My stomach did a complete somersault. I hadn't seen them in the same room since everything fell apart.

I sat between them, which was probably my first mistake. I was trying to protect them from each other, as if my body could be a buffer for ten years of unspoken resentment and silent suffering.

The therapist running the group, someone I didn't know, welcomed everyone and talked about safety, honesty, and brave space versus safe space. All I heard was static. I was hyper-focused on Katie's hands in her lap and my mom's blinking.

I could feel it happening before anyone spoke. The tension in my shoulders. The anxiety buzzed in my ears. I wasn't thinking about my addiction. I wasn't thinking about my healing. I was scanning for triggers like a soldier in enemy territory.

Katie shared something soft and vulnerable about how hard it had been to hold everything together, and her frustration about having to wear masks and not being able to see everyone's faces. Especially not seeing them for so long.

I tried my best to scan the pairs of eyes staring back at me, their hidden emotions behind their masks, trying to figure out if I could get a non-verbal hint of communication. But women are hard to crack in that department, so the added layer of the mask didn't help my mission. That session ended with more questions than answers. And in truth, that's probably the most honest place to begin.

Midway through Family Week, during one of our group sessions, my mom shared how she had removed all the alcohol from her house in preparation for my return. She said it with pride, as if it were a grand gesture of support.

The irony? I wasn't much of a drinker. Maybe a glass of wine during the holidays, but alcohol was not my substance of choice. Still, in her mind, removing the booze was the obvious step. It was her way of showing she cared, of trying to create a safe space for me.

Later, another participant, a husband there to support his wife, shared his discomfort with gestures like my mom's. He expressed how, when people removed substances from their homes without discussing it with him, it felt isolating. It made him feel like a burden. He didn't want others to change their lives because of his past mistakes. He had come to terms with his relationship with alcohol and didn't want to impose his journey on others.

This resonated with a lot of people in the room. I know my mom's actions came from a place of love, but it also highlighted a lack of communication about what I truly needed. It's essential to ask the person what they need or don't need when they come home, because making assumptions can sometimes cause more harm than good, even with the best intentions. Recovery is not a one-size-fits-all journey; it requires understanding, communication, and mutual respect. Sometimes, it's just asking someone, "What do you need?"

Later in the day, I was sitting at a lunch table with my mom and Katie. The atmosphere was tense, filled with unspoken words and lingering emotions. I had been carrying a heavy secret for years, a secret that I'd buried since I was eight years old. I decided this was the moment to tell my mom that I had been molested by a babysitter she had hired. I had already told Katie earlier in the week. A casual lunchtime revelation, right? Because who doesn't drop bombshells over a sandwich? I also reminded my mom that this was absolutely not her fault!

I just needed her to know. Because, for the first time, I was learning that healing meant telling the truth, even when it made everyone uncomfortable.

She didn't believe me.

At least, not at first.

Fast forward to a therapy session with Billie, me, and my mom. I tried to explain the lunch debacle, but it felt like I was narrating a sitcom episode. Billie, always the straight shooter, was like, "Wait, what? She didn't believe you?"

He stood up, hands on his hips, channeling a mix of disbelief and dad energy. "Chris actually came out and was honest during a men's small group, and you're telling me you didn't believe him?" It was like a scene from a TV drama, but with more awkward silence. That moment was decisive for me. I realized I wasn't crazy. I was just unheard.

And then there was the Katie situation. My mom kept bringing her up, like a broken record. It was as if Katie was the plot twist in a soap opera, and my mom was the critic.

I remember trying to address the Katie situation directly, thinking, "I'm an adult. I'll handle this like an adult."

But, of course, my mom didn't want to hear it. She wouldn't apologize to Katie, and that left me stuck, trying to bridge a gap that didn't seem to want bridging. Katie wasn't even in the room, but my mom kept bringing her up. She kept harping on the fact that Katie had brought a notebook with her to Family Week, full of questions and statements, and she felt blindsided and ambushed.

I tried to tell my mom that Katie deserved an apology. I said it once. I said it twice. It was like talking to a wall, though. She just couldn't, or wouldn't, do it. So, there I was, stuck in this weird emotional limbo, trying to be the voice of reason in a room full of unresolved tension and generational trauma.

Billie tried to address the ongoing tension between my mom and Katie. He observed that my mom often brought up Katie during our sessions, expressing her feelings about being attacked or sidelined. Billie made it clear that by forcing me to choose between my wife and my mother, Tracy was putting me in an impossible position..., one that could ultimately damage our relationship.

He added to my mom, "You are putting Chris in a position of choosing between Katie being his wife and you being his mom, and you are going to lose." God knows how much I appreciated Billie saying that, so I didn't have to. It was painfully true and an impossible place to feel comfortable in.

This marked a turning point in my journey. It helped me understand the importance of having a supportive environment whenever you are being open and communicating about past traumas. I also realized how crucial it is to maintain clear boundaries and open communication within my family. Unfortunately, my mom's initial reaction was not what I had hoped for in building a mutual understanding going forward.

This weekend was also the first time I remember truly realizing... *I can't fix this*. I can't make everyone okay. I can't smooth it over. I can't shrink myself anymore, to make space for the wounds I didn't even cause.

All I could do was cry. Silently, at first. Then, not so silently. I heard my mom sniffle. But even then, I didn't feel comfort. I felt grief.

Not just for what was happening. But for how long it had been happening.

The joint therapy session with Billie, Katie, and me was like walking into a three-way emotional car crash, except instead of airbags, there were just tissues, sighs, and the occasional "fuck this."

Katie came in like a calm storm. Not yelling, not emotional, or angry, just... done. The kind of done where someone's clearly walked through the fire too many times barefoot, and now they're standing there, holding a burn kit, waiting to see if you're worth using it on. She laid out her boundaries like they were terms in a lease she wasn't renewing. And they weren't cruel. They were fair. Honest. Unapologetic. Clearer than I had ever seen them.

And I just sat there, feeling like the human version of a trash can on fire. Every word she said, I deserved. Every ounce of exhaustion in her voice, I had earned, like frequent flyer miles to rock bottom.

Then, Billie, you gotta love him, leaned in and gave me this look like he was about to drop a truth bomb with a side of East Coast flair. "My god, Katie, turn back around," he said. "Chris, you are giving that ass away. You are giving Katie away with your addiction. Don't let that ass go!" He was right, and she does have a phenomenal butt.

I blinked, half-laughing, half-breaking. It was such a ridiculous sentence—but it cut deeper than anything else had. Because he wasn't wrong. I *was* giving Katie away. Piece by piece. With every lie, every pill, and every excuse wrapped in charm and half-truths, I was handing over the best thing that ever happened to me, like I was too stupid to know what it was worth.

That session felt like emotional waterboarding. I couldn't tell if I wanted to run, puke, cry, or take notes. Probably all four. But something about Billie's line snapped something awake in me. Perhaps it was the absurdity. Maybe it was the fact that it cut through the fog better than any motivational quote or relapse worksheet ever had. But it landed. Hard.

I was losing Katie. Not because she'd stopped loving me, but because I'd stopped fighting for her. I was giving her away. And it turns out, losing someone slowly, *watching* them pull away while you're too high or too proud to stop it, is a special kind of hell. And I didn't want to be there anymore.

Things started going sideways a few days before I was supposed to leave for Tennessee. I was under the impression that this whole sober-living plan was already locked in: six months in some all-men's facility with structured programming and wholesome bonding.

But then, we had this meeting: me, my mom, Billie, my doctor, and Katie. Honestly, I thought it was going to be a "here's your next steps, good luck out there, champ" kind of chat. Instead, it turned into a full-blown plot twist.

Katie had done what Katie did: the homework. She'd already called the Tennessee place to ask real questions, which was wild to me, because, at that point, I still thought of "due diligence" as something you do before buying a used car. She found out I wouldn't even be allowed visitors until after one month in, which already felt like a red flag. I mean, if you're trying to rebuild trust and connection, maybe don't isolate the guy further?

But the kicker? Katie found out that any money already put down *could* actually be refunded. Fully. Even at the last minute. Which was important, because, spoiler alert, I wasn't going.

And here's where it gets extra messy: my mom had told everyone she *had to refinance her house* to afford the Tennessee program. Let that sink in. A full-blown financial sob story, complete with guilt-tripping undertones and emotional manipulation. Except... it wasn't true. The money *was* refundable. No second mortgage needed. No banks involved. Just more drama on top of an already exhausting situation.

See, my doctor had dug into the program and basically asked, "Why is he going to a place that offers support for things he's already doing?"

I already had a job. I had my own car. I had a place to live. This wasn't some fresh-out-of-jail reinvention story. I was just a guy who needed help staying clean without his life catching fire.

Oh, and then there was the small matter of Suboxone, a big part of my treatment plan. You'd think a recovery program would be prepared to manage that, right? Wrong.

One day, the Tennessee team was like, "We've got you covered, Chris." The next day, they called back and said, "Actually, we don't handle meds. And we think it might be best if you get off of them altogether, anyway."

Cue chaos.

Suddenly, the Refuge staff were speed-dialing every contact they had to find a bed that wouldn't kill me. Billie looked like he was either going to cry or tackle someone.

Meanwhile, Katie was ushered into a weird, dim office full of outdated pamphlets, like it was 2006, and I was pacing, wondering if I was going to be discharged to an actual plan or just vibe it out in Florida with a backpack and a dream.

The new plan? A PHP (partial hospitalization program) at a sober-living facility that could actually handle medication management and didn't treat Suboxone like it was a dirty word. Hallelujah.

Of course, this pissed off the original intervention team. They tried to double down, telling my doctor they agreed with the Tennessee program, that I didn't *need* the meds, which was rich coming from people who hadn't spent ten minutes living in my body.

At that point, even the Refuge was like, "Yeah, we're done with these people."

So, just like that, the Tennessee plan, months in the making, was over. A new one was in place, crafted in about an hour, under pressure, by people who actually knew me.

I remember walking Katie to her car that night. The air was heavy. We were both emotionally hungover from the day.

We sat in her car, laughing through the exhaustion, trading one-liners about how absurd this whole ride had been.

I watched her car pull away, kicking up dust on that long gravel drive. I waved, probably looking like a lost kid at camp drop-off.

There wasn't a big emotional speech or cinematic moment, just a quiet wave and a silent promise to try not to fuck it all up again.

Uncertainty was written all over both our faces. For the first time in a long time, there was also something else: a sliver of hope.

Chapter 12

Frayed, Not Broken

Katie

So, what the heck is Family Week?

Glad you asked! At the Refuge, Family Week is basically four days of "Let's Drag Your People Into This Mess, Too." But in a therapeutic way.

They invite your significant other, family member, or that one friend who still answers your calls (bless them) to join you at rehab for a couple of days. Sounds cozy, right? It's deep. It's weird. It's beautiful. It's all of it.

On paper, it's described as an opportunity to "promote healthy communication," "gain insight into the role addiction plays in your relationships," and "break free from harmful cycles." They hold educational lectures, support groups, and individual family therapy sessions to help everyone unpack how we got here and, hopefully, learn how to avoid a similar situation in the future.

The goal? To show the family and loved ones their role in the dysfunction, not just point fingers at the addict. It's about accountability. Boundaries. Healing. It's about figuring out how to support someone without enabling, love someone without losing yourself, and forgive someone without pretending everything's fine.

It's where the real work starts, not just for the person in treatment, but for everyone else who's been riding shotgun on the chaos train.

So, yeah… Welcome to Family Week.

After James suggested that Tracy and I spend some time apart, we decided to travel to Florida separately and limit our communication to email. Each of us rented our own car and booked our own hotel room. I decided to arrive a day early to visit Chris in the evening, before the program started the next morning, and have dinner at the facility.

As I unpacked my bag in the hotel, I felt incredibly uneasy about seeing/speaking to Tracy, since the weeks leading up to this event had been somewhat emotional. I needed to detach from her with love. The biggest service I did for myself during this time was working on my boundaries. It is okay to detach from people who no longer serve you or who are no longer healthy for your mental well-being. I needed to separate myself from Tracy and her narrative during this time. But that was really hard to do, mainly because all I wanted to do was speak my truth. I felt like I was barely hanging on by a thread, and that single thread that tied us together was completely frayed. I felt jaded.

As I stepped outside for some fresh air around noon, I took a walk to grab a quick bite to eat. I was starving. Once I left the hotel, a splendid, cloudless blue sky and palm trees greeted me, along with an unusually high number of decorated golf carts passing me by. As I walked down the pier into what I thought was a shopping center, I began to feel as if I had been transported to Main Street/Downtown Disney at Disney World.

I was surrounded by clean cobblestone streets, colorful Victorian-style buildings, and vintage streetlamps. The air was filled with the scent of freshly baked cookies and the sounds of live bands playing from nearly every building. All that was missing was Cinderella's castle, a Mickey ice cream bar, and Tinker Bell.

As I sat down to eat, I asked my server, "Where am I? An hour ago, I was going through some sketchy neighborhoods on my drive-in, and now I am in what seems to be a scene from *Stepford Wives*."

He laughed and said, "You are in a retirement community called The Villages."

After getting acquainted with this new 55+ community, I headed to the Refuge. The thirty-minute drive had numerous turns and stop signs, and as I approached, the surroundings became increasingly rural.

As I pulled up, I was surrounded by massive moss-covered trees on both sides of the wide concrete driveway, and I met a closed black-iron gate. After pressing too many buttons on the call box, I sat there for about five minutes until someone finally came on, asked me a bunch of questions, and let me in.

As I parked in my designated parking spot, I noticed a figure getting up from a swinging white chair. He waved and smiled like Forrest Gump did when he saw Lieutenant Dan on the dock. I immediately recognized it was Chris.

We ran toward each other with full force until I leaped into his arms, wrapping my legs around his waist. We laughed and cried as we hugged each other. I am pretty sure we didn't let go for a solid five minutes, but when we did, I was greeted with the biggest shit-eating grin I have ever seen from Chris. He helped wipe away the salty tears from my cheeks.

While we held hands, Chris escorted me to the front desk to check in and have the items I'd brought from home approved, along with some goodies I'd grabbed from the gas station. As we headed down to dinner, Chris gave me a quick recap of the property.

"This is the medical building, where all the magic happens when you arrive and detox. And these buildings are for the people who struggle with eating disorders. This building is where my therapist, Billie, is. Here are the horses and donkeys. This is the tree I sit under when I want to journal, and this is the dining lodge!"

The Refuge can accommodate roughly eighty-four people at a time for its programs. While Chris was there, about seventy people were onsite. The Refuge sits on ninety-six acres in the dense Ocala National Forest in Ocklawaha, surrounded by moss-draped trees and a river along its sides.

I later found out that the Refuge focuses explicitly on trauma and PTSD, along with addiction, depression, and anxiety, so, ultimately, it ended up being an excellent fit for what Chris needed to unpack from his childhood and the darkest corners of his heart. I am incredibly thankful that his family found this treatment center for him, and he was fortunate to be paired with his therapist, Billie.[3]

As we sat down for dinner, I noticed Chris had a few beaded bracelets on his wrist that I hadn't seen before. I asked if he'd made those himself, and he said yes. He took one off and gave it to me, adding how he'd made it specifically for me. While I nervously played with the little beads, I updated Chris on the last few days of unnecessary drama. I opened up about my anxiety about seeing his mom the next day. He felt the same.

After dinner, Chris introduced me to several people who were happy to put a face to a name, and then we walked toward his bunkhouse to show me his setup. I could only peek through the door, as women weren't allowed into the men's quarters without a chaperone. We quickly moved on to his favorite spot: the barn. Chris promptly introduced me to each horse and a random donkey, and I could tell he spent a lot of time along this fence, venting to these well-fed animals.

As the sun began to set, I knew it was time for me to return to the hotel. I hated the thought of spending another night without Chris. Seeing where he slept and realizing how uncomfortable he was with his roommates only added to my unease. On my drive home, I began to pray aloud to God, thanking Him for opening Chris's heart to the long road ahead of him toward recovery and for being so receptive to this experience.

At last, the big morning arrived, and I made my way over to the Refuge to begin the first of the four days of Family Week. The jam-packed itinerary was thoughtfully scheduled for each day, running from 7:30 a.m. to 7:00 p.m.

Once all the visiting family had found their seats in the large community room, they were greeted by their loved ones enrolled in the program. The room buzzed with "I missed you," "I'm sorry," and lots of hugs. Unfortunately, we were still in the throes of Covid, so we had to wear masks, and it was hard to hear one another or see any new faces.

Once Chris's mom arrived, I was cordial and said hello, giving her a hug. I'd even saved her a seat. The first day was very high-level, providing everyone with an overview of the days to come and what to expect, along with introducing us to the facility and staff.

During one of the programs, called "Nuts and Bolts of Trauma," we reviewed specific examples of trauma and were asked to raise our hands if we had personally experienced any of them. When the facilitator mentioned natural disasters, I raised my hand. When they mentioned car accidents, I raised my hand again. I also raised my hand for sexual assault and for knowing someone impacted either directly or indirectly by suicide.

After this session, a staff member pulled me aside to ask if I had good support at home. I responded, "I have dedicated a lot of time toward healing my mental and physical well-being, and the support system I have back home is incredible!" I thanked them for their concern.

One of the most impactful activities involved selecting a handful of clients to write letters speaking directly to their trauma. The experience was incredible; I don't think there was a dry eye in the room.

However, my biggest takeaway from the session was when the facilitators broke down the concept of trauma into three parts: the event, the trauma, and the response. Trauma isn't simply the event itself; rather, it is the shame-based perspective you develop in response to that event.

Dr. Gabor Maté says it best:" Trauma is not what happens to you. Trauma is what happens inside of you as a result of what happened to you·"[4]

For me, the event was Chris's active addiction, along with his lies and manipulation. The betrayal broke the trust in our relationship. My response has manifested as CPTSD, turning me into "Detective Katie,"—constantly vigilant, seeking reassurance, and scanning for danger.

Bessel van der Kolk's book, *The Body Keeps the Score,* helped me understand this.[5] He explains that after experiencing trauma, the nervous system remains on high alert, causing people to perceive danger everywhere. I could relate during Chris's addiction; I spent all my energy trying to catch potential threats before they happened. Over time, this vigilance became embedded in my nervous system.

Even now, with Chris no longer in active addiction, reminders of past trauma trigger me. Fears of relapse can still put me on high alert, creating a need to control the situation.

Trauma also manifests differently, depending on one's childhood experiences. Chris, for example, experienced emotional neglect, which taught him that, "I don't matter." His coping strategies became hyperactivity and controlling his environment to feel safe.

I, on the other hand, learned that withdrawing and tuning out was my safest option. During our fights, we were like two trauma-response bombs, each reacting from old patterns rather than hurting each other intentionally.

Ultimately, we are all still little kids at heart, healing the beliefs we formed in childhood. These beliefs create trauma responses—anxiety, avoidance, rigidness—but they also show our resilience. Techniques like EMDR help reprocess negative cognitions tied to trauma, redirecting them toward healthier responses and fostering growth.

One important insight I gained from Family Week, which focused on addiction, is that many people tend to overlook the various forms of addiction that go beyond just drugs and alcohol. Almost anything enjoyable has the possibility of becoming addictive. These can include behavioral addictions, such as excessive exercise, workaholism, gaming, shopping, gambling, or even sex.

Watching someone navigate addiction opened my eyes to how behaviors, even positive ones, can become compulsive. For example, I personally know people who are obsessed with their routines, like daily workouts. If they miss a leg day, it can throw off their mood or their entire day. Even though the "chemical" involved (endorphins) is natural and positive, the dependence on the behavior can become consuming. I could relate this to the vigilance I carried while loving Chris: I was constantly "on alert," dependent on controlling what I could to feel safe.

For Chris, I saw how addictive behaviors became a way to cope with his discomfort. He used substances to numb from anxiety and shame. The cycle was similar: craving, compulsive need, and temporary relief, followed by more craving. Even positive routines, such as exercise or productivity, can become functional when they are necessary for emotional survival rather than enjoyment.

The crucial point is that the substance or behavior is rarely the root cause of the problem. It's a coping mechanism for underlying discomfort, shame, or unresolved emotions. For instance, a parent may become overly attached to a child, or someone may throw themselves into compulsive exercise, gambling, or shopping, in order to feel control or to escape. In all cases, the behavior temporarily masks pain but doesn't resolve it, and over time, the cycle can become destructive.

Understanding this helped both of us see that healing isn't just about stopping the behavior—it's about addressing the internal discomfort that drives it, building awareness, and learning healthier ways to cope.

Substances are not the root problem; they are seen as a solution. Unfortunately, a destructive one.

During the week, we had the opportunity to participate in individual and family therapy sessions with Billie. He scheduled one session for Chris and me, and another for just Billie and me. There was also a session with Chris and Tracy, one with just me and Tracy, and a final session with all of us together.

I felt the most nervous about the session with just Tracy and me, so I made sure to write down some bullet points in my notes app to help me remember what I wanted to discuss. However, she did not respond well to me preparing my thoughts ahead of time. She interpreted my note-taking as a manipulative tactic, as if I were trying to use it against her. Here is the list I quickly scribbled down on my flight out:

- ⌘ I loved you with an open heart. I forgive you for the hurt you have caused me and my family, but I can't be a part of your narrative. You don't have accountability in recognizing the hurt you are causing. You must earn love; it's not freely given after it's taken advantage of.
- ⌘ You're not allowed in my sandbox. I am putting up some much-needed boundaries
- ⌘ Stop the madness and the gossip about me and my family. You have created horrible storylines that are not true.
- ⌘ I feel you are unavailable for any criticism
- ⌘ I am not actively taking him from you
- ⌘ Are you jealous of my parents or of me taking care of your son?
- ⌘ Stop blaming me, blame your son
- ⌘ Things you say are manipulating and untruthful
- ⌘ My fault Chris's dad was not involved in the intervention. Not true. The intervention team specifically asked for people who knew about Chris's addiction to be present. Why didn't you have my back?
- ⌘ What do you want to ask me about my personal drug use with my prescriptions and with Chris's?

⌘ Why did you tell people you think my parents' house is an unhealthy living place and you think it is deemed bad for Chris to return to?

⌘ Why did you not confide in me about choosing a center together?

⌘ Why did you tell Chris and me that the Discovery Place was nonrefundable? I called, and they said that was false.

⌘ Why did you give me a hard time about ketamine treatment and not ask more questions? I was bothered that you attributed that to Chris's psychotic break, which wasn't true.

When it was time for Tracy and me to spend time with Billie, I was already sweating in places I didn't know I could, on top of the already smoldering Florida humidity. So, I was thankful for Billie's air-conditioned cabin office.

Billie's office was like stepping into the attic of your emotionally intense great-aunt, who was also an art therapist and low-key hoarder. Every single inch of wall space, and I mean every single inch, was covered in artwork, poetry, letters, scribbles, napkin drawings, and even a couple of what I think were papier-mâché masks. No rhyme or reason, just soul vomit taped, tacked, or pinned wherever it could fit. There wasn't an inch of clean drywall visible. It was like an overwhelming visual scrapbook of transformation and torment.

I asked him about it once, pointing at a messy charcoal sketch of a crying child holding a pill bottle that sat on his desk. He squinted at it, puffed on his cigarette (because apparently, fire codes don't apply to seventy-five-year-old men in purple shoes), and said, "Yeah, that one was from a girl who relapsed two weeks after sending it to me. If I find out you've relapsed, your shit comes off the wall."

I half-laughed, thinking he was joking. He wasn't.

He added, "This room isn't a museum of art. It's a museum of survival. I only keep the pieces from the ones still fighting."

It hit me like a sucker punch. This wasn't decoration. This was sacred ground. A monument to pain, resilience, and, in some cases, unfinished stories. It was equal parts beautiful and haunting.

That's when I realized Billie wasn't just eccentric. He was deliberate. Everything had a purpose. Even the pink Polo.

As we sat down on opposite sides of the couch, the tension was palpable. Billie asked me to start, so I began going through each bullet point, asking Tracy questions and seeking her insights. However, we struggled to fully address the issues because she came in with her defenses up. Tense. Guarded. As if she were bracing herself for blame or being shut out.

And I get it. I do. She was watching her son unravel in front of her, and she couldn't fix it. From personal experience, I know helplessness feels unbearable and frightening. Maybe she was trying to find her place in all of this or rewrite her role in the story, so she could be closer to the front lines, like I was. Closer to him, closer to control. And maybe my presence made that feel even further out of reach.

I reminded myself we were both watching someone we loved fight for this new opportunity in life.

This wasn't a competition, and it wasn't about us. But what hurt most was that she never asked me how I was doing. Not once. There was no "Are you okay?" or "How are you holding up through all of this?" It was as if my fear didn't exist. As if the nights I spent awake, worrying didn't count. I wasn't looking for applause or reassurance, but I had hoped, at the very least, for a shred of understanding. Just maybe some small acknowledgement that I, too, was drowning at times.

Billie noticed we weren't making any progress and that the tension was escalating, so he introduced an activity with leading questions: "I hate it when you…," "I don't like it when you…," "I felt frustrated when you…," and "What can I do in the future to address…?"

Ultimately, as our time was coming to an end, I felt more confused and frustrated than I had when I first arrived. Billie recognized we were hitting a dead end and clapped his hands together, saying, "Okay, I think this is a good stopping point. I'm not sure we can cover everything we need to, but I hope we can continue down this path toward being more receptive and listening more."

As it was getting close to dark, Tracy realized she had forgotten her glasses, so her thirty-minute drive back to the hotel would be difficult. I offered, "Well, I can take you!"

Although we often have different points of view, I was still her daughter-in-law, and I wouldn't want her to drive if she didn't feel safe. The car ride surprised me. Somewhere between the headlights and the shared exhaustion, we started to talk, not about each other, but about Chris. About the chaos. The heartbreak. The confusion.

We aired out some frustrations, and for that brief stretch of road, it felt like we were on the same side again. Two women who loved the same man, navigating different roles in the same storm. It didn't solve everything. But for a moment, it reminded me that even strained relationships can have grace between the cracks.

I will never forget what Billie said to me when he pulled me aside after an intense family therapy session. He said, "Katie, I see you. I know the work you are putting in, not only for yourself but also for Chris. And this is only the beginning of what I suppose will be a really tough couple of years for you both, once Chris is discharged.

"But for Chris to get better, he needs to pull his head out of his ass and call out and own his bullshit. He needs to be deliberately honest with no one else but himself, and that is going to take deep internal work. He has allowed his life to become a delusion. He is the only one who cannot see it, and he will need to be the only one who can fix this.

"You didn't cause this. He did. And you won't be able to fix it, no matter how hard you try. This process will help him take a good look in the mirror and become rigorously honest with himself, which will lead to a different, happier life if he surrenders to shame and delusion. I am sorry for the additional pain his family has brought on you, and that is unacceptable, but I am so proud of the grace and forgiveness you have shown. I saw that in our session with Tracy today. Keep it up."

Queue tears and ugly crying. During this time, I didn't get much validation for anything other than it was my fault Chris was addicted, so this was incredibly welcome, to know I wasn't going crazy without reason.

One significant takeaway for me over the weekend came from the breakout sessions for friends, significant others, and family members. While I appreciated the opportunity to engage with others, I couldn't help but feel like something was missing.

On the last day, we had the opportunity to provide constructive feedback on the program, and I suggested what felt glaringly apparent to me: there should be a dedicated breakout group for spouses or partners, not lumped in with parents, siblings, or support people who don't live in the same emotional or physical reality.

Most of the clients enrolled were in their teens or early twenties. The family dynamic leaned heavily toward parents and their dependent children. As a result, nearly all the material, language, and support systems seemed tailored to Mom and Dad, not to a wife preparing to welcome home a grown adult partner with shared bills, a shared bed, and shared trauma.

There was little to no guidance on how to reintegrate after treatment, when you're married to the person coming home. Nothing on how to rebuild intimacy. Nothing on what it's like to live in a house where relapse isn't theoretical, it's personal. I wanted fundamental tools, not just inspiration. I needed an outline, a guide, something to help me prepare for the hard days. For the mess. For the triggers.

What do I do if he relapses?

What words can de-escalate a tense moment instead of igniting it?

How do I honor my boundaries without pushing him further into shame?

These were the questions I had. But they weren't the questions being answered.

I felt less prepared than the moms and dads who attended with their other children. Even Tracy, I could tell, felt unprepared. Though we were both there for Chris, our realities were very different. He wasn't going back to live with her and his stepdad. They saw him a few times a year. I found myself wondering what her biggest takeaways from the weekend were.

Then, just a few days before Chris was supposed to leave for Tennessee, things shifted again. We had a last-minute meeting with Chris, Tracy, Billie, and his primary doctor to discuss the next steps for Chris. These next steps involved reviewing the plan that the intervention team had already put in place. Six months at an all-men's sober living facility. It was presented as if it were a done deal.

But thankfully, this time, I had done the research. I had learned my lesson with the Refuge. I picked up the phone and called the Tennessee program myself, armed with questions to understand their facility and offerings better.

I found out I could visit Chris once a week during family visiting hours, after Chris had been enrolled in the program for a month. I also learned that any money deposited for an individual would be fully refundable, regardless of how close it was to the start date, if the individual decided not to attend at the last minute.

After looking into the Tennessee program himself, Chris's doctor expressed concern. She noticed Chris already had many things in place that the program claimed to help with. Such as finding a job (which he had), saving for a car (which he had), and looking for a place to live when he returned home (which he also had). She was unhappy that the intervention team had enrolled Chris in the program before he'd even arrived at the Refuge, without fully understanding his medical history or consulting with his personal doctors, psychiatrists, therapists, and medical team.

This Tennessee plan came to an abrupt halt when Chris's doctors determined the program could not provide the medical support for his treatment. The program failed to align with the specific aftercare treatment plan Chris required, particularly for Suboxone, which was currently being prescribed and monitored. Also known as *medication-assisted treatment (*MAT*).*

The constant back-and-forth during this time was aggravating. One moment, the Tennessee facility assured us they could fully support Chris's medication management; the next, we received a call from their program director, who stated they did not assist with medication management at all.

Following our meeting with Chris's doctor, I was led into a dimly lit office filled with pamphlets. At the same time, an employee at the Refuge rushed to find an available bed for Chris that would meet his medical needs, since he was scheduled for discharge the following morning. As a result, a new plan emerged: he would enter a partial hospitalization program (PHP) in a sober living community in Florida, rather than the program in Tennessee.

Though I don't remember the exact words exchanged over the phone with the intervention team members, Tracy, and Billie, it was clear they were frustrated with the evolving plan. The Tennessee facility even attempted to persuade Chris's doctors that he didn't need Suboxone and that everything he required could be handled within their sober living program. As you can imagine, tensions increased. Ultimately, the intervention team withdrew further referrals to the Refuge because their original plan wasn't implemented.

After the whirlwind of an afternoon, a bed finally became available, and Chris now had a place to stay for the foreseeable future. It was time to say goodbye. As Chris walked me to my car, I found myself slowing down with each step, apprehensive about getting closer to the door. We climbed into my car, laughing and crying over the events of the past few days, and shared an awkward hug across the middle console.

I couldn't believe I had to say goodbye again, not knowing how long it would be until I would see him or what this new place looked like. Before leaving, we held hands and prayed together, asking for open minds as we entered this next chapter, as well as for Chris's sobriety and my peace of mind.

As I drove away down the long, winding gravel driveway and waited for the gate to open, I glanced in the rearview mirror and saw Chris waving goodbye with a look of uncertainty across his face.

Chapter 13

The Shift

Chris

There was a plan. A whole damn plan, put together by the intervention team and my family without Katie's help or opinion. By the time I had completed the program at the Refuge, my doctors were concerned about this pre-cooked plan, made before reading the directions on the back of my recovery box.

Everyone had ideas about what would be "good for Chris." The idea was that after finishing rehab at the Refuge, I'd head to Tennessee for a long-term, all-men's sober living program. Six months. Structure. Brotherhood. Healing. That kind of thing.

But, plot twist, the Tennessee program didn't offer medication management, and my doctors at the Refuge weren't cool with that. So, the day before I was supposed to leave, everyone scrambled as if it were a fire drill. Suddenly, I was booked at the last minute into some facility in Florida. I had no idea what I was walking into, and neither did anyone else.

So, I showed up at this place, suitcase in hand, heart cautiously optimistic. What I found was... a glorified dorm room. A bunch of teenagers and early twenty-somethings whose biggest life responsibilities were:

1. Don't die
2. Take out the trash (my chore)
3. Go to an AA meeting after sundown

The rest of the day? Fortnite and Mountain Dew. I swear, it was like a halfway house for underage streamers.

I was thirty-three years old. I had a life in Colorado, a career, a car, a wife, and a home. And there I was in a Florida group home, taking out trash bags and watching nineteen-year-olds hack drug tests. The staff was supposed to host bonfires and make dinner. Instead, they were more like invisible camp counselors. So, guess who went grocery shopping and made dinner most nights? Yep, me. The trash man turned Top Chef.

The facility also boasted some "job prep" services. Résumé building, interview coaching, and life-skills workshops. You know, stuff I didn't exactly need. What I needed was peace, structure, support, and a safe place to recover. What I got was noise, teenage drama, and the gnawing feeling I was slipping backward instead of moving forward.

After a week, I called Katie. I was triggered. Not like "ugh, I'm annoyed" triggered. More like "this is dangerous, and I don't trust myself here" triggered. The drugs were around. People were high. The whole thing felt like the blind leading the blind, and I had just enough vision to realize I needed to get the hell out.

And for the first time, we made a decision as a team: to take my control back, as a couple. Screw the noise; we were going to do what *we* thought was best. Katie and I agreed: I needed to come home. But, of course, not everyone clapped.

My family was livid. To them, I was abandoning the plan. To be fair, they were scared. They wanted me well, and to them, Florida was supposed to be the next right step. But to me, staying there felt like gambling with everything I'd just worked for. And that wasn't a risk I was willing to take.

So, I packed up my suitcase and another one I just… found? Look, it was there. Not locked. Not labeled. Don't judge me. I figured, if I was gonna make a dramatic exit, I might as well look like I had options.

Back to Colorado I went. Cue the fallout and the drama. A friend reached out to Katie while I was on my way home, basically accusing her of being manipulative, controlling, and unsupportive. Said she was pulling me away from the "program" and sabotaging my recovery. The rest of the family more or less agreed. Mean things were said. Lines were crossed. And it was bullshit.

Katie had done nothing but support me... More than anyone ever had. She didn't just stand beside me; she *stood up* for me. And I finally stood up with her. It was the first time we stopped letting everyone else dictate what our lives were supposed to look like. It was the first time we said, "No, thank you" to the parade of opinions and reclaimed our power. Not in rebellion. In responsibility.

It wasn't clean. It wasn't easy. But it was ours.

There's this feeling when the plane lifts off and you realize you're not just leaving a place, you're leaving a version of yourself behind. As soon as we were in the air, I felt lighter. Not because I had it all figured out, but because Katie did what Katie always does: she moved mountains while everyone else was arguing over their changed plans.

By the time the wheels hit the ground in Colorado, she had already called (no exaggeration) eight outpatient clinics. *Eight.* And I was enrolled in one before I even picked up my bag. Who does that? Honestly, I was still trying to remember if I'd packed socks.

And this time, for the first time, I wasn't just sober; I was *ready*. Ready to give this clean life a fair shot. Not to impress anyone. Not to tick off some milestone. But because I wanted it. Because we wanted it.

That doesn't mean it wasn't scary as hell.

I was excited, yeah. But there was this weird pressure that came with it, too. Like stepping off that plane meant I was also stepping into a spotlight. Family tensions were high. Opinions were loud. Expectations were louder. It felt like everyone was watching to see if I'd fall on my face or float. And I wasn't sure yet, either.

But then I saw her, Katie, waiting for me at the airport. And all that noise went quiet. I couldn't wait to hug her. I mean, full sprint, emotional airport reunion-level stuff. I half-expected her to be holding one of those cheesy signs. You know the kind: "Welcome

Home from Rehab!" complete with glitter letters and maybe a sad little balloon.

Most people would've assumed it was a joke. I would've laughed. And also... not laugh. It would've been the perfect mix of awkward and true. Which, honestly, kind of sums us up. But she didn't need a sign. Her face said everything. Relief. Love. A little exhaustion. And maybe just a whisper of, "Please don't make me do this part again."

Coming home that day wasn't just a return to a place. It was a return to us. Our mess. Our healing. Our shot. And for the first time in a long time, I believed we actually had one.

Outpatient was... different. For starters, nobody was trying to sneak Xanax in their sock or buy fake pee off some sketchy website to pass a drug test, so already a significant upgrade from Florida. Drinking mouthwash to get a buzz was something only the true rats did in high school. The place Katie found had structure. Real therapists. Group sessions that didn't feel like high school detention. People who actually wanted to be there. Or at least I wanted to be there.

Still, adjusting to everyday life again was a weird kind of whiplash.

There's no guidebook for how to go from, "Hey, I was just in rehab, every meal cooked for me, therapy every day, no life decisions to make, other than what time I was going to put myself to sleep that night," to, "Hi, I'm back at home, taking out the trash, and trying to be a functioning adult." Every interaction felt like it came with a mental asterisk. *Yes, I went to rehab. No, I'm not high right now. Yes, I showered. Please clap.*

The hardest part? Nothing looked different... but everything was.

I was brushing my teeth in the same bathroom. Driving the same car. Sleeping in the same bed. But *I* wasn't the same. And that meant I had to relearn how to live in this life without the crutches I'd relied on for years. There was no numbing, no disappearing into pills or a perfectly curated social persona. Just... me. Sober.

Some days, I felt like I was crushing it—making meetings, meal-prepping, listening to Katie, and setting goals. Other days, I felt like I was one missed call away from unraveling. The shame lingered, too. Like I owed everyone proof that I was serious this time. That I wasn't just on another spin cycle of the addiction and redemption ride.

But Katie never once made me feel broken. She held space for my mess, even while trying to carry her own. She could've thrown the whole relationship out like one of my many rehab-issued suitcases, but she didn't. She stayed. She chose *us*. And that made me want to choose me, too.

Recovery is quiet. It's early mornings with coffee and a journal. It's phone calls you don't want to make. Apologies you don't want to say. Boundaries you don't want to accept. It's sitting in a support group full of strangers and somehow feeling more seen than you did with people who've known you for years.

And it's realizing, repeatedly, that healing isn't linear, but it's possible.

Even in the middle of a mess. Even when your trash chore is over. Even when the glitter rehab sign never shows up. You just keep going. One brutally honest chapter at a time.

Here's the thing they don't always tell you: just because you're not using doesn't mean you're sober. In those first few weeks back, I was clean. I was doing the work, going to outpatient, and hitting meetings. I was checking every box. But something felt off. Like I was going through the motions, but not actually in motion. You know?

I wasn't taking drugs, but I also wasn't really living. I was white-knuckling my way through each day, holding my breath and hoping nobody noticed that I still felt utterly disconnected from myself. That's what they call being *dry*.

Dry is when you're physically sober but emotionally drained. You're not numbing with substances, but you're still running… still hiding. I didn't want to admit it at the time, but I was scared shitless. Afraid to feel anything real. Scared to trust myself. Scared to let Katie back in fully, in case I messed it all up again.

Dry sobriety is like trying to drive with the emergency brake still on. You're moving, but you're burning through energy to stay in place. And eventually, something gives.

The meetings helped. The structure helped. Katie helped. But it wasn't until I started getting honest… like, *really* honest, that things began to shift. I had to stop trying to impress anyone. Had to stop performing "recovery" and actually *live* it.

The truth is, I didn't just need to detox from substances. I needed to detox from shame. From perfectionism. From the constant pressure to prove I was better now. Because sobriety isn't about being better. It's about being real. And that's what I was finally starting to learn.

Coming home wasn't just about recovery, it was also about damage control. While I was gone, my mom had been busy. And not in a helpful, "let's support Chris" kind of way. More like a "let me call every family member and paint my own version of this mess" kind of way.

The version where I was unstable. Where Katie was manipulative. Where everything was being handled wrong. She'd created this wildfire of gossip and speculation, and by the time I got off that plane, I wasn't just stepping into my life; I was stepping into a f***ing PR crisis. If you have ever seen the show or movie *Entourage*, it's the scene where Ari flies a helicopter to a meeting he wasn't invited to, coming to my rescue at this moment.

And the part that gutted me? My little brother. He was living with my mom at the time, along with his wife and their brand-new baby. And he never once called me. Not a single, "Hey, man… What's the real story here?" Not even a text. He just believed her.

That hurt in a way I still don't have words for. It wasn't just about me; it was that no one asked for *my* side. No one fact-checked. They just ran with the narrative that was easiest to digest, even if it wasn't true. Even if it caused more harm. I somehow felt erased.

And maybe the worst part? I couldn't even focus on my own healing, because I was too busy trying to clean up the mess I'd left behind. Trying to explain myself. Trying to protect Katie from the absolute bullshit that people were saying about her, like she was some puppet master behind all my decisions or, worse, the reason I was struggling in the first place. It wasn't just unfair; it was cruel.

She was the one who took the late-night calls. The one who fought for a plan that actually made sense. The one who didn't give up on me when it would've been easier to walk away. And instead of thanking her, my family made her the villain. So yeah, coming home should've felt like a relief. But in many ways, it felt like walking into enemy territory. And all I wanted, more than anything, was to stand in the middle of the room and yell:

"LISTEN TO ME. I'M RIGHT HERE. I'M STILL ME. AND I KNOW I MADE THIS MESS, BUT IT IS MY FAULT! LEAVE KATIE OUT OF THIS!"

But they weren't listening. So, I got quiet. Focused on Katie. On recovery. On our business. On showing up, even when it felt like no one believed in me but her and her family. Because sometimes, the loudest way to speak your truth… is to live it.

Coming home, I had a lot of things going for me on paper: Katie, a house, a job, a car, and a business plan. But inside, I was still trying to catch my breath. Still trying to figure out who the hell I was supposed to be now.

That's when an old high school buddy reached out. He was a few years older than me, someone I'd always respected, a good guy with a solid story who had been through the wringer with addiction and come out the other side. Clean, grounded, and with a good head on his shoulders. He offered to be my sponsor.

And listen, I appreciated it. I really did. But I wasn't ready for the commitment. Not emotionally. Not mentally. Not logistically. I'd just gotten home. I was back at work. Back in my routine. Trying to reenter my own life without tripping over every landmine of guilt, shame, or pressure. The idea of adding nightly check-ins, meetings, and deep talks with an accountability partner? It felt like a lot. Too much. But I didn't say that. I just nodded, smiled, said thank you, and figured we'd feel it out.

Then, one day, he invited me to golf with a few other guys. Sounds simple enough, right? But for me, social stuff was still hard. My nerves were fried. My brain wouldn't stop racing. So, before heading out, I took one of my prescribed anxiety meds. Nothing crazy—just something to take the edge off: a beta blocker. I didn't think anything of it.

But, at some point on the golf course, he looked at me sideways. Asked if I was okay. Said I seemed… off. I brushed it off. Told him I was fine. Laughed it off, even. But later that night, he texted me and said something I'll never forget:

> *Man, I care about you. But I can't stand by you if you're not being honest with yourself.*

That one hit hard.

Because he wasn't wrong. I hadn't "relapsed." But I was still playing it safe. Still keeping parts of myself hidden. Still cherry-picking and choosing which pieces of recovery I was willing to participate in. I wasn't ready to hand over the reins. And that's the truth about this whole process: it's not just about substance abuse. It's about facing yourself.

He didn't ghost me or write me off completely. But the dynamic shifted. And weirdly, I'm grateful for that moment. Because it forced me to ask the harder question: *Am I really all in? Or just trying to look like I am?*

Losing that sponsor felt like my first real failure in recovery. Not because I relapsed. Not because I blew up my life (again). But because I had to admit, for the first time, that I was still full of shit.

I was already hanging on by a thread, trying to keep it together, while Katie and I were building our business from the ground up. Insurance… well, it's actually exactly what you see on TV… An old man fishing with a dollar bill, dangling it in front of you.

So, when I was told, "You need to make this program your life," my immediate response was, "Cool. Do you guys offer vision and dental as part of your health plan? And how much PTO do I get?" Because I was already stretched super-thin as it was. Husband. Business partner. Semi-functional adult. Recovering wreck. The truth was, I didn't want my entire identity to become "that guy in recovery." I wanted it to be a phase. Ya know? Like keto diets, NFTs, and gluten allergies!

But recovery doesn't work that way. It's not something you squeeze into your schedule when it's convenient. It's a whole rewire. And I wasn't ready to give it that much real estate in my brain or my calendar. Plus, I hate plans. Twelve-steps wasn't for me, because I didn't accept my life being "recovery" forever.

I retreated. I backed off and started to pull away. I told myself I was being "strategic," when, really, I was just scared. Scared to admit how much I needed help. Afraid to sit in a room and tell people I wasn't okay. Scared to let go of the version of me that could "figure it out" without anyone noticing I was unraveling. So, yeah, I lost my first sponsor. And with it, a chance to be really honest.

So, the outpatient program? It started to get weird quickly. At first, it felt like they had their shit together. They were all about the group stuff, the community stuff, but then it felt like they were playing some weird mind games with me.

They'd give me my meds for a few days and then say, "Cool. Come back in three or four days, and we'll see where you're at." Which, let's be real, isn't exactly the best foundation for someone who's trying to get sober.

Then, one day, they just stopped doing medication management altogether. It was just, "Here's some community support, but if you need meds? You're on your own." So, I found myself at a methadone/Suboxone clinic, because what's recovery without a little real-world trauma!

The first time I walked into that place, I felt dirty before even stepping inside. They'd give me the dose, I'd wait a bit, and then they'd give me the nod to leave. They were treating you like a very specific flavor of broken. A little too broken for outpatient, but not quite dangerous enough to need a straitjacket. It was an uncomfortable, daily reminder that recovery is more like playing defense than winning the game.

At first, I was there every day. Then, once my urine was clean for a while, I got bumped down to once a week. Progress, right? Except, here's the thing with Suboxone: it's a weird blend of "I'm better" and "I'm still stuck." It didn't feel like recovery; it felt like a Band-Aid on a bullet wound. A weird, chemically-induced limbo where you could still function but never really *feel* like you were living. It was like being dry, but not sober.

I was playing the game, but I felt like I wasn't really winning. So, I decided to take charge of my meds. I went to UC Health to manage everything.

That whole experience was a disaster. No wonder people struggle to recover and still live some version of a life. The entire thing felt like recovery's weird cousin, who shows up at Thanksgiving and tries to sell you Bitcoin while you're trying to avoid a political argument. They were doing their best, but the system was clearly built for someone else.

Slowly, another battle started to creep into the cracks of my foundation. I was struggling in my damn mental battle. I honestly thought the physical battle was going to be the most challenging part of being addicted. But no. I had to have pills on me; I had to have access to them, but I told myself I wasn't planning to take them.

I know, I know. *"Why the hell would you even have them, if you're not going to take them?"* Well, welcome to the mental clusterfuck of addiction. It wasn't about the pills themselves. It was about having them. It was a security blanket. It was the *idea* of control, even if I wasn't actually using them. I wasn't ready to let go of that *what-if* safety net.

I knew it wasn't healthy. But the mental struggle? That was a different beast. And that's when the infamous Detective Katie started snooping around.

Her radar went off, and the *Law & Order* theme song played in the background as she started investigating. I don't know how she did it, but she had a way of getting into my head. She knew something wasn't right. And any time in the future, she would always know when something was off and would catch me.

But in one of those moments, it hit me: I wasn't just trying to get sober; I was trying to convince myself that I was. And I didn't even know how to explain it. I wasn't ready to face the reality that my mental battle was just as dangerous as the physical one.

While all this chaos was unfolding on the outside, I was slowly unraveling on the inside. People think recovery is this journey where you discover your best self on a yoga mat, playing with puppies, on the beach, or while flying a kite. For me, it felt more like running through wet cement while everyone shouted instructions from the sidelines. Katie was still standing beside me. But she was getting quieter.

She was tired. Tired of being "on," tired of wondering if the next discovery would be a bottle cap or a pill or another stupid lie. I could feel her pulling in, shrinking into herself to survive the uncertainty. She wasn't just tired of my addiction; she was tired of being everyone's rock, translator, punching bag, and therapist all at once.

Meanwhile, I was learning just how hard it is to break a habit you've built your life around. I wasn't using, but I wasn't sober, either. There's a difference. I was dry. I still think like an addict. Still trying to outsmart the system. Still looking for something—anything—to take the edge off.

That's when I realized: it's not just about getting clean. It's about learning how to sit in the damn discomfort and not run from it. To recognize that every trigger isn't just physical… It's mental, emotional, and spiritual. And I wasn't equipped yet. Not really.

When you've built a reflex around medicating pain, boredom, fear, or silence, you have to learn how to fill the gaps. With something real. With surrender, but not with submission. That's a line I struggled to define. I didn't want to lose myself. I didn't want to become a shell of a man, walking around reciting recovery slogans like some sober robot. I wanted to fight for my healing and still feel like me.

But I'll be honest: it felt like I couldn't win. The program demanded my full attention. Life demanded everything else. I was trying to help Katie build a business from the ground up, rebuild trust, pay bills, breathe, and sleep, and somewhere in there, I was also supposed to find time to process twenty years of emotional trauma.

It felt like everyone had a playbook for how my recovery should look. Everyone had ideas, rules, timelines, opinions..., especially my family. But no one—not one person—asked what I needed.

Not until Katie finally looked me in the eye and said, "You have to choose what kind of man you want to be. I can't do it for you."

That one landed.

Chapter 14

When the Plan Unravels

Katie

Once I got home, I started planning my month to stay productive and focus on my self-care. I scheduled several therapy sessions, a ketamine treatment, a massage, and a chiropractor appointment. I also made reservations at some restaurants for dinners with my girlfriends.

I was especially excited about a girls' trip to New Orleans at the end of the month, which was finally being organized after lots of discussion and had made its way out of the group chat. I planned to attend a new church in Denver that is a spiritually focused community for people with substance disorders and their loved ones, recommended to me by a friend.

For additional support, I also researched and signed up for various Al-Anon and Nar-Anon meetings, as I hadn't yet found one that suited me, and I was grasping at anything and everything to stay afloat. If you are unfamiliar, Al-Anon is an organization affiliated with Alcoholics Anonymous, specifically for the loved ones and family members affected by those struggling with alcohol addiction. There is also Nar-Anon for loved ones and family members of those struggling with drug/narcotic addiction. The goal of Al-Anon and Nar-Anon is to help people find their own happiness, independent of whether their loved one is drinking or using substances.[6]

Being in a relationship with someone who has an addiction is a choice that comes with the responsibility of understanding what it entails. This support group helped me explore the responsibilities I can control.

I attended three different virtual groups once a week for two months and attended a handful of in-person meetings for one month, both Al-Anon and Nar-Anon groups. There is a time and place for these support groups. I have seen how these groups can serve as an anchor for healing and recovery for loved ones and family members. And if you are feeling alone in your journey with a loved one's addiction and have nowhere to turn, I encourage you to see if it could be a good fit for you! They offer both in-person and virtual meetings at various times throughout the day. For me, though, this did not fill my cup or meet my needs during my journey.

Personally, I felt a negative vibration in every meeting I attended. When everyone went around the circle to share, it often felt like a trauma dump session. Although there is definitely a time and place for that, I would leave the session feeling heavier than when I walked in. There were uplifting moments, and I felt more connected and purposeful when I attended in person than online.

Some of the most valuable takeaways for me were around how to detach with love and the three Cs: I didn't cause it, I can't control it, and I can't change it. Detaching with love can be so painful to do when we see our loved one's potential. They are burning it down over and over, and our gut instinct is to rescue them, but *we* cannot save them.

We need to hold love from a distance and hope to God they find their way through the pain; they are most likely numbing themselves through substances. I know, at times, we think we have the power or control to change them, but they have to do the work themselves. I also believe that having strong support from my friends and family, along with consistently seeing my personal therapist, provided me with a solid foundation to build upon.

It was incredible to see the strength and resilience of those who attended the meetings. This helped me to realize how relatable their experiences were. It made me feel less alone and isolated because they truly understood what I was going through. Occasionally, I stopped discussing Chris and my problems with a few friends, because I felt my struggles were a burden. My path felt too dark for them to see any positive light, especially since they had not personally experienced a loved one struggling with substance abuse. I believe these groups are powerful because they provide a safe space for individuals to share and feel seen.

The following Saturday, I was at my girlfriend's house, celebrating her son's birthday, when my phone vibrated in my back pocket. It was Chris, calling from his sober-living facility in Florida. As I shut the door to an open office, I could tell something was wrong.

Chris had been trying so hard over the last week to remain positive and approach this next step with an open heart and mind. He began to tell me how he was feeling incredibly triggered at the sober living house and didn't know what to do about it.

He described how the past week had felt like the same day repeating itself: he would wake up, eat breakfast, and each guy in the house would handle one chore a day. Chris was to take out the trash. Then, they would wait around until 7:00 p.m. to attend AA/NA meetings.

Some days, they'd sit at the dining room table with the house manager, who would explain how to create a résumé or conduct mock interviews to prepare them for job opportunities. And if they needed a ride to and from work or school, the manager also helped with that.

However, Chris already had a job in Colorado, plus a car and a place he called home, so during this time, he helped the house managers with the younger clients. Mostly, Chris said the residents were teenagers or in their early twenties, spending their days playing video games and secretly doing drugs. They seemed to want to live there to escape their nagging parents.

This was incredibly confusing to me. From what I was hearing, the sober living program presented to us at the Refuge was not at all what Chris was experiencing or what was actually happening. I called the co-founder and operations manager to ask why they thought Chris was a good fit for this program. I explained that the program didn't resemble anything outlined in the pamphlet from the Refuge or what we had discussed over the phone.

There were no weekly campfires on the beach, and there were no adventure-based activities to build community with peers, outside of video games. Chris would go to the grocery store himself during the day and make dinner for everyone each night, paying for his own groceries. After I made that call, the managers seemed to get in trouble for not doing their jobs.

Ultimately, Chris and I made our first decision as a couple regarding his recovery: we both agreed he should come home as long as he immediately enrolled in an outpatient program. While he spoke with the property manager and his family, I began calling intensive outpatient programs to determine whether they accepted our insurance and had any available slots. After four hours and over eight calls, I was starting to feel defeated, but I finally found a place called Continuum Recovery that had availability!

Their program offered on-site psychiatry, EMDR therapy, one-on-one therapy, family therapy, and group therapy sessions multiple times a week. They worked through the Twelve Steps and taught coping strategies for stress and negative emotions, as well as educational workshops on life skills, healthy eating, and stress management. They also had prevention groups to help identify triggers and temptations that could lead to a slip-up, along with strategies to avoid these situations and ensure Chris stayed on track. And the cherry on top was that they would assist him with his medication management.[7]

The people involved in the original intervention plan and process would support this decision for Chris. However, it quickly became clear this was not the case. The situation was harmful, and the new plan caused significant drama and strong opinions from others.

Some people claimed to have our backs, saying they only wanted what was best for Chris. They asked us to let them know if there was anything they could do to help. However, one friend sent me a hurtful text, strongly opposing Chris coming home at this point and criticizing those who might influence him to do so. They accused me of being selfish, manipulative, and unwell, suggesting I was contributing to Chris's struggles. Additionally, a family member labeled me an addict and insisted I was choosing a risky path for Chris, indicating that I needed help. Oh, I'm sorry—did my support not come with a brochure you approved?

I received information that a family member was going around, spreading personal stories about my parents and sisters from our past, claiming that our home was unsafe. Additionally, there were rumors that Chris was stealing medicine from my parents, which was completely untrue.

I reached out to James from the intervention team for some insight, but I learned they could no longer work with us due to an issue that had arisen between Tracy and them. I was also informed that I could no longer contact them. This news was a huge blow, especially since James and I had developed a close relationship, and I'd appreciated having someone to consult when I was feeling overwhelmed or needed advice. I was especially looking forward to their help when Chris eventually came home, as well.

The comments and rumors being spread were unwarranted, unwelcome, cruel, and entirely baseless. My family finally reached a breaking point, and my older sister, Ashley, came to my aid by sending a text to one of Chris's family members that read:

> *I am going to do my best to keep this cordial. But you and your family need to start keeping your comments, thoughts, and opinions to yourselves. The way you are treating my family, my sister, and Chris is utterly disgusting and, quite frankly, is defamation! Unfortunately, yes, my family has a*

history of mental illness... but if you had ever taken a step back and simply talked to ANY of us, you would know that we all go to therapy and are on the necessary medications.

Not one of us has an addictive personality, nor do ANY of us have or ever have had a drug problem! Continuing to say to ANYONE that my sister is ill or has a drug problem is defamation, and you clearly don't know her AT ALL! I love your son with all of my heart, but his addiction is because of past traumas and surgeries, where meds were not controlled properly, not because of Katie. HE brought those drugs into their home, not Katie, and HE has accepted and owned up to that and has done an incredible amount of work over the last 45 days! None of which you have ever praised or given support for.

I saw who you truly are the night we were on that Zoom, and you put Chris's call on speaker for everyone to hear. You are the one with a problem, not my sister, and I sincerely hope you have taken this time and sought a therapist because you have a lot you need to work through. You have used Chris's situation as a means of control and not as a way to help and support him.

I would again take a step back and listen to what Chris is trying to tell you, and you would know the facility he is in now is not a continuation of what the Refuge was and is not the continued help and support he needs! Katie and Chris have done a lot of research and have found an incredible intensive outpatient program where Chris will have the support, therapy, and medication management that he needs. Chris wants you in his life, but if you continue to treat him and his wife the way you are, I promise you, you will lose him permanently.

I am kindly asking you to please be courteous and respectful to my family, especially Katie. She has done nothing but unconditionally love Chris and your family. But please keep your mouth shut, or we will be looking into ways to help you do that.

Mic drop.

I can't begin to express how much I needed this validation, and I didn't even know I was looking for it. After months of betrayal, heartbreak, and isolation, I finally felt something shift. I felt seen. Protected. I thought, thank goodness I wasn't the only one walking through this darkness.

The truth is, there are no detailed instructions for recovery. There is no perfect roadmap, no step-by-step guide, and no one-size-fits-all option. It's great when something like the Twelve-step program works for someone, and I think it does for many. But for us, the journey wasn't linear. And yet, from the outside, it seemed that Chris's family and a handful of close friends believed there was only one acceptable path to recovery, rigidly defined by the intervention team, with little room for questions or deviation.

So, when that initial plan began to unravel—as plans often do—there was no grace. No flexibility. Instead of being welcomed home with open arms, Chris was met with suspicion, disappointment, and judgment. Guarded hearts. Blame. And a silence that spoke louder than words. That hurt more than I'd expected.

While he was trying to rebuild himself from the inside out, the people who claimed to love him the most were still holding onto a version of him that no longer existed or, worse, refusing to believe he could change at all.

Do you think there's only one path to recovery?

I firmly believe there is no "correct" way or single route to recovery. It's okay if the original plan changes, as long as the intention remains the same: Chris wants to improve for himself, not for others. Unfortunately, by this point, the smear campaign had been successful; the ongoing malicious gossip had become toxic. I eventually accepted that I would always be the scapegoat in their eyes, and there was nothing I could do to change that.

Instead of coming home to focus on healing, Chris found himself consumed by damage control, trying to manage a crafted narrative, navigate whispered judgments, and explain himself in a world that had already made up its mind. It was exhausting. What he needed was space to release the toxic patterns that had contributed to years of pain, buried shame, and unhealed trauma. And somehow, even in the middle of that chaos, he created something for me that I hadn't expected... Safety. A sense of being heard, protected, and deeply loved. By standing up for me, his wife. Chris unknowingly began to break the very cycles that had shaped his life for years.

Together, we learned to set boundaries. Real ones. Not to punish, but to protect. We prioritized emotional well-being over outdated loyalties that had become one-sided and conditional. And in doing so, we were slowly ostracized from parts of Chris's family, from the people we thought would celebrate his growth and our survival through this confusing time. When a group of people bond over gossip, triangulation happens, toxic meets toxic. Sides are drawn, and the truth becomes distorted. The worse Chris and I looked, the better some felt in their own reflection. There was a ton of finger-pointing, and the energy it took to defend ourselves became too heavy to carry.

So, we asked ourselves: Do we continue to suffer? Or do we make the difficult choice to cut toxicity out of our lives—no matter where it comes from?

I realized I was burning myself out, trying to belong in a space that didn't make room for me. I kept showing up with olive branches, only to feel pricked by thorns. So, I started to pull back, not out of spite, but out of survival. I stopped explaining myself, I stopped justifying my every move, and I stopped trying to prove that I loved Chris enough, had fought hard enough. I stopped following "the right" plan.

Creating emotional distance wasn't easy. It felt like admitting defeat, like walking away from a bridge I'd spent years trying to build. But I had to protect my peace, my sanity, and the fragile foundation of my own healing. I couldn't keep absorbing other people's fear and grief on top of my own.

The truth is, I was grieving, too. Grieving the life we'd had before addiction took root. Grieving the version of family I had hoped to be part of. But I couldn't keep grieving in a house where I wasn't allowed to speak the truth.

So, I stepped back. Quietly and intentionally. Not to create drama, but to make space for myself and for Chris. For what we were trying to build, without all the noise. And in that space, I found relief.

The pressure to perform, to please, and to mend what I didn't break, it all began to lift. I finally gained the clarity to focus on *our* healing, rather than everyone else's expectations of it. I still held compassion. But I also held a boundary. And sometimes, that is the most loving thing you can do.

Chris also began setting his own boundaries. He spoke plainly and bravely, saying, "This is what I need from you—an apology to Katie. This has hurt my feelings. This is unacceptable." Crickets.

Instead of being met with understanding, Chris was discredited and dismissed. A handful of people chose not to grow. There's no sugarcoating this part of the journey. Breaking free is brutal, and it felt impossible at times. However, we knew we couldn't stay in a cycle that kept us dysregulated in our systems due to the stress and the doubt that crept in as we stood in our truth. Distancing ourselves from toxic family and friends was one of the most painful decisions we've ever made, but the freedom on the other side is priceless. From that place of freedom, we finally began building *our* lives, the ones we wanted, not the ones others expected of us.

I believe Chris learned to hide his struggles at a young age. Struggling with unmedicated ADHD, he learned to mask and overcompensate, which led him to shut down entirely. Through therapy, it's come up that his father was emotionally unavailable while he was growing up, and his mother relied on him heavily for emotional support, placing responsibility on him that he wasn't prepared for. Chris's needs went unnoticed, and he wasn't given space to be a child. Instead, he overexerted himself. He became the kid who fixed everything around him, not because he wanted to, but because someone had to carry the weight.

But because he was only valued for what he did, not for who he was, he carried a deep shame. Shame for the things he forgot, shame for the ways he struggled, shame for feeling like he was never enough. His brain worked differently, and the adults around him made him feel broken. Now, as an adult, that shame still follows him.

When I ask for help, he hears "You aren't doing enough." When his job demands more structure, he hears, "You are incapable." When our life becomes overwhelming, he hears, "You will never get it together or keep up." So, he reacts, gets defensive, and shuts down.

He has spent most of his life trying to keep up and prove himself, fighting his brain against a world that expects so much from him. Now, he is exhausted, trying his best to be present for me, and he almost kills himself to take care of us. But he doesn't know how to slow down without feeling like he is failing.

Chris is now working toward learning how to heal his inner child, since he's carried his own pain far too long without anyone noticing his struggles. He is beginning to understand that his past struggles with drugs don't define him. That he is not broken. It's okay to feel sad or angry, and he is allowed to throw himself a pity party every now and then. That doesn't make him weak. It makes him human.

He, like everyone else, is working to unlearn the shame that's been stitched to him since childhood and to learn to replace it with something softer, like compassion. The right support system isn't just a luxury or helpful; it is crucial for survival. Men, specifically, I think, learn at a young age to tell themselves to get over it, move on, suck it up, or just be grateful. And the result is that they don't feel safe telling people they aren't okay and need help before it's too late.

And to be honest, I think Chris's recovery got more complicated when some family members and some friends decided to define what they thought sobriety should look like for him. They created new expectations, new rules, and new versions of what they'd heard was the "right" path, without fully acknowledging their own unresolved pain or personal demons. And let's be real for a second: *WE ALL STRUGGLE.* We all carry something we are still trying to come to terms with. Chris's addiction was just more visible and aired out for all to see.

Before Chris came home, my mom and I bought and scoured every book we could find on addiction. We read everything, from guides on what to expect when a loved one returns home from treatment to books on codependency, trauma, and the tangled relationship between the two. But as the stack on our kitchen table grew, so did our realization: something was missing.

Few, if any, of these books captured both sides of the story, the recovering addict's journey *and* the emotional rollercoaster of their loved ones' ride alongside them. We flipped through the books in search of answers, guidance, and hope. Instead, we found fragmented information and tried to put together our own path without the intervention team's help or support from Chris's family and select friends.

I couldn't have guessed in a million years that Chris and I would one day become the story we'd been searching for, a book that spoke to that very journey. But at the time, we were just two people trying to find our way back to each other through the fog of everything that had happened. As my mom and I read through the pages, trying to prepare ourselves for what was coming, the weight of uncertainty settled in. Chris was coming home, and we had no idea what that would really mean or entail.

Chris's flight landed late on an April spring evening, and I was giddy with anticipation of seeing him come up on the escalators. I debated making a glitter sign to hold. It was because I didn't trust myself not to use the glitter to write something slightly inappropriate. Like: *"Congrats on Not Dying—Welcome Home From Rehab."*

Yeah… I knew better.

But when I saw him walking toward me, rolling that busted-ass suitcase that wasn't even his, I didn't need a sign. I needed a deep breath. Because this was it. We had made the call. Not the intervention team. Not his family. Not the rehab staff. Us.

And that was the first moment when I felt like we'd taken our power back.

I knew people were mad. I knew they were talking about me behind my back, saying I was controlling or manipulative or somehow sabotaging his recovery.

But I wasn't going to apologize for trusting my gut. Or for choosing a plan that actually felt human instead of punitive. The system wanted him to disappear into another six-month boot camp. I wanted him to come home, be seen, be supported, and try. Really try.

And that's what he did.

He showed up.

So no, I didn't have a sign. But I had open arms. A stocked fridge. A therapy schedule color-coded like a damn war plan. And most importantly, I had his back, even if the rest of the world was ready to write him off.

Because real recovery doesn't come with a hashtag or a thirty-day certificate.

It comes with trash duty, early mornings, messy fights, quiet wins, and loving someone enough to say, "Let's figure this out together."

Even when you're both still figuring yourselves out.

The moment I saw his blue-ball-capped head pop up, I ran through the line of people patiently waiting behind the marked boundary, ducked below the rope, and jumped into his arms. Once he grabbed his luggage, we headed to the car, with Lexi popping her head up once she heard his voice. I thought her tail was going to break the window out of excitement at not seeing her dad for over two months. He was finally home.

I felt a mix of nervousness, happiness, and fear for apparent reasons. The Chris I knew when he left was struggling in active addiction, and now I was welcoming a new Chris who was navigating the challenges of sobriety. He had worked incredibly hard over the past two months to achieve this new mindset, and I couldn't be prouder of him. I hoped to see growth in his confidence and for him to fall back in love with himself and his life. If anyone deserves that, it's Chris.

But what I thought was the end of troubles was only the beginning. Before Chris came home, I was introduced to someone a few years older than me who attended our same high school. He had a history of addiction, but was on a healthy and happy path to recovery. He offered to be Chris's sponsor, and I was thrilled! However, since Chris returned home earlier than expected, we were adjusting to our new reality while I faced the packed calendar I had scheduled before, not knowing he'd be home so soon.

I was hesitant about going to New Orleans for Jazz Fest with my eight girlfriends, but after Chris encouraged me and I noticed the dark circles under my eyes, along with what felt like a permanent trail of salt from crying so much, I decided to go. I later wished I hadn't.

Chris went golfing with his new sponsor and mutual friends over the long weekend I was gone, and I could tell by the way he was talking on the phone that he seemed off. I asked if he was okay, and he said yes and to stop worrying. I remember getting a text from his sponsor saying he couldn't support or stand by Chris if he wasn't going to be honest with himself or him. Chris was telling me one thing, and his sponsor was saying another, and I was once again in the land of uncertainty and delusion and deceit. I didn't know what to believe.

Doubt crept in. Why did it feel like every decision I made was either the wrong one or immediately met with resistance? Maybe I was still enabling him... being too involved, too hopeful, and too scared to let go. I had tried to pull Chris out of one unhealthy, triggering environment, thinking a change of scenery might help. But in the end, it didn't matter whether he came home too soon or six months later. If he wasn't ready to get clean for himself, nothing I did could change that.

Recovery—real, lasting recovery—requires a brutal, radical honesty with oneself. A willingness to look in the mirror and face everything you've been running from. And during that time, I don't think Chris was there yet.

Do I wish I had known that sooner? Absolutely.

One of the ways I tried to support Chris when he came home was by consistently reminding him (sometimes quietly, sometimes out loud) that I knew he was doing his best. This reassurance mattered, especially when things were uncertain.

One of my personal struggles has always been managing expectations, and during this time, I made a real effort to offer Chris grace. I gave him the space to grow into this new version of himself, even though I didn't know what that would look like or how long it would take. We were slow to return to work. Every hour felt crucial financially, but we did our best to ease into it. We understood the pressure from bills, responsibilities, and the life we had temporarily set aside, and I knew rushing wouldn't help and would only make him feel overwhelmed.

Recovery does not happen on our timeline; it follows its own stubborn, uneven pace. And if anyone knows about stubbornness, it's me. If you're reading this and waiting for someone to come home, please give the Adrift time. The process is slow. It's long. And the version of those who return might not match the one you remember.

They may still be experiencing post-acute withdrawal or struggling with anhedonia, that emotional flatness where joy feels out of reach. They might seem distant, unmotivated, or disconnected from the world around them. But please don't mistake that for failure. They're not broken; they're healing. And healing can be quiet, awkward, and messy before it even appears to be strength.

There is a lot of talk about tough love in the world of recovery. And while I understand the place it can hold, especially when boundaries are being crossed or safety is at risk, I don't believe it should be love that doesn't try to fix or force. Instead, it's passion that simply stays and supports. From personal experience with my family, I have found massive personal growth when there is a presence that says, "I see you. I'm not here to rescue you or judge you, but I am here with you, while you find your way back."

There is a difference between supporting someone and saving them. I used to think I had to do both. That, if I just loved him enough, showed up enough, and carried the heavy load for him long enough, he would finally be okay. But I learned healing isn't something you can do for someone. You can't outrun their rock bottom or rewrite their recovery path, or decide there is only one path to recovery.

But you can walk beside them without trying to steer. You can be the steady place to land when everything feels chaotic. Sometimes, love is just not giving up on them. Try cheering quietly from the sidelines, ready to welcome and encourage, not rescue or control.

They are also learning to face emotions they've avoided for years, perhaps even decades. And they are doing this without the only coping mechanism they've ever known. That's terrifying and brave. They are genuinely trying their best. The first few weeks after Chris came home were quiet in a way that didn't feel peaceful. We were both tiptoeing around each other, me unsure of what version of him I'd encounter each day, and him uncertain of who he was supposed to be now.

There were good days, don't get me wrong. Days when I caught a glimpse of the old Chris, with the quick wit, the way he made me laugh unexpectedly, the spark in his eyes. But those moments were fleeting, often followed by exhaustion, irritability, or complete emotional withdrawal. I tried to remain calm and be the steady one.

However, I was grieving, too. Grieving the version of him I'd lost, the version of us I didn't know how to regain.

I had been holding it together for so long through the chaos, the lies, and the silence that, when things finally quieted down, all the emotions I had been suppressing surged to the surface. I had to swallow my urge to control, to overfocus, to obsess, and to overcorrect. Communication was challenging. He didn't always have the words, and I didn't always have the patience. I was learning, too. Learning when to speak up, when to let things go, and when to take a walk to breathe instead of trying to fix something that wasn't mine to fix.

Recovery isn't just for the addict; it touches everyone who loves them, and we need time to recover as well. Looking back, one of the best things we did was allow space—not just physical space, but emotional room for both of us to feel what we were experiencing without judgment or the urge to rush in and make it better. Some days, that looked like making dinner in silence. On other days, it involved falling apart in the middle of the kitchen, sitting on the red rug I made him buy me at Home Depot. We didn't know how to navigate this, and no one had written the rulebook for us to carefully follow like a recipe, trying to avoid a cooking disaster or, in this case, a relapse.

Chapter 15

Dialysis and Denial

Chris

The First Collapse

A few months later, I woke up one summer morning and couldn't breathe.

Not like being out of breath from running or from allergies. I'm talking full-blown elephant-sitting-on-your-chest kind of shit. My body was heavy, my brain was foggy, and I had the kind of exhaustion that no nap or Red Bull could fix.

"Katie," I muttered, trying to sound casual, not like I was actively dying, "I don't feel right. My breathing's weird. I've been super-tired the past couple of days."

I left out a *tiny* detail: I'd taken something I shouldn't have the night before.

The next thing I knew, a paramedic and firefighter team were in our bedroom. After asking me a million and one questions, they helped me slowly down the steep stairs and into the ambulance to take my vitals. Once they got everything strapped to me, they could see my oxygen was extremely low and said I needed to go to the hospital. My anxiety began to skyrocket. I asked if they could give me something for my nerves, and luckily, they did.

The ambulance ride to Parker Adventist was a blur. I remember flashing lights and shame creeping in, even though I was still clinging to the story that this was all just a weird reaction to something. Yeah, that sounded plausible. But deep down, in the corners of my brain where I try to avoid what I know, I *knew* I'd taken something I shouldn't have. And I was holding onto that secret like it was a goddamn life raft, except it was actually sinking me.

Once I was in the ER, I remember feeling like there was a disconnect from my body, and I was somewhere else entirely… floating above it all, trying to piece together what the hell was happening. Someone shouted my name. I think it was Katie. Or maybe a nurse. Or maybe God, but they sounded really worried.

My hands were shaking, but I couldn't tell if I was cold or just scared.

I heard "ammonia." I heard "liver failure." I heard "he's not stable… ICU." It felt like my brain was underwater, and everything sounded slow, stretched, like it had to travel through multiple doors before it got to me.

I remember looking over and seeing Katie sitting next to me. Her hands were clenched together in her lap, barely holding herself together. Her eyes were wide and red, scanning the monitors, then flicking back to me. She wasn't crying, but she looked worried. Like she was stuck in a nightmare and couldn't scream.

I wanted to say something… anything, to reassure her. "I'm okay," maybe. Or, "It's not that bad." But my mouth wouldn't cooperate, and neither would my brain. The words got stuck somewhere between the thought and my inability to move my mouth.

Everything around me was spinning slowly, like I was on a carousel. Nurses moved in and out of the room. Machines beeped, and the lights were too bright, then too dim. Someone kept asking me questions, but they all sounded like riddles. Like them asking me who was the president of the United States, like, duh, it's Obama, you dumb ass. (Was, in fact, Biden.) I looked back at Katie again. Her image blurred as though my eyes couldn't keep up. My eyelids felt heavy, starting to close without my permission.

What was happening? Nothing made sense. I didn't know where I was. I didn't know how I'd gotten there. I was in my body but not in control of it, and I felt like I was drowning. And beneath it all was this sense of dread. The knowing that I'd taken something I shouldn't have. That this might be my fault. That Katie was watching me die, and I couldn't even say I was sorry, and that I loved her.

So, I closed my eyes because it was easier than holding her gaze. The hospital stay was not ideal: liver failure, sepsis, and pneumonia. Triple threat. At one point, I woke up restrained, ankles and wrists bound to like some kind of fucked-up magic trick (and not in a good way). I was literally anchored to the bed, because I kept trying to rip out my IVs. Apparently, near-death me is not a chill guy. My body didn't belong to me anymore. It belonged to the many IV bags dripping whatever needed to be absorbed into my body. And somewhere beneath all of it, I still held onto the lie.

I still kept drifting in and out, half-conscious, catching snippets of conversations that made me feel like a burden, a disappointment. You haven't truly hit a low until your wife and your mom are fighting over your hospital bed while you're hallucinating. I remember my dad coming at some point, with his much-needed laugh to break the heaviness of the day and the restraints.

Finally, I was getting better, and I was downgraded to the general hospital. The doctors were still baffled as to what had caused this officially, but they said there was a liver virus going around, especially in children. I wish I could say that was the moment I broke down and told the truth. But the truth is, I stayed quiet. I let everyone believe the liver-bug story. I didn't reveal to anyone that I had taken a benzodiazepine, and it was covered up on my toxicity report when the ambulance administered Ativan.

No one gives you a manual when you leave rehab. You get a graduation date, a plastic bag with pharmacy labels, and a pep talk about "keeping it simple." I walked in with two prescriptions—one of which I shouldn't have been taking—and walked out with nearly fifteen. Fifteen new ways to sleep, wake, breathe, stabilize, and not feel. Fifteen potential collisions.

No one sat me down and said, "Here's what happens when Suboxone meets a benzodiazepine. Here's why even Benadryl mixed with buprenorphine can quietly turn your breathing into a coin flip."

Looking back, that secret about taking a benzo was heavier than the restraints. Shame has a way of doing that. It doesn't just anchor you; it buries you. I didn't tell Katie. I didn't tell the doctors. I convinced myself it didn't count if no one knew.

The Second Collapse

Mexico was supposed to be a break. A reset. Some sun, some beach, some pretending we were okay. While Katie was at the spa, I walked into a pharmacy and asked a stranger in a white coat to bless my rationalization. Tramadol, he said, "Kind of like an ibuprofen, señor." A diet painkiller.

And I believed him, because I wanted to. There's no such thing as diet heroin. There's only the part of you that wants an off-ramp and the sales pitch that hands you the exit sign.

A few days later, after arriving home from our trip, I took one. It wasn't some significant moment. It was casual. Mindless. I opened that bottle of hell.

I woke up (if you can call it that) on the floor at 4:00 a.m., with Katie crouched next to me. Her voice cut through the fog—steady, frantic, loving, exhausted, but her movements were steady. I couldn't feel my hands. They were completely numb, like they didn't belong to me anymore. My breath came in shallow stabs. My brain kept short-circuiting—filled with panic—then went blank. Panic, then blank.

The paramedics came. Again. I heard them say things like, "His vitals are unstable." They strapped me to a gurney, and off I went in another siren-blasting ambulance. Everything after this point is a haze. Information and my surroundings came in and out in little chunks of time. I heard a voice, almost like a whisper saying, "Stay strong, babe... They said I barely got you here in time... Keep fighting."

Everything buzzed. Not like a sound, but like a feeling, like my body had turned into a drifting balloon. I remember being sweaty, but freezing. I could hear machines beeping. Someone called my name... I think.

Then hands—so many hands—lifting, attaching, inserting. Tubes. A mask. Plastic pressed against my face, blowing air so hard and fast down my throat and nose. I remember wanting to swat it away, but I couldn't lift an arm. I didn't understand what was happening; I just knew it felt like I was suffocating while surrounded by people trying to save me. I was just there, trapped inside myself. Time felt endless, like maybe I'd been there for minutes or maybe it had been hours. I didn't know. Couldn't say.

Katie's voice... was she next to me? Or just in my head? She said my name like it hurt her to say it. Like she wasn't sure if I could hear her or if it even mattered anymore. Or maybe it was a dream. Perhaps I imagined her face, because I couldn't bear the thought of her not being there. Words floated around me, I couldn't connect:

Sepsis. Kidney. Liver. Pneumonia. Organ failure. Unresponsive.

I wasn't in my body anymore. I was hovering just above it, watching the collapse in slow motion, too tired to scream and too ashamed to speak.

Later, they explained it. Suboxone (buprenorphine) was doing its job—holding the door against the worst of the cravings. Then, I'd paired it with a central-nervous-system depressant the first time and with Tramadol the second—an "almost-opioid" with serotonin tricks. Mix that with buprenorphine and you get a silent suffocation called hypercapnia. Your lungs trade oxygen for carbon dioxide, and you begin to drown without water.

No one had told me how lethal those combinations could be—not a doctor, not a nurse, not the profusion of pharmacy labels stacked like trading cards in my bathroom drawer. We found out after I almost died. Twice.

I was in the ICU for five days. At least, that's what they told me. Time didn't exist there. I don't remember much. Just flashes. Foggy little windows that opened and closed quickly and slowly at the same time.

At one point, I swear my niece was there, sitting on my knee. I was bouncing her, smiling, entirely sure it was real. Was she ever even there?

The ammonia in my blood was poisoning my brain, turning reality into a dream. I couldn't tell what was memory or what was hallucination.

After the ICU, they moved me to the general hospital. The confusion didn't go away; it just changed.

One time, I looked across the room and saw a red balloon floating by the window. Gently bobbing like it had somewhere to be. But when I blinked, it wasn't a balloon. It was my late grandfather. Or at least I thought it was. Standing there, quietly watching me, not judging, just… waiting. Like he knew something I didn't.

(I was very close to my grandfather, who'd passed away a couple of years before this. It wasn't like a dream, and it wasn't like a hallucination... It felt like he was there to take me somewhere or tell me something important.)

I wish I could say these moments woke me up. Even in a hospital bed, hallucinating, I was trying to make sense of a life I hadn't yet decided to live fully. You'd think the gravity of my situation would've sunk in. It didn't.

On the floor unit, I turned petty rebellions into ritual. I started stealing drinks from the nurse's station. Like, a lot of drinks. Gatorade, apple juices, whatever I could get my hands on. I also hoarded Jell-O like it was currency. Red was my favorite. Here's the kicker: I wasn't even *supposed* to be drinking fluids. My kidneys weren't turned back on yet. Every sip was basically me flipping off their medical advice with a bendy straw.

Some of it was impulse, some of it was boredom, but most of it was denial. Like, "There is no way my organs are shutting down, and I need to stay hydrated."

I was not ready to face the truth, so I found ways to rebel against the idea that my body had shut down. For some people, it's sneaking out of the house. For me, it was hoarding apple juice. But in those moments, it gave me control. And when your body is failing and your dignity's been checked, with your ass hanging out of your gown, sometimes you reach for whatever scraps of freedom you can find. Even if it's Jell-O.

October 21 felt like the day my story stopped being a bad dream and became a reality. I was faking urine output with a jug—yes, that low—convincing myself and trying to convince the nurses my kidneys were waking up. That's how deep I was in the bullshit—so committed to the lie, I almost convinced myself it was working.

I don't remember the exact words the doctor used, but I remember it felt like someone had throat-punched me, and I couldn't get air. The room was getting smaller.

Permanent port.

Dialysis.

Kidney hasn't turned back on.

I wanted Katie there, but I was also relieved she wasn't. Kay, my mother-in-law, was in the chair, asking the questions I couldn't hold in my head.

This was the first time I let the full math in: I had nearly died twice, and the bill was coming due. I remember this moment like a scene from a movie. My doctor was such a kindhearted guy, and he did not want to give me this news.

One of the only questions I was able to muster was, "So, what do I do now?"

His face said everything before his words solidified my sentence. "Well, we can get you onto a donor list right away…"

I stopped him. "So, am I going to die from this?"

He looked at me through his glasses and didn't break eye contact as he calmly said, "Not today. And hope is your best medicine right now."

My mother-in-law, being a retired nurse, had already seen this writing on the wall, and she knew the medical facts as they were. I would be on dialysis for the foreseeable future, and ultimately, I would need a lifesaving transplant in a matter of single-digit years, if my kidneys didn't turn back on. Unfortunately for her, she was the one who had to witness me, as I initially came to understand my fate.

I have never experienced a heavier moment. My life flashed before my eyes, not on the brink of death, but on the edge of barely existing. I had lived my life to the fullest and was so fortunate to have experienced all that I had. But just like that, I had replaced all those beautiful memories with this image of me dying in a chair.

My first intentional thought went to Katie. If this was going to be my ending, I wasn't about to let it be hers.

Let me say this plainly. When I left rehab, I had fifteen prescriptions. Fifteen chemical levers for my brain and body, each with its own fine print and hidden trapdoor. I don't blame anyone; I blame the blueprint. There's a gap between acute care and actual life where education should live. No one said, "Benadryl—yes, over-the-counter Benadryl—plus Suboxone can slow your breathing into a dangerous lull."

No one warned us that anxiety meds in the ambulance could mask the origin story of a respiratory crash. We were undereducated, overmedicated, and very politely congratulated. A whole year passed before a doctor finally looked at my chart and asked out loud what no one had asked: "Why is he still on all of this?"

Later, when Katie walked into the room, sore from taking a back injection, I couldn't even meet her eyes. I knew she saw right through me, through the fear and the deflection and the unknown. She always did. I didn't have words, so we just sat in silence.

That night, she curled up on my hospital bed, quietly trying to be supportive. I heard the beat of Taylor Swift's new album in her earbuds, something familiar in a moment when everything felt like it was unraveling. And even though I couldn't say it then, I'll say it now: I was scared shitless. I was cracked open.

The next day, I had to get the permanent port in my neck, and I asked for no sedation. I felt like I had earned something. Like a badge. Like I could at least say, "Yeah, I'm falling apart, but I took that like a champ."

It was stupid, honestly. I think I was trying to prove I still had some control over something. Anything. Plus, this was the first time in a while that I was adamant about not being given drugs to relieve pain.

Then came the lengthy list of rules. The diet. The fluids. The annoying changes. Melissa, our case manager, was like a coach preparing us for a marathon I'd never signed up for. And my RN broke down the math of what I could eat and drink like it was nuclear code. But here's the truth: I didn't give a shit. Not really. Not then.

I started sneaking more drinks from the community fridge and stashing them in the cabinets, as if they were my rations for survival. Was I supposed to be restricting fluids? Absolutely. Did I care? Not enough. Katie would find my stashes and sigh. Sometimes, she laughed. Sometimes, she cried. Sometimes, she just walked out, because I think, if she didn't, she might've thrown a ginger ale at my head.

Katie carried the weight of my body and then the weight of the room it occupied. She learned to pack hospital bags with grace and humor: chargers, ChapStick, gum, boundaries. She played Taylor Swift in one ear while the other listened for monitor alarms. She said less as it got harder, because language frays when you use it too much on the same wound. She also laughed at the wrong time with me, which is to say the right time. She didn't make me a project; she kept me a person.

Eventually, she started leaving the hospital in the evenings to keep herself sane and let my family take over. That's when I really pushed the envelope.

One night, my family snuck in a BLT my mom had made—mayo, mustard, and crispy bacon. I ate it like it was my last meal. Honestly, it might've tasted better than anything I'd eaten in months. I wasn't supposed to have it since it had too much sodium, phosphorus, potassium... Basically, everything I was told could kill me. But at that moment, I didn't care.

The next morning, a nurse chewed Katie out, as she thought she had personally made the bacon. I felt awful. Not because I ate it—I still don't really regret the sandwich—but because I put her in that position. Again.

She tried to make light of it in the family group text, something like, "*Believe me, a BLT is my favorite sandwich, too, but his body can't even handle that right now.*" Classic Katie, trying to be funny and gentle at the same time. But it didn't land. Things exploded.

A few nights later, something else happened. I won't get into the details, but someone visited me and tried to record our conversation. It got so heated that Katie had to involve security. One of my family members was not allowed to come back to see me.

Thirteen days. That's how long I was trapped in that hospital room, wired to machines, poked at, and pumped full of things. So, when the nurse told us a chair had finally opened up at a dialysis center and I'd be discharged the next morning, it didn't feel real. But the next thing I knew, Katie was stuffing hospital belongings into bags so fast, it felt like we were escaping a crime scene.

The air outside that night felt amazing. It was oxygen that didn't smell like antiseptic and Jello. We didn't talk much on the ride home, and we didn't have to. For the first time in weeks, no machines were beeping, no doctors with grave news. Just me, Katie, and silence.

But the second we walked into our apartment, everything came rushing back. The denial, the near-death moments, and the weight of what I had put her and my body through. I wanted a shower. Just something normal. Something human. But nothing was normal anymore.

At the apartment, I peeled off my shirt and watched Katie freeze at the sight of my bruises and the tunneled line sewn into my neck. We had a reality check.

She looked at me with those glassy eyes and whispered, "I'm so sorry. This is so scary."

And it was. It really fucking was. We slid to the floor. We cried the kind of tears you don't have language for—grief, shame, relief, terror, all sharing a glass.

We fell onto the floor and cried like we had both been holding our breath for weeks. Because we had. I didn't know how much weight I was carrying until I finally let it hit the floor beside us. Eventually, we got up. Katie grabbed the waterproof bandages and medical tape, and I tried to brace myself for what was to come.

But I couldn't help myself. I did what I usually do when life is hard: I laughed. Most of the time, it's inappropriate. So, right as she leaned in, all gentle and focused, and slowly reached out to start replacing this huge bandage... I winced dramatically and let out a fake yell, as if she'd hurt me or damaged this giant tube hanging out of me!

She screamed and flailed, then almost backhanded me right in the port. We started laughing. I could barely breathe. Tears ran down both our faces, but this time not from grief or fear. Just relief.

That's when she looked at me through her tears and said, "Thanks for always being you." And in that moment, bruises, tubes, kidney failure, and all, I felt like I still was.

The next few months of my life were dictated by a dialysis machine. Twice a week, every week, like clockwork. I'd walk into that clinic and see a row of faces (most of them older than me), hooked up and hollow-eyed. I was the youngest guy in there by a long shot. It was heartbreaking.

At first, I tried to crack jokes and make everyone laugh, to lighten the mood. But as the weeks passed, something shifted in me. The labs kept coming back the same or worse. My kidneys weren't waking up.

I'd sit in that stiff vinyl chair, tubes coming out of my neck, and watch a machine do the job my own organs couldn't. I wanted to believe it was temporary. That, any day now, I'd get some good news. That maybe I'd piss like a racehorse, and my numbers would start getting better. Hope began to drain from me.

But a month later, we finally got *the* call.

I was lying on the couch, feeling defeated, when my nephrologist's number glowed on my phone's screen. It was daunting. "Am I dying? Or does he miss me?" I will never forget the words he relayed, ones I'd desperately been praying for.

"Your kidneys are starting to work again."

I didn't cry, but something inside me cracked open. I was still weak and still sore from the port sticking out of my neck like I was some cyborg, but my body had finally decided to fight. I felt like myself again, not just as a patient, but as a person. Hope slowly reemerged.

Getting that damn port out of my neck, with no meds by choice, was like taking back a piece of my control and power. It was a quick but excruciating procedure. It was like my battle scar was finally closing.

The nurse offered something to take the edge off, but I shook my head. I needed to *feel* it. I needed to remember this moment, be fully present, feeling every tug, every burn, every wince. Because this wasn't just about removing a piece of plastic from my body. This was about reclaiming my life.

I walked out of that clinic lighter. No more dialysis. No more 7:00 a.m. chairs, cold fluorescent lights, or comparing creatinine levels with eighty-year-olds who had been doing this longer than I'd been alive. No more machines.

The day the port came out, I stood in the shower and let water find the places tape had irritated. I watched bruises lift their purple into yellow and called it a sunrise. I did not feel invincible. I felt invited.

I started telling the truth out loud, not as a performance, but as a way to keep oxygen in the room. Dry is what happens when you remove the poison but refuse the water. Sober is what happens when you say yes to the whole glass—the ache, the joy, the boredom, the want, the ordinary miracle of breath.

Here is the math I refused and then learned: Suboxone saved my life and also could have ended it when I fed it the wrong friends. The first collapse was a "one-time" anxiety pill on top of a maintenance medication and a body that had memorized scarcity. The second collapse was a "one-time" Tramadol, the diet painkiller that wasn't. Each time I reached for control, I fell on my face. I wanted to call that stubbornness. It was arrogance braided to fear.

Here is the other math: I did the things the brochures promised—therapy, in-patient, outpatient, doctors, groups, and still a year passed before anyone asked why I was still taking enough prescriptions to rattle an elephant. That's not an accusation; it's a diagnosis of a gap. The system excels at crisis and struggles with the quiet choreography of "after." I don't want a new villain. I want a better map.

If you are reading this because you love an Adrift, ask the pharmacist to draw you pictures. Ask the doctor to explain the interactions as if your life depends on it. It might.

If you are in recovery and you feel empty while you're doing everything "right," it doesn't mean you're failing. It might mean you're dry. There's a difference. You are allowed to want abundance, not just absence. You are allowed to ask for teachers, not just rules. And to the people building the systems that kept me alive: thank you. Now, please add a map to the bag.

Chapter 16

Edge of Collapse

Katie

A few months after Chris came home from Florida, the following July, I started to notice something wasn't right. He had been sleeping excessively for days, but that morning felt off. He seemed disoriented and was taking shallow breaths. Alarm bells went off in my head.

I went downstairs and woke up my mom, hoping she could come upstairs to help evaluate the situation, since she was a nurse. Without hesitation, she grabbed her stethoscope and blood pressure cuff. I snagged a fingertip pulse oximeter, and she followed me back upstairs.

Chris was so lethargic that he could barely sit up in bed. My mom wrapped the cuff around his arm and pumped it, her eyes quickly scanning the gauge. Then, she put the oximeter on his fingertip, waiting for it to calculate. I'll never forget her expression. She looked up at me, her face concerned, and said, "I think we need to call an ambulance. His oxygenation is extremely low and in the low 80s." My heart dropped. Generally, a healthy oxygen reading would be between 95% and 100%,

As I began dialing 9-1-1, a ton of questions flooded my mind. *Does he have a virus? Did he take something he shouldn't have? Am I overreacting? How much is this ambulance going to cost us? Did I wait too long to call?*

Ten minutes later, four large paramedics and firefighters made their way up our steep stairs into our low-ceiling bedroom. They didn't seem too concerned at first. In fact, one of them said he didn't believe my mom, insisting there was no way Chris's oxygen could be that low.

Since Chris could barely stand, two of them assisted him downstairs. After running a few quick tests in the ambulance, though, one of the paramedics came back to talk to us. His tone had changed.

"I'm sorry," he said to my mom. "I didn't believe you, but you were right. We need to take him to the hospital." I asked which one, and they said to Parker Adventist, which was just seven minutes away. Before driving away, they told us that Chris appeared to be experiencing severe anxiety, so they'd given him some medicine to help.

Everything about that morning felt surreal, marked by panic, helplessness, and the frustration of not being taken seriously. I wasn't sure what would come next. Yet I was surprisingly calm. I knew how to compartmentalize, so I shut off the panic button long enough to stay functional. I've been told, and now deeply believe, that individuals who have been exposed to consistent emotional distress often develop tools for coping in crisis situations. Yay for hidden superpowers? I wonder if I will use it for good or evil.

In a messed-up way, my years of learning how to dissociate allowed me to stay calm while the ground beneath me began to crumble. I quickly packed a bag, grabbed some snacks—because you never know how long you'll be there—and updated my family and took off in my white Subaru. Soon after, the ambulance rolled away down our driveway. As much as I hate what I've been through, part of me thanked the survival mechanisms that kicked in.

Once parked, I ran inside through the Emergency Room entrance, my sneakers slapping against the run-down tile. I quickly scanned to see if there was any sign of Chris. But then, through two double-glass doors, I glimpsed the ambulance parked in the back alleyway and Chris being rolled into a room on a stretcher. I felt like I had been punched in the gut.

I hurried to the security checkpoint, where a police officer began rummaging through my purse. He didn't need to ask questions. He could read the worry on my face. Without saying a word, he picked up the pace, quickly handing me back my bag, and told me to go through the security gate. Every second was heavy with urgency, and I hoped the security alarm wouldn't go off. The officer glanced at his computer screen, pressed a button to open the double doors, and directed me to room 7. The smell of the ER hit me hard as I turned the corner, unsure of what I was about to walk into.

As I passed each triage bay, I couldn't help but peer in, seeing each patient lying atop the uncomfortable blue ER beds and quietly guessing why they must be there. "Oh, the poor kid broke his arm. Yikes, that guy is hacking up a lung in there. Oof, that was a lot of blood." Until I reached Chris's room.

When I walked in, nurses were bustling around him, attaching monitors, and one of them started an IV. They quickly found out how much Chris hates needles and isn't the type of patient who gets a gold star or a sticker for good behavior.

Once I found a chair, I set it next to his bed, grabbed his hand, and noticed he was coming in and out of consciousness, with his body twitching every few seconds. As I fought back tears, a doctor came in and introduced himself, quickly typing on a standing monitor, barely looking up as he asked about medications and his medical history.

I brushed over the fact of his history with substance use and said, "He was recently in treatment… He just came home a few months ago." It felt like a confession I was unprepared to make. How were we here? What was happening?

He told me they were monitoring his vitals closely, that they were ordering an ultrasound and a CT scan, and then they were going to run a toxicology report. As they rolled Chris away, I was immediately introduced to a hospital case worker who needed to gather insurance information. Once the tests were complete, the results began to come in, and we gained a better understanding of what was happening. I finally felt ready to send an update to our friends and family, as I didn't want them to worry if this wasn't too concerning.

I quickly typed,

> *Chris is currently experiencing acute liver failure and pneumonia in his left lung. His ultrasound looked okay, and he had to be given medication for his CT scan because he was twitching and moving a lot. That medication showed up on his tox screen since it falls under the benzo class, but his tox report otherwise came back clean. The CT scans of his neck, head, and chest all came back clear. He's being treated with antibiotics for pneumonia and medication to help flush his liver. Right now, he's not coherent and is very confused. He's being admitted to the ICU for the night and will be in room #251. I'll keep you updated with any changes or new information as soon as I hear anything. Thank you all for keeping Chris in your thoughts.*

Leading up to this point, Chris and I weren't on speaking terms with his mom, Tracy. Their relationship had cracked after he and I had decided together that he would come home early from the sober living house. As you know, it wasn't an easy decision. So, when I sent the update about him being in the hospital, I knew it might stir things back up. I hoped that sharing information, whether timely or not, would be enough. It sure wasn't.

Within what felt like minutes, Tracy appeared on the ICU floor, her face full of panic and anger. She confronted me, demanding to know why I hadn't called sooner and why she was just now finding out that her son was in critical condition. She also requested to speak to his doctor and not to me.

I stood there, exhausted and emotionally fried, and tried to hold it together. Each sentence hit me like a wave full of accusations and questions laced with fear and unresolved drama.

I lost it. I screamed behind my medical mask that I was doing my best, trying to respect what I thought Chris wanted. However, the answers I was giving her weren't good enough, and she wanted a second opinion from his medical team.

She didn't believe the diagnosis I told her. She wanted more answers. She wanted control. But deep down, I knew she was scared. Still, it felt like all my efforts weren't enough, and I'd barely had time to process what was happening. I had barely eaten or drunk anything throughout the day, despite packing snacks, and I was exhausted. Defending myself only made things worse. The rest of the night blurred.

I decided I needed to go home, grab a change of clothes, and get a quick bite to eat. As I closed my car door, I looked up at the night sky and saw a thin crescent moon shining through the clouds. I didn't even realize I was holding my breath until it came out in one loud, broken sob. It took me a few seconds to notice I was gripping the steering wheel with all my might. I shook back and forth between my back's weight and the steering wheel, crying out in anger.

After I calmed down, I pressed my forehead against the steering wheel, begging God to make it all make sense. I knew I couldn't sit there much longer, since I had to go home, change, drive back, and keep it together for Chris. But for that one moment, I released some built-up frustration. And that sliver of moonlight became a tiny thread of hope in my chaotic day.

That night, I didn't sleep. The ICU had a long, blue couch against one window that faced southwest toward the Rocky Mountains. It was just barely wide enough for me to lie down. I grabbed the scratchy, once-warm hospital blankets and tried to get comfortable. The pillow deflated almost as soon as I lay down. Instead of listening to my home white-noise sound machine, I heard the steady, low beeps of all the machines hooked up to Chris. I don't remember getting any solid sleep that night. And in the grogginess of the following morning, I knew I couldn't sleep there again. I needed to be strong for Chris and the unexpected, so I left at 10:00 every night and came in at 7:30 each morning, ensuring I wouldn't miss the doctor's rounds on each of the remaining days Chris was in the hospital.

One of the most challenging experiences I faced was when Chris awoke from the haze of those first few days. He woke up like the mighty Kraken monster coming to life, thrashing into his new reality. (I love the movie *Clash of the Titans.*) Of course, on this particular day, Chris's dad had come to visit. I think he was hoping for a moment of calm together. Unfortunately, what he walked into was sheer chaos. Did I mention how Chris is not an ideal patient in hospitals? Chris was trying to pull out IVs and was confused, so he gave the nurses no other choice but to restrain him.

I can't even begin to express the heart-wrenching experience of seeing a loved one forcibly held down and strapped to a hospital bed. I know the screams and words that Chris was yelling weren't from the man I married. But this was his reaction to waking up in the ICU, wanting to go home, and coming out of his confused state. His dad, Jeff, and I felt helpless.

This was also a time when someone else could finally see Chris's manipulative tendencies firsthand. He tried to convince his dad to loosen the constraints around his wrists. This moment is etched in my memory because I found myself in the corner of that ICU room, wrapping my arms around my shins and trying to stay strong and reset, while I watched the man I loved unravel in front of me.

Luckily, after some intense and challenging days, Chris was successfully downgraded from the ICU and transferred to a general hospital floor! His symptoms started to show noticeable improvement. I felt like I could finally let out a massive sigh of relief.

The pneumonia had cleared, and Chris was becoming more coherent. However, the doctors were still uncertain about the cause of his liver failure. They suspected it might be a hypoxic liver injury, resulting from a lack of oxygen. They also mentioned a virus that was circulating the hospital that had affected other patients' livers, specifically young children.

Even though we didn't get a straight answer, we were so grateful to hear that he could be discharged. As we walked out of the hospital, Chris breathed in the fresh air for the first time in over a week. We were beyond ecstatic that we were both headed home. But little did I know, Chris was holding a secret close to his heart, and I wouldn't find out what it was until months later.

As summer slowly transitioned to fall, Chris and I decided to plan a mini, postponed honeymoon in Mexico, just the two of us in October, at our favorite resort, the Viceroy Riviera Maya, for what felt like the promise of a fresh start. This jungle resort is nestled in serene private villas, each with its own private plunge pool. You get your own butler, receive personalized, hand-carved soap upon arrival, and they perform a healing ritual called a *temazcal*. We had waited so long for a little break in the chaos, and I sincerely wanted to believe this would be a turning point.

One morning, I walked along the resort's peaceful stone paths toward the spa for a long-awaited moment of self-care. I remember the smell of the ocean air as I lay there during my massage, and I finally felt my guard drop. For the first time in what felt like forever, I let myself breathe.

Meanwhile, Chris went into town. When I returned to our villa later that afternoon, everything felt off. I noticed an edge in his demeanor, in the way his pupils darted when I asked what he had done while I was at the spa, and how his words weren't quite lining up. My gut twisted, and my Detective Katie hat went on. He confessed he had bought some Tramadol while I was gone. Just like that, the serenity of the spa was a distant memory. I was back in the storm.

We argued. It wasn't the quiet kind of disagreement you can brush past on vacation. It was raw, emotional, and loud. We were lucky not to have any neighbors close to our walls, because it would have been a scene. I felt like the foundation I had just started to rebuild was crumbling beneath me. In an effort to control the situation, I took the pills and placed them into a locked bottle I'd brought for emergencies. I thought that would be enough. But it wasn't. I wouldn't find out until days later, after arriving home, that Chris had broken the bottle. And by that point, it was too late.

At about 4:00 a.m. on October 14 (the day before my birthday), I shot up in bed with a sudden jolt, like someone had shaken me from a deep sleep. I turned groggily toward Chris's side of the bed, expecting him to be next to me, but he wasn't there. A sick, sinking ache spread through my cheeks, and I knew something was wrong.

I jolted out of bed and ran around the corner to our living room. That is when I saw him, face down on our blue-and-purple shaggy rug, not moving. I rushed to his side and turned him over, but his body was heavy and limp. He was breathing low, shallow, uneven breaths, and just like in July, panic surged through me.

He'd thrown up a little on his sweatshirt, and his skin was clammy. Chris awoke and cried out in pain, saying, "I can't feel my hands, Katie! It hurts." His voice was filled with raw worry, and he cried out again, trying to grasp his hands, but they wouldn't close.

Everything in me wanted to start asking him a million questions, but there wasn't time. I went into autopilot, my hands shaking as I dialed 9-1-1 for the second time this year.

I ran downstairs and woke up my mom, yelling that something was wrong and she needed to come upstairs immediately. As we bolted up the apartment steps, we walked into Chris, still yelling out in pain. He was so disoriented, it was terrifying.

The medics and firefighters arrived quickly, and when they came in, they said Chris looked familiar and that they recognized the house because of our long, curvy driveway. This time, I was better prepared; I gathered all of Chris's medications and lined them up on our TV stand so they could write down the dosage and information. I also asked them not to take him to Parker Adventist again and asked if they could take him to Sky Ridge, instead. I preferred this hospital, even though it was an additional fifteen minute' drive away.

In my mind, I told myself this was just like last time: a liver virus, something the hospital could treat. But as they took Chris down the steep stairs on a stretcher, I knew, deep down, this time was different. The energy felt heavier and more serious. Like whatever we were stepping into now… might not be something we could walk back from.

This time, there wasn't time for me to pack snacks as I raced to my car to follow the ambulance. Once I pulled up near the Emergency Room, I threw the car into what I thought was park and bolted out without thinking.

A few steps later, I heard this slow, creeping noise behind me… Yup. I'd left it in neutral. My car was just casually rolling away as if it had its own plans. Once fully parked, I ran through the sliding doors to meet security, who rifled through my purse, and then I was clear to head back to the last bay—the one closest to the ambulance entrance. That's where I found Chris.

No one looked up when I walked into the confined, cold room. There were more nurses this time, and space was limited. I felt like I was in the way, so I sat in the rigid ICU chair behind Chris's left shoulder and just observed quietly, holding back tears. My gaze remained on Chris's face, searching for any flicker of reaction to the needles and monitors being administered to his limp body.

Whenever his eyes fluttered open, he looked right and left with no comprehension of where he was and never focused on my face, even to notice the scared tears falling down my cheeks. He kept waking up, lifting his arm in the air, and playing with his green hospital gown. Then, he would immediately fall back asleep. It was unbearable to watch him in such a state of confusion and daze. Each time he opened his eyes, I leaned in closer, telling him he was safe and that we would figure out what was wrong. I also reminded him, over and over, that I was right there. I don't think he heard me.

More tests were ordered. And no one was actually telling me what was going on. I tried my best to listen to the muddled medical jargon behind their medical masks, but I struggled to understand what they were saying. I remember stopping one nurse and begging her to tell me what was happening.

She said they were doing everything they could for him and that Chris was struggling to breathe, so they had to place a tight, pressurized mask over his face to help force air into his lungs. They told me that, if he couldn't start breathing on his own soon, they'd need to intubate him. My husband was lying there, unresponsive, and I was back in that limbo between hope and the unknown.

I kept asking for updates, but no one would give me a straight answer. Every person I spoke to seemed to talk in circles, and I grew more desperate by the second. Finally, I pulled a nurse aside, tears streaming down my face.

I begged her, "Is he going to be okay? What is happening? No one will tell me anything."

She looked at me, her eyes steady over the mask, and said plainly, "He was minutes away from dying. You got him here just in time. But now… Now he's fighting for his life. He's in complete organ failure. He has sepsis and pneumonia, and he's not breathing well. His potassium levels are very high, which tells us his kidneys are failing, so that's why we just gave him some insulin and sugar to kind of suck the potassium back into his cells. His liver enzymes are elevated again, in the mid-3,000s."

I shakily replied, "Yeah, they were 3,500 in July."

She quickly replied, "Yes, technically, he is at 3,300, so it's the same picture as last time. His chest X-ray seemed clear, but I am going to scan his chest, abdomen, and pelvis to see if there are any abscesses and also to evaluate his liver. We will also conduct some urine studies. And we might need to do a straight catheter, but because he is not waking up or following commands, we are going to give him meds to calm him down. We are waiting for a bed in the ICU, where the care there will be two-to-one (two nurses for every one patient), whereas on the floor here it's one nurse for every six patients. The ICU is also bigger."

I asked, "Why do his organs keep failing?"

She replied, "That is what they need to evaluate, and to check whether he ate something in Mexico, because he also has some infection. That's why he was sweating so much. So, we will pump him with antibiotics, as well."

It was so matter-of-fact and quick, I had to sit down. I felt like the ground had disappeared under me. Everything sounded muffled, as if someone had just put on noise-canceling headphones. I was in a complete daze.

As they rolled Chris away to transfer him to the ICU, I was left in the messy aftermath, looking down at the white-tiled floor, littered with tubes, gloves, papers, trash, and medical wrappers. The stillness in the room was suffocating, yet I clung tightly to my quiet prayer to God, asking Him to bridge the gap between Chris and me in my absence, while he was made comfortable in the ICU.

Once again, I had to send a cryptic text to Chris's family, but this time I only texted Chris's dad and brother. After what had happened in July, Chris told me that if something like this happened again, I should not tell his family and should keep all sensitive information between us. My hands shook as I typed, and I knew, once I hit send, it would make everything real. This was serious, and I was the one delivering the scary news.

While the medical team worked to stabilize Chris, I was escorted into a large waiting area just outside the ICU, big enough to hold families waiting for their loved ones to get out of surgery and a holding tank before being shuffled back to the ICU. I sat down, numb, eyes locked on the floor. I couldn't stop thinking, *How did we get here again? Why does this keep happening? Did he really almost just die? This wasn't supposed to happen. I thought he was getting better.*

I contacted his little brother, Kyle, and thankfully, he showed up quickly and sat with me while we waited outside the ICU doors. We tried our best to fill the stiff, quiet moments, but we kept staring into the distance, trying to disconnect from this new reality. I was so thankful he showed up quickly and sat with me while we waited. I really needed a hug and didn't want to be alone.

After an hour and a half had passed, I couldn't believe we weren't allowed back yet. I knew Chris was being stabilized and they needed to insert more tubes, but why was this taking so long?

I quickly stood up, went around the corner to pick up a phone at the entrance to the closed ICU doors, and waited for a nurse to stop the ringing.

I asked about Chris, and she said, "Oh, honey, he has been ready for a while now. Come on back!" Trying to hold back my annoyance, I yelled around the corner to Kyle, letting him know we could head back.

As we made our way down the long hallway to the farthest room on the east side of the ICU, my heart raced with each step and grew heavier the closer we got. Just as we were about to enter, a nurse stopped Kyle and me in our tracks.

"Hold on," she said firmly. "We're still placing his catheter. Please give us a few more minutes." Once she'd slowly drawn the curtain shut, I turned to see a big group of people headed in our direction. My heart dropped.

Michelle, Kyle's wife, arrived with their adorable newborn, Melody. Behind her were Chris's mom and stepfather, who didn't even acknowledge me as they walked right past as if I didn't exist. I was already exhausted and terrified, but at that moment, the fear crashed down on me all at once, and I felt so alone.

I stood there, frozen and staring at the closed curtain, wishing I could see and speak to Chris to tell him I was sorry, and that I had tried my best to respect his wishes regarding his family. I felt a surge of anger because I felt so alone and was angry that he'd left me to defend him and me by myself once again.

Every emotion I'd been trying to keep at bay since 4:00 a.m. came rushing through me, and I collapsed to my knees in front of the nurses' station, sobbing uncontrollably. Michelle, bless her sweet soul, came over, kneeled down beside me, handed me a tissue, and gently asked what she could do for me. She was the only one who even asked.

I sobbed even harder, telling her I was so scared. Seeing sweet Melody in her carrier instantly lifted my spirits, and I thanked Michelle for her kindness.

Once we could enter Chris's room, I made a beeline to the chair in the corner of the cold room, where it was quiet. I wanted to give the rest of his family time to gather around his bed and support him in their own way. But my gaze remained fixed on Chris's face, searching for any movement as I yearned for a sign that my vibrant, witty husband still lived in his motionless body. There was no room for sleep, no space for panic to seep in, and no amount of social media or reading would allow my mind to turn off. Staring at the floor was all the energy I could muster.

I don't know what time it was, but there were very few visitors, and it was dark outside, too, when the nurse told me, "Katie, you need to prioritize yourself during this time. We don't know how long he will be here, but you can't sleep here. Go home, take a shower, and try to get some solid sleep. We will call you if anything changes."

Tears welled up in my eyes. I agreed and double-checked that he had the correct phone number for me, mentioning I had written it down on the whiteboard near the door.

He seemed confused at first, then looked at me and said, "We can only have one emergency contact."

My immediate thought was, "Well, of course," and I glanced at the board to see that a family member had written *their* phone number above mine with a star next to their name. I was livid. I wanted to scream at the top of my lungs, *"I AM HIS WIFE! What else do I need to do to prove myself?"*

Instead, I took the edge of my tear-stained sweatshirt and dragged it across the phone number written above mine, erasing it. "I am his emergency contact," I said, and then thanked the nurse before grabbing my purse and walking out.

Once I got home, my mind wouldn't turn off. I kept replaying the day and questioning everything. I don't remember getting much sleep, but I was excited to take a warm shower. The next morning, I woke up early because I wanted to be at the hospital in time for the doctor's early rounds.

My little sister was so sweet and supportive. She drove all the way to Parker that morning, bringing coffee from Starbucks. She had written "Happy Birthday, Katie!" on my cup and drew balloons and confetti. That's right, happy birthday to me… *Oof,* worst birthday ever. In those moments, though, nothing else mattered except for Chris. It was just him, unconscious in his hospital bed, and me, trying my best to hold it together.

As my mom, sister, and I stepped quietly into Chris's ICU room, I could hear the steady beeping of monitors and saw that Chris was still in a deep sleep. Then I noticed a slight movement in the corner. It took me a second to see, but it was Chris's mom, curled in the chair by the window.

I quickly said, "Oh, hi!"

Two thoughts hit me at once. The first was compassion: she must've stayed the night… She must be exhausted… I know how scared she must feel. But almost immediately, the second thought crept in, louder, sharper: *Where have you been? You haven't tried to be part of his life for months. You only show up when he's at his worst.*

Before I could say anything, she stood up, slung her purse over her shoulder, and walked right past us. No hello. No eye contact. No acknowledgment. Just… gone. The sting of that silence was brutal, and the air between us was thick, filled with everything that had been unspoken.

At that moment, I kept wondering if I had somehow failed, if my trying to protect Chris and handle everything alone had backfired. The emotional weight was unbearable, but I reminded myself I was here. I stayed. I fought. I showed up for him and was trying my best to honor his wishes. And in that moment, that had to be enough.

While we waited for the doctor, the room was quiet, and I soon grew sick of hearing the slow, rhythmic beep of Chris's monitors, while the weight of the unknown was palpable. But my little sister did what she does best: she started talking, filling the heavy silence with one of her hilarious, animated stories. I caught myself smirking in gratitude for her and my mom and how they'd shown up for me today, somehow softening the sharp edges of the heavy situation.

I silently thanked God for my family, for their constant support, unwavering presence, and unconditional love. They were always there… truly there… for me. But nothing could prepare me for what the doctor was about to divulge regarding Chris's toxicity report.

The doctor came in and quickly introduced himself, barely looking up from the chart. He asked me about Chris's medications, substance history, mental health, and specifically how long he had been on Suboxone. I tried to answer the best I could, my voice cracking as I explained what I knew and what I didn't.

After he gave a slight nod, he explained they'd found an opioid in Chris's system, asking what it could have been. I told him about our fight in Mexico and Chris getting Tramadol, but that I thought I had removed this from his possession. I was wrong.

This was the first time I was informed that mixing opioids or benzodiazepines with Suboxone is extremely dangerous and should never be done under any circumstances. The doctor explained that even using this combination just once while on Suboxone can be fatal, and it is the leading cause of overdose deaths among individuals in medication-assisted treatment. He said that because Suboxone partially activates specific receptors and blocks others, a person's tolerance can be unpredictable. Mixing these substances could result in slow or stopped breathing, and even lead to a coma.

While this doctor had probably seen this story unfold a hundred times, I felt this news bulletin shout across my head, "*Breaking news!* Please be wary of Suboxone and mixing certain types of pills. Today, we have a specific case unfolding behind us. The patient nearly died, but let's see what is about to unfold…"

I immediately wondered if this was the cause of our ER trip in July, and Chris still wasn't being honest with me.

The doctor gave a slight nod, as if that explained enough, then continued to provide me with a comprehensive update on Chris's symptoms. He said, "Chris has severe kidney damage and failure, which is a byproduct of his muscles breaking down and the lack of oxygen. If his kidney doesn't turn back on in the next few days, we will need to begin dialysis. He has pneumonia in his right lung, and his liver enzymes are slowly going down, which we hope will improve over the next few days. He also has ammonia, which is causing him to fade in and out, and he will be pretty out of it for a few days. Chris will most likely get moved to the general hospital floor, hopefully soon, but right now, we are just pumping fluids and antibiotics."

I was barely processing what was coming out of his mouth. I thanked him for the update and was in shock, as my mind raced to a conclusion.

I immediately cried. The type of cry that wasn't pretty or polite, with uncontrollable gasps of anxiety, hoping to catch my breath. As my shoulders heaved, I finally released all control and everything I had been holding for the last few days. Shit, maybe even the previous few months. Or fuck, perhaps even the last few years. It all came pouring out at once.

I whispered to God, "Please… please help me. Help Chris."

Something in this moment of panic bubbled into something else I can't quite explain. It was a moment of doubt. A profound grasp of the universe, asking God, "Are you still here? Are you listening? Why have you been so quiet?"

I felt that if I weren't so caught up in my stress, I would have probably heard a quiet whisper in my heart from Him, saying, "I am still here. I love you. I never left. You're okay."

After my anxiety attack subsided, anger rushed through me that boiled my blood. I turned to my mom and sister and said, "What in the absolute fuck just happened? Is this for real? I have tried everything! No matter what I have done, whether it was getting a safe for my prescriptions, locked bottles with interchangeable codes, locked bottles with time stamps once shut, me writing locked notes in my phone to track my medicine to make sure I am not missing anything, to my head being on a constant swivel, with bouts of being Detective Katie, going through his sock drawers, clever hiding places like on top of his ZYN can, and pockets. Dear Lord, do you know how many pockets there are? Shorts, pants, shirts, sweatshirts, jackets, bags, backpacks. To catch him and make sure he isn't ingesting anything.

"I wonder every time he leaves the house to run an errand if he is lying to me and is meeting up with a drug source. Instead of him getting a hug hello when he walks through the door, he is met with me swarming up to him, picking apart his pockets to see if there are drugs in them. No matter what I do, he always finds a crack in my system. Even when he is overly sleepy, I can't help but wonder if he took something! Why did it have to be drugs? They are so fucking small and inconspicuous. Is this truly the rest of my life?"

All they could do was cry with me and hold my hand.

When you are in the hospital, nothing passes the time. You can try watching a TV show or reading, but your mind is too restless. All I could muster was listening to music, staring off into the void, or shutting my eyes. And every time I opened my eyes, I glanced over at Chris, still hooked up, still quiet, barely moving, still here. I thought that was enough for now.

After my mom and sister left, I had to make a gut-wrenching decision to uphold Chris's wishes. I had to pretend to his family as if I didn't know the real reason Chris was in the hospital, hooked up to machines and multiple drips of medicine, with organ failure.

I am an awful liar. It literally rips my soul apart when I have to lie. I had to ensure the loose ties wouldn't unravel when discussing his medical team and what they could share with his family, if they asked.

I found Chris's nurse and told her the situation. She had never encountered a situation like this before, so she asked if she could get back to me after speaking with her manager.

A little while later, the nurse came back to me and handed me a small slip of paper with a five-digit code written on it. Seems so simple, but it may have been the lock to my secret diary. She explained that under HIPAA privacy laws, anyone who called would usually need that code, but in my case, it also had to be presented *in person*. No exceptions.

You'd think holding this tiny piece of paper with a string of numbers would give me some power that came with such control, but it didn't. It was a quiet reminder that I had to be the keeper of Chris's secret, while balancing the roles of his wife, his primary communicator, and his advocate, all while I was barely holding myself together.

Chris's family began arriving one by one. Soon, the room was bustling with love and concern. Everyone knew this went beyond typical ICU guidelines, not to mention all the Covid restrictions. Yet, considering the gravity of the situation, the nurses seemed to turn a blind eye for a short while. Later, they told us only two people could enter at a time, in the future.

Then, in a moment I can only compare to when Snow White gets her true love's kiss, which felt like a dream, Chris suddenly fluttered his eyes open. After days of being unconscious, his energy filled the room, as if his spirit had come back into his body. I will never forget when someone placed baby Melody into his lap, and, for a few magical moments, laughter grew louder than the slow beeping of his monitors.

I found myself in the corner of that room, feeling paralyzed, despite being surrounded by so much love. My body was there, but, emotionally, I felt a deep burden of mixed emotions, ranging from anger to heartbreak and fatigue. I observed as people engaged with Chris, their eyes rarely meeting mine. Some had distanced themselves from me for months, while others had ignored me completely. Yet there I was, putting on a brave face, nodding along, hiding the tears I had shed just hours before with my sister and mom.

Fortunately, my medical mask hid the dark circles under my eyes. Inside, my emotions swirled, but I had to swallow my longing to speak up and cry out, "Do you see the struggles I've faced for you, Chris? I wish I could tell them everything without their judgments. I wish they could see the pain you have unintentionally caused." I also wanted to scream *"HAPPY FUCKING BIRTHDAY TO ME!"* No one had remembered.

I wished someone would recognize the many challenges I, too, had endured while fighting for his recovery. But I stayed silent. When you're the strong one and the Anchor, you learn to smile through the pain, even when the world is falling around you. You quietly support others while holding onto your own battles, wishing for your strength to be acknowledged, yet you continue to stand firmly in love. I desperately needed some form of acknowledgment for what I'd had to put up with, but even then, I knew I would never get it.

Instead, I received a rush of questions:

"Katie, I saw on your Instagram that you let Chris drink in Mexico. I read somewhere that he shouldn't do that on Suboxone."

"Katie, can you tell us more about what the doctor was thinking for a potential reason as to why this happened to Chris?"

"Katie, I read an article. I will send it to you, and the symptoms he is experiencing seem like he mixed something with his Suboxone." Apparently, I wasn't the only detective in the group.

I lost my composure. I glanced at the family member who'd mentioned Chris drinking a beer on our vacation, looked directly into their eyes, and said, "*Let* him? Let him drink? Chris is his own person. He is an adult, and I am not his babysitter. He decides for himself, and lately, he has made many decisions that weren't the smartest. But yeah, I *let* him drink alcohol because that is my problem and my fault."

I grabbed my bag and walked out to wait for the rest of their visit alone, in the waiting room.

I knew they were all scared and concerned, but instead of being able to hold space for one another, it felt like I was on the opposite side of an invisible battlefield, vastly outnumbered. I wasn't just Chris's wife in that moment... I had somehow become enemy number one, the gatekeeper of information and secrets, and the one to blame. If you visit your loved one in the hospital and the situation is intense, maybe bring their significant other a coffee. Ask if you could get them lunch, or ask how they are doing and if there is anything they can do to help. It will go a long way. They are also trying to survive this stressful situation.

I left the hospital earlier than I wanted to, but my mom, dad, and sister weren't taking no for an answer and were determined to celebrate my birthday. Every year, we always carved pumpkins after the birthday dinner, and they weren't about to let this year be an exception. Once home, I poured myself a glass of my favorite white wine and felt strangely comforted, being around everyone at the table. My little sister carved a beautiful and intricate beehive with bees in midflight, while I focused intently on creating a delicate cat silhouetted against the moon and stars. I channeled every ounce of my fury and fear into that pumpkin, as I cut away at the emotions I didn't know how to express.

After dinner, my mom brought out the cake, white confetti with chocolate frosting, my favorite since childhood. She lit the number 3 and number 5 candles, and everyone gathered around to sing. I followed my little tradition, crossing my fingers and holding them in front of my lips. Closing my eyes, I made the loudest wish I've ever made in my life: "I wish Chris would walk out of the hospital in better health than when he went in. I hope, when he comes home, drugs won't be a problem anymore. I hope our marriage will be okay."

It's incredibly hard to blow out candles when your eyes are welling up and your nose is dripping. But I did it... somehow. Because that's what you do. You make a wish, even when you're not sure you believe in them anymore.

In hopes the wish fairies heard my wishes, I walked into Chris's room the following morning with more pep in my step. My lifted spirits were quickly quashed. Chris needed to have a temporary PICC line in addition to the other four IVs already jammed in his arms for fluids and medicine drips, to administer access for him to begin dialysis. Dialysis is a procedure that filters blood to remove waste and excess fluid when the kidneys are unable to function correctly. Think of this large machine as an artificial kidney, helping maintain a healthy balance of electrolytes, removing waste products and excess fluids (including water) from the blood, and regulating blood pressure.

Since Chris's kidneys hadn't turned back on, his body could no longer filter toxins on its own, so the large, noisy machine beside him was doing what his kidneys could not. Keeping him alive. Chris's body had also become super-swollen. The doctor told me this was called edema, a common side effect of kidney failure. Fluid was beginning to build up in his tissues, and since his kidneys weren't able to filter out fluid by urination, his legs, feet, hands, and face swelled.

A new sound was added to the rhythmic beeping as the dialysis machine's steady hum whirred, cycling his fluids in and out of his body. It was oddly hypnotizing to watch his blood circulate, and I couldn't stop staring at the machine. Finally, something to stare at, other than the dirty hospital floors. Chris kept getting flushed, so I wetted cold cloths for his forehead.

Four hours later, my mind filled with worst-case scenarios, and I felt ill-prepared for the helplessness I was feeling. I sat there, trying so hard to be strong and have faith, but deep inside, I was slowly unraveling in light of the new nightmare possibility that this machine could be our reality for the foreseeable future.

Chris had to stay in the ICU for five days. To say we were exhausted would be an understatement. However, on October 18, Chris was finally moved to room #6125 at the general hospital level. Unfortunately, he continued to experience bouts of ammonia, which caused him a significant amount of confusion. At one point, my thoughtful aunt and uncle in California sent a beautiful fall-themed bouquet along with a balloon shaped like a hedgehog that read, "A hedge HUG for you!" Who doesn't love a good pun? The balloon bounced each time the air conditioning turned on, and Chris mistakenly thought the balloon was his late grandpa in the corner and started talking to it. I found this incredibly entertaining and unsettling at the same time.

We also encountered a challenging situation when Chris's wedding ring became stuck on his finger after significant swelling. At one point, I overheard a nurse say they would likely have to cut the ring off, but I was determined to prevent that. The ring was quite expensive, made of platinum, and held immense sentimental value. Fortunately, my mom, a nurse, came to the rescue with a clever trick she had learned during her early years of nursing. She carefully wrapped a string tightly around Chris's finger, from the tip down to the ring, to help compress the swelling. Then, she threaded the loose end of the string under the ring and slowly unwound it to guide the ring off. And voilà, it popped right off!

Oddly enough, Chris's hands were still not working well. He could not write, and I received a phone call from him one evening after I left, during which he yelled at me for messing with his phone settings. I told him I would look at it the next day. The following morning, when we were pressing buttons together, I noticed it wasn't a phone issue… It was a combination of Chris's fingers shaking and his ammonia levels still being relatively high, so he was struggling to make things work. He was beyond frustrated, and I hated seeing him move so much slower when, usually, he is a rapid thinker, with all four cylinders firing at all times.

On October 21, the atmosphere felt heavy, as if the air had been sucked out of the room. The truth seemed to finally settle in for all of us, especially for Chris. Until that moment, he had been fighting against the reality of his kidney failure, even going so far as to fake urination in a desperate attempt to convince his nurses his kidneys had turned back on.

Whenever I tried to discuss Chris's toxicology report with him and ask questions, I was met with anger. He was trying to deceive himself and me about the truth: that he had taken something he shouldn't have and was lucky to be alive.

I believe it was a moment of divine intervention when I couldn't be present at the intense meeting held with the doctor that day, when he delivered the latest news to Chris. Instead, my mom stepped in for me, while I attended another doctor's appointment.

When I arrived later that afternoon, still sore from my back injection, I walked into a room full of unspoken fear and understanding. My mom greeted me at the door, asking if we could talk in the hallway, and from the look on her face, I knew I was walking into an intense day ahead. Dialysis was no longer a possibility. This had become a certainty. A permanent port was scheduled to be placed the following day, and outpatient dialysis was now going to be added to our new routine.

The options we now had to face were either dialysis for life, a kidney transplant, or a miracle that his kidneys "turned back on." So, that night, I began the grueling process of learning the steps to put Chris on a transplant list for a new kidney.

Despite the challenges we faced, we also had some small victories that brought us relief. One was that Chris no longer required 24/7 oxygen or needed to go to in-patient rehabilitation. Then, a new challenge arose. We had to wait for an opening at a dialysis clinic before Chris could begin his treatments, which he needed two or three times a week. He couldn't be discharged until a chair became available. Fortunately, later that evening, two bright moments lifted my spirits. First, as I lay on the stiff couch, trying to be quiet while Chris rested, Taylor Swift released her album, *Midnights*, which became a welcome distraction from our new reality. Second, my older sister, Ash, was on a plane to visit Chris and support me, after recognizing that my mental and physical health were slowly deteriorating.

After Chris got his port inserted into his neck (with no assistance from drugs—Chris's brave choice), we worked closely with our new case manager, Melissa, who guided us through this new and uncharted territory, along with Chris's RN, who instructed us on how to follow Chris's strict renal diet, once we returned home.

That period felt like I was living in a pressure cooker, barely holding it together. I would often find ginger ale cans and Jell-O cups stashed like little awards in Chris's cabinets, taken from the community fridge behind the nurses' backs. Chris always found the cracks within any system, and he kept challenging the boundaries of his new renal diet. There were days when he tried to ignore the strict fluid restrictions, because he really enjoyed Gatorade or a cold Coca-Cola. Unfortunately, this led to him swelling up, disrupting the delicate balance his body now demanded. It was frustrating, but sometimes all I could do was laugh, because, if I didn't, I would have fallen apart.

To protect my sanity, I often left the hospital in the evenings and wanted his family to take over for the night shift. But this meant losing control over the one thing I was desperately trying to manage: Chris's care and diet. One morning, I was confronted by one of Chris's nurses, who scolded me for Chris having eaten a homemade BLT (which is off-limits on his renal diet for dialysis) with mayonnaise, mustard, and crispy bacon for dinner the night before, when his family visited. So, his sodium, phosphorus, creatine, and potassium levels had skyrocketed.

I tried to handle it gently in the group text, and added humor, saying, *Believe me, a BLT is my favorite sandwich, too, but his body can't even handle that right now.*

Unfortunately, that did not go over well. It became just another spark in a situation that was already too heated. To make matters worse, there was an awful incident one evening involving a family member that required me to involve security. As a result, that family member could no longer visit Chris in the hospital.

Thirteen excruciatingly slow days passed, filled with sleepless nights, awful medical updates, and emotional turmoil, before a chair finally opened up at a dialysis center with a 7:00 a.m. slot. We packed up Chris's hospital room in a blur of relief and urgency, eager to bring him home.

The evening air felt crisp, and I remember watching him take it in. That first deep breath outside the walls of the hospital wasn't just air. It was a sign that, maybe, just maybe, things might improve sooner than later. We didn't say much on the car ride home; there was no need to. We were simply grateful to be heading home together. No sirens, no stretchers… Just us. The weight of the past week hadn't fully settled yet, but in that quiet moment, all I felt was overwhelming gratitude that Chris was alive and we were finally headed back to our bed, our home. It felt like reclaiming a small piece of normalcy after so much chaos.

Once back in the familiarity of our apartment, the reality of everything began to settle in. Chris, wishing for a shower, had to work carefully around the new dialysis port in his neck. When he peeled off his shirt and revealed his bruised skin and the small tube stitched in place, I froze. The weight of it all—the trauma, the fear, the unknown—hit us like a tidal wave.

Tears filled my eyes as I wrapped my arms around him and whispered, "I'm so sorry. This is so scary." We sank to the floor and cried together, releasing everything we had been holding in. Eventually, we got ourselves together, and I gathered the medical supplies to waterproof the port.

Chris, being his humorous self, couldn't help himself. He flinched dramatically as I reached toward him, pretending I had hurt him. I shrieked, jumping in the air, and then I almost smacked him in the chest near his port. We both collapsed into laughter. Through his watery hazel eyes, I saw the same old Chris I'd fallen in love with, always resilient, playful, and still himself.

I smiled through my tears and told him, "Thanks for always being you."

We have all taken advantage of our health at some point in our lives and often forget to be *THANKFUL* for it. For most of us, sickness will be a quick inconvenience that comes and goes, and then we move on. For others, sickness is a way of life. It can last for a season while recovering from something serious or for a lifetime when the ailment is chronic.

Being grateful every day will change the way you see life. And in the following weeks, we had to ease into this new reality. Some days, Chris would come home from dialysis feeling invigorated and full of energy. Other days left him completely exhausted, where he could barely make it up our steep stairs.

After thirty-two draining days filled with fear, pain, and endless waiting, we finally received the call we had been praying for. Chris's kidney doctor called with incredible news. Based on his most recent blood work, Chris's kidneys were beginning to function again!! The dialysis had worked, and his body was finally responding. He could have his port removed the following week.

Chris looked pale and exhausted from the toll it had all taken, but as the news sank in, his entire face lit up. A huge sigh of relief was finally exhaled, and for the first time in over a month, there was hope. Real, tangible hope shone behind his eyes. Which we clung to until the following July.

Chapter 17

From Jail Cells to Wake-Up Calls

Chris

I thought I knew what rock bottom looked like. I almost died… twice! I had lived through things I shouldn't have. Everyone has a low point, sometimes more than one. I had a physical rock bottom, and an emotional rock bottom. What follows is the culmination of both.

There are many sayings in recovery. Most of them only make sense the hard way. One of them is, "You're not done suffering yet." It sounds cruel, because it is painfully true. When someone relapses or drifts off the path, people say this. I was not done suffering, either. Every giant red button you are told not to press, I still had to test for myself.

I kept collecting "time," because that is what we do. I had lost more than once, but this time I was nine months sober. Katie and I had taken our power back. We set up an office. I was working again and feeling like myself in small, steady ways.

We moved into our newly updated condo. Fresh paint. New floors. A space that felt like a reset. Boxes were still stacked everywhere, mostly in the corners. Lexi paced the small rooms, confused, already missing Grandma and Grandpa and their acreage.

For the first time in a long time, there was quiet. There was stability. And then, I wrecked it.

Two days in, Katie found the pills. They were in my pocket. My stupid, selfish pocket. I thought I had hidden them well enough, but nothing gets past her… Not really. She knows me too well by now. She sat down slowly when she found them, like her legs couldn't hold the weight of it all anymore. My stomach sank, not just because I got caught, but because *I hated myself* for what I had done to her… again.

I told her the truth. A source had reached out from a new number. I met up. People think dealers disappear when you get clean. They do not. They send feelers. It does not matter how many numbers Katie blocked. This world and the devil find a way back in. And I let it.

But this time was different. Katie didn't scream. She didn't throw things. She didn't storm out. She just sat there, eyes wide, and listened. I saw the pain I'd caused. But I also noticed something else. I saw someone choosing grace over anger. I saw someone who should've given up on me but didn't.

And I realized that *shame* is the thing that almost killed me. Not the drugs. Not the cravings. Shame. It's what made me lie. It's what made me hide. It's what made me think that I'll always be broken. And in that moment, sitting in the middle of our brand-new condo that already felt heavy with old mistakes, I promised her I'd try again. Because, if someone's willing to shine a light when you're buried in darkness, the least you can do is stop digging.

Around Christmas, we always head up to the cabin with Katie's family, then ski through New Year's. In January, I was back at work. Long day, big meeting. I wore a ski jacket that I had brought down from the cabin. Anyone who skis obviously knows that those coats are built for secrets. Pockets inside pockets. The last time I'd worn it, I had tucked a tiny, powerful pill into one of the many pockets. I found it that morning while looking for my phone.

I pulled it out and stared at it like Golem from *Lord of the Rings*… "My Precious."

Yet there I was… in the bathroom of my collaborative office space setup. I was holding this tiny pill like it was *the one ring to rule them all*, and the toilet bowl contained the fires of *Mount Doom*!

The *Lord of the Rings* trilogy is a phenomenal analogy for addiction. There is this incredible power that is sought after by all but truly intended only for some. Despite the good it could do, it causes chaos and destruction everywhere it goes. And every *ring bearer* has a love/hate relationship with it. Fortunately for me, I was more Frodo than Golem, so I flushed that sucker down the toilet, and that was the end of that! The end.

Just kidding! If you've seen *The Wolf of Wall Street,* you will be able to paint a clear picture of this event. Also, if you haven't seen that movie or read the book, you're missing out. I kept the pill.

I put myself through eight hours of misery. With four hours of promised relief in my pocket, I made a deal with myself. Finish the list. Nail the 6:30 meeting. Then reward. At 6:57 p.m., I texted Katie that the meeting went well, and I was going to stay late to get ahead.

Waking up in my office that next morning wasn't part of my master plan. The office walls were glass, with neighbors on both sides, so there was no hiding. The property manager woke me. Fresh shave. Coffee in hand. My feet were numb from being up on the desk. I muttered that I was fine and left.

When I was younger, I'd black out from drinking. I have overdone a lot of things. With painkillers, though, I was careful. I kept count. I never drank on them. I never drove on them. But I did not account for what a long hiatus would do to my tolerance. I did not make it far. I barely made it at all.

I saw missed calls from Katie and panicked. I knew I'd scared her. I knew I had no good reason for staying.

I went home and crashed.

A few days later, an email arrived from the property manager. I had been expecting it. He had reviewed camera footage of me stumbling through the kitchen and common areas. The office contract was clear: no one on the property after midnight. They had to open an investigation. The news hollowed me out. Something felt cracked beyond repair.

Shame rose like a wave, mixed with a tight fear that stole my breath. I had potentially jeopardized our office, Katie's trust, and our future. Katie watched me in silence. No yelling. Just heartbreak. That silence cut deeper than any scream.

I was not fooling anyone anymore, not her, not myself. For what? A hit of fake comfort. A small selfish escape. I wanted to crawl out of my own skin. I thought about telling her everything—the jacket, and the contact—but fear sat in my throat.

Then it did not matter. She found the pills in my pocket again.

Her face said everything. I told the whole truth. I did not plan to take more, and I did not throw them out. The contact reached out, and I'd said yes. Then, I lied. And lied again. Now I stood in our kitchen, heart racing, palms sweating, while she stared at me like I was a stranger.

I told her the truth. Finally. I whispered it like a prayer I didn't deserve: *"I'm so sorry."* I tried to explain. I tried to make sense of something that didn't make sense even to me. I could feel her unraveling.

And then she exploded. I don't blame her. She screamed. She threw things. She said the words I always feared: *"I'm done. I can't do this anymore. Maybe we should separate for a while."*

The worst part? I believed her.

I had taken everything we'd worked for and lit it on fire again. And this time, it wasn't just a mistake. It wasn't just a relapse. It was the domino that toppled everything: our business, our office, our foundation. And the look on her face told me this wasn't just heartbreak. It was *broken.*

What I did was not just a mistake. It was a domino that could knock down our business, our office, our foundation.

We ended up on the kitchen floor. Me, begging. She, numb. I could feel the weight of every lie I'd told sitting between us. I wanted to promise her the world. I wanted to say, *"This is it. This is really the last time."*

Then, she disappeared into the bathroom. I didn't follow. I didn't beg through the door. I just sat there in my wreckage, thinking, *This time, I might have really lost her.* I don't remember the exact words Katie said when she came out of the bathroom that night. But I remember the angst. I had pushed her past the point I never thought she'd go.

She called her mom. We went to the hospital. In the ER, Katie did the talking. The caseworker split us up. The hospital said I was not "acute" enough to stay. No bed. No detox. A referral. Some prescriptions. Good luck. We went home.

I wanted to tell Katie how sorry I was, how broken I felt, how scared I was that I might not make it next time. But all I could do was stare at the floor.

When we got back to the condo, I collapsed into bed. My whole body was wrecked. I didn't deserve sleep, but my body shut down. Meanwhile, I knew Katie was out in the other room, doing what she always does: fixing the mess I'd made. She found us a place to go. A rehab center. The last one on the list. I don't remember getting into the car, but I recall my head pounding, and I felt like I was unraveling from the inside out.

At the facility, I curled up on the floor in the waiting room, cold and shaking. Katie wrapped her jacket over me. It smelled like home. It made me want to cry.

When I heard her arguing with the staff at the front desk, I felt sad. Not because she was frustrated, but because I knew she shouldn't have to be doing this. I should have gotten help before it got to this point, before the call to her mom.

When those heavy wooden doors finally opened and they called my name, I stood up and walked in, not knowing what would come next. Honestly, I was prepared to go back out into the waiting room and find that she was gone for good.

Barely through the interview, Katie came running in, yelling that we were leaving. I was so confused. After we went home, I didn't say much. I didn't have the energy to. My body felt like it was turning itself inside out. I couldn't get warm, my legs were still burning, and every sound, every movement, felt like sandpaper on my brain.

By the time we got home, I went straight to bed. I curled into myself, sick and shaking, trying to ride out the wave. The withdrawal was rough, but the shame was worse. There's no medication for the moment you realize your wife is drowning in the fallout of your mistakes, while still fighting for you to make it out alive.

I don't remember much about the next couple of days. Just sweating through our sheets, lots of cold showers, and pacing around the condo. Katie kept checking on me, but I could tell she was running on fumes. I could see it in her eyes: exhaustion.

Then came the shift. The shakes stopped. My appetite came back. I could stand without feeling like I was going to collapse. The fog that had been pressing down on my skull started to lift. And with it came this crushing awareness: *She hasn't left.* She was still here. All I could say was, "I'm sorry," because I was.

I told her I was done screwing up. I felt the weight of what I'd put her through. I didn't want to be the guy who kept breaking promises and patching them with apologies. That I *meant it* this time.

She just looked at me, tired but clear-eyed, and said, "You can't just say sorry and expect that to be enough anymore, Chris. I want to believe you. God, I really do. But you need to show me something different. Not for me, but for yourself."

And damn, she was right. And something about that moment felt different. Heavier. But also, more real.

That next week, things started to shift. Tiny glimmers of hope. We met a new couples therapist, Madison Mehlman. She did not tiptoe. She asked hard questions and held space for the version of me I wanted to become. I did not know it yet, but she would help save our marriage.

Jason came next. Katie had been seeing a functional medicine doctor, and he gave her a referral to a guy named Jason. He was a guy who had helped him and others with alternative healing. Jason started talking about microdosing psilocybin for managing inflammation, trauma, and mental health. Katie leaned in. I watched her eyes light up with curiosity. And when she asked if I wanted to try this out, I was on board. Something in me said yes before my fear could say no. Because I was willing to try something new. Because the old way was killing me. And because I wanted to meet her in the healing.

Something shifted in me that week, not just emotionally, but spiritually. After years of trying to get sober for Katie, for my family, and for friends, I finally understood why none of it stuck. I had never done it for *myself*. And I couldn't fake it anymore. I didn't want to. That quiet conversation in our condo, the look in Katie's eyes when she said, *"You need to show me something different,"* it hit differently this time. I didn't feel defensive. I felt determined. I was honestly scared by how good I felt, to the point where I was scared to go to bed and wake up losing that steady, reassuring feeling.

I wanted to get clean and not just exist between relapses. Not just white-knuckle my way through guilt and regret. I wanted to heal. So, for the first time, I became my own advocate. I picked up the phone and called CeDAR—the same program I had been referred to in that ER. I got involved immediately. No prompting. Not waiting for Katie to do something about it. Just me, doing the thing I knew needed to be done.

I talked to someone in admissions. Told them everything. I didn't sugarcoat it, didn't sell a shiny version of myself. I told them I was done letting shame steer the ship. I was ready for the work. Whatever it took. Finally doing it, not because I had to, but because I *wanted* to.

I also did a huge disservice to both Katie and myself by not educating myself better about Suboxone and mixing it with other medicines. I was lucky to survive it once. Miraculous to survive it twice. But I was going to make sure there wasn't going to be a third time. And from that moment forward, I knew: If I was going to stay alive, I had to get educated, stay accountable, and take my recovery seriously. No more excuses. No pills. No numbing. No backup plan in my pocket just in case the feelings got too loud. And slowly, quietly, things started to settle. Time was the only thing I could count on.

I started to feel my own rhythm again, giving me enough strength to start putting my pieces back together. Katie checked in on me without hovering, and that helped. Her energy shifted, too: not entirely back to trust, but out of the emergency zone.

Every day that passed, I didn't just feel "sober." I felt more present. I honestly hadn't realized how much the pills had blurred everything, from the colors of flowers and the weight of people's words to the feeling of someone's hand on your shoulder. It was like this dull, thick fog had finally lifted its emotionally numbing veil.

There were still moments when I wanted to run. There were times I caught myself reaching for something to escape. But I didn't. Instead, I sat in the discomfort. And for the first time in years, I didn't feel like a walking apology. I was slowly rebuilding the life I deserved, even though it wasn't perfect or even pretty. But it was honest.

Then, a Denver number lit up my phone.

"This is Detective Grace from the Denver Police Department, returning your call." I had reached out to fix my mess. I wanted to explain.

My attorney, Joe, was the first person to call this what it was. A *relapse.* He did so with such care and humanity, in a way that wasn't degrading or belittling. It was Joe who gave me the courage to accept that relapse was a part of my recovery, and that I didn't need to shy away from admitting that truth or that detail.

Being honest with myself and proactive with the officer was the first intentional act of my recovery. No one forced me. My lawyer didn't drag me in. I did it because I was done running from the truth, done rehearsing the right words to soften the wrong choices.

Joe told me, "If you'd just used a different verb in your statement, something lighter, less broad and self-incriminating, this whole thing would've been dropped."

But I couldn't do that. Not anymore. I was tired of bending language to dodge accountability. I had lied to myself for years, dressed up chaos in nice sentences. This time, I wanted to tell the truth, even if it hurt. Especially if it hurts.

So, I walked in, signed my name, and let them cuff me. Cold metal. Warm shame. That sharp click of finality that says, "You're not in control anymore." The air inside the station smelled like bleach and stale coffee, and for the first time in a long time, I didn't try to make sense of it. I just let it happen. I let it *be*.

"You don't look like you should be here," the officer said. Maybe he was right. Maybe not. Either way, I didn't want sympathy. I needed a consequence. Because consequence is where truth finally starts to breathe.

The holding cell was a fluorescent purgatory. Ten feet of concrete and regret. Men detoxing, pacing, yelling. I sat with my thoughts for twenty-four hours. Silence became its own detox. I replayed everything. The pills, the lies, the shame, the look on Katie's face the night she found me unraveling again. Every scene looped on repeat. But then, somewhere between self-pity and surrender, something shifted. I stopped hiding from the pain. I asked, "What if this is the line between the man I have been and the man I can still become?

It was not cinematic. It was quiet and real. I found a kind of peace I'd never known, the kind that comes when you stop running from the mirror.

The whole process was chaotic. You wait and wait and wait, until they call your group for processing. You're herded through like cattle. Stripped. Bagged. Labeled. Talk to one nurse. Talk to medical. No one has updated your file. No one follows through. I told them I was on Suboxone. They nodded and kept moving. I never saw a real doctor; they didn't administer the suggested medication I needed.

The holding courtroom felt like a DMV with consequences. Four desks, a judge behind plexiglass, an air of "do not mess this up."

The DA looked at my file. "You were in your office. A medical event. No record. You called the detective yourself. This is not where you belong. I am sorry you had to go through this." There was a program for borderline cases. I fit the criteria.

The judge said, "You are getting out today. I do not want to see you again."

Relief? Yes. But then, I had to sit in a holding area next to thirty other guys whose cases weren't so lucky. The awkward tension? Palpable.

Back in the unit, I kept to myself. Tried to stay invisible. One guy bumped into me and tried to start something. Another muttered, "Of course, the White guy walks." The tension was thick.

I didn't eat; in honesty, I couldn't. Everything smelled like mold. Even the peanut butter and jelly came on moldy bread. My cellmate ate it anyway. Peeled the green off like it was nothing.

That place wasn't rehab. It wasn't justice. It was punishment, even for people who didn't need punishment. One guy told me, "I come back because I don't get anything out there."

And I believed him. Just before I got discharged, one of the guys from my original holding cell pulled me aside and said, "I know that dude who was messing with you. He's nothing. If you ever end up back here (God forbid), use my name. Might keep you safe."

His nickname was Tío. Spanish for uncle. Or cousin, depending on the situation. I laughed. He didn't. Never had a referral like this before.

I didn't belong there. And I knew it. But so many of those guys did, *not* because they were bad, but because the world outside had already thrown them away.

That night in jail? It taught me three things:

1. The system is beyond broken.
2. I never want to go back.
3. I had officially hit rock bottom.

When they finally released me, the air outside felt almost foreign. I expected relief, but what I felt instead was gratitude.

Heavy, grounded gratitude. I'd been given another chance. Again. And I knew there were men in that cell who wouldn't get one.

Katie was waiting in the car. She didn't say a word when I opened the door. Total silence. But it wasn't the cold kind of silence. It was the sacred kind, the kind that holds space for truth.

Then, after what felt like forever, she looked at me with that sideways smirk and said, "So…, what gang did you join?"

I couldn't help but laugh. It was absurd and perfect. That one joke cracked something open in both of us. It didn't erase the pain, but it reminded me that we were still here. That somehow, after everything, there was still room for laughter.

We drove home mostly in silence, but it wasn't heavy anymore. It felt clean, like breathing new air.

I used to think rock bottom was a personal low. Now, I think it is the moment you finally realize you've been given more chances than most people ever get, and you *still* almost threw them away.

That night in jail broke something in me, but maybe it also reset something, too. It made me sick to think I'd almost lost everything… again. That I'd hurt Katie. I could have been swallowed by a system that does not care if you are trying to change.

Back at home, I made no big declarations. I didn't promise the world. I didn't say, "This time will be different." I just showed up.

That week was packed—appointments, work meetings, commitments I could've easily canceled. I wanted to crawl into bed, disappear, and pretend I wasn't the guy who had just spent a night in jail. But instead, I went. To every single one.

I showed up to the meetings. I showed up for dinner plans. I showed up to life.

And that's when I realized: recovery isn't about grand gestures or perfect days. It is what you do when no one's clapping. It is showing up when you are humiliated and scared. Those days did not fix everything, but they built something new. Consistency. Integrity. Self-trust. A quiet confidence that does not shout. It stays.

Because if you only heal when it's convenient, you are not healing. You're managing. I had managed my wreckage long enough. I wanted to live. Intentionally.

I kept thinking about the guys in that cell. Some will never see the light of day again, not because they didn't want to change, but because the system is not built for it. One man heard I was getting out and said, "Must be nice."

He wasn't wrong. It was nice. It was unfair, too. And it lit a fire under me. Because if I was going to walk out of there, I needed to make that freedom mean something.

I called what I was doing "intentional recovery." Not reactive survival. Not just white-knuckling sobriety or apologizing my way through life. But actually *choosing* how I wanted to live, moment by moment, breath by breath.

Reactive survival is what got me there. It's what made me lie, hide, and scramble for control I never had. Intentional recovery was different. It wasn't about control at all. It was about surrendering to honesty. Doing the next right thing, not because someone was watching, but because you've finally started watching yourself.

Every step since that day, every conversation, every hard truth, has been a small act of intention. Those acts, strung together, are what keep me alive.

I used to think healing was about getting back to who I was before addiction. Now I know it means building someone new from the wreckage, piece by honest piece.

So, I turned myself in. I faced the humiliation. I laughed in the car with my wife. Then I showed up. Again, and again.

Sometimes, recovery does not start in a hospital bed or a treatment center. Sometimes, it begins in a cell where you stop running from your reflection and start walking toward the man you want to be.

That is what I did. One moment, one breath, one choice at a time.

Chapter 18

Fault Lines

Katie

With me emotionally recovering and Chris physically recovering from the whirlwind of 2022, we did our best to get back into the groove of work and find our footing in our busy lives. Since we wanted to buy a new home for a fresh start, we decided to sell my condo in Cherry Creek North. Unfortunately, it sat on the market for months with little interest.

As a solution, we decided to completely gut and renovate the condo with the help of our mutual friend, Kim, who owns a reputable interior design business called the Design Project. This felt like the perfect reset. The renovation was completed in just a few months, and I thoroughly enjoyed selecting new flooring, tiles, paint, countertops, cabinets, and appliances. When we moved in July, we were filled with excitement, even though I faced a significant downgrade in closet space. It felt like the promise of a new beginning. Or so I thought.

Two days after we moved into our updated condo, still surrounded by unpacked boxes and finally catching our breath, I discovered Chris hiding a stash of new pills in his pocket. My heart sank. He told me a source had reached out to him from a different number a few weeks ago, and he'd decided to meet up with them.

All of those awful times when I had to sneak through his phone to block any contacts with conversations about drugs suddenly felt like a waste of effort. Apparently, drug sources go through many burner phones, which means multiple numbers would contact

Chris. No amount of blocking numbers ended the relentless temptation to meet up and get drugs. The walls of our freshly renovated condo suddenly felt tainted, and, despite the already small square footage, they felt like they were caving in.

Instead of reacting like I had in the past when I'd encountered hidden pills, by screaming and yelling and slamming doors, I just sat on the ground and listened. Chris was honest with me and expressed his remorse, saying how sorry he was and that he needed help.

By this stage in Chris's journey to sobriety, I'd learned that reacting harshly to a relapse only drives the person further into their shadows. Relapse isn't just the act itself, but it also includes doubt, self-sabotage, temptation, self-pity, moments of weakness, and, most difficult of all, shame. Shame is the kindling fire that fuels the cycle and is the most significant part of this complicated puzzle. I think it keeps many people from seeking help because they are reluctant to admit they are struggling. I feel like the shame keeps them from getting better.

I understand how easy it is to get completely caught up in anger, frustration, and betrayal, and to stay stuck in the lies and absolute chaos of it all. It's raw, infuriating, and heartbreaking. Here I was yet again, standing there with the weight of everything crashing down around me. *AGAIN*!

I wanted to feel some control in the turmoil, but any rules, boundaries, or consequences felt insufficient.

Over time, working with our therapist, we created a relapse plan—a framework that clarified boundaries, expectations, deal-breakers, and responsibilities for both of us. Looking back, I wish we'd had this insight during those early relapses. It would have given us a roadmap when everything felt chaotic and maybe spared some of the anger, guilt, and helplessness we both carried.

For example, our plan included:

- ⌘ Radical and constructive honesty: sharing everything relevant, but only if it supported the relationship rather than escalating conflict.

- ⌘ Clear boundaries and deal-breakers: We are both committed to upholding them consistently.
- ⌘ Ongoing one-on-one therapy: no exceptions, with open communication between therapists, if needed.
- ⌘ External support system: ensuring we each had people to turn to outside of the relationship, for guidance and emotional support.
- ⌘ Drug testing agreements: deciding together how to monitor and maintain accountability.

This plan became a tool to navigate the chaos without being consumed by it, and it allowed me to practice forgiveness intentionally. Not because it's easy, but because it's the only way forward. Forgiveness doesn't mean you forget or excuse the behavior. It means loving someone through the darkness when they can't see their way out.

And I know how hard it is to hold a flashlight to shine a little light for them while you are desperately grasping to protect your own little bit of sanity. Please don't forget about yourself in this mess. You must also take care of yourself, and protect your peace fiercely. Whatever that looks like for you.

Believe me, I've had to do both. I've become someone who can look at the worst moments and say, "Okay. He messed up… again, but he is still willing to try again to get clean." Getting sober isn't a linear process; it's not a clean break or perfect. In fact, from my experience, relapse is more of a rule than an exception. And that's one of the most brutal truths to accept, especially when you're watching someone you love hurt themselves repeatedly, as well as hurt you. As long as they're willing to do the work, to sit with the discomfort, the shame, the guilt, and come back to say, "I want to try again, I'm so sorry," then I must respond with a decision of my own.

For me, that decision has been to keep showing up, to remain honest, and to continue choosing love, even when it's complicated. After another long and intense conversation, where everything was laid bare and we both sat in the weight of the truth, we did what we could. We sat in the heaviness. He admitted it. Said it out loud.

And when the silence finally broke, I just asked, "Are you still willing to try?"

He nodded yes.

So, I grabbed my keys, went to the store, and picked up what we needed to detox: electrolytes, crackers, Epsom salts, Pedialyte, and ginger chews. With no panic, just numb familiarity. When I returned, I didn't say much. Chris had drawn himself a bath, and I could see the disappointment in his eyes, like the scared kid who just didn't want to drown. He was quiet and exhausted.

Let me be clear about one thing. I do not recommend detoxing from opioids or benzodiazepines at home. It can be incredibly dangerous. The safest way to detox from these substances is under the supervision of medical professionals in a rehab facility or by going to a hospital. And this time was different. It wasn't as severe as when he went to the Refuge. We caught it early, and it felt more like a physical reset than a full-blown medical crisis.

I watched him closely. We monitored his vitals and ensured he was hydrated, supported, and not alone. However, if you ever find yourself in this situation, please do not go it alone. Don't try to tough it out without support. Mostly, when it comes to detoxing, I'd say you can't do it without medical help, so it's not something I'd recommend doing on your own.

For the rest of 2023, things improved for a bit. After coming back from enjoying a much-needed relaxing few weeks at the cabin with our family and celebrating our third anniversary on New Year's Eve, we returned home, looking forward to the opportunities that 2024 would bring. In full work mode, Chris found himself working late nights at the office.

One night in January, Chris told me he would be home late, so I went to bed at a reasonable hour. When I awoke and looked over to his side of the bed, I only saw Lexi sprawled out next to me. I called out anxiously, "*CHRIS*! Did you fall asleep on the couch again?"

There was no answer. I sprang up and looked around the corner to see a blanket I had left on the couch the night before, but no Chris. I nervously called Chris, but there was no answer. I dialed three more times, but still no answer. I tapped on his name to see his location on the map, and the little "C" was hovering over our office.

I sighed anxiously, then looked over at our dog and whispered, "Oh, man, your dad is constantly keeping me on my toes." Just then, my phone vibrated, and I looked down to see he was returning my call. He sounded exhausted and scared.

"Katie, oh my God, I am so sorry. I fell asleep at the office. Please don't be mad! I can't believe I did that. I'm going to pack up now and come home."

I didn't have the energy to be upset, so I simply replied, "Okay, I was really worried. See you soon."

When he finally came in the door, he hugged me and said, "I think I'm going to lie down for a bit. I didn't sleep well," then he unmade the bed to lie down.

While scrolling through my phone to check emails, my heart suddenly dropped. I came across something disturbing that stopped me in my tracks. I'd received an email from our office building management containing video footage and screenshots of Chris walking around communal shared areas at 2:40 a.m. The email stated they were opening an investigation to file a report. They requested an explanation for why he was on the property in the early hours of the morning.

Panicked, I immediately ran to our bedroom and woke up Chris to tell him about the email. He sat up in shock as I read the email aloud. After I asked him a million questions, he said he would immediately craft an email offering clarification regarding last night. Obviously, I already knew what had happened, and the reality was he had relapsed.

In his email, he sincerely apologized, explaining how embarrassed he was to have fallen asleep in the office, and he hoped they understood this wasn't normal. He deeply regretted how this may have looked. He acknowledged the broken trust and offered to make amends in any way they saw fit, asking for the chance to speak with them in person.

Unfortunately, due to the terms of the lease, they decided to move forward with an investigation. We had to move out of the office by the end of the month.

Even though Chris had sent an apology, and I stood by him in front of the property managers, something cracked deep within me that day. It wasn't just the relapse. It was the continued breach of trust. I found myself in the position of having to fix another thing he'd caused, and I had to be the one to pack up our office on my own. And I also needed to find us a new office space by the end of the month.

We had to find a defense attorney for Chris because we didn't know what charges would be pressed, if any.

Professionally, the timing couldn't have been worse. Our business had finally started gaining momentum, and we had built a reputation for integrity. Suddenly, I found myself worried about what others might say, whether our office neighbors would know, or if the news would spread beyond those four walls. I felt the tension every time I walked into the building, anticipating side glances or polite smiles that might conceal judgment. It was unsettling.

One of my biggest fears about taking the step toward writing this book was the slight chance that people would read about our honesty regarding a topic that is taboo and complicated. I worried that they wouldn't see past Chris and me and our imperfections, and that they wouldn't want to work with us. But hey, their loss if they decide not to work with us. We are all imperfect, sinful humans. We just decided to share intimate details, but I think that makes us brave.

At the same time, sharing our story feels necessary. Addiction and recovery are often hidden in silence, shame, and misunderstanding, and by telling our truth, we hope to offer connection, understanding, and encouragement to anyone navigating similar struggles. Our imperfections don't make the message less valuable; they make it real, human, and relatable. This book is not just about what we went through, but about what we've learned, what we continue to navigate, and how love, resilience, and hope can coexist with imperfection.

On top of everything else, as if my nervous system wasn't already fried, my Detective Katie radar was going off, and I went on a hunch. I caught Chris hiding pills in his pockets. A handful of them.

Chris looked at me, distraught. Speaking softly and full of shame, he said, "I'm so sorry." He went on to explain he had found pills in a ski jacket while we were at the cabin, and when he got home, he'd had a source reach out, and he'd acted on it.

My body went completely still. I honestly don't think I even blinked. I wanted to scream. And boy, did I. I was furious. I threw things, I packed a bag because I couldn't bear to look at him, and in the heat of the moment, for the first time, I said, "I'm done. I can't do this anymore." I was tired of riding this never-ending rollercoaster, with its unexpected drops that left me gasping for air.

Remember when I mentioned I felt like I was walking through a paradox in how I perceive the world and its hypocrisies? In this moment, I became a walking hypocrite. Earlier in the chapter, I discussed being calm and understanding regarding relapse, as well as being forgiving. But right then, I was losing my shit. I felt like a dragon, ready to unleash my fury. Welcome to the contradictions and cognitive dissonance of addiction.

Chris kept begging for forgiveness and for another chance, saying it would never happen again. And somewhere between his apology and my silence, we sat there on the cold kitchen floor, unsure of what to say or do to fix it this time. This wasn't just a bad decision or a mistake at the office that could be corrected. It was a whole storm brewing beneath the surface, raging full of lies, shame, and deceit. I could feel the sirens going off in my head for the tornado warning for the irreversible pain and damage my cruel tongue was about to deliver.

Instead, I ran and locked myself in the bathroom, where I texted my older sister, Ash: *9-1-1- emergency!!! I need you to call Mom and tell her to get down here immediately. NOW please!!*

I needed my mom. I took a deep breath and knew what we needed to do.

Despite Chris's progress, his addiction had washed over our marriage, our home, and now our business like the tide, and it felt like it couldn't be stopped. I wish I could have just sat in the bathroom's darkness, in my happy, disassociated space, but I knew I had to keep going, even with my broken heart.

So, as I peeled myself off our new marble-tiled floor, I knew where we had to go. The hospital. Chris was getting the help he needed. And the person I needed most was on their way to pick up the broken pieces of her daughter. This was my rock bottom.

Once my mom arrived, we all piled into her car and headed to Anschutz Medical Center's E.R. On the car ride over, I don't think I had ever been so mad. It was hard to be compassionate toward Chris, and it felt hard to grasp. Beneath all that rage, there was a deep punch of confusion. How did we get here again? How did I get here?

When we arrived and checked in, we waited to be called back so that he could be assessed. Once they took us back into a closed room, they asked us multiple questions. I felt he needed a mental health evaluation based on some comments made after I suggested we separate, along with their help for him to detox.

Eventually, the caseworker separated us because they could see the hostility boiling between us. Over the next two hours, the caseworker went back and forth like a pinball between Chris and me, relaying our conflicting information. By 1:00 a.m., the news hit me like a punch to the gut: the hospital was going to discharge Chris.

They handed him a piece of paper with a referral to a program he qualified for called CeDar (Center for Dependency, Addiction and Rehabilitation), for him to follow up. Apparently, this program would help Chris craft a personalized outpatient treatment plan to help his mental and physical health needs for his substance use disorder.

The hospital claimed they couldn't assist with his detox and saw no medical reason to keep him overnight. I sat in that stiff plastic chair, completely overwhelmed, holding my mom's hand as we waited for the few prescriptions that they sent him home with, something for the body aches and something for the anxiety. They explained that, because Chris wasn't showing full withdrawal symptoms and already had a prescription for buprenorphine (medication for opioid use disorder), there was no reason to keep him.

It felt like the system had slammed a door in our faces. I couldn't believe it. After everything, we were sent home to figure out the scary situation ourselves. It was now our responsibility—or should I say *my* self-assigned responsibility—to find him a bed in a rehab facility. One that could safely help him detox and give him another chance at recovery. It felt impossible, and it ultimately turned out to be chaotic.

After my mom dropped us off, Chris went straight to bed, completely exhausted. I didn't have that luxury. My mind racing, I opened my laptop and started Googling for recovery centers. I left voicemail after voicemail, hoping that by morning one of them would call back with the words I was praying to hear: "We have a bed available."

In the meantime, I also began filling out intake forms for couples therapists in the area. I typed as honestly as I could, hoping they would sense the desperation in my words, even though I wasn't exactly sure how to express it. I just needed someone to help us make sense of the chaos. We required an unbiased third-party individual to help bear the burden I could no longer manage alone and to see whether we could fix the broken pieces that weren't falling into place.

As I crawled into bed, I knew the night ahead would not be fun, but we did what we could. The next morning, I received voicemails from a handful of recovery centers stating that there weren't any beds available, but to keep calling back each day to see if the situation changed. Any remaining hope slowly drained from my body.

When my phone rang, it was the last center that hadn't called me back. They said they were close to capacity, but we could come for an interview later that evening, at 6:00, to see if Chris would be a good fit. The day dragged on, but when it was finally time to head south to the recovery center for his appointment, we packed a bag with a change of clothes and some toiletries and headed to the car.

Chris was not in good shape. He was shaking, had a horrible headache, and was nauseated. Once we checked in with the front desk, I noticed how disorganized they were. They said they would get us when they were ready.

As we watched the clock tick to 7:15, my annoyance and frustration grew, especially as I saw Chris lying on the carpeted floor, using our packed bag as a pillow and my jacket as a blanket, shaking in pain. I stood up quickly and marched to the front desk, demanding an explanation. The nurse informed me they had accidentally given our reserved time to someone else, but they were wrapping up the current interview, and assured me it would be any minute.

Between the sleep deprivation and the stress of the last few days, my patience was wearing thin. I told her that if we weren't seen in the next fifteen minutes, we would leave. As the clock struck 7:30, I had had enough and started to help peel Chris off the floor. Just then, the woman at the front desk cried out that they were ready for him. I was disappointed to learn that I was not allowed back with Chris during the interview. As I watched the two heavy wooden doors close slowly behind him, I let out a tiny sigh of relief.

With time on my hands, I did more in-depth research on the facility, reading the comments people had made regarding their experiences and stays. Almost every review I read mentioned disorganization and unprofessional behavior among the staff. Multiple individuals mentioned they needed additional therapy after their experiences there, due to the trauma they'd encountered.

As alarm bells went off in my head, I immediately demanded they open the doors so I could grab Chris and leave. Once in his small room, I pulled Chris aside and told him I didn't feel comfortable with him staying there and that we were going home. I was convinced that people were watching us through the double-paned window.

Moments later, two staff members arrived and said, "After our evaluation, we don't think Chris is a good fit. He mentioned that his legs felt like they were on fire and tingling, which is beyond our area of expertise."

I thanked them for wasting our time, and we quickly left for home. I couldn't help but think how ridiculous the last two days had been and how broken the system felt. It seemed almost set up to fail. Where you try to get help from the hospital, only to be turned away, and then you search for a bed at a recovery clinic, only to find they are all full. What on earth would we do if we hadn't had a safe, warm place to sleep that night?

We left feeling defeated. Chris was experiencing withdrawal and desperately craved our bed and a warm bath. As I approached the ramp on our way home, I was tempted to turn left to see if another hospital could help us, but I decided to turn right and head home on the highway instead. The next day, I had a glimmer of hope when I received a call from one of the therapists I had contacted. She asked if I had a few minutes to talk, to see if we would be a good fit for couples therapy. I thought the call went well; I believe she could sense the desperation in my voice and agreed to meet with us the following week. I felt relieved.

After a few long days had passed, I noticed that Chris's withdrawal symptoms were lessening, and the fog seemed to clear, with Chris gaining more energy. I had completely forgotten that I had scheduled a nail appointment with a new technician at an independently owned nail salon in the Whittier neighborhood called Acronychous. Since I didn't want Chris to be alone, I called my mom to help me out for a few hours and keep him company.

I will never forget my first appointment with Nikki. I felt like Elle Woods in *Legally Blonde* when she sat down at the nail salon after Warner dumped her for not being serious enough and seeing her diamond ring on another girl's finger.

I didn't have the energy to put on any makeup to cover the deep, dark circles under my eyes, but I ended up pouring out all my feelings of frustration and sadness to Nikki. She just sat back and listened without judgment while bringing my cuticles back to life. I swear, nail technicians should have to get a psychology degree, since they listen and give so much advice to the mess of a client in their chair.

Once home, I relieved my mom of her duty, thanked her, and told her how much I really needed to get out of the house and have a little "me" time. After walking her out and walking back into our condo, Chris was standing with his hands in his pockets, waiting to talk. I could tell he was in deep thought, so I just sat back and listened.

He told me how incredibly sorry he was and that he was done messing up. I knew he felt ashamed and guilty for what had unfolded over the previous days, and he was ready for change.

I replied, "You can't just say sorry and expect that to be enough anymore, Chris. I want to believe you. God, I really do. But you need to show me something different. Not for me, but for yourself."

He nodded and agreed, his head in his hands, rubbing his eyes. Not much was said, but I could feel the moment opening up to the hopes of a new beginning and the belief that we could rebuild what had been broken. I don't know why, but this time he felt heavier, with a different tone and demeanor. Healing, like relapse and addiction, is also not linear. It is complex and difficult to comprehend.

Over the following week, we had a few glimmers of hope that helped bolster my sanity. The first was meeting our new couples therapist, Madison. She didn't know it yet, but she would become a significant reason we could start to climb out of the depths of the holes we had dug. I believe she played an essential role in saving our marriage.

The second glimmer of hope came from my functional wellness doctor, who introduced me to someone named Jason, who had helped him and other clients tremendously with alternative medicine options for managing inflammation. Jason wanted to meet me to discuss microdosing (taking tiny amounts of psilocybin mushrooms) and see if I would be a good candidate for it.

One day, I asked Chris if he wanted to join me for coffee to see if he could benefit from this approach, too. I had read a few articles suggesting that microdosing psilocybin had been explored for addiction recovery and mental health, so I thought it was worth a shot! And boy, was I happy he came along.

We really hit it off with Jason, who was incredibly professional and genuinely cared about us and our situation. He provided us with a sample of our first dose to gauge our reaction, and after about thirty minutes, we went for a walk. Time slowed down a bit, and I noticed tiny pieces of light shimmering through the trees as the wind gently lifted a few flowers, making me feel lighter. It was a subtle but noticeable effect.

Jason's advice was that the key to microdosing is to be mindful of the reasons for taking it. It helps to pair it with a specific intention and to take "breaks" in between doses. For example, we could do five days on and two days off, or four days on and three days off, and so forth. Chris really embraced this new opportunity, and I believe this was the first time in a long time when he felt truly in control. His busy mind seemed to quiet down.

Unfortunately, our sunny walk around Cherry Creek ended with us needing to answer a phone call from an attorney named Joe, whom we had contacted earlier in the week. He said he'd be happy to meet with us the following morning to discuss what had happened at the office.

After meeting our new defense attorney, we hired him on the spot. After reviewing the Denver Police report, it became painfully clear that we needed someone in our corner who could help ensure that Chris's voice wasn't lost or distorted.

The weight of everything we were carrying—the shame, the fear, the unknown—came crashing down in that office. But at least now, we weren't facing it alone.

Nothing could brace us for the news we would receive from Joe a few days later. Chris had to spend a night in jail.

Chapter 19

Beyond the Prescription Pad

Chris

I didn't get clean the "traditional" way. I didn't collect chips or memorize Steps by heart. I went to meetings, sat in smoky church basements, and drank the bitter coffee. I listened to stories that felt both too familiar and too far away. But my recovery didn't come with a map or a sponsor who held the compass. It came through people I never expected, through trial and error, and through grace, the kind that looks like chaos while you're living inside it.

For a long time, I believed that meant I wasn't really in recovery. That I hadn't earned the right to say I was healing. I told myself, unless I was doing it *by the book,* I was faking it. That my version of sobriety didn't count. If you are at the beginning of your own walk toward recovery, you'll know this feeling. You'll feel pushed to choose a side.

For me, that decision was heartbreak in itself. Because I loved my life! I was exactly where I wanted to be, just before it became too much. Selfishly, I wanted it back. I accepted my surrender to substances, but I did not accept or want to surrender the life that was waiting for me.

Here's what I've learned: there isn't one book. **There is no single path to sobriety.** There's only the road that keeps you alive long enough to remember that you're worth saving. Mine took turns I never saw coming.

Another part of this process was realizing that recovery had to be for me, not for Katie, not for my family, and not for anyone watching or waiting for proof. As much as I wanted to make everyone proud, to give the people in my corner the win they deserved, I had to face a painful truth. Even Katie, the person who had stood by me through everything, who more than anyone deserved to see me sober, couldn't be my reason. It broke my heart to admit that. Because if love alone could have saved me, I would have been healed long ago.

For a long time, I tried to heal on other people's timelines. I wanted to make everyone proud, to move fast enough to earn forgiveness, and to show progress that could be seen and measured. But healing doesn't work that way. Recovery happens when you're ready—not when someone else thinks you should be. It took me time to understand that doing the work for myself wasn't selfish. It was the only way it would ever last. Because, when you start doing it for yourself, that's when it finally sticks.

For me, it started with Suboxone.[8] Suboxone is a combination of buprenorphine and naloxone, a medication designed to quiet the brain's craving without creating the same euphoric high. It's like rewiring a circuit that has been sparking out for too long. It doesn't erase the addiction, but it gives your body and mind enough calm to begin the real work.

It helped pull me out of the fire. It didn't save me entirely, but it built a bridge between life and death when I was too far gone to make one myself. It gave me distance from cravings and from the self-destruction that had become my comfort. It wasn't a crutch; it was a seatbelt. And some days, that was the only thing keeping me alive.

Eventually, I began to feel ready to take another step, slowly, carefully. After years of using Suboxone to stabilize, my doctor and I worked together to taper down through the Sublocade shot, an injection in my stomach that released the medication gradually. It wasn't easy. There were moments when my body ached for the old patterns, and my mind tried to convince me that comfort meant control. But what I learned through that process was that healing doesn't mean cutting everything off overnight. Sometimes, it's about loosening your grip one finger at a time until you can finally stand on your own two feet.

I'm on buprenorphine now. I don't plan to be forever, but for now, it's part of what keeps me steady, and it gives me balance. I'm living, not surviving, and that's something I never thought I'd say. This version of recovery is quieter, but it's mine. It's proof that progress doesn't have to be dramatic to be real.

Medication-assisted treatment, or MAT, often gets misunderstood. It uses medications like Suboxone, Sublocade, or buprenorphine to reduce cravings and withdrawal symptoms so people can stabilize long enough to rebuild their lives. These aren't "replacement drugs." They're lifelines. They give your brain and body a chance to heal without the constant chaos of survival mode. MAT doesn't take away your accountability; it provides you with the space to finally practice it.

MAT is not a weakness; it's accountability. But it's hard to admit that. People hear *medication-assisted treatment* and assume you're not sober, as if the only recovery that counts is the one where you suffer the loudest.

That thinking nearly killed me. Because shame is the most dangerous drug of all.

Shame tells you that your progress doesn't count. That your recovery only matters if it fits someone else's definition. It whispers that whatever you're doing isn't enough. That if your doctor says one thing and an article on Google says another, you must be faking it. That if you haven't done the Steps, gotten a sponsor, or hit the right milestone, you're just spinning your wheels. My favorite would be when I felt like I dared to speak about my progress to my family, I was met with Google articles contradicting what I'd told them, basically saying, "Well, the world disagrees, and this doctor in India thinks Suboxone is bad for you..."

But I had to drown out that kind of noise, because it wasn't helping me heal. It was keeping me stuck. Eventually, I got curious about what else was out there. And yeah—I mean, *really* curious.

But here's what people don't tell you about medication-assisted recovery: it's lonely. You live with a quiet chorus of judgment, from the world, from others in recovery, and sometimes from yourself. Everyone has an opinion. Everyone wants to fix something they don't understand. But eventually, I learned to tune out the noise and start listening to my own body and, for once, to the people who truly cared if I lived.

That's when things started to shift.

When I finally made peace with the fact that healing could include medicine, I started to wonder what else it could consist of. What other paths might lead to wholeness beyond prescriptions and protocols? Recovery has a way of humbling you.

That curiosity opened the door to something I never expected, an entirely different kind of medicine. One that didn't come from a pharmacy, but from the Earth. From stillness. From spirit.

Ketamine. Microdosing. Kambo. Bufo. Each of these experiences peeled away another layer between me and the truth.

And the truth was simple: I wasn't just addicted to drugs. I was addicted to escape. To avoid my own reflection. To believing that healing was something I'd *find* instead of something I'd *fight for*.

The first time I tried ketamine therapy, I wasn't looking for a high. I was looking for clarity. For quiet. For a way to sit with my pain without it consuming me. I didn't want to escape anymore; I wanted to understand.

Ketamine therapy came first. It scared me. But fear didn't mean stop; it meant pay attention. And I did.

The medicine gave me enough clarity to remember who I was. It helped me see where I'd gotten lost. When that window of awareness opened again, I took one small step toward God, and He blew my world open.

It's still the most humbling experience I've ever had. To feel welcomed home by the Lord when I was as far gone as I'd ever been. I felt unconditional love through Him. And in this life, I experienced it again through Katie, the kind of love that is human, flawed, and holy all at once.

After ketamine, I started to understand that healing wasn't just about removing pain. It was about learning how to sit with it without letting it swallow me whole. That's when microdosing came into play.

Microdosing is the practice of taking tiny amounts of psychedelic substances, like psilocybin mushrooms, to improve mood, focus, and emotional regulation. It's not about tripping. It's about tuning in and gently rewiring the pathways that years of chaos had burned out.

At first, I was skeptical. The old me would have laughed it off as some Boulder hippie thing. But when you've walked through hell, you stop caring how unconventional the road out looks. Katie and I approached it intentionally, guided by people who knew what they were doing and with clear boundaries in place. We weren't chasing escape; we were chasing understanding.

For me, microdosing became less about the medicine and more about the mindfulness it required. It asked me to pay attention to my emotions, my patterns, my energy. It slowed my racing thoughts just enough for me to hear myself again. Some days, it felt like therapy in motion: the fog lifted, and for the first time in a long time, I could breathe without fear that the next moment would collapse.

That practice reintroduced me to patience. It taught me that small doses of intention can create significant shifts in healing. And over time, I noticed it wasn't just my mind getting lighter, it was my spirit.

The world around me started to look different. Colors felt warmer. Conversations went deeper. I began to notice the way light hit the trees, how the wind carried a sense of calm I'd forgotten existed. I wasn't floating outside my life anymore; I was back inside it.

After microdosing, something in me softened. I stopped trying to bulldoze my way through healing and started to listen instead. I wanted to understand my pain, not outrun it. That openness led me to something ancient, medicine that didn't come in a bottle, but through ceremony.

Kambo came next. It's a detoxification ritual using the secretion of an Amazonian tree frog, known for its cleansing properties. I'd read that it could help purge physical and emotional toxins, but nothing could've prepared me for the experience. It wasn't gentle. It was intense and humbling. Within minutes, I felt the fire race through my veins, and my heart was pounding. But beneath the physical discomfort was a deep release as if my body were expelling the residue of the chaos it had carried for years.

On the second day, though, I fought it. The shaman had told us that many people get off all medicine after doing kambo, but I wasn't ready for that. I had finally found a regimen with my doctors that was working and a balance that kept me steady, and I wasn't about to risk that progress. So, I silently protested. I didn't want to go for another round, and honestly, I was exhausted. My body felt like it had run a marathon it never trained for.

Meanwhile, Katie had the opposite reaction. She was buzzing with energy, bright-eyed, grounded, almost electric. I was lethargic, heavy, barely able to move. The shaman told me that it was normal, especially after years of substance use. My system was still finding its rhythm again.

Even though I didn't participate that second day, I decided to come out and support Katie. The shaman had warned us this would be the most intense day, and I wanted to be there for her. I'm glad I was. When she was deep in the medicine, I held her, steady, quiet, and present. It was the first time in a long time I felt like I could offer her strength instead of taking it.

On the third day, something in me shifted. I decided to give it another shot. This time, I surrendered. No resistance, no fear. And what happened next felt like a proper release. My purge wasn't clear liquid like before; it was thick, black, charcoal-dark. It felt ancient, like something I'd been carrying for years was finally leaving my body. I knew, without a doubt, I had released something heavy and dark that had been living deep in my gut.

When it was over, I felt empty, but not in a bad way. It was the kind of emptiness that makes room for light.

If kambo was a purge, Bufo was a rebirth. Each experience peeled away another layer I didn't realize I'd built between myself and the truth.

And the truth was this: I wasn't just addicted to drugs. I was addicted to numbing. To avoid my own reflection. To believe that healing was something you found, not something you fought for every single day.

When you start living your life on purpose again, it's amazing how things and people all come together at the right time, and usually when you need them most. A friend of ours, Jason, is a magnificent human who came into our lives at the right time. Meeting him set in motion a series of events that have ultimately led me back to my most confident and true self.

Not all these alternative methods work the same for everyone; not all of them worked for me. But many did, and the most powerful experience for me by far was during a Bufo ceremony. A true shaman from South America had made the long and expensive trip to Colorado to share his gifts and culture. He brought with him a rarity like I'd never seen or heard. He was from a long lineage of healers, raised in community and in nature. His knowledge, experience, and connection to the world around him radiated off him, and you could feel it.

I did not know what to expect from this ceremony. I had done a little research, and our host shared so much with us. But now that I have experienced it myself, I don't know that I could prepare someone else for what was about to come or what may come.

The medicine comes from one of the rarest creatures on Earth, a toad, and it is sacred. Before ingesting this substance, each of us met with our guide, one-on-one. I walked into the room and sat down with a smile, and he laughed. He was disarmingly kind and socially aware enough to let me know that it was okay not to know what to ask of him. He asked me a series of questions, and I answered each one. Very quickly, I knew what my question (and therefore my intention) was.

I told him I was on a path back toward myself, but I didn't feel I had the same tools I once did. I was missing some parts of myself that were too important to move forward without.

He said, "Your confidence is your weapon and armor. It has always been your anchor in your greatest storms."

I didn't say anything, simply nodded in agreement.

Then he cut right through me and said, "Do you really want to take a path *backward* to get closer to yourself?"

In complete awe of him and his insight, I shook my head, *no*.

He went on, "Your confidence has never left you, but it's been badly weakened, and in its place, something much stronger has been grounding you!"

I was confused by this, but still, I did not speak. I didn't understand how my confidence could be my greatest strength, yet by losing it, it had been replaced by something much more substantial. I finally asked him, in true American form, "So, ugh, what exactly is stronger than my confidence, and how do I harness that?" He laughed again and said that was what he hoped I would find out.

The ceremony itself is a beautiful experience. The medicine is not meant to be disrespected or misused. No drug or mind-altering substance that I have ever experienced could have prepared me for what I was about to pass through.

In a comfortable, quiet, dimly-lit room with great company, I took my first deep breath inward, filling my belly with the medicine. I exhaled and then inhaled once more, only this time I seemed to be falling backward in a calm, slow motion.

I don't know how to illustrate what "there" looked like to me, but I knew I was "there" when I got there. Everything that I was, that I am, and that I could be, where I felt all emotions that I was able to experience simultaneously. I suddenly found myself in this blissful state of contentment, knowing I was exactly where I was supposed to be, and that I was going to be okay.

It also showed me an actual visual version of myself that I'd forgotten existed. One who wasn't desperate, ashamed, or drowning. One who had survived and then thrived!

In that space, I saw Katie. Not her body, but her essence. She was radiant, calm, and steady, the same light that has guided me through every storm. She wasn't saving me; she was standing beside me. It hit me then that love, real love, isn't rescue. It is presence. It's the quiet strength that says, "I'll walk with you, but you still have to take the steps yourself." And she was sitting right next to this new version of me, simply holding my hand.

When I came back from that experience, I didn't feel "fixed." I felt *awake, enlightened,* and I know this might sound weird, but I was angry. Because, for the first time, I could see just how much of my pain I had been clinging to. I wasn't powerless. I had never been. I just didn't know how to use my power without destroying myself. My victim-mentality bubble had popped! I was seeing things very clearly. I had all the tools I needed. I had all the opportunities I needed.

I had the most fantastic woman in the world beside me, still, after all this unnecessary suffering. She was the anchor in my storm when I couldn't be. There are no words that would even scratch the surface of my gratitude for her. Words aren't really necessary at this point; it is all about what I, and what we, do from here.

That was *the* moment I stopped asking, "How do I stay sober?" and started asking, "How do I stay alive?"

Because being sober isn't the same as being alive.

For a long time, I was dry; not using, but still hollow. Still angry. Still carrying all the noise that led me here in the first place. Sobriety without growth is just another kind of cage.

And if there's one thing I've learned, it's that you can't medicate your way out of unprocessed pain. Pills can't teach you how to sit in silence. They can't teach you how to forgive yourself.

But Katie could.

She was my secret sauce, the constant in a world that never stopped spinning. She didn't save me by force. She saved me by refusing to accept anything less than the man she fell in love with. There's something powerful about being seen by someone who knows your worst and still stands by your side. That kind of love doesn't enable you. It demands the truth from you. It's hard and refuses weakness!

Katie was never the kind of person who softened the edges of my pain. She held me accountable to my potential, not my past. And that's what saved me. Over and over again. She balances love, grace, and walking the line.

It wasn't about being perfect; it was about being present. Every time I fell, she didn't just ask if I was okay; she asked if I was ready to stand up again. And when I finally did, it wasn't for her. It was *because of her.*

There's this moment that sticks with me, not one of the relapses or hospital stays, but something smaller, quieter. We were sitting on the couch, months into my recovery. No chaos, no crisis, just stillness. She looked at me and said, "You're here. You're *really* here this time."

And she was right. I was.

I had finally stopped reacting to my pain and started responding to it. That's the difference between reactive survival and intentional recovery. Reactive survival keeps you alive. Intentional recovery lets you *live.*

The interesting thing about growth is that it isn't always obvious. Sometimes, it's a whisper. Sometimes, it's showing up to the appointments, keeping your word, eating the proper meals, taking your meds, calling your therapist—not because someone's watching, but because *you* finally care enough to follow through.

The truth is, the medical system didn't give me that. Rehab didn't give me that. The prescription pad didn't give me that. They all gave me tools, sure. But they didn't provide me with purpose.

Purpose came from learning to face myself and from the woman who never stopped seeing the good in me, even when I couldn't.

I used to believe recovery was about erasing the damage. It's not. It's about learning to live with the scars and still build something beautiful anyway.

When I think about everything we went through—the hospitals, the ambulances, the withdrawals, the near deaths, the night in jail—it's tempting to call those the low points. But the real low point wasn't any of those moments. The real low point was every time I chose silence over honesty. Every time I chose shame over connection. Every time I believed that I had to fix it all alone.

Recovery is a strange teacher. It doesn't reward you with peace for doing things "right." It gives you peace when you stop pretending you ever could.

If there was a "secret" to all of this, if there was something that pulled me through when nothing else did, it was this: love without illusions.

Katie didn't love the version of me who promised things and broke them. She loved the version who kept showing up to try again. And that's what real love looks like. It doesn't protect you from consequences; it walks beside you through it.

So no, there's no pot of gold at the end of this story. There's no finish line. There's just life. And life, I've learned, is what you make of the moments between falling and standing back up.

Every day, I still wake up with a choice: to be reactive or intentional. To chase the noise or sit with the quiet. To reach for a pill or go for patience. Some days, I still screw it up. Some days, I surprise myself. But every day, I try.

And that's the work. That's life. That's the point.

Recovery isn't linear. It loops. It circles back. It tests you. It teaches you. You think you're healed, and then life shows you another layer. Another lesson. Another version of yourself you're still learning to love.

But every time I look at Katie, I'm reminded that the cycle doesn't have to be punishment. It can be practice. It can be progress.

And if you ask me now what recovery looks like, I won't point to a date or a milestone. I'll point to the life I get to live because of it—messy, imperfect, and entirely mine.

The truth is, none of this came with a manual. There's no single formula, no one-size-fits-all cure. Recovery isn't about choosing the "right" path; it's about staying on yours, even when it twists and turns through the unexpected.

For me, that meant medication. It meant faith. It meant sitting through ceremonies, swallowing my pride, and learning to trust my own body again. It meant grace, forgiveness, and work. Real, relentless work.

The kind of work that doesn't end when the relapse stops. The kind that starts when the noise fades and you're left with yourself, your thoughts, your triggers, your truth.

Every morning, when I wake up, I don't promise perfection anymore. I promise to try. To stay awake. To love fully. To be accountable.

And that's the point. That's recovery. That's life.

Because healing isn't about returning to who you were before the storm. It's about becoming who you were always meant to be.

Katie and I have both learned that love isn't the absence of pain, it's the courage to face it together. We've fallen, we've rebuilt, we've risen, and through it all, we've learned that redemption isn't a destination. It's a daily decision.

There's no finish line. Just the steady rhythm of trying again, showing up, and believing that even when everything breaks, beauty still finds a way through the cracks.

That's how you go *beyond the prescription pad.*

That is how you heal.

Chapter 20

From Frog Poison to Prayer

Katie

I never imagined I'd be the kind of person who would seek healing through psychedelics. At one point, I believed healing had to look a certain way. You talked to a therapist. You saw a psychiatrist. You took the medications they recommended. White coats and prescriptions filled at Walgreens. I didn't question it. I didn't think I needed to.

I am a rule-follower at heart, always responsible, and I thrive in a structured environment. So, I did what Big Pharma told me and I didn't second-guess. But what I didn't realize back then was that some of the very medications prescribed to help me were also quietly numbing me. Dulling my spirit. Dimming the connection that I had to myself, to others, and to the world around me.

They may have helped me survive, but they didn't help me *feel*. And eventually, that became its own kind of suffering… A life lived in the ambiguous gray, going through the motions, disconnected from anything real or sacred. I was spiritually malnourished. I didn't need more prescriptions. I needed to be cracked open. I desperately needed to get out of the gray.

Eventually, my window of tolerance became unmanageable, and I felt disconnected from my emotions and body. I realized it was time to explore alternative medicine options beyond couples or my individual therapy. My dissociation was debilitating, and I had lost my connection to my authentic self.

It wasn't until I fully surrendered, truly surrendered, that something began to shift.

And to be clear, this isn't about rejecting medicine. I was raised in a family with a history of mental health struggles, and I've seen firsthand how life-saving psychiatric care and prescription medication can be. For many, that traditional path is valid and it's essential, and I honor that deeply. This chapter of my story isn't about discrediting that kind of healing. It's about exploring what happened when that approach wasn't enough for *me*.

Five years ago, I might have politely smiled or secretly judged if someone told me they were working through trauma using plant or animal medicine. But pain has a way of humbling you. Of cracking you open just enough to consider that maybe, just maybe, there's more to healing than what we've been taught.

I didn't go looking for psychedelics. They found me when I was finally willing to listen. Not just with my ears, but with my heart. These medicines—ketamine, psilocybin microdosing, kambo, Bufo—were not shortcuts or escapes. They were silent teachers. Mirrors. A welcome invitation back to the parts of me I had long abandoned. They asked me to trust. To soften. To believe that healing wasn't just possible, but sacred.

This chapter isn't about tripping. It's about returning. Returning and reconnecting with God in ways I never expected. Returning to tuning into my body and to the truth buried underneath the societal norms and roles I had played and the multiple masks I had worn.

I'm not here to preach. I'm simply here to share what I've learned, in case it opens a door for someone else. I'll share what the medicines are, yes, but more than that, I'll share what they revealed. Because the most powerful part wasn't what I saw. It was what I remembered.

They helped me come home to what has always been true. Because these journeys didn't just help me feel different. They helped me remember who I really am and helped me peel back the layers of pain, fear, and performance, until what was left was something raw, honest, and reverent. What follows isn't meant to impress or convince you. It's simply what I've lived. A spiritual path that has been both mysterious and deeply personal.

And so, I said yes. Carefully and prayerfully. I stepped into the unknown, not as a rebel, but as a seeker. Not to escape my life, but to finally step into it more fully. My first experience was one I'll never forget.

It began with ketamine-assisted psychotherapy (KAP).

I don't remember exactly when I discovered ketamine, but I was intrigued by it. Although I had heard friends mention ketamine in the rave scene, referring to it as "Special K," that made me nervous, and I knew I would never participate in that. However, as I conducted my research, I learned that ketamine was introduced in the 1960s as an anesthetic. It is a dissociative anesthetic with hallucinogenic properties.[9]

Nowadays, practitioners use intravenous ketamine treatments alongside integration therapy to address issues such as depression, anxiety, PTSD, personal trauma, and other related conditions.

I discovered a woman-owned clinic, and after our initial meeting to determine if I was a good fit, I left feeling seen and understood. I am incredibly grateful to have found Balanced Mental Wellness on my healing journey. If you decide to try this treatment, I highly recommend asking Char to guide you through your journey and be your therapist for integration; she is magnetic, caring, and incredibly wise!

I believe administering ketamine in low doses without setting an intention and following up the next day with integration is less effective. The goal is to create a long-term impact on your mental health. Combining ketamine with therapy allows you to discuss and analyze the deep thoughts or feelings you experienced during your journey. It also provides a change in your brain, promoting neuroplasticity and rerouting neural pathways to establish new, healthy habits. I signed up for the recommended program of eight to ten sessions, which consisted of two ketamine sessions paired with integration each week for up to two months.

I will do my best to explain the treatment and experience, but please remember, it can differ for each person. Before your journey, you need to avoid eating for four to six hours and inform the clinic about all medications you are taking, so they can advise whether any might interact with ketamine; or you need to refrain from any medications or supplements before the treatment.

The journey typically lasts between thirty and forty-five minutes. Wear comfortable clothes and bring an intention or focal point for that session. They will make you comfy in a recliner and provide a blanket, noise-canceling headphones with specially selected music, and an eye mask. (I usually bring my own) I've decided to share a few journal entries from my previous journeys, as I think they might give you some insight into what I've gained from the treatment. (Please be kind.)

February 24, 2022—3rd Ketamine Session

Today my intention was: I feel more peace, and I release my pain

And my mantra was: I am safe and protected

There was a moment when it was completely dark, and I was spinning, and I felt like I was spinning out of control, and I prayed to God. I talked to Him during this session like I really talked to HIM.

He told me I am safe, that it is okay that I am hurting, and it is okay that I have been more silent lately, and He's never left. Then, at one point, everything immediately went to darkness.

I have felt this feeling before. The Devil snuck in and took away my time with the Lord, and he made me feel like I was lost, and that conversation didn't just happen. All within seconds of this moment I'd just had.... I ALLOWED this power to take over my time with God.

And I said, "Go away, you aren't welcome."

And I saw a light in the corner and focused on that. Then, I saw a lighthouse. Not too far away, but suddenly I was looking up at this big object in front of me...towering over me. And the light was shining on the other side and not toward me. And I couldn't reach it.

Every time I go in, I think to myself, there can't be anything more! It's been so amazing and deep already. I got to find me again, little Katie. Finally, I felt a moment of pure euphoria and just smiled and started crying. All my pain had left my body. I got to ask my inner child what are her fears, and what are her needs?

I need to be kinder to myself. I have been through so much. I feel lighter and just so incredibly grateful for this experience and excited to see where it goes.

Everyone in life, I think, tries to think of a word that encompasses who they are, and today, Char and I found mine. It's soft. *I have a* soft *soul.*

Char said something to me after my session that made my day. She said, "Katie, I want you to know you have a kind spirit and can tell that you are finding yourself. I don't know you, but I just want to let you know you are really beautiful. Your heart is so gentle and kind, and your energy is very calming."

March 8, 2022- 6th Ketamine treatment

Today, my intention was: I feel more peace, and I release my pain.

And my mantra was: I will focus on the current moment, and I will meet whatever arises with presence and faith.

As I leaned back in the black recliner, set up with an eye mask and noise-canceling headphones with music, I felt my body sinking deeper in the chair, and as I shut my eyes, I went into my mind to explore and waited for the medicine to kick in. It didn't take long.

Right when I felt the medicine take effect, I already felt like my body was grounded and my spirit and soul were lifted and being healed. I got to talk with God again today, and it was so beautiful.

I asked Him to come over me and help heal the *pain that I've been feeling in my body and my heart. I told him that my heart* was *very heavy.*

He said, "Katie, I know." He asked me, "OK, well, what can we do about that?"

And I said, "Let's peel back the layers."

And He replied confidently, "OK, let's do that."

So, I literally was peeling back flower petals from my heart, and with each one that I peeled away, He would say, "Good job, Katie. I love you. Thank you. Good job, Katie girl."

I've also been having a feeling of spinning every session, and today's was different, I finally can describe it...

It's as if God and I were two little girls in a field, hands crisscrossed and just spinning as fast as we can put the most weight on our feet and using each other's weight, but we never let go, and He never let go.

And then suddenly, I felt this rushing spirit come through my body, and it was focusing through my heart and into my back. It was kind of like an axis just circling, trying to heal that area. I got a little selfish in the session and asked God, "Can I have that throughout my head and where my neck hurts?"

He laughed and said, "No, Katie, we're only focusing on this area for right now."

And I said, "OK, I understand." I then told Him, "I'm in a marriage right now, and I'm really struggling and hurting, and I know that Chris is, too."

And He goes, "Yes, you both are hurting, and I am so sorry."

I asked Him if I would have children, and He said, "No, Katie, I am sorry you can't and won't. But you will be an amazing aunt/friend to other people's children." He then went on to explain that there were going to be some really dark times ahead for me, and it wasn't in the aspect of my life but regarding the world.

He said, "Katie, you're going to need to be very strong through that, so you need to keep going no matter what. Can you promise me that?"

And I said, "Absolutely anything, of course."

Then, suddenly, I felt the Holy Spirit come over me, and I felt like I was being lifted up, but my body was grounded to the chair, and my little petals of hurt were just beaming up from my body into the sky, and I felt lighter and healed without any pain.

I then ask Him, "God, I'm really still feeling pain in my right side."

And He replied, "Yes, Katie, this is a problem, and you need to promise me you'll get this fixed." (It's my S1 and Sacrum*)*

And I said, "OK, I will."

Then, suddenly, I could feel His presence leave, and the presence of Jesus took His place. We walked through grass and just sat down together. We sat in silence. There was no face, no gender, nothing to let me know what Jesus would look like. It was just a feeling.

I told Jesus that I was so thankful and appreciative that He died for my sins and died for me every day. I can't imagine how difficult that was for Him.

He said, "I will do anything for you, Katie, always."

And we just sat together. I have never felt like this before. Excited for what's to come. I'm ready to surrender.

March 17, 2022 – 7th Ketamine Session

Today my intention was: I feel closer to love and not disassociation

And my mantra was: I am patient and resilient

Today's treatment was confusing. Immediately, I felt absolutely nothing. I would ask my mind, "Can I talk to God" "Can we talk or address my pain?"

And my mind just kept slapping every thought away like a flyswatter. Saying, "No, Katie, this is not going to serve you right now."

I have these moments when I blank or just stare, and I am literally not thinking of anything. That's what happened. I think the last month and a half has been so traumatic, with Chris away and the way his family has treated me. This session was about shutting down any expectations or pain and allowing my body to catch up with my brain. A calm breakthrough.

I pray for healing and that fear would flee from me. Good things have to come.

During integration, Char explained to me that, in a disassociated state, your brain can calcify and put a veil on that memory and trauma, making it harder to process. Our reptilian brain, which is in the brain stem and where our instincts live, and mine is hurting, and our internal dragon is taking care of business, and it's not you.

The internal dragon is a metaphor for the voices and beliefs that hold us back from seeing ourselves truly and achieving our full potential. Because of my disassociation, I am no longer in the present. The reptilian brain is the portion trying to keep us safe. We must retrain our dragon and pause and practice, and when I feel an old pattern, I need to retrain it from freezing or folding.

I need to rewire my nervous system and take a pause to understand what I am feeling and what I need. I need to figure out what just happened inside of me.

PAUSE. Keep writing quietly inside these messy pages. Don't be apologetic. Just be you, beautiful you, shifting and becoming YOU.

I hope you can see the insights I've gained from my sessions and how they can be applied to your daily life to help improve your mental health. It's really helped me recognize patterns and emotions, or establish a new boundary.

The real work and growth occur between sessions. It's not solely about what happens during the sessions; it's about how those insights influence your day-to-day life. I think that's what life is all about. It's about recovering and rediscovering yourself over and over. We are constantly evolving, and so are our needs. You need to tap into what those are. And if you are like me, who disassociates often, ketamine provides a safe space for you to dive into and search within, even if you fear what you might find.

At some point, my nervous system encountered something it perceived as overwhelmingly distressing. When it tried to respond, it didn't work, leaving me in a state of perpetual dysregulation. To cope, I would tell myself that, since I couldn't stop or escape the situation, I could put on my "numbing cloak" to disconnect from my feelings.

This strategy enabled me to detach from my body and become less aware of my surroundings. The downside was that I often wouldn't remember what had happened. I did try to avoid overwhelming experiences, but there were times when the situation was unavoidable, and my body would just shut down.

The stress from Chris's addiction took a toll on our marriage and my health. I lost my hair, gained weight because of high cortisol levels, and experienced changes in my thyroid function. My hormones felt unregulated. I had a constantly hazy mind, and I was a wound-up ball of anxiety. Despite telling everyone I was "feeling fine," I finally decided it was time to prioritize my health after being unwell for a long time. I needed someone to help me understand the connection between my body, mind, and spirit and to guide me in healing from within.

Trivida Functional Wellness played a massive role in my journey. They conduct extensive blood tests to assess various aspects of health, including nutrition, cardiac health, diabetes, liver and kidney function, thyroid levels, hormones, blood counts, autoimmunity, genotypes, calcium scores, toxicity reports, and gene-drug interactions. They believe that the best approach to mental health issues incorporates both psychological and biological factors. Their holistic approach encompasses nutrition plans, exercise, supplements, medication, meditation, and alternative therapies, all designed to help patients lead more fulfilling lives.

While the program is costly and not covered by insurance, it has changed my life from the inside out. I believe Western medicine often falls short by pushing surgeries and medications without addressing root causes. For instance, I discovered that I had a hypothyroid condition that my primary doctor's blood work hadn't identified. I also learned about food sensitivities that were causing unnecessary inflammation, and we are working to address my adrenal fatigue and hormone regulation.

I've come to realize and agree that "health is wealth." Without good health and energy, it's challenging to function correctly. My journey to this understanding has been lengthy, and there is no quick-fix solution, so it's essential to be patient with yourself as you begin to heal. Acknowledging that there are aspects you need to work on—whether physical, mental, or both—can lead to significant improvements in your life.

I eventually broke through the dense fog I had been in and discovered multiple pathways to rediscover my health in ways I never knew existed. I did not realize the heaviness I was carrying in my body from past trauma and how it affected my nervous system, leading to overworked adrenal glands.

Before Trivida, I didn't know healing could look like this.

I had never even heard of kambo or Bufo. It was Jason, our practitioner—essentially our spiritual guide and eventually our friend—who opened the door to a different kind of medicine. After introducing us to microdosing, he gently suggested that we consider two additional ceremonies that could support more profound healing: kambo and Bufo.

When he first mentioned kambo, I was intrigued but hesitant. The idea of applying frog secretion to tiny burns on my skin and then purging in a sacred ceremony sounded intense, to say the least. I wasn't someone who signed up for discomfort on purpose. But something in me stirred. Not a loud yes, but a quiet knowing. A whisper that said, "Time to go deeper."

So... what is kambo?

Technically, it's the secretion of a frog native to the Amazon. The medicine used in our ceremony was ethically sourced from the Matsés tribe, which has used this sacred tool for generations.

Our shaman, Robert, explained that kambo has been used by over fifty-four tribes for thousands of years, not just for physical healing, but to clear *panema*—a kind of spiritual heaviness or energetic blockage that can dim your spirit.

Science tells us that kambo contains over 200 bioactive peptides, which trigger a massive physical detox and reset the immune system by helping the body release deeply stored emotional and physical toxins. But I've come to believe that while science explains the how, spirit reveals the why. And for me, kambo wasn't just about flushing toxins. It was about facing what had been emotionally pushed down for years; it was about facing myself.

It offers pain relief, boosts immune function, and stimulates deep physical cleansing.

Kambo also helps with your energy. As the body releases what it no longer needs, it clears out stuck or stagnant energy. It resets your entire system—emotionally and spiritually—creating space for new patterns, new insights, and a more aligned version of yourself. It's like a full-body soul reboot. I wish we could have a button for that.

This process expands awareness. When the noise is cleared, you are left with clarity. You begin to sense things differently. Feel things differently. Kambo doesn't just empty you. It opens you.

Our shaman, Robert, told us kambo had been used to support healing in cases of addiction, depression, chronic pain, cancer, and more. But the key message? The medicine is not the healer… *We* are. Kambo helps guide us back to ourselves.

The ceremony spanned three days. Each morning, we prepared our bodies and minds for the day ahead. Though kambo itself lasts only twenty to forty-five minutes, the whole experience spans several hours (usually four to six), depending on how the medicine progresses.

Robert held our ceremony in a traditional *mesa* style, creating a sacred, focused space right inside our condo. No need to fly to the jungle! We rolled out our yoga mats, laid down blankets and pillows, and made the space our own. It was intimate, raw, and powerfully grounding.

Preparation for kambo is essential. Each night, we would do an eight-to-ten-hour dry fast, which meant no food and no water. The next morning, we showed up with a gallon of spring water. Before receiving the kambo, you drink about half a gallon, with the rest available during the ceremony. The water helps induce the purging and bile flow, to expel toxins. If you've taken a lot of medications over the years or your liver is sluggish, the body responds quickly, and the experience can be pretty intense.

Before receiving kambo, Robert introduced us to another sacred practice: *rapé* (pronounced *rah-PAY*). It's a fine brown powder made from holy plants, seeds, and strong Amazonian tobacco (*mapacho*). It's blown into the nostrils using a special pipe (*tepi*), designed to ground, cleanse energy, clear blockages, and bring alignment. You should start taking this medicine before you begin the kambo.

The first time I experienced it, I didn't know what'd hit me. It stung badly. My instinct was to resist, to scrunch up my face, and to push it out. But within seconds, something shifted. My energy shot up sky-high. My mind cleared. It felt like a surge of electricity went straight to my brain.

Then came the second blow, up the other nostril, and suddenly everything softened. The stuck, swirling energy in my head cleared. I felt grounded, calm, and somewhat buzzed, like there was a subtle, energetic hum between my ears. It opened something within me. They often discuss the "third eye" in yoga classes, and I used to nod along without fully understanding what it meant. But at that moment, I finally got it. That inner sight, that feeling of deep presence, it all clicked into place.

Then came the frog secretion.

Kambo is applied to small, round burn marks on the skin, created quickly with a smoldering stick. As soon as the medicine enters the body, it begins to work. It finds you wherever you are. Your skin flushes, your heart races, your blood rushes, and you start to tingle as circulation opens. Energy rises. Your kundalini wakes up. You feel it in your fingers, your spine, your breath. It's not subtle.

As Robert reminded us: *Sit up straight. Let the energies activate. Let the medicine meet you where you are. Breathe. Relax. Trust.* And I tried to do just that, to surrender without understanding. To trust something older than my fear.

The process is layered and slow. On the first day, I received five burn points on my right shin. Chris chose his upper arm. On day two, I added seven more points. Day three, five down my spine. Each point deepened the process. The energy rose. The purge came.

Let me be clear. This isn't just nausea. It's not a stomach bug. It's your body remembering what it needs to release… physically, emotionally, energetically. Vomiting, shaking, sweating, crying, trembling—these aren't just side effects of the medicine; they *are* the effects. They are the medicine doing its work. Your body is removing what it no longer needs. Sometimes, bile comes up. Sometimes, energy releases heat, movement, tears, or occasionally, sounds.

The second day hit me the hardest. We began with *rapé,* followed by seven points of kambo, and then repeated the *rapé.* At one point, the medicine became overwhelming as it surged through my body, and I had to take off layers of clothing. I was burning up, my hands constricted, and it felt like my body was having convulsions. It felt like something ancient was clawing its way out of me.

I wasn't scared, but I wasn't exactly calm, either. Robert was a huge help during these moments, to help move my energy and the medicine.

Robert moved through the space with such steadiness. He used flower essences, alcohol claps, and mist over our heads to help shift the energy when we got stuck. He reminded us that the mind will try everything to resist. It will create stories, fear, or doubt. It will panic. But the real healing happens when you move through the resistance, not around it.

After each session, we rested. Showered. Nourished ourselves. Slept. Robert explained that most of the healing continues after the purge. The ceremony cracks something open, but it's the integration that seals the transformation. Where Chris felt the need to sleep off the experience, I was buzzing. Alive. Clear. I felt reawakened, energized, rebooted, and full of vivacity.

Yes, it's intense. Yes, it's emotional. And yes, it's beautiful. Kambo doesn't just push out illness… It stirs up the truth. It asks you to meet what you've been avoiding and helps you let it go.

For me, kambo unearthed my buried anger. Old resentments I thought I had rationalized away poured out of me in waves, tangled and unforgiving. But once it moved through, I felt lighter. Like my body had exhaled for the first time in years.

The medicine didn't heal me. It showed me what I needed to heal. It reminded me that I am capable of healing what was buried deep within. That God lives in my willingness to show up. And I did! For three straight days. With no escape route. And I left changed.

Not fixed. Not finished. But freer.

I've heard it said that Bufo isn't something you seek out. It finds you. It arrives when you're ready, maybe not in your mind, but in your spirit. That's how it felt for me. I wasn't searching for toad medicine, but if it shows up in your life, it's because the universe is telling you that you're open and ready. I knew I couldn't ignore it.

Our introduction to Bufo came through Jason, who connected us with Paulo, a visiting practitioner from Brazil. Paulo would guide Chris and me, along with two other couples, through a sacred ceremony held in Jason's beautiful new space in Denver: Qwantify Wellness Collective.

Before the ceremony, we met Paulo on Zoom. I took pages of notes, knowing one day I'd write about this.

His words didn't just inform me–they stirred something in me. He explained how Bufo, like many other sacred plant and toad medicines, calls us to awaken, a call we often don't know we've been preparing for until the moment arrives. It urges us to break free from the conditioned noise of modern life and return to the sacred rhythms of the Earth and the more profound truths within ourselves.

He reminded us that we live in a world filled with noise, materialism, constant distraction, and loud opinions from others. It's easy to forget who we are, and we lose connection to our essence. Bufo helps us remember.

We are the artists of our own lives, and medicine invites us to reclaim that creative power. Our soul asks us to examine our stories, release what no longer serves, and realign. Paolo emphasized that this medicine is not merely a tool; it is a teacher. It guides us to the places we've hidden from ourselves, the wounds we've buried. And in those dark places, we uncover the gifts meant not just for our own healing, but for sharing with others. We were also told it can help reduce anxiety and PTSD, and help deal with substance abuse.

The journey with Bufo, though powerful, can be arduous. The medicine takes us deep into the shadows, where discomfort, grief, and long-held pain reside. But it's here, in the heart of that darkness, that true transformation is possible. We may discover our suffering and the ways we try to hold onto pain, as it may have become an integral part of our identity. Yet the medicine gently tells us there is another way. It asks us to surrender, to trust, and to step into the healing process.

The ceremony took place under a full pink moon in Libra, a sign of emotional balance and transformation. That felt significant. Chris and I moved through the morning slowly, with intention. You're meant to arrive on an empty stomach, so we had a nourishing breakfast, took deep breaths, and cleared space in our minds.

That evening, we stepped into the candlelit room and were warmly welcomed by Paulo. The energy was calm and focused. Each couple brought an intention, and Paulo invited us back one by one to speak with him privately. When it was my turn, he asked, "What's your relationship like with your family? Let me know of any traumas from your past."

I laughed in my head. *Where do I begin? How long do we have?*

He then asked for my birthday and shared that my Mayan spirit animal is the bald eagle. It struck me as fitting, constantly scanning from above, trying to see the whole picture, and always trying to protect. We reviewed my personal mantra together:

I shed, I soften, I surrender. I trust the magic of my becoming. I uphold my light, even around the shadows of the heart. I feel, I learn, I rise. I embody love, truth, and divine responsibility. I am aligned. I am free. I am the light. I am enough.

I meant every word.

With the group settled on our mats, wrapped in blankets, holding space in quiet devotion, the ceremony began. I brought a small glass of water in a Mason jar to place on the altar and later charge under pink moonlight. We started with *rapé*, the same sacred tobacco blend used in our kambo ceremony, to ground us and prepare the body to receive the Bufo. My mind was calm yet alert, as if it knew something significant was about to happen.

We drew numbers out of a bowl when we arrived, and I happened to pick 1. So, I was to go first.

I had tried Bufo once before, briefly, after a kambo session with Robert. But this time felt different… more intentional, more sacred, more whole.

Bufo (also known as toad medicine) contains 5-MeO-DMT, one of the most powerful naturally occurring psychedelic compounds. It's found in the milky secretion of the *Bufo alvarius* toad, which is scientifically known as *Incilius alvarius* and commonly referred to as the Colorado River toad or the Sonoran Desert toad.[10] When smoked, it quiets the mind, dissolves the ego, and floods the body with light, allowing you to reach a blissful, euphoric state. People often refer to it as a "ten-minute conversation with God."

That doesn't even begin to cover it.

The dried toad secretion is inhaled and smoked slowly, much like sipping through a straw. You breathe it deeply into your belly and hold it in for as long as possible. The moment it entered my lungs, I felt my mind stretch open. Bufo immediately cleared any mental blocks and began to soften the sharp edges in my mind. My body surrendered. I sank. There was no turning back. And in this vulnerable space, I opened. I met everything I had been avoiding. It came crashing through the walls of my heart and wouldn't let me push it back down.

I was wailing, crying harder than I ever had. Again and again. I was offered Bufo five more times, and after each inhale, I returned to this place. Each round cracked me open a little wider. Each wave of surrender dragged up what I had buried for so long.

Grief. Rage. Shame. Longing. Love. Sadness.

As if it stormed through the fragile walls of my heart. There was no more pushing it down. What happened next is almost impossible to explain. It felt like a portal opened inside of me, a doorway into everything I had avoided. The medicine pulled me face-to-face with my grief, my longing, my pain. No matter how hard I tried to resist, Bufo demanded I let go.

I folded forward, my forehead pressed into the mat, sobbing from a depth I didn't know existed. The cries tore out of me, raw and unstoppable, echoing from a place I had waited years to be heard.

And then, the words carved into my heart began spilling out. They came like gasps for air, loud and unfiltered, pouring into the space around me. It was my soul speaking out loud, refusing to stay hidden any longer.

I AM LOVED.
I AM BEAUTIFUL.
I AM FORGIVEN.

I FORGIVE CHRIS.
I AM MAGNETIC.
I AM SO SORRY, KATIE.
I AM FILLED WITH GOD'S LOVE AND LIGHT.
I AM ENOUGH.

Each cry was a release; each breath marked a rebirth of my ego. I shook as old sadness left my body, and both resentment and fear poured out. The medicine cracked me wide open and cradled me as I let go of what no longer belonged or served my purpose.

When the tears finally stopped, what remained was stillness, peace, and hope. I had surrendered fully, and in return, clarity came. I was emptied. I then crawled onto Chris's mat and melted into his arms, and we lay there, cuddling gently, with the unspoken promise that we wouldn't be the same after this.

Bufo had reflected my own light like a mirror. It revealed to me the parts I had overlooked, the pieces I had hidden. It helped me remember that I am not separate from the divine, but a living, breathing extension of it.

In the days that followed, I could still feel the medicine moving through me. It softened the sharp edges in my thoughts, rewired old patterns, and reopened parts of my heart I thought I had lost. Colors looked brighter. My capacity for joy, for trust, and stillness all came rushing back. And there were moments, days even, when I cried for no reason. Or maybe for every reason. My heart was finally opening again.

Bufo is often referred to as "rocket medicine" for its ability to dissolve the ego and propel us toward truth. It gave me the courage to confront myself and the grace to accept what I found.

I didn't come back from that ceremony fixed or finished. I came back remembering who I really am. Bufo showed me what it means to be truly alive. Not just to exist, but to be awake. To come home to myself. Me.

And from that place, anything felt possible.

When we began exploring these alternative medicines, Chris and I were in a new phase of recovery.

He had gained a good understanding of his addiction and was able to maintain a significant period of sobriety without a relapse. For the first time in a long time, I let my guard down, and I could exhale. I could stop scanning the horizon for danger. I didn't need to be Detective Katie anymore. And that allowed space for something I hadn't dared to touch: my own emotions.

I had spent years focusing all my energy on supporting Chris in his recovery. But when he stabilized, I was forced to stop, observe myself, and genuinely feel. And what came up was everything I'd buried: grief, sadness, anger, disappointment, resentment.

Because I hadn't felt safe in the relationship to express these emotions, they had festered, tucked away in the corners of my mind and body. Every disagreement felt like a potential explosion. I had built a whole narrative around my pain. I let it define me. But the medicine cracked something open. It helped me release those emotions, and in that release, I felt the permission to rewrite the story I'd been living in.

The healing didn't come all at once. I feel like it rarely does. But the space these ceremonies created gave me quiet moments to ground myself and just be. Small moments of awareness added up to real, lasting change.

What I learned is that triggers aren't the problem. How you respond to them is. There's a split second between what happens and how you react. That space? That's everything. That's where emotional regulation is born. And before these alternative medicines, my emotions were dysregulated entirely and guarded and bolted shut.

Before, my heart rate would spike, emotions would flood in, and I'd go straight into autopilot. I'd lash out, shut down, or spiral into resentment. My nervous system was responding not just to the moment at hand, but to every past moment when I had felt dismissed, hurt, or unheard. I learned that I had to tap into my self-awareness and self-forgiveness, to try to separate the past from the present. Do I let my history dictate my reaction? Or can I pause, recognize the trigger, and choose a different path? Well, hello and welcome to emotional regulation!

Triggers hijack the moment. But with practice, that split second becomes a wide-open space. And in that space, you can finally choose something new. You can stop living in reaction to the past. And recognize the new recovery from the past to the present. With the proper support, they can be understood, processed, and healed. Eventually, you may even come to appreciate them for what they taught you.

I was once told by a masseuse that "your body is innately intelligent." And that is so true. It's doing the best it can with the information you've given it. When you shift physically, emotionally, and spiritually, it can start to heal finally. But sometimes, that healing looks like walking straight through the shit: the muck, the memories, the fights, the tears, the lies, the deceit, the dark nights. Sometimes, you must go through the darkness to find and reach the light.

It's tempting to avoid that. I did it for years. We all have ways of running from discomfort. And I think one way to avoid distraction is through substances, tying to what leads to addiction. The substances can be work, busyness, or even "healthy" things like family or wellness routines. This then leads to the suppression of your feelings, where you stuff your pain so far down that it becomes background noise. And then there's numbing, where we slowly disconnect from the body and spirit, so we don't have to feel the ache underneath.

Our greatest purpose in life is to be true to ourselves and to live authentically. This requires doing the internal work necessary for personal growth. When we do this, we become more connected to others and to ourselves. When unpacking trauma, it will create a ripple effect, impacting your body, mind, and spirit. I don't remember where I heard this, but it's always stuck with me: change is the only guarantee in life, so if change is inevitable, why not choose the direction in which you want to grow?

Over the years, I've also tried my best to develop emotional awareness through therapy, journaling, shadow work, meditation, mindfulness, and prayer. I've wanted to bring awareness to my body through yoga, stretching, bodywork, reflexology, chiropractic, acupuncture, and massage. I've wanted to deepen my spiritual awareness by connecting with God, and perhaps that's not for you, but I'd encourage you to try to connect with something greater than yourself. For energetic awareness, I have tried alternative medicines from ketamine, microdosing, Reiki, sound healing, kambo, and Bufo through energy healing. I encourage you to stay curious about other therapeutic tools available, if you feel led!

One thing that anyone close to me would say is that I have a curiosity for life and am always looking for the next adventure or experience. This mindset keeps life vibrant and full of possibility. That same curiosity has led me into the worlds of functional wellness and alternative healing mentioned above. Each one offered me something different. Some helped me release trauma I didn't know I was holding on to for dear life. Others gave me insight, clarity, and the ability to finally feel safe in my own body again, after years of chronic pain and emotional exhaustion.

But I want to be very clear. These medicines are not for everyone. They are not a magic pill, a fast track to enlightenment, or a shortcut. They require intention, humility, deep, honest, raw integration, and a safe environment.

You need to be careful, because just like any medication or alternative medicine, they can be misused, abused, or misunderstood. Healing doesn't come from the substances available alone. It must come with how you meet yourself in the process, in the weeds, in the humility.

I didn't enter these spaces looking for a shortcut or a quick fix. I came with an open heart and the truth. I have learned to hold these experiences with respect.

Curiosity can open beautiful opportunities and doors, but you must walk through them with your eyes, and your heart *WIDE* open.

And if you are wondering if this is your path, I don't have the answer. But I would say, *listen*. Listen to your body. Listen to your breath. And most of all, listen to any whisper in your spirit that knows you're ready for something more. Because the real medicine isn't what you inhale or put in your body. It is what you're willing to face, once the veil lifts.

The journey toward healing is layered and complex. But with every step, you come home to yourself, one breath, one breakthrough, one brave choice at a time. So, keep trying. One thing you have control over is taking care of yourself, and who better does that than *YOU*?

Epilogue

Drawing Your Own Recovery: No Crayons Left Behind

Where We Are Now

At the time this book was published, the official intervention occurred three years ago. Since then, Chris has returned to use many times, but as of today, he has been entirely free of opioids for one year, ten months, and one day.

That doesn't mean our journey is over. We could have postponed this book to give ourselves more time between those moments, but we felt it was important to share now. Chris's recovery is an ongoing battle, and waiting wouldn't make the story more perfect; it would just delay the honesty, the lessons, and the hope we want to offer.

Addiction and recovery are messy, ongoing, and often unpredictable. There are still moments of fear, triggers, and uncertainty, but there are also moments of joy, growth, and connection that remind us why the fight is worth it.

For us, the focus now is on rebuilding trust, staying committed to each other, and learning how to navigate life together in a way that feels safe, honest, and sustainable. We're embracing the gray, celebrating progress while acknowledging setbacks, leaning into vulnerability, and supporting each other without losing ourselves.

Every day, we make choices to show up, to grow, and to love..., even in the messiness.

Some days are harder than others. Some days, the weight of the past or the fear of what could happen still lingers in the side wings. But even in those moments, we are learning to hold space for each other, to honor our growth, and to trust that love—messy, imperfect, and resilient—can endure!

We don't know what the future holds, but we do know that, as long as we keep choosing each other, keep showing up, and keep moving forward, there is hope.

What to Do with All That Hurt/Who to Blame

Katie: The grief and hurt from being lied to repeatedly created an invisible wound that I couldn't see, yet I felt it every day. It was like an invisible bruise that lived within me. I tried to give that pain purpose, hoping to transform it into something softer. I tried my best to mask it with a smile.

At first, I thought, if I could belittle the ache, it might hurt less. But pain doesn't work that way. John Green said it best: "That's the thing about pain. It demands to be felt."[11]

At times, I tried reasoning with my pain; I even attempted to bargain with it. I begged for it to go away. But the only way out was to stumble through. I had to confront the ghosts haunting my mind, which was filled with the lies, deceit, and manipulation Chris had put there. It just seemed so unfair.

I needed to sit at the feet of Jesus and confess how this experience had shattered me in ways I will never fully understand. In silence and therapy, I was able to repair the loss of time. By taking the time to slow down and honestly acknowledge the weight of my feelings, I found the strength to hand over my burdens to Jesus when they felt too overwhelming. Since grief and anger had settled within me, I began to unpack how my grief was proof of the depth of my love. However, it had turned into resentment.

I am grateful for the alternative methods I sought to help release the constant, resentful feelings I'd tried to bury. Through that resentment, I rediscovered hope. I know how challenging this journey can be, but I want you to know that I'm proud of you for having the courage to start. Here's to taking it one day at a time!

Takeaway: Grief, in its rawest form, can linger, but when we allow it to shape us, rather than define us, we find that healing has already begun ***and is possible.***

Chris: For years, I pretended I was not hurting anyone, and this disease was only affecting me. You try to minimize the damage and tell yourself it isn't *that* bad. That you'll fix it tomorrow. That no one really sees what's going on behind the charm, the hustle, or the excuses.

But eventually, the truth catches up to you. And when it does, it doesn't just knock. It kicks the fucking door in. The hardest part about getting clean isn't the physical withdrawal. It's waking up to the wreckage. It's seeing the look on the face of someone you love who doesn't know if they can trust you anymore. It's the feeling of shame settling in your bones. It's realizing the pain you've caused and the lies you told, the promises you broke, and the nights you disappeared.

And it's asking the same question over and over again:

What the hell have I done? What the hell am I doing?

You might want to point fingers. Blame your upbringing. The trauma. The system. The pain. And let's be real, some of that blame is valid. The medical system is both a miracle and a mess. Rehab centers can save your life or exploit it. They are also in the business of making money. Society judges the addicted as if we chose this for fun as an extracurricular activity on our school schedule.

But at the end of the day, the question isn't about blame. It's about responsibility. No one is coming to save you. And no one can carry the weight of your pain except you. That doesn't mean you have to do it alone. It just means you have to decide you're done hurting people to protect your own numbness.

I used to think I was too far gone. I couldn't forgive myself because I didn't deserve forgiveness. But I've learned that shame is just pain turned inward. And the only way to stop the bleeding is to stop running from it. Feel the hurt, let it teach you the hard lessons, and let it help you rise from the ashes of what you have burned down in your life. The pain? It's proof that there's still a part of you that wants to do better. That part is worth holding onto. Don't let it go.

Even if you feel like shit. Even if your name's been dragged through the mud. Even if you're still shaking from whatever you did last night, there is still something left in you that wants to heal, and that is more than enough.

Takeaway: You don't have to fix everything overnight. You have to stop lying to yourself about the pain you've caused, and the pain you're still carrying.

What Addiction Took and What It Taught Us

Katie: Addiction is a thief that robs us of moments of joy. It takes away trust, safety, stability, time, and peace of mind. It creates financial instability and emotional chaos, miscommunication, and codependency. This process unfolds gradually, making it hard to notice warning signs. When you start to see them, you may feel a sense of denial or be unsure of how to seek help, just as I was.

As the partner caught in the crossfire, I lost myself, trying to save someone who didn't always want to be saved. As a result, I burned out and broke down. I experienced constant frustration and anger, which sadly became my new normal. I lost my ability to feel peace and comfort in our relationship.

Through this journey, I've learned that love can sometimes not be enough, but compassion is more important than I ever realized, along with the importance of surrendering. Addiction has revealed the fragility of trust and how challenging it is to rebuild what has been broken. Yet, it has also shown me my own strength in persevering. I have learned the difference between helping someone and enabling them, as well as the distinction between standing beside someone and losing myself in their struggles.

Addiction has commanded me to understand boundaries, not as punishment, but as standing my ground with respect and my survival needs. I've experienced raw disappointment and hope, and how they can happen in the same breath, on the same morning, or even within the same apology. It has taught me how to grieve for someone who is still alive and how to celebrate them in moments that others might overlook.

Addiction has opened me up and reshaped the way I love, not through fixing or saving, but by simply witnessing, being present, and practicing detachment with deep compassion. I've learned that surrender is not a sign of weakness and that sometimes it is the only path forward.

Addiction has demanded everything from me: my energy, joy, sleep, safety, health, and plans. But it has also given me fierce resilience. This is a type of strength I never wished to earn, but now I carry it like armor. Above all, I have learned that healing doesn't mean everything is okay; it means that *I* am okay, even if everything else isn't.

Takeaway: Love can sometimes not be enough, but compassion is often more powerful. Compassion for yourself, for the person you love, and for the messy, broken parts becomes the quiet force that moves you both forward.

Chris: Addiction didn't just take things from me. It took over my life.

It stole my values, my integrity, my intuition. It stole years I'll never get back, years I spent disconnected from everything that actually mattered. It chipped away at my self-worth until I couldn't tell the difference between survival and self-destruction. It convinced me I needed the very thing that was killing me.

It cost me my health, my freedom, my reputation, and the trust of people I love. It cost me my dignity. It killed me to watch my wife's face go empty from worry, hearing her voice change after finding the pills again, watching her learn how to brace for impact every time I walked into a room.

Addiction is the kind of thief that robs you slowly, and it tricks you into thinking you're in control while it's taking over your life. But as much as it took from me, it also taught me, too. It taught me that rock-bottom isn't always one dramatic moment. Sometimes, it's a quiet, lonely place you revisit over and over again until you finally say, "I am better than this, and I don't want to live in this mess any longer."

It taught me that detox is just the beginning, a relatively small part of the process. The real work starts when everything you tried to numb comes roaring back. It taught me to sit in discomfort and eventually helped me realize that it is okay to ask for help.

I've had to relearn a lot of basics: How to be in my own body without needing to escape. How to rebuild trust, not with promises, but with consistency and *ACTION*. And how to stop measuring worth by the worst things I've done?

Forgiveness for myself has honestly been the most challenging part, because I didn't think I deserved it. You don't have to wait until you feel "ready." You don't have to have it all figured out. You just have to get better.

Addiction took so much from me. But recovery gave me back something better: **a future I actually want to live in.** It also really makes you see who is actually going to be there for you when things do get messy and not perfect.

Takeaway: You might not recognize yourself anymore. That's okay. You get to decide who you become now.

Boundaries, Not Ultimatums

Katie: A boundary is not an ultimatum; it's not saying, "If you do X, I'm gone." A boundary involves drawing a line in the sand, showing what you will and won't accept, and spelling out the actions you will take if that line is crossed. It helps to define what you won't allow in your life and explains how you intend to protect your peace.

Boundaries are acts of love, not abandonment. When you communicate to a loved one that if they choose to continue along a path of addiction, whether it's drugs, alcohol, gambling, pornography, etc., you may tell them you have decided not to engage in the chaos that comes with their decisions. It may be necessary for you to step back for a while, because witnessing their struggles can be too painful.

Let them know you may need to temporarily step back and disengage from the relationship to strengthen yourself. After all, you need to put your own oxygen mask on first, remember? Maybe also remind them you are worried about their well-being, that you care for them, and that you won't turn your back on them. Remind them they are loved and that your offer of help will always remain available. Setting boundaries isn't out of cruelty. It is one of the most loving actions you can take, both for yourself and the other person.

Enabling behavior keeps them stuck, and boy, did I do this. You need to try to break any codependency, which I still struggle with myself. As someone who enjoys helping others, I often feel compelled to solve their problems. However, if you continuously clean up their messes, you are enabling their behavior and preventing them from taking responsibility for their own decisions. When you allow them to face their own consequences, you create the opportunity for genuine change.

Focus your energy on protecting your own peace. Letting go might ultimately be your best option. You can support, encourage, and love them, but you cannot do the hard work for them. I wish I had taken my own advice sooner because, in my desire to help, I recklessly kept Chris stuck in an unhealthy cycle. Don't allow them to drag you down with them.

Takeaway: Boundaries evolve as we grow, and that's okay. What feels like a firm line today might become a flexible link tomorrow. The key is staying true to your needs while navigating life's fluidity.

Chris: If someone you love has started setting boundaries with you, let me be the one to say it out loud: **It's not because they've stopped loving you. It's because they're finally learning to love themselves, too.**

I used to see boundaries as threats. As ultimatums. Do this, or I'm gone. And my instinct was to rebel. Push back. Call it abandonment. I'd tell myself they were giving up on me or, worse, trying to control me.

But here's what I've learned: when someone sets a boundary with you, it's not about them controlling you. It's about *them saving themselves.*

Because addiction isn't a one-person sickness. It infects everyone around you. It makes the people who love you sick with worry. It drains their hope, patience, energy, and joy. And eventually, if they don't draw a line, they lose themselves completely. So, when someone you love says, "I can't do this with you anymore," hear this: they're not punishing you. They're protecting their peace.

And they should have done it sooner. Perhaps you wish they'd hang in a little longer. But trust me, enabling keeps everyone stuck. When you're shielded from the consequences of your own actions, you lose the chance to take responsibility. And if you never take responsibility, **you never change.**

It took me a long time to see it, but boundaries were the beginning of my turning point. Because when Katie stopped saving me, I had to ask myself if I wanted to save myself. Boundaries aren't walls. They're someone saying, "I still care about you, but I'm not willing to destroy myself while you self-destruct."

And if you're still in a place where you can't respect someone else's boundary, it might be time to take a good, hard look at the boundary you've never set with yourself.

Takeaway: When people start to pull back, don't take it as rejection. Take it as a mirror. And ask yourself if you're finally ready to stop burning bridges with the people who still hope you'll find your way home.

The Reality of Loving an Addict

Katie: Loving someone with an addiction comes with its own challenges. You find yourself chasing every high, every moment of clarity, and every hope that "this time will be different." You may convince yourself, if you love them deeply enough, say the right things, or make enough sacrifices, that they will choose you over the substance.

Unfortunately, there are times when they don't. Whether you decide to stay with or leave someone who is addicted does not make you weak. It can feel like a callus is forming around your heart, hardening over time. But if you want the relationship to work, you need to break down that wall again and again. The key is that you have to do this together. I know this process can be exhausting and painful, but it is worth it.

Another harsh reality is relapse. From my experience, I wish I had heard more statistics. At an Al-Anon meeting, someone said it can take up to five years for someone with substance use disorder to fully recover. I'd like to see where they heard this statistic. However, studies show that more than eighty-five percent of individuals relapse within the first year of treatment.[12]

The likelihood of relapse among individuals recovering from opioid addiction is higher than for any other substance. One study reported that up to ninety-one percent of people in opioid recovery experience a relapse. It also found that at least fifty-nine percent of those who relapsed did so within the first week of sobriety, and eighty percent relapsed within the first month after completing a detox program.[13]

Addiction is a powerful disease that does not discriminate. For some individuals, achieving sobriety may require multiple attempts. This journey often involves serious challenges, such as arrests, overdoses, losing custody of children, or facing repeated stays in prison or the hospital. Are you ready to support them, even when the future is uncertain? Are you able to accept that, even after they seek help, sometimes involving significant emotional and financial sacrifice, they could still relapse months or even years down the road? The uncertainty can be frightening, but it's crucial to understand that recovery is not a one-time fix.

Loving an addict is its own kind of addiction that nobody talks about. We become obsessed with "fixing" them, and you chase every high, every promise, every moment of clarity, and every "this time will be different." Then, when they fall and relapse, it destroys you, like a withdrawal. Then, you think things like, "If I just love them harder, do the right things, say the right things, sacrifice enough, they will stop choosing the thing that is destroying us both." But sometimes, they never do, and yet you can't walk away from them.

It is often messy, complicated, and sometimes takes longer and is more challenging than anyone anticipates... And that's okay. You might decide to walk away, and that choice is valid, too. Or you may choose to fight alongside the Adrift. Although the journey may leave scars, you might both emerge stronger from the experience, if you're willing to try. Remember, you are not alone!

Takeaway: Relapse doesn't erase progress. It merely rewrites the story, reminding us that healing is never as simple as one win or one loss. It's the continual act of choosing each other, even when the path is unclear.

Chris: Here's what no one tells you about trying to get clean: it's not just hard—it's frustrating.

You don't just drop the drug. You drop your entire coping strategy. You drop the false confidence, the bullshit illusion of control. And in its place? Raw, unfiltered you, full of anxiety, shame, trauma, doubt, and a desperate need for something to take the edge off. Because that is your coping mechanism.

People think addiction is a moral issue. That if you just wanted it bad enough, you'd stop. But if you're in this battle, you already know: this shit doesn't care how much you love your wife, your kids, your friends, or your future. It only wants you *numb*. That's the hook. It gives you just enough relief to keep destroying yourself.

And when it comes to relapse/return to use? I used to think it meant I'd failed. That I was weak. That I didn't deserve to recover. But returning to use doesn't mean you don't want recovery. It means the pain you were trying to survive with drugs is still there. And sometimes, even with the best intentions, the need to shut it off wins.

I've returned to use during my journey, more than once. I've broken promises I swore I meant. I've felt the shame, knowing I had to tell Katie again that I'd relapsed. That I'd lied. That I'd hurt her. Again. But here's what I now understand: return to use didn't erase my progress. It showed me where I was still hurting. It revealed the holes in my healing that I hadn't yet patched. It gave me a choice to either go down the dark hole of shame or take it as another opportunity to get honest again.

Sorry to say this harsh reality, but addiction recovery doesn't have a finish line. For me, the timeline has been messy, inconsistent, and full of unexpected left turns. But it's real and raw. And every time I chose to get back up, I reclaimed another piece of the man I wanted to be.

To the person still using: you're not beyond help. Even if you've relapsed ten times. Even if no one trusts you anymore. Even if you don't trust yourself. You are not suspended from healing.

And to the person whose loved one keeps slipping? Please know that their relapse isn't a reflection of your failure. Sometimes, we don't even know why we go back… We just do. But the moment they're willing to try again? That's when something real can begin.

Takeaway: Relapse doesn't mean it's over. It means you're still here. Still trying. Still worthy of a life that doesn't require you to be numb just to survive it.

You Are Not Their Savior

Katie: I repeat: You are not their savior. You cannot force someone to get sober, and you can't desire their recovery more than they do. The real change must be from within them. You can't want sobriety more than they do. No matter how much you love them, you can't force them to heal. And at times, their addiction will be the most important thing to them, over everything else, even though they don't intend for that to happen. When that happens, you may face the hardest decision of your life: choosing to step away.

Walking away doesn't mean you've failed them or stopped loving them. It doesn't mean you didn't try hard enough. It means you chose to survive. It means you decided to prevent drowning with someone who wasn't ready to swim. Remember, that decision is also an expression of love. Love for yourself, and perhaps, in time, it could open the door to a new, healthier relationship with them. The day I decide to walk away will be the day Chris gives up on himself and his recovery.

Sometimes, you may hear "I'm sorry" so often that it begins to fade into the background. I know I am sick of hearing it. However, real change can still occur. When words are finally accompanied by genuine actions, healing becomes possible. I know it is hard when you are losing hope, but try to acknowledge any small actions you see as progress, even if it's slower than you wish to see. Change is still attainable!

Also, their rock bottom might be lower than you can handle—you think it can't get much worse, but with addiction, it always can. How far are you willing to fall with them?

Takeaway: You are worthy of love, peace, and joy, whether it's returned to you or not in the form you expect. The love you give is not a measure of your self-worth; your worth is essential, just as the love you deserve.

Chris: I used to think someone or something else could save me. Maybe if Katie just forgave me one more time, or if I found an alternative to drugs, I'd finally get my shit together. But here's the truth I didn't want to face: no one could save me from something I wasn't willing to surrender.

Addiction convinces you that you're in control. And if you're still out there, expecting someone to fix you, love you enough, stay long enough, or hurt deeply enough to finally make you stop… You're not ready. That's not recovery. That's manipulation wrapped in shame and panic.

You'll say "I'm sorry" a hundred times. And you might mean it. But until those words are backed by actions—daily, difficult, and inconvenient actions—it won't matter. And eventually, the people you love will stop listening. They're not cruel. They're exhausted. And rightfully so!

If you're lucky, they'll still hold out hope for you, even from a distance. But whether they do or not, that's not the point. Because here's the thing I wish I'd understood sooner: **recovery starts when you finally stop bullshitting yourself.**

Your partner isn't your rehab. Your friend isn't your therapist. And no one can want your healing more than you do. When people finally step away, it's not because they gave up on you. It's because they realized they couldn't give up on themselves anymore.

And sure, you might be mad and feel abandoned. But if you ever find yourself at the bottom, alone and ready to ask "what now," that's the beginning of the real work.

Takeaway: No one is coming to save you. But the second you stop expecting them to… you just might start saving yourself.

Addressing Guilt and Self-Forgiveness

Katie: But what about the heaviness of guilt? That feeling of "Did I do enough?" or "Why didn't I leave sooner/love better/say less/say more?" Self-forgiveness is often a crucial part of the healing process, too. I know you know how to forgive, because you've probably been giving it even when it wasn't yours to give.

I've had to forgive myself, too, for staying too long, for saying the wrong things, for not knowing how to fix something I didn't cause. Guilt has been a heavy companion, but I wonder if you can replace it with grace, allowing it to slowly take guilt's place. Who you are in this very moment is valid, and you are worthy. Your healing is valid. Your sadness and your grief are valid. You are enough. Your happiness is valid. You have so much potential within you, and you are capable.

We need compassion for ourselves. We need to cultivate so much curiosity instead of judgment and separation. Pick up love and trust beyond logic, and let go of the ego and pride. We need forgiveness and patience that test us over and over again. Ask yourself, what area of your life is calling you to open your heart? Can you open and soften into it? Where could you offer forgiveness?

I know it's been a long and challenging road, and I know you are tired. But try to find some energy to give back to you!

Takeaway: Self-forgiveness takes practice. Try to incorporate small acts of kindness toward yourself every day. Try to reclaim more of who you are and what you deserve.

Chris: If there's one emotion that clings on for dear life after you stop using, it's guilt. The voice saying, *"You ruined everything."* The kind that reminds you of every broken promise, every lie, every time someone looked at you and saw a stranger instead of the person they love.

At first, I thought guilt was part of the price I had to pay. That if I carried it long enough, maybe it would make up for the wreckage I'd left behind. Maybe, if I hated myself just enough, it would prove that I got it. But that's not how healing works. You can't hate yourself into becoming a better person. You can't guilt yourself into being trustworthy again. All guilt ever did for me was keep me stuck, making me feel like I didn't deserve peace or a second chance.

But over time... and I mean a *long time...*, I've come to understand that guilt has a shelf life. That real accountability doesn't come from punishment. It comes from presence. From choosing to show up, again and again, even when the shame tries to drag you back under into the depths of guilt.

I've done things I'm not proud of. Hurt people I care about. Repeated mistakes I swore I'd never make again. But I've also fought my way back from places most people don't return from. I've owned my shit. And I'm still standing, and I think that counts for something.

If you're sitting in the destruction of your choices, I know how hard it is to believe you deserve forgiveness. But **YOU DO!** Especially from God.

Takeaway: Self-forgiveness isn't a *weakness. It's choosing not to let shame define you. It's learning how to love the parts of yourself that you once tried to destroy.*

Finding a Path That Works

Katie: So, here's the big, loaded question: Is there only one path to recovery?

I personally don't think so. Actually, I *know* there isn't. Because I've lived beside someone who didn't follow the traditional route. And it worked. It took longer than I would have preferred, but it worked.

There are many options and different ways to heal. For some, the Twelve Steps are a practical and life-changing approach. They offer structure and community, and they encourage people to speak their truth that once felt unspeakable. For others, therapy, a spiritual connection, creative expression, or a unique, personal path they carve entirely on their own is what works best. Recovery, just like grief or growth, isn't a one-size-fits-all.

What genuinely matters is not the method or the program but the outcome. If your path is leading you toward peace and healing, keep moving forward. Don't allow shame or external judgment to define what recovery should look like for you and your loved one. All that matters is that, as long as you both are on the same page, you can create a safe space where you can be open about any setbacks, cravings, thoughts, and expectations.

I believe that having outside support is essential, whether that's a sponsor, a friend, or a mentor. Having a solid support system with guidance is crucial. Please, please, please don't try not to walk this road alone.

Recently, I met a friend for lunch, and she made an interesting comparison to help me better relate to Chris's unconventional recovery path. She said she prefers working out alone on her own schedule, rather than attending a group fitness class. It got me thinking about how similar it is to Chris's approach to healing.

Recovery is a Twelve-Step program for some people, similar to signing up for a group workout class. You might even have a workout buddy or accountability partner, similar to having a sponsor. The group environment provides motivation and milestones to work toward, whether it's a fitness challenge, a goal weight, or collecting sobriety chips to celebrate or mark your progress.

Just like my friend Iryna, Chris prefers to exercise on his own terms. He found that his journey needed to be more personal and intuitive. He wanted the freedom to tune into his accountability without relying on an external structure that these traditional programs offer.

In fact, I'd argue it takes more strength to heal without the applause. Healing wasn't about showing up at a particular time or following a prescribed path; it was about showing up for himself, even when no one was watching or holding him accountable. I firmly believe that such a self-motivated path can be more challenging in certain ways. You don't have the built-in encouragement of a group or a sponsor to call, no meeting to attend, no chip to collect. You must dig deep for your own reasons to keep going.

You must learn to trust yourself, even through shame and guilt, to know when to push, rest, ask for help, and be. The voice in your head saying, "You're doing it wrong." It's still commitment, discipline, and growth. Just like an athlete slowly building strength daily, Chris was establishing a foundation of recovery rooted not in external expectations, but in deep personal accountability.

Like an athlete showing up every day, building strength from the inside out, his recovery wasn't checking boxes or getting through each step. It was meeting himself where he was and choosing himself over and over again.

This led to significant rifts with some of his family and friends. Some members wanted him to follow *the* plan, the structured, familiar, approved route. And when he didn't, it created tension. Because, when someone chooses a path outside the norm, it can feel threatening to those who stayed inside the lines. It makes people uncomfortable. Sometimes, discomfort means you are actually getting closer to the truth.

Both paths are valid, and both require radical courage. What matters most isn't the method; it's the willingness to keep showing up and the drive to improve every day. Especially when it's hard. I don't recall where I heard this saying, but I agree with it: I think recovery is like trying to fold a fitted sheet. You know it's going to be a struggle, but there's no rulebook for how to do it right.

But seriously…if you have any tips on how to fold a fitted sheet, please send them to me ASAP. The struggle is *REAL.*

Takeaway: Recovery looks different for everyone. Find what works for you, trust your journey, and remember that progress, no matter how small, is still progress.

Chris: You'll hear a lot of people say, "There's only one way to get clean and programs out there that work."

And if that's true for you, all power to you! But it wasn't true for me.

The Twelve-Step program helped in some ways, and it provided me with a language. But it didn't stick, not because I was lazy or rebellious, but because it didn't align with how I needed to process everything. I wasn't interested in earning chips or uttering the steps in a circle of strangers. I wanted to feel again, heal my inner child, and work through intense therapy to address what I was feeling. I wanted to learn how to sit with myself without having to explain, defend, or conform.

What worked for me? A weird mix of things.

I found pieces of myself in therapy. I got uncomfortable in silence. I explored alternative medicine, microdosing, spiritual practices, animal medicine, and functional wellness. I found my rhythm in self-accountability. My walk wasn't flashy and by no means perfect. It wasn't linear, and it wasn't "by the book."

And that pissed some people off.

When I didn't follow the exact recovery plan others wanted for me, it created tension. I get it. They were scared. They wanted a guaranteed path. But here's the thing: there are no guarantees in recovery. Only choices. Repeated, relentless, messy-as-hell choices. My path was more like a solo hike, not a group fitness class. No built-in structure. No coach yelling encouragement. Just me, myself, and I in a brutal, honest conversation with myself every day about what I needed, what I could face, and what I had to leave behind.

Some days, I nailed it. On other days, I barely held on. But I kept showing up. Not to a meeting. Not to a program. *To myself.*

If you're trying to get clean and the "standard" path isn't working, that doesn't mean you're doomed. It means you might need to try something else. Something more honest. And it is not reflective of someone else's expectations.

Whatever path gets you there? That's the right one.

Takeaway: You don't need permission to heal in the way you think is best for you.

Hope in the Dark

Katie: One of the hardest lessons I've had to learn is that relapse is not failure and is part of recovery. No amount of love can do the work for them.

Outside support is essential. Whether it's a therapist, mentor, or trusted friend, we all need someone who can guide us, challenge us, and hold us up when we are tired. Don't try to walk this road alone.

Along those lines, one of the most important things we've learned is the value of having a plan. A real, honest, agreed-upon plan for when things go sideways. Because, at some point, they probably will. Whether it's a relapse, a spiral, or even just a mental or emotional lapse, having something mapped out **before** it happens can be the difference between chaos and clarity.

As a couple, we sat down and had the hard conversations with our therapist. What will we do if Chris relapses? What does support look like in that moment, for him and for me? Because it's not just about one person getting help. It is about making sure we both have what we need to stay safe, supported, and grounded.

For us, that plan includes boundaries. For example, if Chris relapses, I may need time and space to regulate myself. I might not be emotionally equipped to jump into crisis mode, and that's okay. That doesn't mean I don't love him. It means that I am human.

Therefore, we implemented a backup system. I have a few trusted people on speed dial—our "response team"—who know the situation, love us both, and can physically show up if I'm unable to. Whether that means sitting with him, helping him get to a doctor, or just being a calm, compassionate presence in the chaos.

We've also discussed the medical aspect. Having a supportive doctor or mental health professional who is part of that plan can make a huge difference. Perhaps the three of us (me, Chris, and his doctor) can create a "relapse protocol" together, outlining the steps and care options before things escalate. It might sound formal, but it brings peace of mind. And when everything feels like it is falling apart, peace of mind is everything.

It's not a plan because we're expecting failure. It's a plan because we believe in being prepared for the messy, real-life parts of recovery. Because love without boundaries is chaos, and recovery without structure is fragile. Having a plan doesn't make it perfect, but it does make it possible.

I've spent more sleepless nights than I can count. Yet somehow, we're still here, and love still remains. I see Chris trying. I notice the flicker in his eyes that reminds me of who he is beneath the pain. He is kind. He is selfless. He is fighting, even when it's messy and painful. Because of that, I fight, too.

Addiction tried to take everything from us, but it didn't take our love. It has changed us and tested us, but it's still here. We are still writing our story, one page at a time, and now you get to be a part of that!

Healing isn't linear. Some days feel like progress, others like regression. But I've learned to celebrate the small wins: if we had an honest conversation followed by promised actions, getting out of bed, a clean day, a clean week, a clean year, a laugh that doesn't carry the weight of fear, landing a client that we can help at work, and form a lasting relationship. That's our version of success right now. It's imperfect, but it's ours.

And some days, we are taking our marriage one day at a time because of the broken trust. We aren't in a rush to fix everything, and there will be hiccups along the way. It is simply a matter of whether you want to stay and fight together.

Takeaway: We all have the power to rewrite our story, even when we're unsure of the plot. Trust that every step… no matter how small… is leading you toward a version of yourself that you've yet to meet or maybe healing parts of your inner child.

Chris: If you're in the pits of hell right now, in the shame, relapse, withdrawal, regret... this is for you.

You're not broken beyond repair.

I know it feels like you've wrecked everything. I know you've probably burned bridges, lost trust, and hurt people who would've done anything for you. I know the guilt is heavy, the future looks blurry, and the idea of being "sober forever" feels like a prison sentence instead of freedom.

But hear me: **you are not your addiction**. You are not the worst thing you've done. You are still standing, and as long as you're here, you get to keep trying.

When I was deep in it—detoxing in hospitals, breaking down on kitchen floors, hiding pills, having to be hooked up to machines for dialysis, losing myself—I never imagined I'd still have a marriage, a business, or even a voice worth sharing. I thought addiction had already written my ending. But it hadn't.

There's a version of you whom you haven't met yet, and that version gives itself grace and forgiveness. You are staying to fight for a life worth living.

You're not going to do this perfectly. Some days, you'll take steps forward. Some days, you'll fall flat on your face. But if you keep showing up, completely humbled and determined to move through the mess, you will remember who you are before the wreckage.

I see the man I'm becoming. And even though he's still figuring it out, I like him. I trust him. And I'm proud of him. And I know that you can become someone you're proud of, too.

Takeaway: Hope doesn't always feel like it's possible. Sometimes, it's just the decision not to *disappear. Even in the darkest moments, keep going. You are worth the work.*

Closing Remarks

Katie: Sure, this isn't the chapter I imagined for my life. But it's the one I was given. And I've chosen to make it mean something. Chris and I turned rock bottom into a rough draft. And now, together, we're rewriting the ending. This is not the end.

This is the part where you rise. Not because you're unbreakable. But because even broken, messy things can still be beautiful. From the rubble, we've found our strength. And you? You are capable of anything. I believe in you.

Chris: If no one has told you this yet, I see you. I know the chaos, the shame, the constant negotiations you make with yourself just to survive. I've been there.

But here's the truth… Your story isn't over. You still get to decide who you become.

There's no perfect way forward. But there *is* a way. One honest step at a time.

Keep walking. Keep choosing life. And when it gets hard, **AND IT WILL,** remember this: even from your darkest place, you can still build something worth living for. You can still come home to yourself.

Welcome home, friend.

Acknowledgments

Katie

I was terrified to dip my toe into the book world. It's a sacred, intimidating space, and one I've spent so much of my life swimming in, seeking solace in, and getting lost in different worlds and imagination. Books have been my refuge. But stepping into this space as a writer felt daunting. What could I possibly offer to the same shelves that have carried me through my hardest days? But slowly, word by word, I realized… maybe it's not about being perfect. Perhaps it's about being honest. And so, I wrote the story I couldn't find when I needed it most.

Let me start by showing my love for my parents, Kay and Dan Farland. You have never once failed to make me feel seen, loved, appreciated, beautiful, and worthy. It is one of the greatest gifts of my life to be your daughter. When I said I wanted to write a book, you didn't hesitate to give me support. You beamed with pride, you screamed with joy, and you believed in me before I even believed in myself. Thank you for showing me what it means to show up, to love fiercely, and to never doubt my voice. I love you both so much. Always.

To Ashley and Jess, my imagination and love for stories began with you. Thank you for holding me when I didn't have the words, for your friendship, your wisdom, and your steady, unwavering love. You reminded me who I was when I felt like I was disappearing. Thank you for being my safe place. Thank you for picking up the parts of me that were too heavy for me to hold, for supporting me while I learned to walk again.

To my friends who always ask about my writing with such joy, you are my shining stars. Thank you for being bright lights in the darkest corners of this chapter of my life.

Your love reminded me there was still light worth writing toward.

To my husband, Chris. Writing this with you was an emotionally charged, cathartic roller coaster ride. Thank you for digging deep, even when it hurt. Thank you for meeting me on the page with truth, tenderness, and grit. Thank you for standing beside me in the wreckage, for not walking away when everything around us was crumbling. Thank you for not giving me away. We didn't just survive… We rebuilt, and this book is a testament to that. To the words we didn't think we could say, to the love we didn't know would make it, and to the quiet choice to stay, to try, to love, again and again. I love you.

Chris

To my family and friends: Thank you for seeing me and having the courage to offer me the help I was too proud to ask for.

To my whole world, Katie: Thank you for loving me when I'm not easy to love, and for showing me what unconditional love feels like. In your strength and unshakable grace is where I call home. You are the love; you are the heart of my life.

From the Couple

We want to thank those working on the outskirts of modern medicine. You are pushing boundaries with alternative healing methods. Thank you for your courage and your effort to create safe, compassionate environments and for providing a pathway to healing for those of us who needed it.

Your work has made it possible for us to face our trauma, confront our pain, and heal in ways we never thought possible. You have all helped heal parts of our inner child, and she and he are safe and smiling, thanks to you.

To our mentor during the writing process, Jaime, we are truly blessed to work with you. From the very beginning, you took us under your wing and helped guide us through the intimidating first phase of writing this book. Your belief in us was the spark we needed, and your energy carried us through. Even while navigating your own difficult season, you showed up for us in ways we'll never forget, including writing our foreword with such heart and bravery. Thank you for being our champion.

To our mentor during the editing process, Paige, your energy is contagious. Thank you for bringing structure to our chaos, for organizing our wild ideas into something tangible, and for holding space for our story. Your energy kept us inspired; your support kept us grounded. And thank you for reminding us that our voices mattered. I will continue to aggressively simplify! (Let's put that on a T-shirt, okay?)

To Kathryn, our editor at Landon Hail Press, thank you for helping us shape this book into what it was meant to be. You saw the big picture when we were tangled in the details, and your encouragement challenged us to rewrite! This book is better because of you.

To Ashley Dodge, you helped bring our vision to life through your stunning design work and creative insight. You went above and beyond, often working past your original hours, to create a website that truly reflects our story. You also helped design *The Embrace the Gray Guide* with the same care and artistry. Your talent, patience, and attention to detail turned our ideas into something extraordinary. Thank you!

A huge thank you to SJ at Landon Hail Press, thank you for your passion, insight, and for taking a chance on our raw, unconventional story, told by two previously unproven writers. Your belief in this book and in us means more than we can say. We're deeply grateful for your expertise, your brilliant guidance, and your genuine, tangible commitment to bringing our story into the world. We're endlessly grateful. You are one of the few people who continue to inspire us daily. Your spirit is contagious, and your light is so bright. Thank you for helping us break free from the fear we had with writing our story and truth. You made us feel safe and supported the entire way.

To you, the reader. Thank you for spending a bit of your valuable time with us. It's an honor. Thank you for stepping into our story and holding space for our healing. You are the reason we wrote this book in the first place. We hope you find pieces of truth and hope that carry over and stay with you long after the last page.

Finally, to those who decide/have decided to share your stories with us, your vulnerability is a gift we will not take lightly. Thank you for trusting us with your truths and for letting us glimpse the weight you've carried. We see you. And we carry your courage with us, in every word written on these pages. You help us feel less alone. We hope this book does the same for you.

About the Authors

Katie Bowick is a wife, author, entrepreneur, and proud aunt. She was born and raised in Colorado and studied Communications at university. Part memoir, part playbook, her contributions to *Coloring Outside the Lines* are an invitation for others to consider alternative approaches to traditional recovery methods that are often at odds with sustaining love.

When she's not writing, you can find her snowboarding, golfing, collecting art, or snuggling up with a good book and a glass of wine. As a child of God, Katie finds peace in her faith. She is driven by a deep belief in magic and the beauty that exists in both people and the world around her.

Katie has spent over a decade building a successful career in marketing, communications, and client storytelling. Known for her creative problem-solving and strategic thinking, she brings the same energy and empathy to the page that she brought to boardrooms and brand campaigns. Whether she's crafting a heartfelt narrative or helping others feel seen through words, Katie writes with clarity, vulnerability, and purpose.

△▽△▽

Chris Bowick is a husband, entrepreneur, and recovering perfectionist who spent over a decade building a highly successful insurance agency from the ground up. He graduated from Metropolitan State University of Denver with a degree in Business Management and a minor in Finance.

Throughout his career, Chris has earned multiple licenses in insurance and financial services—including Property & Casualty, Life, Health, Flood, and his Series 6 license—and has been nationally recognized with distinctions such as *Agent of the Year*, *Commercial Elite Agent*, and Farmers Insurance's *Championship* and *Toppers Club* awards. Today, he and his wife run their own independent agency, Val Moritz Insurance Group.

But behind the numbers and accolades was a man quietly struggling with addiction. This book marks a new chapter for Chris, one where truth and vulnerability matter more than any award ever could. Through resilience and recovery, he's learned to redefine success not by titles, but by the courage to show up, even when it's hard. He hopes his story offers strength to anyone fighting their way out of the dark and into a life that finally feels like their own.

Outreach & Speaking Engagements

If you're walking this road and want to connect, we're here. We may not have all the answers, but we promise to meet you with honesty, not judgment.

If you're looking for a guest speaker for your podcast, event, or recovery community, we'd love to connect. We speak openly and authentically about addiction, recovery, marriage, and the gray space in between. Our goal is to create honest conversations that bring hope, healing, and connection to those walking similar paths.

We're available for:

- ⌘ Podcast interviews
- ⌘ Speaking panels and workshops
- ⌘ Recovery, faith-based, or mental health events
- ⌘ Book clubs and community discussions
- ⌘ Media interviews or guest articles

If our story resonates with your audience, reach out to collaborate or invite us to speak.

For exclusive updates and behind-the-scenes content, be sure to follow us on our social media platforms. We love connecting with readers and sharing our journey!

Ready to step out of the gray? Scan here to connect with us.

Website:

www.ChrisAndKatieBowick.com

Instagram:

@lovethroughthegray
@kitkat.attack
@chrisbowick

Facebook:

www.facebook.com/lovethroughthegray

TikTok:

@lovethroughthegray
@kit.kat.attack

Resources & Support

If there's one thing our journey has taught us, it's that healing rarely happens in isolation. Whether you're "the Adrift," "the Anchor," or somewhere in between, there are people, communities, and tools out there, ready to walk alongside you. Some may meet you where you are in your faith. Others may offer practical strategies, tough love, or simply a safe space to be seen.

We found our way by piecing together what worked for us—traditional programs, alternative therapies, and a whole lot of trial and error. This list is just a starting point. Try, explore, and give yourself permission to keep what helps and set down what doesn't.

No one else's crayons, no one else's lines. This is your story to color.

Twelve-Step & Peer-Support Programs

Alcoholics Anonymous (AA) — Fellowship for people seeking recovery from alcohol addiction. www.aa.org

Narcotics Anonymous (NA) — Support for those recovering from drug addiction. www.na.org

Cocaine Anonymous (CA) — Recovery for those seeking freedom from cocaine and all other mind-altering substances. www.ca.org

Al-Anon Family Groups — Support for families and friends of people with alcohol addiction. www.al-anon.org

Nar-Anon Family Groups — Support for families and friends of those struggling with drug addiction. www.nar-anon.org

Adult Children of Alcoholics (ACA) — Support for adults raised in dysfunctional families. www.adultchildren.org

Christian-Based Recovery Programs

Celebrate Recovery – Christ-centered recovery program for all types of hurts, habits, and hang-ups. www.celebraterecovery.com

Overcomers Outreach – Combines Twelve-step principles with biblical truth for recovery and spiritual growth. www.overcomersoutreach.org

Alcoholics Victorious – Christian fellowship for recovery from alcohol and drug addiction. www.alcoholicsvictorious.org

Reformers Unanimous – Discipleship and recovery program rooted in the Bible. www.rurecovery.com

Non-Twelve-step & Secular Recovery Programs

SMART Recovery – Self-management and recovery training using science-based tools. www.smartrecovery.org

LifeRing Secular Recovery – Peer-led support without religious affiliation. www.lifering.org

Women for Sobriety – Program tailored to women seeking recovery from addiction. www.womenforsobriety.org

Refuge Recovery – Buddhist-inspired approach to recovery from all addictions. www.refugerecovery.org

Mental Health & Trauma Resources

National Alliance on Mental Illness (NAMI) – Education, support, and advocacy for mental health. www.nami.org

The National Center for PTSD – Resources for understanding and healing from trauma. www.ptsd.va.gov

TherapyDen – Find a therapist who meets your needs, including faith-based, trauma-informed, or culturally specific care. www.therapyden.com

The Trevor Project – Crisis intervention and suicide prevention for LGBTQ+ youth. thetrevorproject.org

BetterHelp – Online counseling platform. BetterHelp.com.

Psychology Today Therapist Finder –Searchable directory for therapists, treatment centers, and support groups. psychologytoday.com

For Loved Ones of Those Struggling with Addiction

Al-Anon & Alateen – For families/friends of people with alcohol addiction. www.al-anon.org

SMART Recovery Family & Friends – Science-based meetings for loved ones. www.smartrecovery.org

Faces and Voices of Recovery – Inclusive support for all paths to sobriety. https://facesandvoicesofrecovery.org/

Codependents Anonymous (CoDA) www.coda.org

Partnership to End Addiction – Resources for parents, caregivers, and loved ones. www.Drugfree.org

PAL (Parents of Addicted Loved Ones) –Support for parents navigating addiction in the family. www.Palgroup.org

Books that Helped Us

The Body Keeps the Score – Bessel van der Kolk
Untamed – Glennon Doyle
Breathing Under Water – Richard Rohr
Codependent No More – Melody Beattie
This Naked Mind – Annie Grace
High Achiever – Tiffany Jenkins

If You're in Crisis

988 Suicide and Crisis Lifeline – Call or text 988 or visit 988lifeline.org – 24/7, free, confidential support.

SAMHSA's National Helpline – 1-800-662-HELP (4357) –Free, confidential, 24/7 treatment referral and information. samhsa.gov/find-help/national-helpline

Crisis Text Line – Text HOME to 741741 – Free, 24/7 support via text. Crisistextline.org

Endnotes

---

[1] However, to avoid stigmatizing language, the Substance Abuse and Mental Health Services Administration (SAMHSA) recommends using the term "recurrence" or expressing a relapse as "a return to substance use."

https://americanaddictioncenters.org/alcohol/relapse-statistics.

[2] Centers for Disease Control and Prevention. (2024). "Understanding the Opioid Overdose Epidemic." *www.cdc.gov/overdose-prevention/about/understanding-the-opioid-overdose-epidemic.html.*

[3] www.therefuge-ahealingplace.com.

[4] Dr. Gabor Maté. *The Myth of Normal: Trauma, Illness and Healing in a Toxic Culture.* New York: Avery, 2022.

[5] van der Kolk, Bessel. *The Body Keeps the Score.* New York: Penguin Books, 2015.

[6] https://al-anon.org.

[7] https://continuumrecoverycenterofcolorado.com/.

[8] Otuonye IS, Banken R, Kumar VM, Pearson SD. "Effectiveness and Value of Extended-Release Opioid Agonists and Antagonists for Addiction Treatment of Opioid Use Disorder." J Manag Care Spec Pharm. 2019 Jun;25(6):630-634. doi: 10.18553/jmcp.2019.25.6.630. PMID: 31134864; PMCID: PMC10398112.

[9] *Drugs of Abuse, A DEA Resource Guide (2020 Edition) Drug Fact Sheet: Ketamine.*

[10] https://pmc.ncbi.nlm.nih.gov/articles/PMC6695371/.

[11] Green, John. *The Fault in Our Stars.* New York: Penguin Books, 2014.

[12] Brandon TH, Vidrine JI, Litvin EB. "Relapse and relapse prevention." *Annu Rev Clin Psychol.* 2007;3:257–84. doi: 10.1146/annurev.clinpsy.3.022806.091455.

[13] Smyth, B. P., Barry, J., Keenan, E. & Ducray, K. (2010). "Lapse and relapse following in-patient treatment of opiate dependence." *Irish Medical Journal. 103(6),176–179.*

www.ingramcontent.com/pod-product-compliance
Lightning Source LLC
LaVergne TN
LVHW050917080826
845145LV00001B/115

* 9 7 8 1 9 5 9 9 5 5 7 4 0 *